# *Finding Susanna*

The story of Mrs Susanna Ingleby
(née Sneyd) 1831-1891

Pam Inder and Marion Aldis

# For our families and anyone who has ever kept a diary

## Acknowledgements

We would like to express our gratitude to staff in the Special Collections section of Keele University Library for all their help.

We also thank all the descendants of the Sneyd family who have helped us so generously with information and illustrative material, in particular, Averil Scott-Moncrieff, Humphrey and Judy Scott-Moncrieff, Ambrose Scott-Moncrieff, Colin and Joyce Shenton, Dr John Sneyd, Roger Wykes-Sneyd and Humphrey Townley. We could not have produced this book without their help.

Our very special thanks also to Dr Alun Davies for the invaluable information on medical history with which he has furnished us, and to Barbara Fishburn for information on all things to do with Ipstones.

We are also grateful to the following individuals and institutions who have, in various ways, furthered our research:

Christopher Armstrong, Mr Ash, Alan Bednall, Bridget and Bob Boyd, Peter and Susan Brandreth, Philip Charles, Peter Cheeseman, Christine Chester, Linda Coleing, Arnold Corden, Angela Davies, Angela Druce, Stephen Freer, John, Jean and Quentin Haig, Mrs Hysel, Christine Jordan, Daniel and Rayne Kruger, Barbara McCarthy, Sheila Lewis, Scott Partridge, John and Jodi Peck, Reverend Stanley Price, Mrs Richardson, Roger Scales, Dr Keith Snell, Mr and Mrs Tunnicliffe, Stephen Walker, Mr and Mrs Wheatley, J. Youle and Co, Rotherham.

The staffs of:

The British Library, London; the Bodleian Library, Oxford; Brasenose College Archive, Oxford; Hanley Library; Torquay Library; the National Newspaper Library, Colindale; the Nicholson Institute, Leek; the Department of English Local History at Leicester University; the Record Offices at Ipswich, Lichfield, Manchester, Norwich, Oxford, Stafford, Preston and Warwick; the London Transport Museum; the Old High House, Stafford; Staffordshire County Museum, Shugborough; Walpole Hall, Cambridgeshire; the National Portrait Gallery, London.

**CHURNET VALLEY BOOKS**
6 Stanley Street, Leek, Staffordshire. ST13 5HG 01538 399033
© Pam Inder and Marion Aldis and Churnet Valley Books 2002
ISBN 1 897949 91 X

# CONTENTS

## MONETARY CONVERSIONS

In various places throughout the book we have converted 19th century prices to their present day equivalents. These conversions are based on tables in a programme supplied by the Drake Software Association (1998). They are reasonably accurate but reflect annual variations which may make some of them appear inconsistent.

## PERSONAL NAMES

These tend to be spelt differently in different sources; for example Susanna's sister in law, Christabel, also appears as Christabelle, Christabella, Chrystabella and Chrystobel! Where possible we have used Susanna's own preferred spelling.

# SUSANNA'S MAIN RELATIVES

**GRANDPARENTS**  William Sneyd 1767-1851, m. 1796 Jane Debank 1772-1840

**PARENTS**   Rev John Sneyd 1798-1873 m. 1. 1822 Penelope Holley 1799-1849
m. 2. 1850 Mary Adams 1827-1908

## BROTHERS AND SISTERS

John William 1822-1904                    Harriet Sneyd 1823-1857
Emily Jane 1825-1901                      Penelope Marianne 1826-1877
Helen 1827-1844                           Ralph Debank 1829-1854
Dryden Henry 1833-1913                    Edmond Lionel 1835-1853
Mary Elizabeth 1837-1854                  Frederick Clement 1839-1864 (Freddy)
Richard Wettenhall 1841-1863 (Wettie)

Gustavus Alfred 1844-1926 (Tavie) m. 1882 Christabel Harris.  No children.

Ada Mary 1851-1911 m. 1871 Robert Ponsonby Carew Hunt.  Several children.

## NEPHEWS AND NIECES

**Ralph De Tunstall Sneyd** 1861-1947.  The nephew, Ralphy, whom Susanna brought up.  Son of her brother John William Sneyd m. Agnes Cotton 1861, who died 1862.  Ralph m. Harriet Brookes 1894.  Four children.

### Children of her sister Penelope Marianne & John Clerk Brodie m. 1848

Penelope Anne b. 1849 (Effie)             John Sneyd b. 1850 (Johnnie)
Anne Catherine b. 1852 (Annie)            Elizabeth b.& d. 1853
Alexander b. 1854                         James Gibson b. 1855 (Jim)
David b. 1856          Frederick b. 1858          Phoebe b. 1862

### Children of her sister Harriet & the Rev Robert Bamford m. 1850

Penelope Dorothea b. 1851 (Dora)          Harriet b. 1853
Robert b. 1854                            William Henry b. 1856

## AUNTS AND UNCLES

Tom Sneyd b. 1800 m. Emma Whitley.

Rev. Henry Sneyd b. 1804 m. 3 times. Only the marriage to Penelope Broughton (d 1855) in 1834 produced children who survived into adulthood.

Mary Sneyd b. 1807 (Aunt Mary) m. in 1830 Clement John Sneyd-Kynnersley of Loxley Park.

Rev. John Holley b. 1805 from Norfolk.  He was her mother's half-brother and father's curate who brokered her marriage to Charles Ingleby in 1860.

# SOME OF SUSANNA'S COUSINS

## Children of Tom Sneyd and Emma (Aunt Tom)

Emma b. 1833 m. 1862 Richard Hoghton Gale of Bardsea Hall, Lancs. 2 sons, one of whom, Richmond, was at school with Ralphy at Debenham.

Caroline Anne (Carrie) b. 1835 m. Robert, Viscount Sherbrooke in 1885. No children. Susanna wrote frequently to Carrie.

Major General Thomas William b. 1837. Inherited Ashcombe Park in 1913. His only son (Averil Scott-Moncrieff's father) was killed in 1st World War, so the estate passed to his brother..

Lieutenant Henry 1838-1920 inherited Ashcombe Park.

Clement John b. 1840

George Edward b. 1846

## Children of Reverend Henry Sneyd and Penelope

William Debank b. 1835 m. Lizzie Coxon in 1860. No children.

Mary Anne b. 1837 m. Francis (Frank) Hand in 1863. One of Susanna's bridesmaids. 3 children to whom Susanna wrote.

Penelope Rosamund (Rosie) b. 1839 m. Henry Kerr Porter Mocatta in 1862. One of Susanna's bridesmaids. 2 children to whom Susanna wrote.

Henry Francis b. 1840 m. Marianne Swete Townsend in 1864 and later abandoned her. Several children. Susanna helped Marianne financially.

Clement Broughton b. 1842 m. 1866 Emily Gillett (sister of Susanna's Abbots Bromley friend, Harriet Pickering). 2 daughters.

## Children of Mary (Aunt Mary) and Clement Sneyd-Kynnersley

Clement Thomas b. 1833 m. Ellen Mallaby in 1858. Several children.

William Henry b. 1835 m. Caroline Adie in 1862. He and Susanna were romantically linked in 1859

Mary Jane (Minnie) b. 1837 m. Dr Fraser, vicar of Alton, c.1854. She left him in 1886. Very close to Susanna, as were her many children.

# PREFACE

*'The art of biography is a despised art because it is an art of things, of facts, of arranged facts'*
(Ormerod Goode in *The Biographer's Tale* by A S Byatt, 2001)

*'A shadow never falls upon a wall without leaving thereupon a permanent trace - a trace which might be visible by resorting to proper processes'*
(Professor Draper quoted in *Psychometry* by Henry S Olcott, 1886)

This is not a profound book. We are historians and we are interested in people - it's as simple as that. We started to research the life of a 19th century gentlewoman and found ourselves meeting all sorts of interesting people who were related to her or who lived in places she had known. It was great fun and we thought if we had enjoyed it so much, you might enjoy reading about it. After all, most of us are curious about other peoples' lives - and most of us can learn something from the way other people live.

So, we present the biography of Mrs Susanna Ingleby, a strong, courageous, rather unlucky, very human, Victorian lady - and the story of how we found out about her. If nothing else, we hope to tell you some things you didn't know about the Victorians and convince you that research is fun, that all historians are not boring and that not all history is to be found in libraries.

We must stress that all this is true. Susanna and her family were real people and they really kept diaries - most of them can be read in Keele University Library. All the quotations we use come from actual documents, though occasionally we have made minor alterations to spelling and punctuation for the sake of clarity. Some of the originals are in the public domain, many are in private hands, but they all exist. We haven't altered or adapted the Sneyd family history at all, however fantastic some of it may sound.

The description of the way we did our research is also entirely truthful. All the incidents actually happened, all the people we met are - or were - real. Sadly some of them are now dead. The events described in the first research visit (chapter one) all happened on that visit and in that order.

Other incidents are presented as they become relevant rather than in the sequence in which they occurred.

We haven't altered any of the place names - you can find all the big houses on the map if you want to - though we should warn you that none of them are open to the public. But we have altered the names of those people alive today who did not want to be identified and we have left the location of some of their homes deliberately obscure.

Marion kept a log during our visits and wrote it up immediately afterwards so we have an accurate record of all the seventeen trips we made. Of course we do not carry a tape recorder with us at all times so the conversations we report are only as accurate as our memories - but conversations very like them did take place. All the time.

Our only flight of fancy is Susanna, although there is solid evidence for everything we have her say and for the character we give her. You get to know someone pretty well when you read thirty year's worth of their diaries and letters. Susanna's story sustained us through six year's worth of our own family troubles - so different from hers in kind but remarkably similar in feeling. The project came to be about finding parallels, about coincidences and timing, about empathy and intuition, about shared experiences, differently interpreted. We were all three of us female, we all had family responsibilities. Our lives became interwoven.

For us, Susanna's intervention was very real. You may choose to see it as a literary device, a figment of our imaginations, the voice of a real person or an unnecessary intrusion. It's up to you. We can't explain what she is, why she should want her story told, or why she should have chosen us to do it. But we do know she was interested in psychometry. What is that? Thought transference. Is that relevant? Perhaps.

We have arranged the facts. You must decide whether we have captured the shadows on the wall.

> *'Linear time is a figment of human imagination'*
> Peter Ackroyd's *London, a Biography*, 2000

> *'History is everything. People in the end will not forgive*
> *you for not having shared theirs.'*
> Thomas Keneally's *Women of the Inner Sea*, 1992

Chapter 1

# Choosing Well

01604 153 - I knew the number by heart.  She had to be in.

'Hi Marion.  How are you?'

'Hello Pam. I'm fine - you, Paddy and the kids?'

'We're all OK - but guess what?  Susanna has left Charles!'

'Never!  How long had they been married?'

'Eight weeks to the day.'

'So what **happened**?'

I took a deep breath..........

For several months we had been working on a collection of diaries kept by a Staffordshire gentlewoman.  Susanna Sneyd was born in 1831 and sometime early in her adult life she began to keep a diary.  Day after day, year after year she recorded the events of her life, some of them momentous, many of them trivial, and as each diary was full she shelved it next to its fellows in the family library.  Eventually they had all been acquired by a dealer in second-hand books who sold them to Keele University.

I had first come upon Susanna's diaries while supervising a group of students doing a local history project.  It wasn't my project - I was simply helping my friend Linda.  We were both costume historians at Staffordshire University.  Linda's students were looking at the types of document, in various libraries in and around Stoke-on-Trent, that might give them information about the making and selling of clothing in North Staffordshire.  Amongst the material that the Keele Special Collections Librarian had found for them was a pile of small, green, cloth-covered diaries, kept between 1858 and 1889 by a Mrs Susanna Ingleby.  She was, as it happened, a talented needlewoman, and the diaries were full of tantalising references - '*I finished Clement's shirts.*'  '*Alice and I cut out my blue silk dress.*' '*Harriet came to borrow the sewing machine*'.  But it was soon clear to me that there was much more in these diaries than a mere record of dressmaking and clothes buying.

After the students had finished I talked to the librarian.  No, no-one had shown any interest in the Ingleby diaries in the twenty years they had been at Keele. Yes, of course I could work on them if I really wanted to - why didn't I take one home to study? And at that point I had rung Marion for the first time.

We had met while studying local history at Leicester University, and, as two mature students in a department full of twenty-somethings, had become friendly. Marion, I remembered, had done her MA dissertation on the diary of a Victorian gentleman and was fascinated by 19th century diaries generally - she had a large collection of published ones. However, by the time I found Susanna's diaries our husbands' careers had taken us both away from Leicester - to Northampton and Hertfordshire respectively - and we had all but lost touch with each other. But I had guessed right - Marion was interested. She was keen that we should collaborate.

I began to transcribe the diaries so we could make sense of their contents, beginning with the 1860 diary - the year of Susanna's marriage. It contained a list of her wedding presents, the names of the guests at her wedding breakfast, and detailed entries about her honeymoon in France. It seemed a good starting point.

Susanna Sneyd married the Reverend Charles Ingleby on April 11th, 1860 and the first few months of that year were occupied with wedding preparations.

*January 5th I went out with Papa and Mary and bought my wedding dress £5-5s*

*February 13th  Mary, Ada and I went out shopping. I ordered the wedding cards*

*February 24th  Mary, Ada and I went  shopping and bought a bonnet and my wreath.  Papa gave me an ornament for the neck £8-10s*

The entries were bland. There was no sense of excitement or any other emotion and it was clear that young Mrs Ingleby's prose style was not going to make enthralling reading. And I still knew virtually nothing about her. The former owners of the estate that was to become Keele University were Sneyds - hence the university's acquisition of diaries kept by someone with that name. However, there was no mention of Keele in the diaries. In 1858 Susanna, *'Papa'*, *'Mary'*, *'Emily'* and *'Ada'* appeared to be living in Leamington Spa. It was some time before we learnt that they had only a tenuous link with the Keele family - as the descendants of a seventeenth century younger son. Susanna's papa was the Reverend John Sneyd, vicar of Ipstones since 1833 and owner of the Ashcombe Park estate near Leek. Emily was her spinster elder sister, Mary was their young stepmother, and

Ada was their eight year-old half-sister, Mary's only child. They were only staying in Leamington for a few months.

By the time Susanna married the family had returned home to Cheddleton in North Staffordshire. *'April 11th Dear Charles and my wedding day we were married from Woodlands at Cheddleton.'*

The Sneyds owned a good deal of land in the area and various big houses - Woodlands was one of the more modest of them. It had been built for one of Susanna's uncles in 1832, in the woods to the south east of Ashcombe, the family seat. For reasons that would soon become clear, Susanna's family had fallen on hard times and could no longer afford to live in the big house.

After their wedding Susanna and Charles honeymooned in France. I was not yet used to her handwriting, the entries were long and criss-crossed each other across the pages of the tiny diaries, and they were full of unfamiliar French place names - a tedious record of compulsive sightseeing, but containing little in the way of real description. One sentence occupied me for a long while. *'We saw the Pyrenees nicely, they were very'* - not 'nice' 'good' or 'beautiful', Susanna's favourite adjectives for the places she saw - at last I had it - *'white'*! I began to have doubts about these diaries. Perhaps other researchers had been right to decide that they were of little interest?

Doggedly I followed Susanna and Charles across France and back to his home in Oakamoor. They arrived *'quite unexpectedly, as no notice had been sent that we were coming'* on May 2nd. That seemed rather odd. And, over the next few weeks I found such entries as *'2 rooms. We each had our own bedrooms' 'Very unhappy' 'I got ready to go to Woodlands but was not allowed to go'.* I began to suspect that there was something very wrong. And there it was - on June 11th - *'Papa came here by the 9.30 train to help me.... I left Wood Bank* [the Ingleby's house] *not to return again'*. I read on in disbelief but it was true. The marriage was over.

'What year was it again?' asked Marion.

'1860.'

'But I thought people married for life then - divorce wasn't possible....'

'Well actually,' I said, having just read it up, 'the law changed in 1857. You could then get a divorce without an Act of Parliament - that was what had made divorce so impossible for ordinary people previously. But there were still very, very few.....'

'So did Susanna and Charles divorce?'

'Not as far as I can see. I've read all of the 1860 diary - Charles made her a settlement of £100 a year, she says, so it seems to have been official. And I've skimmed through the next few diaries and there's absolutely no mention of him - or of any divorce case'

'What on earth can have happened? I mean, wives were expected to obey, weren't they? Rape within marriage was legal, husbands were allowed to beat their wives so long as they used a stick no thicker than their thumb.....'

'Charming!'

'Well, you must remember that lecture.'

'Clearly. I can't think what might have happened either, but Susanna's father came to her rescue and he was an eminently respectable clergyman, very strict, not the sort of man to come and take her away just because she'd had second thoughts or because Charles's leaving the cap off the toothpaste was getting on her nerves. He must have been quite sure it was Charles's fault - and it must have been something pretty dramatic.'

The transcription of the wedding diary took over a month of my spare time - about fifty hours. By the time I reached the last diary, 1889 - when admittedly most of the entries were shorter - Marion and I could read Susanna's handwriting as easily as we could read each other's and transcription time was down to about seven hours per diary. We could also - and this was to prove invaluable - recognise her handwriting when it appeared elsewhere.

We began to be able to gauge her mood by her writing - illness (shaky), anger (pressing so hard that the nib almost went through the page), unhappy (untidy, blotchy). And then there were the few occasions when we could only deduce that Susanna was deeply embarrassed or upset by something she had written. Normally, she crossed out mistakes and corrected them. But sometimes - three times to be precise - she deleted what she had written by scraping away the surface of the paper, over-painting it with white gouache, and ruling an ink line through it. It worked. Not even under ultra-violet light could we see what had once been written. But as time went on we could guess.

With three or four diaries transcribed and some preliminary research done I made one of my regular visits to Keele. This time the librarian had news for me. I rushed home in a panic and rang Marion.

'Hi Marion. Are you sitting comfortably?'

'Ye-es.'

'You know I told you there were thirty of Susanna's diaries?'

'Mmm.'

'Well, there aren't. There are about two hundred - they showed them to me this afternoon - not all her's of course,' I gabbled.

There was a pause on the other end of the phone.

'Whose then?'

Marion sounded excited. That was good.

'Her father's, mother's, grandfather's, brother's, some scrap books, a few bank books - I didn't have the chance to look at them all properly but it's a **huge** collection, probably unique - you need to see it. We must go up to Staffordshire **soon**.......'

At the time of this phone call we were both still hesitating about making our first trip to Staffordshire together. Outside our university department we scarcely knew each other and our lives and backgrounds seemed very different. Would we get on? What would Marion make of my little terraced house in Stoke where we were to stay? I retained a room in the house to use for the one or two days a week when I was working at Staffordshire University - but the rest of it was let, long term, to my friend Barbie. Barbie has a passion for vivid, clashing colour schemes, layers of clutter - and a constant stream of unsuitable boyfriends; Marion is an artist with a beautiful home and an ordered lifestyle. They are both lovely people but they could not be more different and I could not imagine them together.

Marion's husband was less than enthusiastic about being left behind while she went off chasing wild geese - or diarists - with someone he barely knew. I had a globe-trotting husband and an assortment of warring sons, stepsons and dogs who could not be left unsupervised for long. We both had complex work and family commitments and it was easy to delay. But as the project grew Marion and I both knew we had to see Susanna's territory for ourselves. We needed to know whether any of the Sneyd homes survived, whether Susanna had any descendants, what was in the other diaries - whether, in fact, the research I had begun so lightly was worth pursuing.

At last, in the early summer of 1994 we set off. We planned carefully. I still had not read all of the diaries but we knew that Susanna had lived for some years after her marriage breakdown with her widowed brother and his little boy in a place called Armitage, near Rugeley, in mid-Staffordshire. We planned to go through it on the way to Stoke-on-Trent. We made appointments at Keele University to spend three days working on the diary collection and decided to spend a Sunday driving around the area of North Staffordshire where the family estate was.

This would bring an unexpected bonus. The area around Cheddleton and Leek is one of England's best kept secrets - a breathtakingly beautiful landscape of lush wooded valleys amid rolling hills which give way to bleak, high moors with spectacular views - and all a mere thirteen or fourteen miles from the dismal example of industrial decay that is Stoke-on-Trent. The countryside is probably even more lovely today than it was in Susanna's time for then the moorlands were pockmarked with mines, quarries and smelting works.

The little town of Leek still serves a network of villages. There are supermarkets, a Woolworths and a Boots, but also traditional family ironmongers, butchers, and bookshops, as well as the ubiquitous charity shops, building societies and banks. It is well-known for its antique shops and galleries. Susanna shopped in Leek and she would have known well the shops that were there then. In 1873 there were twenty nine bootmakers, thirteen dressmakers, fourteen tailors, the same number of drapers, three chemists, several stationers-cum-booksellers, butchers, bakers, fruiterers, confectioners and provision merchants. Leek also had an umbrella maker, a watch and clock maker, and a sewing machine agent.

On Wednesdays she would have seen the market square thronged with farmers' wives selling butter and eggs, home-reared bacon, farmhouse cheese and whatever spare produce their gardens and hedgerows supplied, season by season. There would have been cabbages, onions, mushrooms, hazel nuts, pears and raspberries and the odd scraggy, pale-combed chicken awaiting its fate as nourishing soup for a sickly gentlewoman. At Christmas there would have been bright-berried holly from the hedgerows and mistletoe from ancient trees; a few months later the stalls would be selling posies of early violets, primroses and wild daffodils, nestling in blankets of wet moss.

On alternate Wednesdays the women's husbands would come to town with them to the cattle market at the end of Derby street, and every six weeks or so that market would become a cattle fair, enticing buyers and sellers from all over the county and beyond. On those days the town's pubs - almost fifty of them - would be full to overflowing, and respectable ladies like Susanna and her friends would stay at home.

But Leek was more than a prosperous market town. On market days, and in between, the little town hummed with the clatter of silk mills. Silk had made the town rich and the centre boasted an unusual number of fine Georgian and Victorian houses. It was a less healthy place for the poor. Their houses were low-lying and damp; despite the countryside on the town's doorstep the infant and child mortality rate in Leek was well above the national average - fifteen per thousand rather than nine. Not until the 1850s was an Improvement Commission appointed and given powers to improve the water supply, provide mains drainage, pave and light the streets and replace the worst of the slums with new houses. Susanna saw, and no doubt approved, the changes.

Now much of the industry has gone and the area is a rural backwater, but Leek is still a pretty, prosperous little place, handy for the Potteries but light years away in atmosphere. And because the area has not changed much in the 20th century, everything Susanna knew is still there - all the grand houses on the family estate - Ashcombe Park, Woodlands, Basford Hall, Sharpcliffe, Belmont - we could find them all on the Ordnance Survey maps. In time we would find the churches where she worshipped, the court in which her father dispensed justice - he was a magistrate as well as a clergyman - the schools where she and her sister helped teach needlework, the inns, farms and cottages she knew - even the office of the family solicitor in Leek. It was quite amazing.

And of course Marion and I got on. What is more, when we were together we became people our families would not have recognised - obsessive, bolder, sillier, more imaginative. We ate all the foods our respective husbands disliked, drank a great deal of not-very-good wine from Mr Shah's mini-market just round the corner from my house, sat up late at night and talked and talked and talked It was, we can now see, an important part of learning to work together effectively - though at the time it was just huge fun, something that was often lacking in our lives as working wives and mothers. And it worked. Between us we seemed to generate a sort of energy that made things happen. In Staffordshire, if nowhere else, we led charmed lives. People were always in when we called, they had the information we needed or knew someone else who had; weddings and christenings seemed to be planned so that we would always be able to see inside churches that were normally kept locked; hitherto unknown individuals who proved to be useful contacts apparently arranged their schedules to coincide with ours. The unexpected always happened.

After a while it ceased to surprise us that, to take just one example, we should decide to photograph the monuments erected to Susanna's father in Cheddleton church at exactly the same time on exactly the same day as the expert from the Victoria and Albert Museum (the only man in the country, he assured us, who knew anything about the firm that made them) was making his one and only visit to North Staffordshire to view them.

Someone seemed to be helping us - we came to believe Susanna wanted her story told. We began to treat her as an invisible colleague. When in doubt we would invoke her help - jokingly at first......

'Come on Susanna, which way now?'

'Now Susanna, please make sure.....'

But after a while the jokes rang a little hollow - it really did seem that she was smoothing our path. But that was too fantastic to be true. Could it be, we asked each other, that we were actually exceptionally clever researchers who just got extra lucky from time to time? Past experience led us to discount that theory. That we had been particularly fortunate in finding such a rich collection in such a stunningly beautiful area went without saying and our local history training certainly stood us in good stead. We had lived long enough to know that we both had good people skills - which perhaps went some way to explaining why everyone was so willing to help us. But still there was an indefinable sense of something else. The long arm of coincidence could only be stretched so far, things simply could not keep slotting into place so effortlessly - it certainly didn't happen in our 'other' lives.

Of course it was impossible that Susanna could be helping us. But as visit after visit produced the same range of unbelievable results we decided we should stop trying to understand and sit back and accept our good luck.

However, on our first trip we still had the capacity to be amazed and on a blazing hot July Saturday we drove to Armitage as planned, on our way to Stoke-on-Trent. From her diaries I knew Susanna and her brother and nephew had lived at Armitage Cottage. They visited the Spodes at Hawkesyard Priory, the Birches at Armitage Lodge and the Wilsons at the Rectory - so we would go in search of those houses. The blistering afternoon heat did nothing to endear Armitage to us. It seemed an unprepossessing little town and Armitage Lodge and Armitage Cottage were nowhere to be seen. We crept around the unfamiliar roads.

'There's Rectory Lane,' said Marion, spotting the unlikely name in the middle of a modern housing estate. We turned into it and saw an imposing Victorian villa, tree-screened and soft red brick amongst the harsh, rectangular, repetitive modern houses.

'And that must be the Old Rectory.'

There was a man up a ladder painting one of the windows - we scrambled out of the car.

'I know this sounds rather odd, but please, may we take a photograph of your house - you see, we're doing research on this collection of diaries...'

Bob Boyd clambered down his ladder, a wiry, athletic-looking, grey-haired man.

'Come in,' he said, 'you must meet my wife, she collects diaries.'

'How many diary collectors can there be in a place the size of Armitage?' we wondered, unable to believe our luck.

Bridget Boyd was sitting reading in the garden: she had indeed read a great many published diaries and was fascinated to see the single one of Susanna's that we had with us. She served us tea in the cool interior of the Old Rectory drawing room - a large, airy room, with pale walls, chintz-covered sofas and two large, friendly golden retrievers. The house had been built in 1861 in a late version of the 'gothick' style and the doors and windows were topped by shallow pointed arches. The then rector, Mr Wilson, had built the house with a grant from Queen Anne's Bounty, the ecclesiastical charity. He was a close friend of Susanna and her brother and on November 13th 1862, a few months after they arrived in Armitage *'we called on the Wilsons, they took us all over the new Rectory....'*.

And now, here were we, seeing over the Rectory, too. On our very first step into Susanna's world we had found ourselves in a room in which she would have taken afternoon tea. The idea caused a tingling sensation up our spines - a sensation we would come to know all too well over the next few years. The garden, the Boyds told us, was very different from the one Susanna would have known. There were originally six-and-a-half acres of it - much of the housing estate we had driven through had been built on Rectory land. Originally a curved drive had led up from Rectory Lane to the front door, and there had been a coach house, huge greenhouses and a large kitchen garden. There was also a wood, a grotto set in a bank at the bottom of the garden, and a big, circular, raised lawn surrounded by a gravel path and borders crammed with rockery plants, shrubs, roses and flowers.

'I could have wept when it was destroyed,' Bridget told us.

We chatted about the house, the village and the whereabouts of the various places Susanna had known, and the Boyds undertook to find illustrations for us of Armitage Lodge and Armitage Cottage both of which had been demolished within living memory.

Then they insisted on driving us to see the churches and hamlets Susanna had visited. Bob was an organist and knew under which stones, in whose gardens, all the local church keys were to be found.

'The roads round here are terrible, you'd never find your way,' they explained as they showed us the paths she would have walked, adding 'that's where we take the dogs.' They took us into Hawkesyard Priory, walked us round the gardens there - a famous local attraction in Susanna's day but now sadly overgrown and neglected. In return we invited them to join us at Keele on the Tuesday to look at more of Susanna's diaries. It was an unbelievably good start, we agreed, as we headed for Stoke.

To my intense relief Marion was unfazed by her first encounter with Barbie - not to mention with the newly-painted fuchsia-pink-and-petunia-purple bathroom and the sunburst-yellow-and-coriander-green-kitchen-with-frieze-of-hand-painted-hopping-frogs - all pervaded with the scent of some exceptionally potent joss sticks from the latest WOMAD festival. Not for the first time I wondered why I had given Barbie free rein to decorate the house as she wished!

'It's your home, Barb,' I remembered saying, 'I can always paint over it if you leave.' But I was beginning to wonder just how many gallons of white paint it would take.

The tiny living room was particularly eccentric - though the hopping frogs in the kitchen now ran it a close second. A terracotta-pink dado was topped by walls and ceiling stippled in a similar shade of pink on white - Barbie has an aversion to white ceilings. The paintwork and carpet were navy blue - another of her favourite combinations - and a broad frieze of multi-coloured ducks on a dark green background swam round the walls. Flame-coloured nylon chiffon curtains, beautifully made with gold ribbon loops - Barbie is an accomplished needlewoman - hung in elaborately draped folds over a pole.

'Isn't it a wonderful colour?' she enthused, 'and only a pound a yard from this stall on Newcastle market. They had all sorts of brilliant rainbow colours.....'

I could imagine that on a bright sunny day in the open air the colour was indeed wonderful, but muted by the navy paint it was overpowering.

Huge panels covered with collages of family photographs dominated the walls, Barbie's two children at every stage from babyhood to adulthood, her little grandson as newborn, as toddler, as schoolboy, her mother, brother, sister, long-dead aunties and uncles. She might have left home but Barbie's family were with her whenever she looked up. Her own paintings, her artist uncle's paint palette, crudely coloured images donated by her Indian neighbours, a Peter Scott wildlife plate, painted wooden ducks from China, an African wooden bust draped in Barbie's beads and scarves, candles, small plastic toys from her 1950s childhood, heaps of artificial flowers, a straw sun hat, magazines and papers littered every flat surface.

Despite the riot of colour and pattern in her home, Barbie's dress sense is impeccable. She makes most of her own clothes and prides herself on wearing unusual outfits in toning colours. Tall and slim with shiny shoulder-length hair, careful make-up and neatly painted nails she always seems to look elegant. I envy her. But she is prone to inexplicable enthusiasms. Around the time of our visit Barbie's latest boyfriend had imbued her with a passion for motorbikes. I had known her for years and motorcycles had never previously featured in her conversation, but in the few weeks of the summer vacation that had passed since my last visit Ken had realised a boyhood dream and bought himself a fearsome looking Suzuki.

'You can't call them Barbie and Ken,' interrupted Marion, laughing, 'no-one will believe you - change one of them - call him Joe or Sid or something!'

'But those are their names,' I objected, 'this is a true story and they didn't want their names changed. We agreed, remember? People keep their own names unless they ask not to be identified. I mean, when she first met him we all made jokes about Barbie'n'Ken dolls and they **liked** it!'

Barbie was now hooked on biking. Luridly coloured leathers and helmets were produced for our inspection and plans for buying and learning to ride a bike of her own were gleefully laid before us, but in between it was clear she was genuinely intrigued by what we were doing. Fortunately she liked Marion - but then Barbie likes everyone - and Marion liked her. Ken, and Thai, Barbie's half-Siamese cat, also took to Marion and I was assured that I could bring her to stay as often as I wished if we discovered there was any mileage in our project.

On Sunday we set out to see if there was. First we decided to explore the area Susanna had known and loved. As my house lay alongside Leek Road, Leek seemed both a possible place to find - we had already discovered that map reading was not one of our key skills - and a good place to start. Its town centre has changed little since Susanna's day and we had no difficulty in finding places she would have known - the market square, St Edward's church, the Nicholson Institute which she saw built, silk mills, now disused, which belonged to family friends - even the office of Mr Joseph Challinor, her solicitor in Derby Street, where the messy business of Susanna's separation from Charles Ingleby was sorted out. But though she visited numerous friends in Leek we could not pinpoint their homes, and the shops she patronised must all have changed hands many times. It was difficult to feel Susanna in Leek. So we set out for Cheddleton and Basford Hall where she had spent most of her life.

Susanna lived in leisured times and the actual work of running her home was in the hands of servants, she had few deadlines to keep and long walks were very much part of her routine. Her visits to Leek usually followed the same pattern *'Took the train to Leek - and walked home'*. Half a mile out of Leek on the Cheddleton road we understood why. 'Always go and look at the place and the terrain,' our local history tutors had told us. For all of Susanna's adult life the Churnet Valley railway operated a regular service - Susanna knew the timetable by heart and recorded the precise time of every train she took or met. Basford Hall stands on a hill above the station - a steep mile climb whichever way she travelled. But the road from Leek to Cheddleton dips sharply - so most of her homeward journey of three miles or so was downhill. It was a tiny discovery but surprisingly satisfying. We were not difficult to please.

As we entered Cheddleton a sign pointed to the station - and to Basford. We followed the road through a trading estate and came to the little gothic station (reputedly designed by Pugin) that Susanna knew so well. By the sort of coincidence that we would soon learn to take for granted it is the only station to survive on the now disused Churnet Valley line and on certain weekends local enthusiasts run a service that chugs a few hundred yards down the valley and back again. Naturally, the service was operating that Sunday. We bought tickets, hoping to get closer to Susanna by travelling a small part of the journey she so often took.

In the little station museum we discovered the newspaper report of the opening of the line and learnt that Susanna's father had cut the first turf when the line crossed his land. He was one of the major landowners in the area and the family was old and well-established. Local people respected and feared the Sneyds. Amongst the preserved rolling stock at the station was a ladies' first class carriage, wooden, rust-coloured and dilapidated, but dating from the 1850s when Susanna began her diary.

'That's how Susanna would have travelled,' said Marion gleefully, 'perhaps in that very carriage.'

We passed the turn to Churnet Grange - home in Susanna's day to a Captain Colvile who hosted the local flower show at which Susanna's gardener won prizes and where she and her nephew exhibited flower arrangements. One year she complained to her diary that the organisers broke her vase. We imagined her, in her full skirts and tight boots carefully carrying her display down the hill and along the drive to the Grange.

Beyond the station sheep and lambs grazed on curiously shaped grassy hills - prehistoric barrows, we wondered, forcing our minds back to that part of our local history course?

The road climbed and forked - round the corner we went - past the cottages. 'Those are early 19th century,' Marion enthused, 'Susanna would have known those. Did I ever tell you I spent a fascinating afternoon with Dr Snell dating houses by the colour, shape and size of the bricks. He told me so much.'

'Spare me! And anyway - those are stone!'

Although we still had not seen a portrait of her, now that we were in the vicinity of her home, had seen where she had caught the train and done her shopping, Susanna was becoming more and more real. A little further on we passed Sneyd Arms Farm and then - there was Basford Hall itself, a grand, grey stone, gabled house, perched on the crest of the hill with wonderful unspoilt views over the Churnet valley in one direction and over the Ashcombe valley in the other, set at the end of a drive of mature trees, surrounded by neatly mown grass and immaculate flowerbeds full of geraniums.

'Susanna's gardener planted geraniums there, too,' I said quietly.

It was Sunday lunchtime and the owners were entertaining. Rows of cars stood outside and we decided now was not a propitious moment to arrive unannounced.

We picnicked in a nearby field and discussed our options. We had not hitherto considered seeing inside the Sneyd houses - we had just been delighted to discover that most of them survived. Now we realised that we needed more than just a glimpse of the exteriors if we were to get inside our diarists' lives. Dark clouds had gathered over the moors and were heading our way. The rumble of a tractor came closer. Marion jumped up; law-abiding by nature she knew that we were trespassing.

'I wonder if you could help us?' she smiled beguilingly. 'We'd rather like to see inside the hall. Do you think the owners would let us? Do you know them?'

'Pigs might fly!' he growled. 'You could try Mrs Scott-Moncrieff, she's the owner's mother. You might get something out of her - she's more or less human - though I wouldn't give much for your chances. Difficult family. Very difficult.'

Obviously we were going to need all our tact and diplomacy if we were ever to see inside Susanna's home. In tune with our mood, it began to rain. Heavily. We dived for cover in Marion's car clutching damp sandwiches. Weather in North Staffordshire, we were to discover, does nothing by halves.

We decided to try something easier. Susanna's father had been vicar of Ipstones while he was living at Basford. It could not be very far away and we set off in torrential rain.

The drive up to Ipstones was breathtaking. A sunken road, overhung with emerald-green ferns, dipped into a valley between boggy pools full of reeds and irises and then rose steeply until suddenly it broke from the tree canopy and stone walls replaced the hedges. Ipstones was high up on the moors. It was along this road that John Sneyd and his family walked to church and back each Sunday, in all weathers.

We found the church was open, a pleasant little building of pink local sandstone and millstone grit, with fine art nouveau panels and screen and a Saxon carving depicting what Susanna's little nephew had called *'the fighting dragons'*. It was not as Susanna would have known it as a child; we knew from her diaries that it had been renovated and partially rebuilt in 1877 and that Susanna herself had donated the east window in memory of her father. There was also a curious monument to her forbears in the tower - two slabs of grey slate with enamel plaques arranged in the form of a family tree. Many were cracked, some had fallen off and the slate itself was in two pieces. Our researches were still at quite an early stage and many of the names were unfamiliar to us so we tried to copy down as much of the information as we could, hampered by the broken and incomplete state of the plaques and the fact that one slab was placed immovably in front of the other.

Then, in the vestry, to our great joy we found our very first family portrait, a photograph of Susanna's father, the Reverend John Sneyd, a thin, ascetic-looking man with a long nose, receding chin and a stern, piercing gaze. At this stage our diarists were still only names. Giving a face to just one of them was hugely exciting.

'Impressive, but certainly not handsome,' I said, 'just look at that nose!'

Soon we would discover that John Sneyd's long, pointed nose was a family characteristic - notable enough to have given rise to a local legend. The Sneyds, it was said, 'took the stars off poor men's broth' - no-one could explain exactly what that meant, but the inference was clear enough. One day, the devil seized a member of the family by the nose and pulled and pulled - to teach him to treat his poorer neighbours with respect. As we read more of the diaries we were forced to conclude that the devil had not pulled anything like hard enough!

'Where next?' Marion asked me as we headed back to the car through the still-pouring rain.

This excursion would have been impossible without her car, I thought. Cursed with extreme short sight I have never been able to drive. And we really were enjoying each other's company, egging each other on - yes, Marion had been a good choice of colleague, I decided.

'Belmont Hall, please. We passed it on the way up here - the Sneyds owned it. John Sneyd often called on relatives at Belmont Hall while visiting his parish and Susanna's Aunt Mary spent her last years there.'

Belmont Hall had been built by Susanna's great-grandfather, another John Sneyd, but his son - her grandfather - had built himself a more imposing new house in the valley - Ashcombe Park. In Susanna's father's childhood Belmont was rented to the then vicar of Ipstones, the Reverend Carlisle, and young John had lived with him for some time to be tutored before sitting his entrance examination for Brasenose College, Oxford. He often recorded swimming in the 'ponds' at Belmont - these presumably were the reedy pools, choked with weed and overhung by banks of trees that we had passed in the valley. In the pouring rain they looked deeply uninviting.

We turned into the drive. Heavy iron gates with 'Private Drive' notices barred the way and the house they guarded was invisible in the trees. For some inexplicable reason this seemed less intimidating than the visitors at Basford and we drove on. As we came through the trees a large white house appeared - and so did two young people under  a large golfing umbrella. Their body language made it quite clear that intruders were unwelcome.....

An hour later, having been shown round the ground floor of the house and having had tea and seed cake (appropriately Victorian, we felt) in the vast kitchen, we took our leave, uncertain quite what it was we had said or done to  change our welcome.  We had been given a brief history of the house, presented with copies of the few documents that the owners had that related to its past and shown the improvements and restoration that they were lovingly carrying out.  There was still much to do and they both held down demanding jobs, so it would be sometime before Belmont was restored to its former glory, but clearly they loved the place and its secluded grounds.

The house, we discovered, was now very different from the place Susanna and her father would have known - a whole wing had been demolished and a porch built - and very different indeed to the house Susanna's great-grandfather had built for himself in 1770.  But the site, the walled kitchen gardens, the careful tree planting and landscaping, the drive with its dripping rhododendrons would all have been familiar to Susanna. In the 1870s and 80s she made regular trips to Belmont from Basford, walking down the steep hill, past the ponds and up the long drive to the Hall to visit her Aunt Mary.

The rain had stopped.

'There's another Sneyd house near here,' I informed my long suffering driver, 'Sharpcliffe Hall, bought in 1846 for Susanna's brother Ralph Debank to farm.'

Ralph died young and the farm was lived in over the years by various of Susanna's siblings.  It was at Sharpcliffe that Susanna was staying when Charles Ingleby first fancied himself in love with her.  The roads to Sharpcliffe have not improved since Susanna's time and grass grew thickly down the middle of the unmetalled  tracks. The Hall sits up on the edge of the moors, behind wrought iron gates, a huge three-storeyed, gabled 17th century pile.  The yard in front was choked with weeds, rusting farm machinery lay in heaps and we concluded - wrongly as it turned out - that the house was derelict. The gates were shut, and we contented ourselves with a photograph from the road.

It was a wise decision. The owners of Sharpcliffe, we were later told, had been refused planning permission for various schemes by Staffordshire Moorlands Council, and, in the time-honoured way of thwarted developers, were letting the building collapse around them. They did not welcome visitors. Sharpcliffe remains the only one of the Sneyd homes that we have been unable to see inside.

'Have you noticed how long this afternoon has seemed?' said Marion. 'We've fitted in an awful lot, more than should really have been possible considering how long we spent at Belmont - and its only six now.'

I nodded. 'I can't believe how lucky we've been. It's almost as if Susanna wants us to know her story.'

Somewhere above us, Susanna smiled knowingly. Time, she knew, could be stretched if the occasion demanded. She was impressed that we had noticed her intervention so quickly.

'I chose well,' she thought, 'already they are beginning to understand.'

The rain had stopped, it was heavy and humid, flies were everywhere. And we were lost. From Sharpcliffe we had hoped to return to Cheddleton and perhaps see the church, locate Ashcombe Park and Woodlands and drive through the village of Wetley Rocks where Susanna and her sister Emily had given needlework lessons to the local schoolgirls. But there seemed to be no relationship between the roads we had travelled and our map and we found ourselves in front of yet another apparently derelict 17th century property about a mile down the track from Sharpcliffe Hall.

Out of nowhere a young woman appeared in a small, newish car. We asked the way to Ashcombe.

'Oh, I'll get my husband,' she replied, 'he plays in a recorder group at Ashcombe, knows the Haigs well.'

In this remote locality everyone knows everyone else, but at the time it seemed an almost surreal coincidence. A young man emerged from the broken-down house carrying a sleeping baby and gave clear, concise directions. The winding, narrow, grass-ridged tracks seemed to go on for miles, but eventually, as predicted, we met the main road. The drive down to

Ashcombe Park runs off this main road and we passed the gatehouse and the impressive gateposts surmounted by carved lions. It was, we decided, too late to visit - we would phone Mr Haig when we got home. But we reached Wetley Rocks church just as evensong was finishing. It was a small, plain, white building with the old school next door and did not detain us long.

'Did you know that Wetley Rocks was one of Staffordshire's sights in the early 19th century when they were into 'picturesque' scenery?' I asked Marion.

The village is long and straggling, built on the valley side with hanging rocks perched precariously above the houses. As picturesque scenery goes, we agreed, it was not a patch on Ipstones.

Our luck held, of course, and when we arrived at Cheddleton we found the church service there ended half an hour later than at Wetley Rocks, so we were able to see that church too - large and dark with wonderful stained glass windows glowing in the late evening sun.

'That looks like William Morris,' said Marion happily. I groaned. She was off! Marion and her husband had recently redesigned their lounge to accommodate a curvaceous, inlaid, art nouveau cabinet that they had fallen in love with in Brussels and imported to the UK at what seemed to me to be enormous trouble and expense. Other, home-grown pieces had been acquired to go with it, their walls had been papered in rich red paper, muted blue-grey William Morris curtains now hung at their windows and Marion had used a panel of Morris's 'Strawberry Thief' fabric as the basis for a wall hanging, adding colour, beads and embroidery to the original design. She was nothing if not thorough. In the process she had become something of an expert on Morris in particular and the art nouveau movement in general.

I did not share her passion but I knew that I had no choice but to allow her enthusiasm to run its course. The window proved to be a design by Burne-Jones - three large angels with ruby wings and agitated drapery - but there were other designs by Morris and Ford Madox Brown. Marion was ecstatic.

Cheddleton church should not have surprised us. William Morris, I knew, had often come to Leek to visit the Wardles. Thomas Wardle had been his dyemaster and many sample pieces of Morris fabric were dyed and printed in Leek. Thomas Wardle was an important man in the locality - indeed, the Sneyds and the Wardles were on visiting terms. Thomas Wardle had many contacts in London and he and his wife entertained numerous influential artists and designers; some worked on commissions for local churches, others produced designs for students at the local art school. Leek was no artistic backwater.

At last I dragged Marion away from the church and we drove round the village, spotting the Red Lion pub where Susanna's father held Petty Sessions in his capacity as magistrate, the canal where she and her nephew went to see the barges, the flint mill and many old cottages. Marion rambled on about brickwork again......

Back in Stoke-on-Trent after a lengthy and unscheduled detour - blamed variously on inefficient road signing and incompetent map reading - we took stock. Parts of Stoke really were dreadful, we thought, and we had seen quite a few of them on the way back to my house. We had begun to devise a game which we would refine as the project progressed; it was called 'See Alternative Britain'.

'Who wants to see the Cotswolds, Devon or Shakespeare country when they could play bingo in Burslem, tour Tunstall or hang out in Hanley?' it went, followed by increasingly crazy ideas about how to entertain an imaginary coach load of Americans in the more dismal reaches of Stoke-on-Trent. We probably got lost so often because we were too busy playing 'Alternative Britain'.

But apart from our excursion through the back streets of Stoke it had been an amazing day, and we celebrated with some barely-drinkable white wine from Mr Shah's as we recounted it to Barbie and Ken. Thai purred on my lap. Monday was to be spent at Keele - Marion had yet to see the diary collection as a whole - and a careful phone call to Mr Haig at Ashcombe Park produced an invitation to visit at six o'clock in the evening. He seemed wearily tolerant of people wanting to see his house.

Marion had visited Keele some years earlier when she was earning her living by selling her pottery at craft fairs. 'It was delicate high-fired stoneware,' she told me, 'very 18th century, decorated with lots of lustred and enamelled flowers, butterflies and dragonflies - but Keele was awful, no-one ever sold very well there.'

She remembered the university buildings as heaps of decaying 1960s cement, and it was an accurate memory, we agreed, as we searched for space in the crowded car parks. Despite its rural, woodland site, much of Keele University is deeply unattractive.

'That's quite interesting though,' said Marion indicating the chapel, a solid wedge of a building with narrow vertical windows like arrow slits and two massive round towers crowned with curious little steeples. 'It's got a fairy tale quality about it somehow. And look at those wonderful slate-grey bricks!'

'Not bricks again, **please**. Come on, we've work to do! '

The librarian was pleased to see us and had set out the diaries for us on a trolley in the Special Collections room. It was Marion's first sight of them.

'Oh wow! Amazing!' she beamed, clapping her hands and reacting to them like a child in front of an enormous light-spangled Christmas tree, then sobering..... 'but the work! Look at all the **work** we shall have to do!'

The day spent in the Special Collections Library was soothing - we were used to working in libraries. The diaries were fascinating. Many were red or brown leather-covered volumes with pockets in the front. Susanna's mother, Penelope, kept snippets of her children's hair in hers, carefully folded in slips of paper bearing dates and ages. At three, we discovered, little Susanna was a mousy blonde.

Her father, the Reverend John Sneyd, and grandfather William Sneyd, kept lists of the people to whom they owed money, lists of their servants and what wages were due to them and details of the beer being brewed in their cellars. There were odd letters, newspaper cuttings, and in Penelope's diaries, cut out paper animals and tufts of the fur of favourite pets.

Most appealing of all were the scrapbooks Susanna had made with her little nephew, Ralphy. He was her eldest brother's child, Ralph De Tunstall Sneyd, and Susanna had looked after him after his mother died. It was interesting to see just how little pictorial material was available to a child in a comparatively well-to-do home in the 1860s and 1870s. Most of the 'scraps' were in fact drawings done by Susanna or Ralphy. Even as a little boy he had a fertile imagination, and, aged five or six, he was drawing machinery and strange imaginary creatures. Susanna's drawings were much more pedestrian but often they connected with things we knew about Ralphy's childhood - it was particularly moving to come on a sketch, signed by Susanna and labelled *'Jennetta'*. Jennetta was Ralphy's pony, a present to him when he was three years old, and there she was, immortalised for all time on pink paper, a fat little Shetland with short legs and a thick mane.

Susanna, we knew, was a keen gardener, and stuck in the scrapbooks were pages from seed catalogues from Sutton's of Reading along with the cover of a price list from the family grocer in Rugeley. Ralphy's father,

John William, was passionate about shooting and the most colourful images in the scrapbooks were wrappers from his gun cartridges, *'Curtis and Harvey's Hounslow Gupowder'* printed in bright red and blue, each with a picture of a different type of game bird. And at last we found a clue as to what Susanna looked like in the form of a figure of a woman, cut from a fashion magazine and labelled by Ralphy *'I used to call this picture Aunty Susan'*.

We were loth to leave but at half past four we had to tear ourselves away to brave the Stoke-on-Trent rush hour, the fiendish one way system and the total absence of useful road signs and find our way across town and out to Ashcombe Park, allowing plenty of time for the inevitability of getting lost.

Cheddleton was quiet and peaceful but the drive down to Ashcombe was overgrown, the gates unpainted, so we should have been prepared for the Hall - but still it came as a shock. Ashcombe was the Sneyd family seat, a large, foursquare, grey stone house with a neo-classical porch, which Susanna's grandparents had built in the early 19th century in the valley below Wetley Rocks. Magnificent once, it stood now with stained walls, peeling paint, shuttered and shrouded windows blind to the unkempt garden. It looked like the setting for a horror movie. Nervously we rang the doorbell.

Distant barking echoed through the house and a tall grey-haired man limped to the door, still buttoning up his shirt. Though he was expecting us John Haig seemed suspicious at first, but the sight of Susanna's diary - which would have lived for so many years on one of the shelves in his library - worked its charm, and soon we were being greeted by his wife and their two large, amiable, smelly Newfoundland dogs whose sole aim in life seemed to be to stand on visitors' feet. Their heavy coats were not designed for hot weather and they scratched unhappily.

Mr and Mrs Haig could not have been more kind. They were a surprisingly modest couple to inhabit such a grand house, we thought, as they showed us round the home they so obviously loved. Its former grandeur was evident but it now sadly needed restoration and redecoration. They allowed us to take photographs - apologising profusely for the array of empty coke and beer cans on a trestle table at the foot of the magnificent flying staircase, the remnants of a Scottish country dancing evening the night before.

We thought about previous dances that had been held at Ashcombe -

in the same rooms, no doubt, with guests taking refreshments in the same hallway, stars glittering above them through the little cupola. Susanna's father had come home to Ashcombe when he was a pupil with the Reverend Carlisle at Belmont to take lessons with his sister Mary from Mr Fritsch, the dancing master. In the early years of the century William and Jane Sneyd had held dances at Ashcombe for their friends and neighbours; we pictured them, dapper men in skin-tight trousers wearing colourful, embroidered waistcoats, extravagant cravats and swirling tailcoats; pale, plump women with bare necks and arms in high-waisted dresses of magnificently embroidered muslin or fragile silk, a local band sawing away at the foot of the stairs, curry-coloured Indian shawls and lacy stoles draped on chairs as their owners swayed and curtseyed on the dance floor. It was not such a far cry from dancing eightsome reels to the tune of John Haig's recorder, we decided.

His recorder-playing skills were clearly much in demand. Within half an hour he was explaining that he had to go and give a recorder lesson to Mrs Scott-Moncrieff over at Rock Cottage. We realised with a start that she was the mother of the owner of Basford Hall to whose tender mercies the man on the tractor had recommended us the previous morning. Her telephone number, we had found the night before, was ex-directory, so we had planned to write to her with a view to meeting her on a future trip.

'Could you possibly take her a note?' I asked, scribbling frantically, 'We really want to meet her.'

Now we might have an introduction. We had obviously made a favourable impression on John Haig and he was willing to talk to the family at Basford Hall on our behalf. It was almost too good to be true. Emboldened by one success we enquired about the neighbouring house, Woodlands, which we had still not located.

'Next door? No problem - use my private road - then there's a public footpath. They won't like it but they can't stop you.'

It all sounded rather ominous.

We took our leave and drove the short distance to Woodlands. Susanna had married from there and had lived there with her sister Emily for two years after her marriage failed. Seeing the stone gateposts and the winding path gave us a frisson of excitement - we were really beginning to feel that we were stepping on her territory, seeing the places she would have known. As we stopped the car a bull thundered menacingly across the nearby field and stood panting heavily, watching us over the low stone wall. And in the steamy heat caused by Sunday's downpour a frenzied cloud of recently-hatched black flies descended on the car, completely obliterating the windscreen. We were back in the horror movie. For a few seconds we faltered....

'Do we really want to see Woodlands?' we asked each other nervously.

We were committing no crime, harming no-one, but there is something inherently improper, impolite, very un-English about calling on strangers for no better reason than an interest in the history of their property - an interest which they may well not share.

'Yes, we do,' said Marion, breaking the mood, 'come on.'

The rhododendron-lined drive curved gently, obscuring the house. As we rounded the corner a pretty pinkish-grey building of local stone came into view - but it wasn't Woodlands. The remains of coach house doors indicated stables - children's toys showed it was now a dwelling house. A few steps further - and there was Woodlands. We stood in stunned silence. The house was painted bright orange - all over! A barking dog signalled our arrival and through the scullery window an elderly man viewed us antagonistically. He shuffled to the door, tall, thin, his loose black trousers held up by braces, a wide black leather strap supporting his wrist.

'What d'you want?' he asked tetchily.

We explained, showed the diary we had with us and waited. He was neither impressed nor interested.

'Help, Susanna,' murmured Marion, and as if in answer, his wife appeared at the door beside him.

She was tiny, almost dwarf-like, thin, with a child's straight cropped page-boy haircut to her thin grey hair, baggy fawn cardigan, thick grey woollen knee socks and pink fluffy slippers. Strange she may have appeared but she was friendly and in no time at all had us past her still-grumbling husband and into her living room - a 1960s time warp with two fires blazing even on that tropically humid evening. She took us through to the front of the house where the full glory of the orange paint could be seen and pointed out the eighty-two windowpanes with their bright yellow frames.

'Will painted them all himself,' she said with obvious pride and affection. 'Does everything here himself. Pity you missed the rhododendrons - beautiful they were a few weeks back.'

Marion took photos, trying to avoid the small modern tractor parked incongruously in the landscaped garden. Pink and purple flowers against the orange and yellow house might have appealed to Gauguin, but we felt we could live without them. Will meanwhile had, at his wife's request, moved a large, rusting water cylinder from the front doorstep to improve the view.

'He's putting in a new water system,' she told me lovingly.

Only later did we learn that he was then over ninety. Why such an elderly couple should choose to live in such a huge, isolated house was inexplicable. More so was their decision to paint it orange. Will was clearly anxious for us to go, despite his wife's desire to chat, and it was obvious neither of them really understood our interest in their house so after a few minutes we took our leave. It was still early and there was one more place I wanted to see.

Susanna's husband, Charles Ingleby, had lived at Woodbank in Oakamoor, about ten miles away by road.

'How do you feel about driving to Oakamoor tonight?' I asked Marion tentatively. It had been a long day and I did not want to strain a friendship that was beginning to blossom nicely.

'Why not?' she replied amiably.

Soon we found ourselves in a hidden, enchanted landscape, a deep, wooded valley with steep, narrow, high-banked roads winding down into the village. Woods encircled the place and every house was on a slope - anyone of them could have been called Woodbank. We pulled up at the roadside.

'You lost?' called a man walking a greyhound.

He directed us to a large, pretty villa, high up the far side of the valley above the church. We viewed it curiously - the Inglebys had obviously lived in some style. But it was nearly dusk; no time to go calling on strangers - we were beginning to develop our own rules for what approaches we could and could not make. We set off for home.

'I can't imagine why so many people are willing to help us,' I said. 'We could be anyone - burglars, con artists. Yet people keep letting us into their homes and showing us round. Think of the couple at Belmont. Or the Haigs. I mean, that chap with the dog just now - he even told us the name of the people at Woodbank - we could turn up and pretend to be long-lost relatives or something.'

'But we don't look dishonest,' Marion objected, 'and we're not, are we?'

We began to consider our image. Marion is slightly older than me, a small, pretty, plump blonde with short, thick hair, piercing blue eyes and a taste for flowing garments, mostly in black and purple, worn with unusual silver and pewter jewellery. She trained as an art teacher but started her own pottery business when her children were young. Now she organises craft fairs which are the source of some of her more exotic outfits. Years of dealing with exhibitors, the owners of grand houses and the paying public have taught her diplomacy and she is at ease with most people and with herself. She is intuitive, with a breathtaking ability for lateral thinking - except when it comes to finding her way around the country. Never before have I met anyone who gets lost so often or so completely.

'I don't know my left from my right,' she explains, 'I'm partially dyslexic, remember.'

Her spelling certainly bears out that diagnosis.

'Well, I can write out a word half a dozen different ways,' she will say, 'and they **all** look right to me!'

I see myself as much less flamboyant - peahen to Marion's peacock. I took a history degree, straight from school and became a museum curator.

'Mind you, in my day it was a much more bohemian world than most people envisage,' I told Marion, trying to make myself sound interesting, 'nowadays entry to the profession requires a first degree and a post-graduate qualification in Museum Studies - all very laudable I suppose, they're all a lot more professional than we were - but when I first went into the business it was full of oddballs, colourful characters with chequered backgrounds and peculiar enthusiasms.'

'Not that I was ever particularly colourful,' I went on sadly.

Marion peered at me over the top of her reading glasses. 'Peahen? Colourless? Don't you ever look in the mirror? Shades of Guinevere or Marianne in the Moated Grange come to mind when I think of you!' she said tartly.

Nonetheless, in my relationship with Marion I am the practical one, the one who can be trusted with the boring jobs - constructing an accurate family tree, creating a map of the family estate, decoding legal documents - that sort of thing. I am larger and clumsier, bespectacled, and my mousy brown hair is scraped back into a bun. It probably doesn't suit me - Marion keeps urging me to cut it and wear it loose - 'It would make you look ten years younger!'

But its comfortable and a lot less trouble my way. Her exhortations to wear makeup also fall on deaf ears. I don't even think I look better made up - wearing lipstick always makes me feel like Barbara Cartland. Only my clothes echo Marion's. I too choose clothes that make a statement, preferably in flowing black to disguise my rather-too-ample figure and with lots of jewellery to distract attention from my shape. I don't feel I fit in anywhere, most of the time, but I like people - the stranger the better. And I'm a good lecturer, I comfort myself. As my own family required more and more of my attention I left museum work and did a series of part-time lecturing jobs - the one in Stoke has been the most enduring.

Together we must present a pretty unusual spectacle.

'But there's an energy between the two of you,' Barbie once observed, 'you spark each other off. It's quite different when I see you separately.'

It also helps, we have decided, to be middle-aged and female. Middle-class accents and a respectable car play a part and the fact that we are both rather plump, coupled with our eccentric dress sense makes us seem dotty and unthreatening, but on reflection it is the age/gender combination that is our greatest strength. Younger women, men of any age, even a middle-aged couple would find it much less easy to be accepted.

But nonetheless, we agree, unscheduled visits should only be made in daylight.

We returned to Stoke and a brief round of 'Alternative Britain' as Marion experimented with a new way of getting lost.

'Hi, you had a call while you were out,' called Barbie, poking her shining, hennaed head out of the kitchen as we entered, 'someone called John Haig. You are to be at Basford tomorrow evening at seven thirty. Is that good? Now tell me about your day.'

We were overjoyed. Basford was truly Susanna's home; she was born there, died there, and lived there for forty seven of her sixty years. We could not wait to see it properly.

The next day we returned to Keele and the diaries, trying to account for Susanna's marriage breakdown. This, we felt, was what made her story exceptional. We speculated wildly but found nothing of any substance. We extended our version of her family tree using Burke's *Landed Gentry*, Susanna's notes and various other papers we found in the library, and dipped in and out of the some of the family account books. We began to suspect that the Sneyds' finances were in fact very rocky. Our understanding of the family was growing. Bob and Bridget joined us for an hour or two.  True to their word they had already located a sketch of Armitage Cottage and they brought us a photocopy of it.

In the evening we made our way to Basford with only a short unscheduled detour in Cheddleton.  The tractor driver's words about how difficult the Scott-Moncrieffs were still rang in our ears and we were apprehensive as we drove along the tree-lined drive.  Only later would we learn that he was their tenant and deeply resented his landlord having returned to live nearby after years of uninterrupted possession of the Hall grounds.

John Haig was waiting for us with his camera - and photographed us. 'For security' he joked, but we knew he was serious.  We were completely unknown to him and he was responsible for introducing us to friends in another big house.  His caution was entirely understandable.    The housekeeper was equally suspicious, unwilling to let us in at all, then, suddenly, a tall, slim man - in his late forties, we guessed - bounced into the hall and the atmosphere changed. Humphrey Scott-Moncrieff had arrived.

'Come in, do,' he urged, smiling, welcoming us like old friends.

The past glory of the other houses had been evident from the outside, clearly showing the local status of the Sneyd family, but unknowingly, we had saved the jewel until last.  Basford was gloriously restored, loved and lived in, full of antique furniture, family portraits and photographs, china and ornaments everywhere.  It shone with life and colour, every room lovingly furnished and polished.  Soon we were being taken all over the house and shown family treasures - a wonderful cream silk dinner dress, books, photograph albums, portraits of Susanna's sister, cousins, father and uncles - and Humphrey Scott-Moncrieff himself was every inch a Sneyd. His features mirrored those of his ancestors - a posed photograph tucked into the frame of a picture of Susanna's uncles Tom and Henry demonstrated just how close the likeness was.

His wife and their delightful two year-old twins joined us - Alexandra, talkative and demanding, William, sweet and solemn. They had escaped their mother's attempts to put them to bed and come to see what these unknown visitors were doing in their home.  Judy Scott-Moncrieff followed them apologetically.  She was some years younger than Humphrey and quite stunningly beautiful, tall and slender in tight jeans and a simple black t-shirt. She had the face of a young Elizabeth Taylor, glossy dark hair, wide-set eyes and bright red lipstick, and exuded unbounded warmth, intelligence and enthusiasm. Basford was the perfect setting for her; Judy was born to entertain. The most inconvenient and unexpected guest (we suspected we probably fell into that category) is made to feel enormously welcome, her hospitality is apparently effortless, her energy unlimited.

After John Haig had left - another country dancing bash needed him - we all retired to the kitchen to drink wine, read stories to the twins, talk and await the arrival of Humphrey's mother, Averil Scott-Moncrieff, Susanna's great-grand-niece.

A car screeched to a halt in the yard - Averil's husband had been a racing driver and she had been driving sports cars for decades. Though over eighty she was lively, warm and as welcoming as her son and daughter-in-law had been, treating us as if we were doing them all an enormous favour by taking an interest in their family. Judy introduced her-

'Meet my lovely mother-in-law.'

Averil beamed. She was tall and slight, rather frail and with a curiously engaging lop-sided smile. The wine flowed and we were told anecdote after anecdote about the Sneyds. Soon we were on Christian name terms and, at last, we felt bold enough to pose the question we had spent so much time discussing.

'Averil,' I asked hesitantly, 'do you know anything about Susanna's marriage? Why did they separate so soon? Did anyone ever talk about it?'

There was a pause.

'Oh!' she chortled, 'yes, absolutely! Indeed they did! She was the one who married the hermaphrodite, wasn't she? The one who sewed himself into his nightshirt on his wedding night! Just too astonishing!'

In the cadences of her speech we began to glimpse the reluctant 1920s debutante that had been Averil Sneyd. She had eloped with her racing driver and broken her mother's heart but she still sounded like the aristocrat she had been brought up to be.

We gasped. It was amazing and improbable but a hundred and thirty years on the hermaphrodite story was still quite widely known locally - we would hear it a number of times from different sources. It would take several more years and more extraordinary encounters before we could put the record straight.

I noticed Marion yawning - it was past midnight. Our body clocks are entirely different, we were discovering. As I come alive at night,

Marion is ready for her bed. Early morning, when she is at her best, I am dead to the world - or exceedingly bad tempered. I love to drink in the evenings and over years of conference junketings with my husband have built up a healthy tolerance to all forms of alcohol. As the sole driver, Marion has to restrict her intake. We were still trying to find ways of accommodating each other's needs. At last we tore ourselves away with insistent invitations to visit again soon and promises to find other treasures for us to see. Overhead, unpolluted by town lights, the sky was black velvet, star spangled.

Susanna smiled approval. 'I chose well, very well indeed.'

Wednesday was our last day and we were due to go back to Keele to continue work on the diaries. Now we had got the feel of them we were making many discoveries. There was financial data, information about the Sneyds' involvement with copper mining in the area, details of social etiquette and business practice which seemed to contradict historically accepted norms. Almost by accident we had stumbled on an archive of unbelievable richness but one which would take many years of work.

We needed time and we needed funding. We would make further trips to Staffordshire - there was no question about that now - but no way could we leave our husbands and families for the length of time this research would require. We had accomplished more in the four days we had been away than we had ever dreamed possible, but it only served to point up how much more there was to do.

On Wednesday morning we had a meeting with the Special Collections Librarian. He was interested, sympathetic, but unable to suggest any source of finance.

'But,' he said hesitantly, 'I suppose it would help if you didn't have to keep coming here to look at the diaries? Perhaps I should let you take more than one at a time?'

'Oh yes,' I replied, fingers firmly crossed behind my back, 'we'd get on so much more quickly. And of course we could let you have copies of our transcripts for future researchers - to save wear and tear on the original documents, you know,' I added as what I hoped was an inspired afterthought.

We held our breath and waited. It would indeed help enormously - but university librarians and archivists are normally unwilling to let items out of their keeping - I had been amazed that we had been allowed to borrow the diaries one at a time.

'How many do you want then?' he went on.

'As many as you feel you could let us have.'

The impossible was happening again as he packed over a hundred of the precious volumes into a box and carried it out, past the checkout desk, to the car. Had we had a bottle of champagne handy we would have celebrated there and then, but tea and almost-edible cake in the students' union cafe had to suffice.

On the drive back we planned how we would split the volumes and who would do what, conscious all the while of the enormous trust the librarian had shown in us.

'We'll have to be ever so careful,' I warned Marion, my twenty years as a museum curator taking over, 'the leather on some of those diaries is getting quite dry and the pages are brittle - and some of them have got leather rot.'

'What's that?'

'Well its when the leather starts to go to powder - there's nothing you can do about it, we'll just have to  treat them very gently - he shouldn't really have given them to us.....'

Marion looked at me hard. 'And how else are we going to work on them?  Less of that....'

We agreed that I would continue transcribing Susanna's diaries since I was getting used to her handwriting, while Marion would start work on John Sneyd's, her father's and we would both read some of old William's - as we were beginning to call Susanna's grandfather - and her mother, Penelope's.  We had already skim read a number of these and it did not look as if they would be very useful - but we needed to be sure.  We would keep each other up to date with what we were finding and exchange transcripts. There was no going back now - we were hooked.  We worked and thought very differently, saw different things and made different connections - but we were a good team.

'We really could do with some funding, though,' Marion said. 'This is going to cost an awful lot of money.  Can we afford to do it?'

'Can we afford not to?' I answered. 'I'll have a trawl through the grant directories next time I'm in the university library.  I'm sure something will turn up.  Perhaps Susanna will help us - if she really does want her story told!'

Susanna Ingleby in June 1873.

*I had tic-doloreux*

**NOVEMBER, 1874.**　　107

**19 Thursday**

Very stormy. Scott the sweep came to sweep the kitchen chimney & to clean away the soot which had coming fire in the dining room grate. John Wm went to Leck about his canal bridge. Dear Ralph was dressed for the 1st time.

**20 Friday** Fine. I worked at my black merino dress. Harriet ? I had our dinner up stairs, my face was bad. Emily came in the afternoon & read the ? John Wm went to Coniscliffe to get his rent.

**21 Saturday** Fine. I worked. Emily came in the ? John Wm went to Captain Colvile's, & to Cheddleton. I wrote in the evening to Wm & Clark, at Messrs Marshall & Co.

A page from Susanna's diary

The Sneyd diaries at Keele University.

Penelope Sneyd, Susanna's mother

William Sneyd and Jane Debank Sneyd, Susanna's grandparents.

The Reverend John Sneyd, Susanna's father.

Penelope Marianne Brodie (née Sneyd).

Dryden Henry Sneyd.

Frederick Sneyd, (Freddy).

Gustavus Alfred Sneyd.

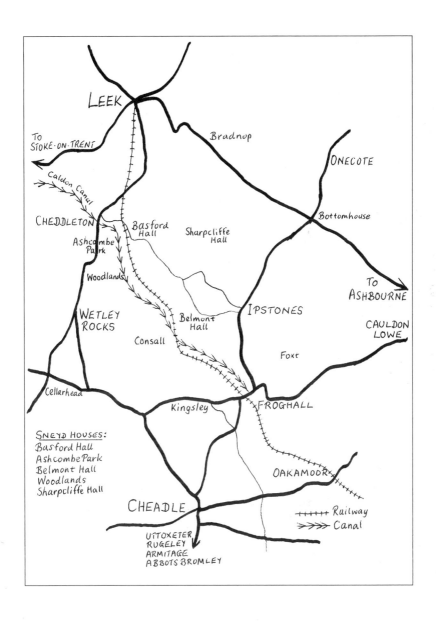

LEEK

TO STOKE-ON-TRENT

Bradnop

ONECOTE

Caldon Canal

CHEDDLETON

Basford Hall

Sharpcliffe Hall

Bottomhouse

Ashcombe Park

Woodlands

TO ASHBOURNE

IPSTONES

WETLEY ROCKS

Belmont Hall

Consall

CAULDON LOWE

Foxt

Cellarhead

Kingsley

FROGHALL

SNEYD HOUSES:
Basford Hall
Ashcombe Park
Belmont Hall
Woodlands
Sharpcliffe Hall

OAKAMOOR

CHEADLE

+++++ Railway
>>>>> Canal

UTTOXETER
RUGELEY
ARMITAGE
ABBOTS BROMLEY

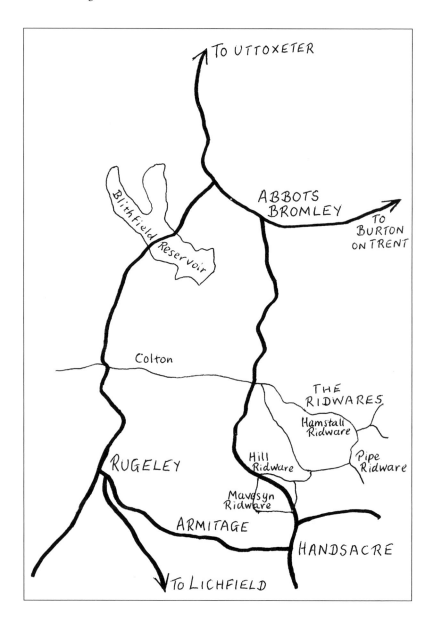

Chapter 2
# The Sneyds of Ashcombe Park

Over the next few months we stuck to our respective tasks, keeping each other constantly updated about our findings. Photocopying costs and telephone bills soared. At our respective homes amusement at our new hobby rapidly turned to irritation -

'It's Marion for you **again,** Mum!'

As we showed no signs of losing interest, irritation became weary resignation or, very occasionally, mild interest.

We knew we had found an extraordinary resource. Diary-keeping was a popular Victorian activity. It was seen as a useful exercise in self-discipline, a way of organising one's memories, recording expenditure, keeping track of calls made and received, and, particularly amongst young women, as a way of sharing confidences with trusted friends. Children were urged to keep diaries to practice their writing skills. Many religious groups encouraged it as a way of charting one's spiritual progress - record offices are awash with diaries of this type, full of pious reflections and anxious self-scrutiny. It was quite common for individuals to keep daily diaries for many years, but what is unique about the Sneyd collection is that so many diaries kept by members of the same family survive together - and we know that there are others that have been lost.

Susanna, for example, recorded helping her sister Emily Jane with her diary on more than one occasion. We have seen some of Emily's letters and her handwriting is impossible - demented barbed wire, made even more illegible by her idiosyncratic way of dividing words *'Wentfor a long w alkin the w oods'* and her frugal, spinsterly habit of always crossing her lines - turning the completed page through ninety degrees and penning another row of lines across the ones already written. Our recurring fear is that Emily's diaries will one day surface and we shall feel obliged to try to interpret them. Fortunately the other family diarists present fewer palaeographic challenges.

Of the diaries that do survive, Susanna's and her father's are the most informative, though her grandfather, old William Sneyd was probably the most prolific, keeping a diary almost continuously for over sixty years.

There were nuggets of information to be found in his early diaries, but for the most part they are a tedious record of visits made and received, meetings attended and family births, marriages and deaths.  Susanna's mother, Penelope, started a diary every year between 1820 and 1837 but seldom completed more than a few months. One diary apiece survives from Susanna's brothers John William and Frederick as does an almost blank diary owned by her uncle Ralph. John William's diary describes 1844, the year he was twenty-two, in Wales with his family, a partner in the family mine, happy, confident and newly adult. Frederick's diary details 1863, the year his younger brother died and he himself became ill and had to be sent abroad to Mentone with his uncle and aunt to recuperate.  The early part shows him as a young man of twenty-four, actively involved with the family estate, but the later entries are painful to read *'Walked about this town'* or *'Did nothing this day that I can remember'* day after day after day. He was sick and lethargic - within a year he, too, would be dead.

There is a family style discernible in all the Sneyd diaries; for the most part the entries are spare and factual with little description and virtually no personal comment. Usually they start with a description of the weather - a much more important factor in people's lives when most journeys were made on foot or on horseback and when much of the family income was directly dependent on agriculture. It was thought important to list all the people one had met in the course of a day, so an evening party was likely to be recorded as a string of names, leaving no space for any comment on what was eaten or drunk or what the main topics of conversation were. Similarly, the men of the family record all the meetings they attended but scarcely ever tell us what happened at them. Sunday entries give the biblical reference to the preacher's text.

They could be very pedantic.  In Susanna's diaries train times are always given in full - never 'the 8 o'clock train' but the '8.02'.  The latter part of Frederick's diary represents the extreme of diary-keeping-as-pointless-exercise but the conscientious Sneyd diarist always wrote something, however banal - Susanna in later years frequently produced such entries as *'A wet day. I did not go out'* or simply *'I worked etc'*. Nonetheless, as we read the diaries, day by day, year by year, lifetime by lifetime, a surprisingly detailed picture emerged.

But first we had to come to grips with all the people and places our diarists mentioned.

'What do you suppose Wettie is short for?' I asked in one of our ever-lengthening evening phone calls, having just come across a batch of entries about *'poor dear Wettie'*. 'Or it might be Hettie - or Nettie.'

'Henrietta? Harriet?'

'Possibly, but I think it's a he.'

It was sometime before I found that it was Wettenhall, actually Richard Wettenhall, also sometimes known as Dick, just to add to the confusion, and that he was one of Susanna's younger brothers and had been crippled as a child with arthritis. 'Tavie' turned out to be her youngest brother, the grandly-named Gustavus Alfred. 'Feddy', Marion discovered from the Reverend John's diaries was not a mis-spelling for Freddy, but his nickname. Perhaps that is how he pronounced it as a toddler. John William, the eldest brother with whom Susanna was to spend much of her life, was 'Jonkey' in his father's diaries until he was about ten years old, and when their little half-sister, Ada, was born her father referred to her as 'Ickey'.

'That tells us all we need to know about baby Ada, doesn't it?' Marion remarked. 'Delightful!'

For the most part the Sneyds led lives that were very like those lived by many others in their strata of society. They saw great events - the French Revolution, the Napoleonic wars, the nationalist uprisings of 1848, the Great Exhibition of 1851, war in the Crimea - and experienced enormous changes. The industrial revolution was well under way when Susanna's grandfather began his diary. He saw the canals built and lived to see the coming of the railways. Other relations fought in wars, travelled to the corners of the empire and described their experiences in letters home.

But the Sneyd diaries only mention such things obliquely. Most diarists - unless they are politicians with an eye on future publication - see no reason to record national events, but they do tell of their own involvement with their family, friends and locality. The Sneyds were no exception. They wrote of attending enclosure meetings, and taking shares in canal and turnpike trusts; of shopping and prices; of visiting, going to balls, the theatre, circuses and wild beast shows. They were magistrates and sat on Poor Law committees. They dealt with poachers, beggars, petty theft, rape, murder and John Sneyd even attended the inquest of a young woman travelling dressed as a young man.

'I've come across that in novels,' I said, 'girls travelling alone -

usually when they shouldn't have been - dressed as boys so they wouldn't be molested. Interesting that it sometimes happened for real.'

The Sneyds administered the law and fell foul of it. They subscribed to local charities and made clothes for the needy. They travelled, and described their complicated journeys and the changes that came as the railway network spread across the country. They farmed, and kept farming accounts. They built schools and churches. They made jam, collected recipes and had problems with the servants. They had their teeth filled, were bled with leeches, swapped recipes for chilblain lotion and had operations performed on them under the newly discovered gas, chloroform. Their diaries describe the minutiae of everyday life in the 19th century, and there are many surprises, even for  historians.

'We have to do something with all this,' we kept saying, 'it's far too good to waste.'

There was, however, a problem which only became apparent when we began the search for a publisher. No-one had heard of Susanna Ingleby and her family. However fascinating their story (and everyone agreed it **was** a fascinating story) no firm we spoke to was prepared to take a chance.

'Readers will only buy biographies if they are of someone well-known,' we were told again and again.

We had not expected it to be easy - no-one had heard of us, either - but we had hoped that someone, somewhere, would be able to see the value of the resource we were uncovering.

'After all, the Edwardian Lady wasn't exactly famous, was she?' grumbled Marion as publisher after publisher rejected our suggestions, 'nor Parson Woodforde, nor Samuel Pepys, come to that...'

We knew we needed advice, an agent, somebody, but we'd just have to trust to luck - or Susanna.

'First we have to explain the family background,' I said.

'I suppose so,' groaned Marion, anxious to get on with what she saw as the interesting part. She's not a patient person.

The story the diaries tell begins in 1792, but the Sneyd family history dates much further back than that. The family tree is complicated; the same Christian names re-surface generation after generation, families were large, second families and marriages between first cousins were common. The detailed family tree that we had so carefully constructed on our first visit to Keele became an essential tool, always open on our desks.

As we have already seen, the Ashcombe Sneyds were a cadet branch of the more illustrious Sneyd family of Keele. They in turn - with an optimism shared by many 19th century genealogists working for gentry families in Mercia - claimed to trace their ancestry back to King Alfred. Susanna's branch of the family was descended from a 17th century younger son of the Keele family whose father purchased land for him, and who went on to marry an heiress who brought him lands in the Staffordshire Moorlands. His grandson was Susanna's great-grandfather, the John Sneyd (1734-1807) who built Belmont Hall, the large white house near Ipstones that we had visited in the pouring rain on our first Sunday in Staffordshire. Once the house was complete he set about the extensive planting of the grounds and the valley below, and won a Royal Horticultural Society gold medal for his efforts. Two-and-a-half centuries on the trees are mature and in the autumn the colours in the valley are magnificent. We had driven through an avenue of his planting on the way up to Belmont, the trees around the pools, and probably the pools themselves, were his, as were Belmont's huge kitchen gardens. Georgian landowners had vision and faith in the future.

This John Sneyd was the father of William Sneyd, our first diarist, who was born in 1767 and was Susanna's grandfather. As a sixteen year-old he joined the 38th Regiment of Foot as lieutenant and later became an aide-de-camp at the Prussian court, but by the time we encountered him through his diaries he was very much the English provincial gentleman. His was a leisured life. He had all the trappings of wealth and privilege, including a man servant, John Birch, for whom he paid a *'powder licence'* of a guinea a year which entitled Mr Birch to wear a powdered wig. He travelled to London, enjoyed visits to the theatre and the spa at Buxton, and shot grouse and blackcock on the moors every autumn. In London he was very much the young man about town, bent on pleasure.

Marion was delighted when she found the entry *'brothels - 3s'* in his diary. We peered at the cramped handwriting. Could he possibly have written that down? He had, there could be no other reading of it. And there was another entry *'to a boy at ye opera - 1s.'*

'Do you know about the boxes in 18th century theatres?' I asked Marion. It happened that I had recently had a conversation on the subject with one of my husband's PhD students who was writing a thesis on an obscure 18th century playwright.

'No?'

'Well, apparently many of them had exits to 'private chambers' where all sorts of sexual services were on offer.'

'So you think the boy at the opera....?!'

'Well, a shilling was a lot more than you paid someone to hold your horse or carry your coat!'

In 1796 William married an heiress, Jane Debank, only daughter of Simon and Elizabeth Debank of Stafford. It was an arranged marriage - an attempt by the Sneyds to stave off their financial problems.

'They seem to have done this generation after generation,' I said, 'find an heiress, marry off your eldest son, watch him spend all her money!'

Though the Sneyds and the Debanks knew each other, the couple's formal courtship consisted of one meeting and the exchange of three letters. Before the wedding William referred to Jane in his diaries as * - the symbol he later used when his mare was covered or his bitch went to stud.

'Unbelievable!' said Marion when we realised what the asterisk meant.

'Horrifying,' I agreed. 'Poor Jane Debank!'

* was a disturbingly accurate comment on William's attitude to his wife. She bore him eleven children in the first thirteen years of their marriage. Five died in infancy. He was a robust husband. We shuddered at the entry in his 1797 diary - *'paid old Mary to draw my wife's breasts'* - when Jane had mastitis after the infant daughter she was breast-feeding had died and she was already pregnant again with their first son. We could only guess what old Mary had done - but it was almost certainly painful.

He was equally pragmatic in his approach to Jane's confinements. In 1802, he recorded that *'Mrs Sneyd and I went for a drive and returned at 2. At 3 my wife was delivered of a son'*. Presumably the ride in an ill-sprung coach over rutted roads was intended to speed up the contractions.

'Poor Jane!' we said again.

The little boy was named Clement and he died of whooping cough at the age of five. After the death of their youngest son in infancy in 1809 William and Jane led almost entirely separate lives. As their children grew up - five sons and a daughter survived into adulthood - the boys became his companions while daughter Mary did her best to pacify *'the Mrs'* as she called her opinionated and difficult mother.

'We need to know a good deal more about Jane Debank,' I told my colleague one evening.

'We certainly do,' she replied. 'She crops up everywhere in the Reverend John's early diaries and really seems to be the power behind the family and difficult to boot. And he seems to take after her - he really was the most unpleasant man.'

'Well, how about another trip to Staffordshire soon? To Stafford Record Office - didn't we find they had a copy of her will?'

Jane Sneyd, always known as Jane Debank, even after her marriage, was a powerful woman. She had brought money into the family and she retained as much control of it as possible, while William spent whatever came his way. His wedding present to her was a beautiful coach. Humphrey showed it to us on one of our visits to Basford. It still stands in the coach-house, along with the family's cars, too fragile to use now, but a splendid sight in canary yellow with the Sneyd crest on its doors. In all probability it was this coach which was used to speed little Clement's birth in 1802.

'A few weeks after the wedding he presented her with the bill,' said Humphrey. 'At least that's what we were always told!' It figured.

Starting in 1806, William demolished the old house - Botham Hall - on his land, and set about building a new one, Ashcombe Park - again with Jane's money. The architect was young James Trubshaw; this was his first big commission and he seems to have allowed his client's formidable wife a good deal more say in the design than a more experienced man might have done.   Despite its deteriorating condition, the exciting thing about Ashcombe, at least for those interested in architecture, is that so little of the original building has changed.   The shutters, detailing, even the door furniture are still just as Jane Debank planned them.

She also took charge of paying Mr Trubshaw's workmen, arriving each week carrying a little black silk purse from which she extracted coins to ensure that each man received his exact wage. It was more than a gesture. Small coins were in short supply in the early 19th century and the normal practice was to pay groups of workmen in sovereigns - which then had to be taken to the local public house to be changed into sixpences and shillings to pay each individual his due. In return, publicans expected some of that money to be spent on beer, with the result that the pittance the workmen received would have dwindled before they even got home to their families.

As her sons grew up, Jane Debank kept them in her power. She built and endowed a church at Wetley Rocks so that her philandering son, Henry, could have his own parish. She interfered in her other sons' lives, calling doctors when she thought they were ill even when they were grown men with homes and families of their own; she organised where they should live and expected them to dance attendance on her. She wrote her own will, in her own hand - draft after draft survives in Staffordshire Record Office.

Despite the fact that he was a busy man with a growing family, a parish to run and magisterial duties to attend to, her son John, Susanna's father, was expected to spend day after day helping his mother with this will. He dared not refuse. The final document is seventy-five pages long and ties up her affairs so tightly that neither her husband nor her sons could get their hands on her money. It must have seemed a wise precaution at the time but it laid the seeds of later disasters, as lack of ready money never stopped the Sneyd men from spending.

Old William Sneyd led a comfortable life, and he thrived on it - despite blood-curdling references in his later diaries to *'haemorrhaging kidneys' 'fever'* and *'spasms in the bladder'* - and lived to a healthy old age. He died in February 1851, aged eighty-three, but that January he was still able to attend church, visit his solicitor in Cheadle and entertain friends. His last diary entry was made in a firm, clear hand on January 27th. Susanna was almost twenty when he died and she and her siblings had visited him regularly, walking down the hill and across the fields that lay between Basford and Ashcombe. Through her grandfather Susanna had a link to an age that was very much more settled and certain than her life would ever be.

Old William was succeeded by his eldest surviving son, Susanna's father, the Reverend John Sneyd (1798-1873). He went to Brasenose College, Oxford, and his undergraduate diary shows him as a typical, reckless, spendthrift student, spending his time rowing, throwing champagne breakfasts, buying glass and fine linen to enhance his reputation as a host. He did just enough work to get by until his last year when he had to spend the whole summer in Oxford, cramming all the Greek and Latin he should have learnt previously, in order to re-sit his finals. It was a stultifyingly boring curriculum and relied very heavily on rote learning rather than analysis.

'Those diaries would make an interesting little publication in their own right' said Marion 'I wonder if Brasenose would be interested?'

They weren't.

'Perhaps Susanna didn't think his behaviour when he was an undergraduate was in keeping with the position he later occupied in life,' I suggested. 'She doesn't want them published.'

Marion snorted.

In 1822 John Sneyd married his first cousin, Penelope Holley, daughter of his father's sister Mary Anne. The couple had spent much of their teenage together as Penelope's mother had died when she was a baby and her father had remarried and produced a new family. *'Little Pen Holley'* was often sent to stay with her Staffordshire relations. Penelope brought money to the marriage but it is obvious that this was also a love match. For some reason Jane Debank disapproved and for three years she did not visit John or receive Penelope.

'Why not?' I asked Marion.

'Maybe she didn't bring enough money,' she guessed. 'Or maybe she just didn't like her. Maybe she was just being cussed because old William was fond of Pen. It wasn't until John's elder brother, William Debank, died - he was the one who died on the day he should have married - remember? John became the heir and everything changed. Jane had to accept Penelope then, I suppose.'

John became a curate at Odstone in Leicestershire but his heart remained in Staffordshire. He and Penelope did a prodigious amount of travelling between the two counties, moving to a curacy in Drayton, nearer the county boundary, in 1824, and then back to the family estate in 1825, where he set about rebuilding a 17th century house, Basford Hall, as his family home. In 1833 he secured the living of Ipstones, up on the edge of the moors and about four vertical miles from Basford.

'How much did he earn?' I asked.

'Not enough to support his family - about £150 (£8000) a year - the job was about status and influence, not cash. He had an allowance from his father to live on - I suppose it was like drawing an income from the family business. And of course his mother doled out money when she felt like it. She set up a trust fund for her granddaughters' dowries, for example.'

Penelope, meanwhile, was producing a child every year or two. She was a healthy young woman and between confinements led a hectic social life with her husband. Her diaries herald the approach of each new baby by recording a few weeks of rest and quiet and the arrival of a nurse - her favourite was a Mrs Gee. The doctor would only be summoned if there were complications.

Penelope's confinements were remarkably trouble-free. Between 1822 and 1844 she had thirteen children - a son, John William, four daughters, Harriet, Emily Jane, Penelope Marianne and Helen, then at last a second son, Ralph Debank; then Susanna, Dryden Henry, Edmund Lionel, Mary and three more boys, Frederick Clement, Richard Wettenhall and Gustavus Alfred. Her diaries show that she breastfed most of them herself; within weeks of the births she and John had resumed their social life, visiting friends and staying overnight - a necessary part of visiting in a scattered rural area before the railways speeded up communications - always with nursemaid and baby in tow.

'Remember that letter we found in one of her diaries?' Marion asked.

In the front of Penelope's 1835 diary was an undated letter from *HH* at Fox Earth inviting John and Penelope to dinner and to stay the night *'for I am happy to be able to offer a room for your nurse and baby'*. Fox Earth was near Cheadle and was the home of the Reverend Charles Hassells and his family.

'The baby would have been Lionel, I suppose,' I said, consulting the family tree.

Penelope's diaries are full of gaps but she usually records weaning the latest baby at about eight months. Then she and John would have a holiday, and within weeks or months she would again be pregnant. She records only one miscarriage - the result of *'riding my Arab mare'* in the early weeks of a pregnancy in July 1824 - and no stillbirths. None of her children died in infancy. One son was crippled from early childhood with arthritis, five children died in their late teens or early twenties, but at Penelope's death in 1849, in her fiftieth year, twelve of her thirteen offspring were still alive, ranging in age from twenty-seven year-old John William to five year-old Tavie.

'There can't have been many women who were as lucky as that, can there?' I said. 'Think of the infant mortality rate. What did they call it in that awful book we had to read on our course?'

'Maternal wastage,' answered Marion, 'only a man could come up with a term like that!'

Penelope's diaries show her as a sentimental mother, writing of *'my*

*Darlings', 'dear little', 'my precious little'* - but, once her babies were weaned she had little contact with them. Their day-to-day care was in the hands of nursemaids and governesses, and some of the children seem to have virtually lived with relations; little Harriet, for example, spent most of her childhood with Miss Broughton, a cousin in Uttoxeter, while Susanna was with her Aunt Mary at Highfields much of the time. It was quite common for large families to farm children out in this way though it seemed rather heartless to us.

John Sneyd, was energetic and ambitious. Unlike his own father he actively sought public office and was heavily involved in local affairs - as a magistrate, as a member of various turnpike committees, as a shareholder in the local railway, as a subscriber to numerous local charities, as a canvasser for the would-be Conservative MP David Watts Russell, as an innovative farmer and founder of Staffordshire's first agricultural school and as a mover-and-shaker in church affairs.

He was probably the most important man in Leek in the middle years of the century; everyone knew him, and he was respected, feared and disliked for his imperious behaviour. At John Sneyd's say-so men could go to jail, families could be refused Poor Law relief, publicans could lose their licenses, men could be evicted from their homes or sacked from their jobs. He had real power over people's lives and he used it. Though he was able and hardworking, he was also deeply flawed, opinionated, inflexible and given to litigation. His father had also been involved in various law suits, and his sons were to be equally prone to take their neighbours and each other to court. The firm of Challinor and Shaw in Leek thrived, generation after generation, on Sneyd litigiousness.

'Do you remember Jarndyce versus Jarndyce in Charles Dickens's *Bleak House*?' Humphrey asked us out of the blue one day.

'Sort of. Wasn't it a case in Chancery? A case that rumbles on and on and nobody really understands what it is about any more, let alone remembers how it started.

'That's right. And the case only came to an end when there was no money left and the entire value of the estate had been used up in litigation costs. Well, I was in the solicitor's recently and someone showed me a letter, framed and hanging on the wall in the office...'

'Yes?'

'It's from Charles Dickens to William Challinor, Joseph Challinor's brother and partner. It seems to imply Dickens knew him.'

'**Really?**'

'Well, it's quite possible. Challinors had a London office and they certainly had lots of connections. Leek was quite an important and prosperous town in the Victorian era when the silk trade was at its height. And Dickens did visit Staffordshire. Anyway, I was told that the Sneyds were thought to be his inspiration for the Jarndyces, always taking each other to court!'

It was a wonderful story. Could it possibly be true? We tracked down the letter - it was a simple, undated note of thanks to William Challinor for sending a pamphlet. William Challinor had written two pamphlets *The Court of Chancery* and *Chancery Reform*, both in 1848. Had Dickens used them when he was writing about the Jarndyce case? It was certainly possible. When was *Bleak House* published? 1853. Could William Challinor have talked to Charles Dickens sometime previously, over dinner perhaps? Growing more and more indiscreet as the port circulated and trying to impress his famous companion?

'The things we lawyers have to deal with, Mr Dickens! Human nature at its worst! Some of our cases are just like your books. Indeed, you could do worse than to set your next story in court. Chancery? A capital idea! I'll send you a copy of my pamphlet on the subject.

There is a family in Leek for example - not my own clients of course, my brother Joseph represents them. The head of the family is an old man, and he won't be with us much longer. And when his heir takes over completely - well, I dread to imagine what will happen. Already his fortune is at risk - an ill-considered mining adventure in Wales. Too headstrong to take advice. Only a matter of time, my brother says. His character? Well, outwardly he is a well-respected reverend gentleman, but much given to litigation, refuses to listen to reason, you could as well scrub black white as to get him to change his mind if once he has made it up. He is a JP and he imprisoned a brother clergyman - yes, back in 1839. Some quarrel about a pamphlet. And he has quarrelled with various members of his family too - his brother moved to Devonshire to escape him. He insists my brother seek legal advice from Counsel in London about all sorts of trivial matters - and the cost! Have you heard of heriots? No, well, let me explain...'

For a few minutes we let our imaginations run riot. There is no proof but it was an intriguing idea. And not impossible.

Fortunes were being made in copper-mining in the early part of the 19th century. The mine at Ecton, only a few miles from the Ashcombe estate, made vast sums for its owners, the Dukes of Devonshire. John Sneyd decided that this was the way to make money. He and his father and uncles became partners in the Mixon mine, high up on a stony hillside on Bradnop moor. There was copper in the Mixon and some huge lumps of ore were found, some *'as big as a horse's body.'*

'How do we know that?' asked Marion. 'I don't remember that bit.'

'You know those notes Ralphy made? After Susanna's death he went round asking people what they remembered about her and the rest of his family and wrote it all down, signed and dated. He had people like us in mind, I suppose. Old Mr Brindley told him about the mine.'

In the first year John Sneyd took £20,000 worth of copper out of the mine - nearly a million pounds worth in today's money. It was a promising start, but much of the ore was below the water table and therefore not economic to extract and eventually the mine lost the Sneyds around £10,000.

'That's about half a million,' said Marion. 'Don't you think you should put the conversions in each time? In italics, perhaps?'

'Most people can divide by two,' I objected, 'and most of them can multiply by fifty, come to that. That's the simple way of converting Victorian prices into modern money. Not entirely accurate but a useful rule of thumb. But if you insist I'll put some prices into modern money from now on.'

The Sneyds also became shareholders in the ill-fated High Rake mine in Derbyshire which, in total, lost its shareholders over £60,000 (£3,000,000). Not content with these losses, the Reverend John followed his dream into Wales, taking as partners his father and eldest son John William. The whole Welsh escapade was disastrous and in total the Welsh mining venture cost the Sneyds £32,500 (£1,879,645). Coming on top of their other losses it all but ruined them.

Perhaps fortunately, Susanna's mother, Penelope, died in 1849 before the crisis really came to a head. Within a year, John Sneyd had acquired a new young wife, Mary, and within two years he had started a second family which must have made his impending bankruptcy all the more disastrous.

The crash came in 1852 and John Sneyd had seen it coming. Within weeks of his father's death, in February 1851, he tried to mortgage the estate, only to find it was his only for his lifetime. The lands were entailed to his son, John William, and the Reverend John could not raise money against them without his son's consent. This John William refused to give. He no longer trusted his father's business acumen and feared that if John Sneyd had his way there would be nothing left for himself and his siblings.

The Reverend John was not a man to brook opposition, least of all from one of his children, and they quarrelled bitterly. John William was turned out of Ashcombe in the pouring rain, late at night, and fled to his married sister, Penelope Marianne Brodie, in Scotland.

Eventually, in 1853, father and son reached an unhappy compromise. Part of the Consall estate was let on a ninety-nine year lease to Thomas Adderley and John Holley - both relatives - and they paid John William £100 (£5241) a year for it. John Sneyd mortgaged the rest of the estate and let the grand houses. For the rest of his life, the Reverend John, Mary and their only child, Ada, lived a peripatetic existence, staying with relatives, travelling, abroad, in lodgings or staying at Woodlands, the smallest and least grand of the family's homes. John Sneyd was never reconciled with his eldest son.

'We're running ahead of ourselves,' objected Marion, 'none of this is in the diaries.'

'But we have to explain it now,' I argued, 'otherwise the story doesn't make sense. We'll describe how we found out later....'

In his diary John Sneyd disguised the reality of his quarrel with John William with the bland statement *'John William left Ashcombe'*. Later references to *'my faithless son'*, curt comments about writing to John William to give him notice to remove his property, and discussions with his lawyer about *'John William's business'* gave us clues, but it was not until we discovered a cache of family documents that the full story became clear. We guessed that the mining disaster held the key but it would be some time before we would uncover all the details. At the time we were transcribing the first huge batch of diaries we could only speculate about what had gone so disastrously wrong.

But we were learning all the time. The Sneyds had been one of the most important families in North Staffordshire and many local people had information to give us. We met dozens of people who had stories to tell of

Susanna's nephew, Ralph De Tunstall Sneyd. He had died in 1947 but his exploits were still remembered with much affection and amusement. He was 'a real gentleman' but a very eccentric one, who conducted Druidical rituals on the Staffordshire Moorlands, dressed up in Arthurian armour, and who experimented with a sequence of increasingly unlikely religions. We heard about the little boy who believed he had seen God outside Thor's cave - only to be told by his parents that he had come upon Ralph De Tunstall Sneyd meditating. And about the two boy scouts camping in the woods near Leek in the 1930s who were terrified by the appearance of Ralph De Tunstall and two of his acolytes gliding through their camp dressed as Benedictine monks, looking neither to the right nor to the left as they headed along their accustomed route to Basford Hall. The boys - one of whom is now chairman of the Cheddleton Historical Society - were convinced they had seen ghosts.

And we were told about Ralph's visit to a pre-war circus in Leek.

'How much to get in?' he asked.

'Sixpence.'

'But how much for gentlemen?' persisted Ralph, mindful of the class distinctions of his father's day.

'Sixp—- oh, half a crown, sir!' came the reply.

Ralph had been brought up by his Aunt Susanna, so in a way these stories were a direct link back to her. We could well see how trying straight-laced, conventional, sensible Susanna must have found her oddball of a nephew.

It took us some time to find his house but we had persisted. We were directed to visit old Ralph Critchlow, 'the only compus mentis eighty year-old in these parts,' who, we were assured, would tell us everything we needed to know about Ralph De Tunstall Sneyd.

'Isn't it interesting how the gentry names were used by everyone else?' I said. 'Ralph is a pretty uncommon name, but there seem to be dozens of them round here. And did I tell you that when I was checking through the 1891 census for Cheddleton I actually found someone who must have been named after Susanna's brother, Dryden? Dryden Henry Blore! Poor chap!'

Old Mr Critchlow was used to visitors - his house was a listed building and totally unspoilt.

'They comes round every year to make sure I've not made meself comfortable,' he chuckled, but it was scarcely a joke. The main room of the cottage had changed little since it was built. The only concessions to modernity were a stone sink with a cold tap, probably put in in the early 1900s, a bare electric light bulb, an antiquated electric cooker and a television set. An ancient rag-rug lay on the bare flagged floor between two threadbare armchairs.    Photographs and a garish modern calendar brightened the dark panelled walls - sepia prints of Mr Critchlow as a young man and on his wedding day, 1950s black-and-white school photos of his children, wedding groups, modern colour pictures of children and a large framed photograph of his granddaughter in her Keele graduation robes. A roaring fire fought a lost cause and water dripped in the sink.

Mr Critchlow, in a well-worn jacket, layers of pullovers, boots and a cap which looked as if it never left his head, chatted to us amicably, standing with his back to the fire thus blocking out the little heat that escaped the chimney. He was a big man, still active despite his years. He remembered Ralph De Tunstall well.

'A real gentleman, dressed fine, always dressed fine.  He built defences up at Fairview for when the invasion came, you know.' Ralph Critchlow did not elaborate on which invasion, there seemed no need, but he did remember the old builder who had done the work. He knew exactly where the house was and gave us clear directions. It was growing dark and outside it had started to snow - odd flakes fluttered through the wide gap under the front door and settled inside the threshold. They did not melt. Standing on the icy flags our feet grew numb and we were anxious to retreat to the warmth of the car heater - and besides, we wanted to reach Fairview while there was still some light left.

'Come and see the Tudor roses.  They all like to see them.'  Mr Critchlow urged us into the passageway that separated his kitchen from his equally comfortless living room.  He pulled aside a row of anoraks and oilskins that hung on Victorian hooks screwed into the oak panelling. Beneath them was a row of simple carved roses, the patriotic work of some 16th century Staffordshire craftsman.

'Do you want a photo?  They all photograph these.'  Ralph Critchlow's house was clearly a Mecca for historians of vernacular architecture - he found it difficult to comprehend that we had a different agenda. Obediently, Marion took a photograph, though she had little hope that it would come out - it was almost pitch dark in the passage. Then, shivering, we escaped to the car.

'Susanna would have recognised that,' said Marion. 'I suppose a lot of the cottages she visited were just as bleak and cold - no carpets, little in the way of heating.'

'You can see why she got chilblains.'

We arrived unannounced at Fairview late that bitter February afternoon just as the sun was becoming a watery red streak on the horizon and snowflakes were drifting on the icy wind. The view was fast disappearing into darkness - and Mr and Mrs Henshall, the owners, were walking towards their car. Our timing could not have been worse, but they were friendly and happy to talk. They pointed out the chapel, with its pink windows and lead lined walls (why lead? - no-one knows) and the lengths of stone on the front lawn that had come from the Giant's Causeway.

'Would you like to see the sacrificial altar?' asked Mrs Henshall, in much the same tone of voice that would have invited us to view a new three piece suite or admire a flowering cherry. She led us round to the side of the house, and there it stood, Ralph's Druidical altar - a huge circular stone slab, eight feet in diameter and several inches thick. Seed trays and flower pots littered the surface - it was surreal.

'Move them if you want to take a picture,' she urged.

We did.

'How often do you get invited to see a sacrificial altar in someone's back garden?' we asked each other gleefully. 'And how on earth do you think he got it up there?'

Ralph Critchlow had told us tales of how, in Ralph De Tunstall's day, the house and outbuildings had been full of his collections - Buddhas, mummies, curiosities from all around the world - of how he claimed to have been pursued across Africa by natives demanding the return of some religious artifact he had acquired and of his adventures with werewolves in Transylvania. The Henshalls showed us photographs of the interior of the house as it had been and gave us a press cutting with a contact address for one of his grandsons - all this in the fifteen minutes or so that they could spare us before they went out for the evening. It was a typically serendipitous encounter.

A few weeks later we followed up the contact we had been given. Ralph's grandson lived in a comfortable, detached, mock Tudor house in a quiet suburban road. As far as we knew he was Ralphy's only surviving descendant, a softly spoken, bearded man with thinning grey hair and the unmistakeable, Sneyd nose. On his drawing room wall hung an oil painting of a family group in a room which we recognised as the library at Ashcombe Park. We guessed that the elderly man in the armchair was old William and the tall thin man in the foreground was definitely the Reverend John.

'And that, I think, is Susanna,' said Dr John Sneyd, pointing to the young woman on the right of the portrait.

I looked closely.

It is very easy to date Victorian women's costume; fashion changed quite rapidly but at any given date all women who had any pretensions to respectability followed the prevailing mode. I had spent over twenty years working as a costume curator and was very familiar with the appearance of mid-19th century garments. I had handled hundreds of them and been called in frequently by my colleagues in the fine art department to help them identify portraits in exactly this way. I was quite sure that the lady in this picture wore a dress of the 1850s - the tightly gathered, but not too full, skirt, ruched 'v' shaped bodice, low pointed waist and slightly over-long sleeves all pointed to the early part of that decade. And she wore a wedding ring. Susanna did not marry until 1860 when dress shapes had changed subtly, waists were higher and straight, skirts were fuller but pleated at the front, sleeves were fitted in a different way. And there was no reason for Susanna to have had her portrait painted with her father and grandfather.

Besides, her diaries make no mention of sitting for a portrait and Susanna even recorded the details of having her photograph taken - we can date most of her surviving photographs to the precise day. Perhaps most conclusively of all, the family was not living at Ashcombe in 1860. No, I was sure this was Mary, the Reverend John Sneyd's young second wife, probably painted very shortly after their marriage in 1850. It was a carefully posed portrait, in the family home, with the old head of the family, William, in the background, and the heir and his new wife, her wedding ring prominently displayed, in the foreground. William was eighty-two in 1850, John and Mary were living with him, their daughter would be born at Ashcombe the following year - it all added up.

The present day John Sneyd looked a little deflated and I was concerned that I had been tactless in putting my case - he had no reason to trust my opinion on so brief an acquaintance. But he took us into the kitchen and brought out other things - packets of letters, books, cards and a series of framed photographs.

'Now this definitely is Susanna,' he said, just a touch defiantly.

We gasped. This woman was strong and striking, not the plain, mousy person we had been expecting. Beautifully dressed in heavy mourning, crêpe on her dress and a jet chain about her neck, Susanna gazed at us with calm, sad eyes. There was a companion portrait of John William; handsome, bearded and young-looking, not the sour, embittered man we had envisaged.

Susanna congratulated herself on our reaction. It was quite a flattering portrait, she acknowledged, the photographer had managed to touch out some of the lines on her face so she looked considerably younger than her forty-two years. And John William really had been a good-looking man, she thought, enjoying our surprise.

The portraits bore a name - Elliott and Fry of Baker Street, W1, one of the major London photographic studios of the day. We recognised it. These had been taken in June 1873 (on June 4th to be precise), when Susanna and John William were in London. Their father had died in February, hence Susanna's mourning. John William was having treatment for his throat - he looked surprisingly well, considering what he was suffering at the hands of Dr Morrell MacKenzie, thought Susanna.

Dr Morrell Mackenzie was **the** throat specialist of his day; he had founded the Throat Hospital in Golden Square in 1863 and had rooms at 19, Harley Street. Dr Mackenzie practised galvanism, a fashionable form of electric shock treatment which was both useless, expensive and exceedingly painful. Susanna had recorded in her diary, straight-faced as ever, *'John William was galvanised'*.

The photographs, we knew from Susanna's painstaking accounts, cost a guinea (£43) for eighteen. John seemed impressed that we could date these photos so accurately - we showed him the references in the diaries - and he unpacked more and more items for us to see. His mother had recently moved into an old people's home and he had taken charge of most of the family memorabilia.

There were photographs of Ralph De Tunstall Sneyd as a boy, as a young man, with his wife - a plump Edwardian beauty - again as a new father and again as an old gentleman. He was a handsome, upright man, tall and thin like his grandfather, with a thick shock of hair even in old age - and the distinctive Sneyd nose. There was another framed photograph of Susanna as a young woman, probably about the time of her marriage, photographs of Ralph De Tunstall's four children, a delicately beautiful daughter and three boys looking like little Lord Fauntleroys in velvet suits and lace collars, a photograph of the Reverend John Sneyd in old age with paunch and eye patch. Lots and lots of them. There was also a beautiful watercolour portrait of a lovely, serene, young woman in a blue crinoline - John William's ill fated wife Agnes - and a fine portrait of the Reverend Sneyd as a young clergyman. He was a striking young man, despite the nose; the intimidating, hawk-like gaze developed in later life.

In the boxes were family letters, many to Susanna from Emily Jane, barely legible in her spidery barbed wire script, and several from Dryden to his sisters describing life on his New Zealand station. There were books Ralphy had had as a child - one volume on the history of fungi had a handpainted cover he had made for it, a sensitively painted picture of red and white toadstools. There were Christmas cards he had been sent by friends and family in the 1880s. Christmas cards became available commercially in 1862 but the Sneyds did not begin to send or receive Christmas cards for another decade - and even then they were not sent to everyone but were a substitute for a present, usually for a child, pretty pictures to frame or put in a scrapbook. Susanna communicated with most of her friends and relations at Christmas time, either by visiting them or by writing a note, but not until 1888 did she send Christmas cards in any number - that year she despatched forty-five.

Most exciting of all were a batch of Susanna's account books detailing her personal and household expenditure for most of the 1860s, 70s and 80s. We dipped in and out of them, fascinated.

'Look, how much coal they were getting through!'

'Mainspring of watch 5s - that was quite expensive, wasn't it?'

'*Edgworth's Parent's Assistant*, 3s-6d, February 1866 - Ralphy would have been four - six volumes of improving bedtime stories!'

'Nutcrackers - 1s-6d.'

'What on earth do you suppose Spanish Juice was? It cost 6d.'

It was clear that we were going to have to spend a fair bit of time on these accounts. Susanna, we realised, tried very hard to be modern, to acquire new gadgets as they became available. In 1871, for example, she purchased a sewing machine for £6-7s-6d (£287) from Wilcox and Gibbs and a Green's Patent twelve-inch lawnmower for £3-10s (£158). In 1870 she bought a new patent reading lamp with a green shade for 15s (£36). By the late 1870s her household accounts included quantities of tinned Australian mutton and American bully beef which were becoming available in increasing quantities.

'What a good job we can both remember pounds, shillings and pence,' observed Marion. 'There are some advantages to age, after all!'

And finally, John showed us Susanna's black papier maché pedestal work table, painted with enamels and inlaid with mother-of-pearl. It had a removable tray for silks and tools and a capacious pocket of pink silk for work in progress. We were sad to learn that the items it contained had been his mother's, not Susanna's. Nonetheless it was in beautiful condition; later we would discover in the account books that Susanna had bought it for £1-10s (£72) in April 1870.

'Lunch is ready,' called John's wife Sue, 'come through to the kitchen.'

Home-made pizza and salad lay on the table. Sue served us and she and three of the family's five daughters listened with polite interest while we chatted to John about his ancestors and the papers we wanted to use. No-one grumbled, no-one interrupted, and when they had finished the girls drifted away quietly to get ready for church. Ralph's Roman Catholicism was still important to this family.

'They were all so well-behaved,' I said to Marion later, 'so polite. Not like my lot. They'd all have been clamouring for attention, cracking jokes about their ancestors' appearance, complaining that they wanted pepperoni or anchovies and comparing my offerings unfavourably with Pizza Hut.'

'Girls are easier,' she soothed. 'Simon was unmanageable but Maddy was always well-behaved. Strong-willed, but good. You should have had a girl. Five sons under one roof was never going to be easy, now was it?'

'Not my choice,' I replied, 'Paddy can't do girls, remember?' My husband had produced seven sons by two wives and was himself one of five brothers, most of whom also had sons.

'You'd have been considered very fortunate in Victorian times - no daughters to find husbands for,' Marion went on.

'Huh!'

Susanna would have approved of John's ladylike daughters, we decided. At last we felt we were getting to know her and the people who were closest to her. Two weeks later we would return to Staffordshire and meet more of them.

We had arranged to visit Averil at Rock Cottage to see more family pictures and meet her old and very dear friend Edward 'who knows **everything** about local history'. We were excited as we drove past Basford Hall - empty and shuttered as Humphrey and Judy were away - and down the precipitous winding track between hilly, water-logged fields where mournful cattle stood hock-deep in mud.

'No wonder Susanna had rheumatism,' we observed, 'even this high up its a quagmire. And its not even been particularly rainy lately.'

Rock Cottage is built into the rocky hillside at the bottom of the track. Averil waved enthusiastically at us through the window and came to the door to usher us in. She was nattily dressed in smart black slacks and a red sweatshirt with 'Rock Cottage' emblazoned across the front; her friend Edward hovered behind her. He had the air of a nervous schoolboy trying desperately to please and laughed a lot in an effort to conceal the fact that he was almost totally deaf. We wondered whether we would ever be able to communicate with him. They led us through a dark sitting room crammed with dilapidated antique furniture - we glimpsed an 18th century dolls' house and a vast, framed family tree - and then we were in the kitchen.

This was clearly the main room of the house and it was indescribable - low ceilinged, an old Rayburn, microwave, dishwasher, two tatty armchairs covered in rugs and sleeping cats, a lovely seventeenth century refectory table, original family portraits, dozens of birthday cards, bunches of flowers, still in their wrapping paper, wilting in all sorts of odd receptacles, bottle upon bottle of wine and gin, balloons, open tins of cat food, newspapers all over the floor under cats' dishes and litter trays - and junk, junk everywhere. The old, faded, green silk curtains had shrunk to three inches above the window sill and the antique wallpaper painted with bamboo and birds barely clung to the walls. Averil moved piles of paper and cats to find us a space to sit.

'It was my birthday last week,' she offered by way of explanation, waving vaguely at the cards and flowers. 'I was going to put some clean newspaper on the floor for you,' she went on, 'but it didn't seem worth it.

Only gets dirty again,' she giggled. 'Time for a snifter, I think.'

Marion winced - it was only half-past ten in the morning. Slowly but with a precision born of years of practice Averil mixed two enormous gin-and-tonics - she and Edward already had glasses to hand.

'Is that too much tonic? You can never have too much gin!'

But her sunny, carefree personality and the warmth of her welcome to two total strangers on a nuisance errand was magical. The house conformed to no expected standards but hers. It had, we discovered, been her eighty-second birthday, but she was ageless, still childlike in her enthusiasm for life and people. We felt enormously privileged. People like Averil are thin on the ground.

Edward finished his gin and went off to a christening and Averil began to show us things.

'That's John William as a boy,' she said casually, pointing to a large watercolour of a young teenager holding a gun and surrounded by dead birds.

Glasses in hand we followed her up the steep narrow stairs and - we knew Averil's gin was strong - but that looked like a racing car in the room opposite, dark green with a leather strapped bonnet.

'It was Bunty's, my husband's. I used to drive it and then I couldn't bear to part with it. They brought it in through the wall from part way down the hill,' she explained, as if a racing car in the bedroom was a perfectly ordinary piece of house furnishing.

She showed us portraits of Harriet, Emily Jane and Penelope Marianne, Susanna's sisters, as teenage girls and a portrait of their father as a boy, another that was probably their sister Helen and a view of Basford Hall with a tiny figure of a woman and child in the garden - presumably Penelope and little John William. Then she let us loose on a wooden trunk of family papers while she went to make lunch. The papers were a mish-mash, some relating to Susanna's immediate family, many not, but amongst them was an album of photographs. This was what we wanted to see - and better still, most of the photos had names on the back. There was Susanna herself as a young woman, her brothers Freddy and Gustavus - Freddy an amiable, bovine young man, Gustavus cocky and self-satisfied - and her brother Dryden, a tall, lanky, chinless wonder with huge dundreary whiskers. It was difficult to imagine him as a settler in New Zealand.

Susanna peered worriedly over our shoulders. She'd always thought Dryden rather handsome.

There were pictures of John William, Agnes and the Cotton relations, Ralphy as a little boy ('Oh, bless him' thought Susanna), her nephews and nieces, Aunt Mary, and numerous cousins and their offspring. And there were also Victorian photographs of family portraits - we were delighted to see what old William and Jane Debank looked like, albeit in faded sepia. But some members of the family were notable by their absence - there was nothing of Penelope Brodie, nothing of Emily Jane as an adult, nothing of stepmother Mary, nothing of little Ada and perhaps most surprisingly of all, no photograph of a portrait of Susanna's mother, Penelope.

Basford Hall would yield two large portraits of Penelope Brodie and a lovely one of her three eldest children as toddlers with their pet rabbits - they were important to Basford as Humphrey's title to the Hall came through Averil who was Penelope Brodie's great granddaughter. We had already seen the portrait of Mary Sneyd, Susanna's step-mother, newly married, seated in the library at Ashcombe with the Reverend John and old William, at Dr Sneyd's, and we would eventually find a photograph of a portrait of Penelope Sneyd, Susanna's mother, with a distant relative in the Lake District, but Ada's and Emily's pictures elude us to this day.

Many of Susanna's siblings died before photographs were readily available. The earliest portrait photographs date from the 1840s but there are very few, produced by a handful of enthusiasts. Daguerrotypes on glass were around in the 1850s, but they were not very satisfactory. They were difficult to see, could not be kept in albums and broke easily. Not until about 1860 did photographs become cheap and fairly commonplace. The elder Sneyd children had their portraits painted but if pictures were done of the younger ones we have been unable to locate them.

'Tomato soup all right?' Averil called up the stairs. 'It's ready.'

We went down, expecting Heinz. As we scraped a space on the cluttered table she brought a motley collection of cutlery and dishes and a huge bowl of soup. We had misjudged her. The soup was home-made and delicious, served with white bridge rolls, still in their packet and a catering-size tub of margarine. She poured wine and ladled cream into the soup.

'I've made some salads too. Hope you like garlic - I love it,' she said moving slowly to the fridge with her curious sideways gait weaving through the cats and their food bowls. We later learned that Averil's recipe for a healthy lifestyle comprised gin and cigarettes in large quantities and garlic in everything.

We were deeply touched that she had gone to so much trouble for us. Edward returned from the christening.

'Was it any good?' bellowed Averil.

'Oh, I expect so,' he replied. 'Food was good. Service a bit strange - mind I couldn't hear it. Batteries have gone,' he tapped the hearing aid in his pocket.

We already knew that Averil had a nap after lunch and Edward was to be our guide for the afternoon. We feared he would be very hard work.

Marion was to drive - Edward had given up his car years previously and walked the four miles each way to see Averil almost every day. He had been friends with her and Bunty for over fifty years. 'We want to see the Mixon mine,' we yelled at him - several times.

At last he understood; yes, he thought he knew where it used to be. He was a good navigator and the nervous laughter subsided now he had a purposeful role. He pointed out landmarks and interesting local names as he led us up through Ipstones and on to the moors. Halfway up a bleak hillside littered with what appeared to be a complete railway track, ran a stony path.

'That's Mixon Farm,' he said, 'we'll go there.'

The track was awful and the piles of junk and stony soil screamed poverty. A boy appeared on the track astride a reluctant ram which he was urging away from the farm - we explained we were looking for a mine. It sounded ludicrous.

'Better ask me dad,' he said, 'he knows everything round here.'

In the huge, comfortless farmhouse kitchen the farmer sat bottle feeding a lamb while another bleated piteously in a box by the range. Sacks and clothing hung from a wooden drying rack near the ceiling. A small child stood at the table playing silently with a handful of lego bricks. But the farmer knew where the mine was - Edward had been right about the location but we had to go round and approach it from another direction.

'You'll watch the track, mind,' he warned, 'worst track for miles.'

Marion cringed; it was her car.

He was not wrong about the road, but soon we found what we were looking for - grass covered spoil heaps and bell shaped dips showed where mining had taken place and where the Sneyds had made and lost tens of thousands of pounds. And it had obviously been quite a small mine. Edward was now leaping up and down the hillocks with wild enthusiasm -

he was fun as well as knowledgeable, we decided, warming to him. And now we knew where the mine had been we had a much better picture of the difficulties the Sneyds would have had and the distances they would have had to carry their ore for smelting over inhospitable terrain. *'Papa and Freddy went to the Mixon mine'* took on a whole new meaning.

Next we were to meet Averil at Edward's cousin Christine's house in Foxt, for tea. We were not quite sure why but it soon became apparent. Christine Chester was an expert on all things to do with mining in the locality - and a keen local historian. She was a sturdy, no-nonsense woman with shrewd, intelligent eyes and a fund of local knowledge. Her husband had been a farmer and she still lived in the old farmhouse, with her motley collection of dogs and cats, while her son worked the land. She lent us pamphlets, recommended books and talked and talked. I wrote down as much as I could! She provided endless tea, generous sandwiches and plates of home-made cake. Stephen, Christine's lodger, an earnest, forthright, little man, was a retired butler, and served us assiduously, passing plates and refilling cups before we were aware that they were empty - he must have been brilliant at his job. It was quite bizarre to receive such professional service in such a homely setting.

Like Christine, Stephen had attended a family history course at Keele. He was passionately interested in the Trubshaws, a Staffordshire family of architect, because for much of his working life Stephen had served in a Trubshaw house. And - of course - the elder Trubshaw was the architect favoured by the Sneyds. They even summoned him to Wales to build an engine house for their mine that any half-way competent local builder could have erected from a plan sketched on the back of an envelope.

'You know he designed Basford, don't you?' I heard Marion say partway through their conversation.

'I **knew** it, I **knew** it! shouted Stephen, triumphantly, 'I always thought he did but I never had proof - you say it says so in John Sneyd's diary?' He went on to describe many houses built by the Trubshaw family.

Local historians develop the strangest obsessions, I thought, imagining the conversation from an outsider's point of view, but I suppose people think we are just as odd.

Stephen's encyclopaedic knowledge of Trubshaw's work would save us a great deal of rather tedious research. The evening was proving extremely fruitful.

Chapter 3
# 'My seventh child to be named Susan.....'

'I do wish we knew a bit more about Susanna's childhood,' I said one evening during another lengthy phone call. 'It's going to be very difficult to do this book unless we find something.'

'**Which** book?' asked Marion.

We had discussed it endlessly. Our original plan had been to write a book telling the story of all the diarists, but we had soon realised that even if we used only a fraction of the material we were gathering we would produce a tome that would make *War and Peace* look lightweight. Now we were toying with the idea of two books - the trouble was, we kept finding more information. And the other trouble was we still didn't have a publisher.

We examined what we did know of Susanna's early life. It wasn't much.

Whereas William and John Sneyd were Georgian gentlemen, John's children were true Victorians. Susanna was six when Queen Victoria ascended the throne and her eldest brother, John William, was still a fifteen year-old schoolboy. The country they grew up in was changing. First of all the population was increasing apace. There were twice as many people in England and Wales when Susanna was born as there had been when her father was a baby, and by the time she died there were nearly three times as many. Many of these people lived in towns, and those towns were linked by a network of roads, canals and railways which made travel easier and faster than ever before. Electric light, chloroform, refrigeration, Darwin's theory of evolution, and the novels of Charles Dickens were all new in her lifetime. Little by little society was becoming more tolerant and humanitarian; a succession of factory and building acts limited the worst excesses of the industrial revolution, sanitation was introduced into cities and elementary education became available to all. Little Susanna was born into an age of progress and optimism.

But up at Basford Hall her birth was not greeted with much enthusiasm. Almost wearily her father recorded '*1831 Saturday July 9th My 7th child to be named Susan was born at about 5 minutes before 5 o'clock.*'

'I expect they'd have preferred a third son,' I observed. 'Seven children and only two of them were boys......'

She was apparently healthy, as were most of Penelope's babies, and there is no further mention of her until her christening on November 16th '*I baptised and christened our youngest child Susanna. Tom Kynnersley, Mary Anne Kynnersley and Maria Carlisle were sponsors. They and Mr and Mrs Carlisle and Louisa Carlisle dined with us*'.

'Were sponsors the same as godparents, then?' asked Marion.

I thought so; Susanna had used the two terms interchangeably.

Susanna peered over Marion's shoulder at her father's diary. Was that really all her parents had had to say about her birth? She read on with interest. Neither of their diaries made many references to their younger children. In May 1832 she found that she - '*little Susan*' - and her two year old brother Ralph Debank were very poorly and Dr Bourne visited on a number of occasions - but clearly they both recovered. On July 29th when she was a year old Penelope reported, probably with some relief, '*I weaned my little darling, Susanna*'. Within six months there was another child on the way and by September 1833 Penelope's '*darling Baby*' was her long-awaited third son, Dryden Henry, and any intimate relationship she had had with little Susan was at an end.

Susanna shook her head - she couldn't remember any of this, of course, nor could she remember life without her little brother Dryden. She did remember that the new babies were always being taken to Mama - but not until she was much older did she understand why. She'd never watched her mother feeding them - it was far too intimate and undignified a process for Penelope to want an audience. In fact, it was difficult to imagine Mama doing any such thing, she was always smartly dressed, tightly corsetted, her hair elaborately curled in the latest fashion - how did she manage wondered Susanna?

'Did many women of Penelope's social class breastfeed?' asked Marion. 'I thought they went in for wet-nurses.'

'Well, she certainly had a wet-nurse for Harriet,' I answered, 'but I seem to remember that the Duchess of somewhere-or-other fed her own babies and breastfeeding became fashionable for a time. There's a cartoon - a nursemaid holding a child which is sucking frantically at its mother while she ignores the whole process. I imagine Penelope was a bit like that.

Sentimental but neglectful.'

Susanna thought about it. Her parents hadn't seemed neglectful to her. Of course when she was little she'd been looked after by nursemaids - there had been lots of them, none she could remember clearly - but that was only to be expected. Her family were rich - there had been twelve indoor servants when she was a girl, and a governess. But she'd spent time with her parents. She remembered going for walks with Mama, helping water the plants in her garden. There was that heath seat that her mother had been so fond of, well, it was a sort of bank, really, covered with thyme and camomile and sweet smelling herbs. It had never been very comfortable - too prickly. She wondered what had become of it. She had helped her mother plant seeds, too - actually Harriet, Penelope and Emily had done most of it. Mama never seemed to have time to show you how to do things. 'Just stay there Tooket,' she would say, 'and watch the big girls.' She was always called Tooket at home - she couldn't remember how it had started.

'Perhaps from the nursery rhyme 'Polly put the kettle on, Susie took it off again,' suggested Marion when we discovered the letter from John William addressed to 'My dearest Tooket'.

Susanna nodded. John William had been such an affectionate brother, she thought. Harriet had been kind too. Penelope Marianne was bossy, Emily Jane self-righteous, Helen sweet and gentle.

Another memory came unbidden into her mind. She was thirteen to Helen's sixteen. They'd been quite close, had drawing lessons together - Helen had the makings of quite a talented artist.

'Not like me,' thought Susanna sadly.

But Helen was sickly, she coughed a lot, tired easily and eventually had taken to her bed. Susanna would go and sit with her sometimes, tell her what was going on outside, what the little boys were doing - three year old Wettie was so sweet, the devastating illness that would cripple him for life had not yet taken hold, little Feddy was learning to read.

And then there was that awful February day when she was told to go and see Helen. The older girls had already been in and come out crying so she knew it would be something bad. Papa was looking sad and scolding everyone who crossed his path; Mama had taken to her room. And Helen was white, so white, barely able to move. Her eyes were hollow and her wrists, sticking out of the voluminous sleeves of her white cotton nightgown, were thin as chicken bones. There was this little pile of things on her bedside table - a pin cushion she'd made, a little box in the shape of a shoe that she'd always liked, scrapbooks, toys, pictures.

'This is for you,' Helen whispered, motioning the nurse to give her a sketch book. She had one just like it. Helen's lungs rattled as she gasped for breath, her face twisted with pain from the effort of speaking. 'To remember...' Helen began to cough, dreadful, agonising, racking coughs and the nurse ushered Susanna out. Her sister died in the night and the next time Susanna was allowed into the room Helen was still and cold; she looked peaceful - but Susanna had not been able to bear to look at her properly, or to kiss her as she was told to do. She could still see the white coffin coming down the stairs.

'I didn't know white was the colour for mourning young girls,' Marion said, 'think of all those pictures of funerals - people are always in black.'

'And I hadn't realised that women didn't go to family funerals,' I replied.

Tears welled in Susanna's eyes. She could not attend her sister's funeral and neither did her mother and sisters. Funerals were thought to be too distressing for the women of the family so they did not see Helen go to her grave in the white coffin, carried by seven of the family's female servants and Mrs Nixon, an old family friend, all dressed in white as befitted a virgin's mourners. 'Dear Mrs Nixon....' thought Susanna.

Mama had often taken her to tea with Mrs Nixon in Leek she remembered. That was something else they did. Every so often Mama would choose four or five of the children - they would have to put on their best clothes, covered with clean pinafores, see their boots were polished and their hair neat - and they would walk, or go in the carriage, to visit one of their relatives or one of Mama's friends. They would be given milk and cake or fruit and were expected to sit still without fidgeting, answer questions politely and clearly but speak only when spoken to, say please and thank you, not eat too much.

These expeditions were not really much fun, nor were they meant to be. You were learning how to behave in polite company. There was no playing or chasing each other on the way - you had to stay clean and tidy. If one of the younger children spilled their milk or got stains on their pinafore or was sick in the carriage - Wettie was often sick - Mama would be cross and scold. Going to see Grandmama was always frightening, she was so strict and cold; Grandpapa was kinder - or at least he noticed you less. Dear Aunt Mary was always welcoming, would find interesting pictures for you to look at and toys to play with. 'Children will be children, Pen,' she would say. And Mrs Nixon - well, she always made us cakes and jellies and took an interest in what we were doing.

Papa. It was difficult to know how to remember Papa, thought Susanna. She'd been in awe of him as a child. *'You think him as infallible as the Pope,'* John William had once written to Aunt Mary; *'time back I myself almost agreed with you....'* That described it pretty well, she thought. He was tall, energetic, imposing, he had those piercing eyes that seemed to look right through you and **know** what you were thinking; he was clever with words, all his children had been reduced to tears by his tongue-lashings at one time or other; he expected instant obedience; and he was a clergyman so you felt his dictats came direct from God.

Papa had rules that seemed strange to other people. At Basford the family had fasted, not eaten meat, on alternate days. John William claimed it had ruined his digestion for life - she smiled to herself. And Penelope Marianne - well, of course, after she was married she was very wealthy and the Brodies lived luxuriously - she complained to her own children how badly she had been fed as a child and how there was never time for second helpings. Now she thought about it, Susanna saw they were right; it hadn't worried her at the time but when she thought about the meals she had insisted on for dear Ralphy...

'But if Papa was on your side he made you feel ten feet tall.' That was why John William had loved him so much, she mused, and why he had been so hurt when his father wouldn't treat him as an adult, wouldn't listen to his point of view, rejected him, banished him from Ashcombe, disinherited him. It had probably hurt Papa just as much, she now realised. John William had been the apple of their father's eye, bold, daring, not caring when he fell off the hay wagon or got bitten by that badger they caught; being so brave when he had that terrible accident falling out of a tree on to a spiked fence - he nearly had to have his legs amputated; joining the Yeomanry with Papa; going shooting - she remembered Papa taking ten year-old John William out of school to join the men rook shooting; even as a child he was always a good shot.

And Papa treated his daughters well, she remembered. She had particular reason to be grateful of course - but that was when she was grown up.

'One or other of us used to go with Papa when he went to meetings or to see his solicitor,' she thought. 'I suppose he enjoyed company on the walk. And on the way back he would explain what had happened - or gone wrong - at his meeting. He was always in the right, of course; funny how we all believed him. None of us would have dared to question what he said.'

'Walking with Papa was hard work', she recalled, 'he had long legs and was impatient with daughters whose long skirts and tight boots made it difficult for them to keep up. Perhaps that's why I've always walked fast,' she thought.

He'd encouraged his daughters to do archery, to ride.

'There was even that Yeomanry drill sergeant who used to have us all out on the grass in front of Basford doing exercises - that was in the 1840s. I'd have been about ten. Papa believed in educating girls, unlike many men of his generation. We all went away to school for a while and back at home there was dear Miss Blagg, the governess. Mary Tudor, from Tudor's farm was a bright little girl and Papa paid for her to go to school when her own father thought it a waste of time and money. Papa could be so kind...... and he always celebrated our birthdays. Children didn't get presents then, not like my Ralphy, and I suppose there were so many of us; but we always had special birthday feasts.'

'Papa and the boys used to kill and pluck hedgerow birds to eat', she remembered.

'And Christmas Eve was a time when our parents, we children and any guests all dressed up and played games together. Snapdragon, Blind Man's Buff, charades. One year we all blacked our faces - he thought it so funny. Papa would wear his 'Scotch dress' and orchestrate the festivities.'

'Averil's mother wrote in her diary that a kilt of some *'strange pattern'* was discovered at Ashcombe in 1915 or thereabouts,' I recalled. 'She said John Sneyd wore it when he visited the Brodies in Scotland.'

'Whatever do you suppose he looked like?' answered Marion. 'He was tall and gangly - I can't imagine he looked his best in a kilt!'

'Perhaps that was part of the fun at Christmas - the one time of the year when it was OK to laugh at Papa?'

Susanna nodded. They were beginning to understand.

Of course the whole family went to church at Ipstones every Sunday. It was a long walk, mostly uphill, four miles each way. Mama and the youngest child rode in the gig but everyone else walked; it was a struggle to keep up with the pony and in wet weather boots got soaked through and the hems of the girls' skirts got wet and muddy. They got colder and colder as they sat in church, listening to one of Papa's interminable sermons and their chilblains started to itch.

'But he was a good speaker,' thought Susanna fondly, 'so certain, so compelling. No-one dared to fidget when he was speaking.'

Then there was the long walk home with the prospect of a final ordeal at the end. In the 1840s John Sneyd had built the Bath House, down on the river below Basford Hall. It was ingenious - a bakehouse for bread which supplied heat to heat the water for the laundry next door. There was a schoolroom 'Bath Lodge' for those children being educated at home - and a plunge bath. Each Sunday after church Papa and most of the children - those who couldn't plead colds or chills - took a dip in the icy plunge bath before toiling back up the hill to a meagre Sunday lunch. It had never occurred to Susanna to question this regime or the religion in which she had been brought up. It remained a source of comfort throughout her often difficult life.

What else had happened when she was a child that might interest them? wondered Susanna. She had a dim memory of the summer of 1835. She was four, in the nursery with Harriet, Emily, Penelope Marianne, Helen, Ralph, Dryden - was Lionel there too? - John William wasn't, he'd been sent away to Ashcombe. The blinds were drawn, she had a headache, her eyes hurt and she was hot and thirsty. Mama was there and someone in a big white apron that she didn't know.

'Just imagine,' Marion said, **seven** of them, all with measles! Poor Penelope. No wonder she had to employ a nurse for the duration.'

'That's right,' thought Susanna, 'I had measles.'

Her mind went back to the nurseries on the top floor at Basford. There was a long corridor with rooms opening off each side, bedrooms for the children, the nursemaids, the downstairs servants and a big room with views out across the valley where the children played during the day. At one end of the corridor was a little balcony - the children used to peep over it when their parents had guests to see people arriving and the servants bringing them food and drink. That floor had been damp when she and John William returned to Basford, they had only used it for storage. The roof leaked - the valleys between the gables got choked with leaves each autumn and the gutters soon overflowed. It had been damp in her childhood too. 'No wonder we were ill so often,' she thought.

The roof still causes problems. 'Do you remember Humphrey telling us how he went out on the roof to clear the gutters and the skylight blew shut and he couldn't get back in?' I asked Marion. 'He always takes his mobile when he goes out there now.'

Susanna found it rather comforting that some things remained the same. It was nice that Humphrey and Judy were so interested in her story and so helpful to the two women. It amused her that the workmen Humphrey employed to keep Basford in good repair were so often the descendants of families Papa had employed.

'See here,' Humphrey would say, taking a page of the transcription of John Sneyd's diary out of his pocket. 'your great-great-grandfather repaired this for my great great grandfather - let's see if we can get it right this time, shall we?'

He was a bit like Papa in some ways, thought Susanna, much gentler, of course, and less dogmatic - but a successful businessman who could be ruthless if he had to be and did not suffer fools gladly. Times had changed, she thought, no-one now seemed to command the sort of respect Papa had expected.

She forced her thoughts back to her childhood. Papa bought us books and read to us, she thought, remembering the volume on mythology he had once brought her as a surprise present. He could be so kind, she thought, remembering another surprise he had bought, this time for her sister Harriet. Papa and Mama had been in Cumberland and they had been fascinated by the new drawing implements that they saw made in Kendal - thin lengths of graphite encased in wood. 'Pencils' they were called. Harriet had always been fond of drawing so Papa had bought her one - 5s-6d (£13) it had cost. We had all sorts of toys, she thought, and there was that huge dolls' house.

We had seen the doll's house at Averil's. She told us it had been made for Susanna's grandmother, Jane Debank, to teach her about housekeeping. Aunt Mary had played with it as a girl, so had Susanna and her sisters, but under supervision, with strict instructions to be very careful. Judy's little girl, Alexandra, was only allowed to play with it when a grown up was with her - something else that hadn't changed.

Funny the way that doll's house had captured the family's imagination, Susanna thought. They'd had it with them in London during the second world war and whenever there was an air raid the little dolls were taken down into the shelter with the family. 'Grandmama would have thought them foolish and sentimental.'

'We played outside a lot too, games of tick, games with balls, skipping. And the boys rode ponies.' She remembered one of her brothers - which one? - riding his pony full tilt straight down the hill to the Bath House for a dare. It was a steep slope and of course the pony couldn't stop at the bottom and carried on into the deep water where it had to swim. And the only damage that was done was that her brother's hat blew off into the water.

'Mr Brindley described Susanna to Ralph - you know, those notes he made, decades later - as a kind little girl, good to her baby brothers and sisters, gentle to the family's pet rabbits, a sweet natured, likeable, merry child who laughed a lot,' I said. 'He said she had beautiful long brown hair that she wore loose and that streamed out behind her when she ran and jumped - you don't think of little Victorian girls doing much running and jumping, do you?'

Susanna was surprised. 'They do have some odd ideas about us. What else would interest them?' she mused. Mentally she rummaged through the 'treasures' that she'd kept in a trunk, all sorts of photographs, documents, letters, that sketch book Helen had given her on her deathbed, lots of things of Ralphy's - she'd have to make sure that Pam and Marion got to see those sometime. She knew where they were, it was lucky Ralph had been such a hoarder. There wasn't much that dated from her childhood. There was the piece of patchwork that she'd made as a four year-old. Mrs Nixon had had that, then gave it back to her when she was in her fifties, to remind her that she'd always been a good needlewoman. Just as well - Susanna's mind wandered - all that patching and mending, embroidery, dressmaking.

What else? She recalled Mama's letter. As a small child, at school at 'Bath Lodge' one day she wrote letters home to her father and mother in careful childish print, telling them about a birthday party they had had for her friend Fanny.

Papa had not replied, of course, but Mama had. It was a stiff little note, but it was the first letter she had ever received and one of very few that her mother sent her. She'd kept that.

*Basford Hall Nov 24th*

*My Dearest Susan, I was very much pleased with your nice little letter and your Papa was very much pleased with the one you sent to him, you forgot to tell me what present you made dear little Fanny on her Birthday, I think she must have been very much pleased with the attention of her little friends. I sincerely hope she may enjoy many many years of health and happiness. I am very thankful that poor Clement Sneyd escaped so well from the shipwreck. He has not yet come to Huntley. I dare say your sister has told you all the news, therefore with kindest love to your dear little friends and kindest love to Sophia, and Mary, Sally and Cook, believe me My Dearest Susan, your truly affectionate Mother, Penelope Sneyd.*

*All here send their kind love to you, we are all quite well, dear Baby can very nearly walk alone.*

'Dear Baby - which of them would that have been - Mary,' she supposed.

She'd puzzled over the bit about Clement Sneyd - he was her great uncle, the Rear-Admiral, but she scarcely knew him. Clement, to little Susan, had meant her cousin, Aunt Mary's son and she couldn't understand how he had been involved in a shipwreck. In fact she wasn't even sure what a shipwreck was.

Aunt Mary; if they are looking at my childhood, she thought, they need to know about Aunt. She had spent a good deal of her childhood with Aunt Mary at Highfields near Uttoxeter, sharing a governess with her cousins. Aunt was a widow. Her husband, Clement John Sneyd-Kynnersley had died in 1840, when Susanna was nine.

Mary Sneyd-Kynnersley was then just thirty three and was left with three young children, Clement who was Susanna's age, and William and Minnie who were younger. Aunt Mary had grown up with her own parents at odds and with a houseful of quarrelsome brothers. She had become a natural peacemaker, mediating between Papa and Grandmam when she disapproved of his marriage, trying to heal the breach between Papa and John William, lending Papa money after things went wrong in Wales. Aunt was younger than Mama, less stressed, sweeter-tempered, more tolerant.

'I learnt a lot from Aunt Mary,' thought Susanna fondly.

'They need to know about Wales, too,' she decided.

In the summer of 1844 the family had decamped to Wales to a rented house near the Snowdon mine which Papa, Grandpapa and John William had leased in their final, disastrous, copper mining adventure. Susan and her sisters had visited beauty spots, attempted to make friends with the neighbours and attended church services in Welsh. She remembered the lilting words, mysterious, musical and completely incomprehensible. They had rowed and fished and gone for picnics. Gustavus had been born that summer and when he was ten weeks old Mama had brought him to Snowdonia. For the most part it was an enjoyable holiday, though it had its darker side. As English incomers they were not welcomed by all the neighbours, the miners plainly despised them, lawyers refused to act for them.

'Listen to this,' Marion said, reading from John Sneyd's 1844 diary. 'This is his first Sunday in Wales - '*I read prayers to the colony*' - the **colony**, I ask you! They were all Welsh speakers and probably Methodists to boot - no wonder they didn't like him.'

Susanna sighed; Papa could be difficult and insensitive.

At just thirteen, Susan was included with her three elder sisters and brother John William in an expedition to climb Mount Snowdon with their father. Dressed, she recalled, in a full-skirted dress worn over layers of starched petticoats, boned corsets and voluminous cotton underwear, stout boots, striped woollen stockings, a poke bonnet and a warm shawl, she had set off with her family on the steep, stony path to the top of the mountain. It was a strenuous climb. Once at the summit they ate a picnic supper, settled down to watch the sun set, and, shivering as the night grew colder, they huddled together and tried to sleep. In the morning they watched the sun rise and then set off down the mountain home for breakfast. She had thought it an exhilarating adventure.

'My cousin says it's still the custom,' remarked Marion 'if you want to thrive in Snowdonia you have to see both a sunset and a sunrise from the summit.'

'Didn't do much for the Reverend John, did it?' I answered.

Susanna had to concede that I was right.

By late summer it was clear to her father that not only was he not going to find his fortune at the bottom of the Snowdon mine, he had gambled with his family's future and lost. The mine had proved much less profitable than he had anticipated. His miners had taken him to court in a dispute about setting wages - he believed he had agreed to pay them a lump sum for a completed job (payment 'by bargain') they claimed he had agreed to pay a daily rate. In Staffordshire no solicitor would have supported workmen who opposed him but his Welsh lawyer was not so accommodating.

Both solicitor and miners spoke Welsh which he did not understand and both were united in their dislike of high-handed foreigners from England. It gradually dawned on him that he would lose the case.

'If only he had explained,' thought Susanna.

'When we were in Wales,' said Marion, 'I got talking to someone at the Sygon Mine - that's the one that's open to the public - we went down it. Well, there have been some recent excavations at the Snowdon Mine and they found a back entrance that's not on any of the plans.'

'You mean.....?'

'Well, they seemed to think that the miners had been taking copper out that way for their own use.'

'So they were defrauding John Sneyd - and he never knew!'   I laughed delightedly - John Sneyd seemed to me an arrogant snob and I was sure I would have disliked him intensely. The Welsh miners had my full sympathy.

Susanna listened aghast. 'Had they really done that?  Poor Papa.'

Her father had soon realised that the whole venture had been an extraordinarily expensive mistake. A disaster, in fact. In November he headed back to Staffordshire with her grandfather, mother, John William, and most of the children. For some inexplicable reason, Susanna and her nineteen year old sister Emily Jane were left behind for several weeks to deal with hostile servants, the family's creditors, threatening miners and the dank Welsh winter. It had been a frightening time, remembered Susanna, and they really hadn't known what was going on.  They had finally got home to Staffordshire just before Christmas.

'In a way, it marked the end of my childhood,' she thought, 'things were never the same again.'

'Well, we haven't got much, but it will have to do,' I said. 'It'll make a short chapter, then we'll just have to start with the first diary, the 1858 one, when they go abroad.'

'But we'll have to give our readers a bit more background,' said Marion, 'describe what happened between the Welsh mining disaster and 1858.'

Between 1844 and 1858 the family saw many changes. Penelope died in 1849 worn out by childbearing, and the following year John Sneyd married Mary Adams of Shrewsbury. She was twenty three, the same age his daughter Helen would have been had she lived. A year later Mary bore him a daughter, Ada Mary. Over the next few years she had several miscarriages and stillbirths but no more live children. Little Ada became the apple of her mother's eye and was denied nothing.

'She was a spoilt little madame,' thought Susanna crossly.

Penelope Marianne, John and Penelope's third daughter, married in her mother's lifetime, and married well. In 1848 she became the second wife of John Clerk Brodie of Idvies in Forfarshire who was Crown Agent for Scotland. She bore him nine children only four of whom survived into adulthood. The Brodies were rich and well-connected and Penelope was soon to look down on her Staffordshire relations.

In 1850, the year after their mother's death, Harriet, Susanna's eldest sister, married the Reverend Robert Bamford of Mickleton in Oxfordshire. Over the next six years they had four children. In 1857 Harriet became ill and Susanna went to Mickleton to nurse her and help with the children. Harriet died later that year.

Both Penelope Marianne and Harriet had married before the financial disaster of 1852 and the ensuing quarrel between their father and their brother John William. We do not know how this rift was viewed in the Bamford household. Perhaps Harriet was too involved with her growing family to have energy to spare for her eldest brother or perhaps Robert Bamford did not feel able to go against the wishes of a brother clergyman who was also his father-in-law. Certainly in later years John Sneyd was charitably received by this son-in-law and for a time he, Mary and little Ada even lived in a cottage owned by the Bamford family.

But wealthy Penelope Brodie had no such scruples. When John William was evicted from Ashcombe he made his way to Edinburgh to stay with the Brodies and consulted solicitors recommended by his brother-in-law.

Back home in Staffordshire Emily Jane bravely fought her brother's cause, smuggling a carpet bag of belongings to Cheddleton station for him at his request. Unfortunately for her, their father intercepted it, slashed it open, read the letters it contained and confiscated the other contents.

'Poor Emily,' thought Susanna. 'Papa cut her allowance after that; she always got less than the rest of us. And in many ways she was so like Papa - always sure she was in the right, always stubborn, always quoting the Bible to prove her point.'

1852 was a traumatic year in the Sneyd household and one from which the family never fully recovered. The Reverend John was left on the verge of bankruptcy with a new young wife, a baby and huge family commitments. To his married daughters he was committed to pay an annual allowance of £50 (£3,000) apiece. John Clerk Brodie absolved him of this responsibility in respect of Penelope Marianne but Robert Bamford was a struggling young clergyman who probably needed Harriet's £50 to help support their young family.

More substantial provision had to be made for the younger sons. Ralph Debank, the second son, had wanted to farm, and in 1846, with a loan from his sister Mary, John Sneyd had bought Sharpcliffe Hall for Ralph to run. The property cost £8,400 (£450,000) and in 1852 John Sneyd was still paying back the loan.

'Aunt Mary was so worried about lending him that money,' thought Susanna, 'he should never have asked for it. Sharpcliffe was always a burden. And Ralph was already ill with consumption in 1846; he never made a living from the farm. Dryden did the right thing when he sold it - and he made a handsome profit.'

Her brother Dryden sold Sharpcliffe in 1876 for £22,655 (£985,000).

In 1851, another brother, Lionel, aged just sixteen, had set sail for America where he was to work on Bryant's Station in Milan County, Texas, learning about stock with a view to farming on his own account. No doubt Lionel had read stories of life in the Wild West but the reality was rather different. Being raised as an English gentleman was no preparation for the hot, humid Texan climate and the rough and tumble of life amongst cowboys and outlaws.

'Poor Lionel was bitterly homesick,' Susanna remembered. 'He wrote letter after letter home to Papa pleading to be allowed to return.'

At length John Sneyd agreed and despatched the £20 Lionel needed for his fare home. It arrived too late. Lionel was already ill and died of yellow fever aboard the Emma Watts, off New Orleans on July 26th 1853. John Sneyd was devastated and rushed to Liverpool when the ship docked to meet Captain Dearborne and see the exact spot where poor Lionel had breathed his last.

In October 1852, nineteen year-old Dryden set sail for New Zealand aboard the Minerva to take possession of the lands his father had purchased for him at Kaipoi near Christchurch. Dryden did his best to settle into New Zealand life. He called his new farm 'Ashcombe' and the area surrounding it 'Keel' in deference to his Staffordshire ancestors, but from the start he had difficulty making it pay. His land was adjacent to the Waimakariri river which regularly changed course, flooding his crops and the neighbouring township - so badly that on one occasion some of the coffins in the graveyard were washed up and bobbed down the main street to the horror of local inhabitants. Dryden struggled on in New Zealand for fourteen years writing brave, newsy letters home to his sisters but eventually he gave up his farm and came home. But his name remained behind. 'Keel' is now known as Sneydstown.

1854 must have been a desperately sad year for the family. Ralph Debank, always a frail young man, and his seventeen year old sister, Mary, both died, of consumption. Emily remembered how Mary asked to be carried to her brother's room to see his body. Two days later she too was dead. Susanna and the others must have been sorely grieved by the loss of their three siblings. We know she was keeping a diary by this point - the shell of her 1852 diary survives - just the covers, with *'Susanna Sneyd'* inscribed inside the front.

'I do so wish we had Susanna's account of the disaster years 1852-4,' I said. 'Susanna gives us much clearer pictures of the characters of her brothers and sisters than John and Penelope do.'

But we had been lucky in another way. During the months that we had been reading the diaries I had been busy on another front. I had been writing applications and filling in forms and sending them off to all sorts of likely and unlikely grant-giving charities. There were charities that gave money for every sort of research you could imagine. My favourite had been one that supported female history researchers over the age of forty-five - sadly, they hadn't felt quite the same about me. But at last I had got positive results. Once again I rang Marion.

'Sit down and take a deep breath. We have **money** - not a fortune but enough to fund a good few trips. The Wellcome Historical Foundation want us to look into the medical stuff in the diaries - what illnesses they all had, what they died of, the remedies they used - well, we've done a lot of it already, really. We'll have to do a report at the end but only five thousand words. **And** the Local Population Studies group - remember Dr Snell told us about them - they're something to do with the Cambridge History Group - they've given us a free hand so long as we write something for their magazine.'

Marion whooped on the other end of the line. From then on I would be known as 'respected colleague' even if we both suspected that it was not all entirely down to me.

'**Definitely** time for another visit then. Now, when are you free?'

Chapter 4
# 'We all left Dover by the eleven o'clock steamer'

Our next Staffordshire trip started, as they all would, with the drive from Northampton to Stoke-on-Trent. It was February and the weather was as bitterly cold as the first trip had been unbearably hot; typical, extreme, Staffordshire weather. The journey gave us a couple of hours in which to distance ourselves, mentally as well as physically, from our everyday lives. Time to exchange news, talk about our worries, and gradually tune ourselves back into our project and our strange, magical Staffordshire existence; time to discuss what we had done and what we wanted to find out; time to meet Susanna again.

'Give me a resumé of everything we know about her as I drive,' said Marion as we headed into Stoke-on-Trent. 'I've been concentrating on the Reverend John and Susanna's slipped away a bit from me.'

I took a deep breath and rattled off: 'Seventh child of family of fourteen; parents wealthy and eminently respectable; classic early Victorian childhood - very strict father, lots of church, mother too busy producing babies to bond with any of them, all brought up by nursemaids and governesses or farmed out to relations; she spent a lot of time at Uttoxeter with her aunt.

Don't know much about her education but most of her brothers went to public school. Big gap in our knowledge until we got to her first diary - lovely description of a family foray abroad, all being very English and supercilious. Came back to Sharpcliffe with sister Emily Jane while her father, stepmother and little stepsister stayed abroad. They had a high old time at Sharpcliffe entertaining brothers and cousins, and Susanna had a fairly serious fling with her cousin William. Was then courted by local vicar Charles Ingleby who was aided and abetted by her aunt and uncle in Devon.'

'Why? Was he a good catch?'

'Fairly. And she was twenty-eight, almost on the shelf, one broken engagement behind her, her father was flat broke and the Inglebys had pots of money.....'

'Fine.'

'Anyway she married him, too hastily it would seem, and it all went wrong very rapidly. Averil says he was a hermaphrodite!'

'Yes, I remember that bit. But I don't believe it. I looked it up in the British Library - there have only been twenty or so recorded cases of true hermaphroditism in humans. Mind, there were several papers published on it in the 1870s. But no, I think it must have been something else. I wonder if....'

'Do you want me to go on or what?'

'Sorry.'

'Anyway, she left Charles and went back home, had a pretty miserable time for a couple of years, then her eldest brother, John William - you know, the one who had the almighty row with their father - married and his wife died of puerperal fever leaving him with a baby boy. Susanna went and lived with him as his housekeeper and foster mother to the child - Ralph De Tunstall, they called him....

'What a mouthful!'

'Well, Ralph was a family name - all the eldest sons were Ralph, William or John, if you remember - it was the same in the Keele family.'

'Same names?'

'Yes - horribly confusing. What's more, usually there were younger sons who got given whichever of the family names the eldest didn't, if you see what I mean. Old William's next two brothers were John and Ralph. The Reverend John had an elder brother William Debank and a younger brother Ralph who both died as young adults. The first of his sons was John William, the second was Ralph Debank....'

'Help!'

'And Humphrey and Judy Scott-Moncrieff called their little boy William John Sneyd! But, back to Ralph De Tunstall; the first written reference to a Sneyd in Staffordshire is to someone who rented lands in Tunstall and Chatterley in the early middle ages.'

'So that's where the De Tunstall bit comes in?'

'I suppose so. They called him Ralphy when he was little though. Susanna obviously doted on the child and did all sorts of things with him - remember the scrapbooks? They lived in Armitage first - 1862 to 1870 - and seem to have had a pretty good time, made lots of friends and went out a lot. Kept in touch with the family; she wrote lots of letters and went back to Cheddleton a couple of times a year, without John William and Ralphy, usually. Certainly they never visited papa, but she did. The surviving brothers and sister visited Armitage but Ada didn't.'

'Ada was Mary's child?'

'Yes. Then Susanna had an admirer called Mr Palmer but it all fizzled out because they moved to Abbots Bromley in 1870. Doesn't seem to have had as much fun there and Ralphy got sent away to school. Father died in 1873 and about a year later they moved back to Basford. Then it's downhill all the way, really. She was ill a lot, so was John William and he got old and crotchety and had rows with his younger brother Dryden who inherited the estate instead of him; Ralphy grew up and was a selfish little so and so, upsetting John William. Any of this sound familiar?'

'Very.'

Between us Marion and I knew all about teenage sons!

'Then there was trouble of some kind with her youngest brother, Gustavus; but I'm not quite sure what yet. Lots of people borrowing money from her - family, mostly. Lots of penny-pinching. Paying the servants very little so they keep leaving and she has this cook who drinks. More and more ill health - rheumatism, bronchitis, heart trouble, neuralgia, chilblains.....'

'Chilblains?'

'Yes, so bad she couldn't go out sometimes, complained she couldn't dress herself, or sew - they must have been on her fingers as well.'

'Heavens!'

'Anyway, she died in 1891 aged sixty - the last diary is 1889.'

'Mmm. Not a laugh a minute, her life, was it? Now tell me about the foreign holiday from her point of view - that's the next bit, isn't it? I already know what the Reverend John had to say about it.'

'Not now. You need to concentrate on where we're going or you'll get us lost and it'll be 'Alternative Britain' again. We'll have a look at the two accounts over a bottle of Mr Shah's finest tonight and see if we can write up that chapter.'

It took us more than one evening of course, and many bottles, but over the next few days we put together an account of the Sneyds' foreign trip. Susanna watched us from a distance. There was not much she could do to help us with this chapter - the diaries would tell us all we needed to know.

The Sneyds were a provincial family. They had relatives all over the British Isles and made regular visits to London but foreign travel was new to them. John's father, old William, had spent some time at the Prussian court and his diaries record one other brief foray abroad in 1791, travelling through France to Salzburg and back home again by way of Luxembourg and Belgium. His diary simply lists how far he travelled each day and where he stopped at night. Had he dissuaded his son from going abroad with tales of ill-made roads, flea-ridden inns and incomprehensible johnny foreigners? What had the young Tory landowner really understood of what was going on in France on the eve of the French Revolution? It would be fascinating to know.

When John and Penelope Sneyd were young the Napoleonic wars made European travel hazardous and later, for whatever reasons, they chose to holiday in Britain. But by the 1850s a young man called Thomas Cook had brought the European holiday within reach of adventurous middle-class tourists. Not that the Sneyds saw themselves as tourists, or middle-class, or even particularly adventurous, and they made their own travel arrangements rather than taking a package tour, but it seems likely that the increasing popularity of foreign travel coloured their decision to go abroad.

However, the chief reason for the trip was financial. The family was still short of money following the crash of 1852, though ruin had been averted by the kind, if not wholly disinterested, intervention of two of John Sneyd's closest friends - his lawyer, Joseph Challinor, and the vicar of Cheddleton, Mr Boucher.

'I don't really understand what they did,' said Marion.

I wasn't sure myself.

'I think they clubbed together to buy the estate,' I said 'they were both pretty wealthy. John Sneyd stayed on as a sitting tenant and bought it back from them through a mortgage he took out with Mr Challinor's firm. They probably undervalued the estate deliberately so they could buy it and he could afford the mortgage - but I'm only guessing. As the mortgage was paid off he gradually got bits of the estate back - I don't think he ever got it all. They would both have made a handsome profit, of course.'

It was a face-saving deal for John Sneyd who continued to manage the estate as if it were still entirely his own. But though the arrangement was discreet and between friends, rumours must have circulated. The reasons for John Sneyd's quarrel with John William were certainly public knowledge; John William made sure of that.

And in 1857 there had been another episode which damaged John Sneyd's reputation. Christine Chester had told us about it. We had no documentary proof but the story was current when Christine was young and she knew the family in question.

Apparently William Weston, a miner from Consall Forge, got drunk one cold spring evening. John Sneyd happened to be passing in his carriage, words were exchanged; history does not repeat what they were but John Sneyd was outraged by Weston's drunken insolence and took the law into his own hands. He dragged the man all the way up to Ipstones and clapped him in the stocks for the whole of one bitter, frosty night. John Sneyd was nearly sixty, he was a magistrate and had been dispensing justice on his own authority for many years. Thirty years earlier his high-handed treatment of a labourer would probably have gone unremarked, but times had changed. The Weston family complained to the bishop who insisted that Sneyd pay the man compensation.

The whole affair was hushed up - no reports appear in the local papers of the time - but legend has it that the compensation was sufficient to enable William Weston to buy a farm - and certainly by the 1860s there was a farm at Kingsley owned by a family called Weston.

Even without the Weston incident the Reverend Sneyd would have had good reason to decide to spend time away from Staffordshire and the gossip-mongers. Nonetheless, for the first three months of 1858 the Sneyds socialised as actively as ever. John Sneyd paid for *'a treat to the Ipstones Church Singers'* on February 9th and on the 20th the family gave a dinner party for twelve people. They were not anxious to advertise the change in their fortunes.

It was generally reckoned to be cheaper to live abroad than to live in England - though of course that is not what John Sneyd would have told his friends and family. It would have been easy enough to present their excursion in a favourable light - travel was educational, they would all benefit from a change of air and the girls would be able to practise their French. So John Sneyd decided to rent out Ashcombe Park and Woodlands. The servants were laid off except for Blair, a maidservant who would travel with them. There were fewer children to think about now. Helen, Ralph, Lionel, Mary and Harriet were dead. John Sneyd had all but disowned John

William. Dryden was in New Zealand; Frederick was an ensign in the army serving in Ireland. Wettenhall, the handicapped son was to be left in the care of a trusted servant and Gustavus was a boarder at Rugby. Of the surviving daughters, Penelope Marianne was safe with her husband and in-laws in Scotland and the remaining three were to travel with him.

Susanna's diary recorded the preliminaries:

*'1858 March 24th The Daglishes fixed to take this house at £150 a year, they left here about 3 o'clock.....'*

Mr Daglish was soon to rent a good deal more than the house and his rent rose to £400 (£20,000) a year. Woodlands was let to a family named Holland, presumably at a lesser rent than the Daglishes were paying.

There were numerous trips to visit friends and relations to *'say good-bye'* and on April 5th their father even gave his permission, probably grudgingly, for Susanna and Emily Jane to go over to the Harracles on the other side of Leek to bid a tearful farewell to John William.

Harracles Hall is a large, imposing Georgian farmhouse of red brick standing alone on a hillside near Horton. From Susanna's earlier diary entries it is clear that the sisters met John William quite often in Leek and occasionally visited him at the Harracles without actually asking their father's permission. This however was a special visit - they would not see him again for many months.

On the 6th three of the family's ponies were sold, raising a few more pounds towards the trip. At last, on April 23rd, some three weeks after their luggage had arrived, the Daglishes took up residence at Ashcombe and the Sneyds decamped to Highfields to stay with Aunt Mary.

On the 24th, John Sneyd went to see John William. Susanna simply recorded *'Papa and John William met'*. They certainly did not resolve any of their differences but it would seem that even John Sneyd could not set off on their great adventure without a final sight of his eldest son. Next it was time to say goodbye to Gustavus at Rugby. They set off on the twenty-sixth and stayed with him for a few hours. *'He told us he had moved up about 25 times and was about 50th from the bottom, there are about 380 boys there'* wrote meticulous Susanna.

They then went to London *'where we arrived at about 1/2 past 6 and we found William Sneyd who had got the lodgings for us £2-15s per week'*.

William was Susanna's cousin, son of her father's brother Henry, vicar of Wetley Rocks. They spent a few days in London shopping, sightseeing and going to the theatre, and then on May 3rd ' - *came to lodgings at 27 Marine Parade, Dover £2-8s per week'*

Susanna religiously recorded their expenses and the price of lodgings. Although she was unable to help her father in any practical way she was deeply concerned about his financial state, though it is unlikely that she fully understood it. Even by Victorian standards John Sneyd was an extremely authoritarian paterfamilias; he would never have admitted to his family that he himself was in any way to blame for their misfortunes - it was all the fault of the *'Welsh devils'* and *'my faithless son, John William'*.

They stayed in Dover for nearly a month. It is interesting to note that both in London and in Dover there was a network of people to visit, almost all of whom had some connection with Staffordshire. In London they visited the Childs and the Antrobuses, spent time with cousin William who was a member of the Inner Temple, and saw one of the Boucher sons and Miss Helen Carlisle, the daughter of the former vicar of Ipstones, John Sneyd's boyhood tutor. In Dover they called on the Baddely Childs through whom they met the Spenser Stones and a family called Ottaway, both of whom had children Ada's age. *'Mrs Stone is sister to Mrs Hood of Blore'* wrote Susanna, happy to have placed her new acquaintance.

A French teacher was engaged to help the girls brush up their French. John Sneyd did not join them - speaking foreign languages was an accomplishment for young women. The military were in town and the family socialised with the officers - Susanna even gave her photograph to one of them.

'Perhaps John Sneyd hoped to find husbands for Susanna and Emily on this trip,' I said, 'maybe that's why they stayed in Dover so long - he hoped a romance might blossom with one of the officers.' If so, he was disappointed.

At last, on May 27th they set sail for Ostend. *'We all left Dover by the 11 o'clock steamer to go to Ostend which we did in about four hours. Papa and Emily were ill, the rest kept quite well. Ada slept all the way.'*

For all of her adult life Susanna wore the cumbersome, full skirted dresses, over tight corsets and crinolines or bustles, that we associate with the Victorian period. When she travelled across Europe, crinolines were at their widest, and that is what she and her sisters and their stepmother would have worn, crushed into railway carriages, blowing provocatively in the breeze on board the Channel ferry, or hitched up over stout boots and brightly striped stockings on their long walks through the countryside.

'Wouldn't that have been horribly uncomfortable?' asked Marion.

'A bit inconvenient, but actually they were quite easy to wear - they were much lighter than the layers of petticoats people had worn previously. They were frames - of steel or whalebone - so they kept your skirts away from your feet - and they squashed into small spaces fairly readily. There were all sorts of cartoons in *Punch* about crinolines, you know.'  I had worked with museum costume collections for years and needed very little encouragement to share my knowledge.  Marion still looked interested so I continued....

'Cartoons showing ladies in huge crinolines trying to get through small turnstiles, be-crinolined ladies in a high wind, rear views of ladies on the beach bending over to collect shells, fathers using their daughters' discarded crinolines as garden cloches - and ladies sitting down carelessly so that their crinolines balloon up in front and show everything they've got - they didn't though, we tried it once.  To sit down delicately you were supposed to make the crinoline concertina flat - you sort of pinched it at the sides - but actually you'd got so much stuff on top it didn't matter if you sat down carelessly.  Anyway Susanna would have been used to managing long, full skirts.'

Susanna's diary entries were long - too long for the spaces allotted to them - and they were cramped and difficult to read.

*May 28th We arrived at Ostend a little before 4 o'clock and went directly to the Carlton house where they very slightly looked over our baggage - we arrived at Bruges at about 7 where we soon had breakfast, after which Papa, Mary and Ada went to bed - in the afternoon we all went with a "Valet de Place" to the Cathedral, the Church of Notre Dame and the Academy of Routieres.*

*29th Mary, Emily, Ada, Blair* (their servant) *and I went to the Cathedral and saw there an Ordination of Bishops, etc., etc., after which we walked about the town and a good way round by the Canals. Emily and I went to the Church to see pictures and the chase of St Ursula, we also went to the church of St Sang to see the Casket with the Holy Blood in it. In the evening we all went to see the chimneypiece in the Palace of Justice and went to the Cathedral and Notre Dame.*

*31st (Ghent) Emily and I walked about the town. I bought two pictures -*
*[and] went to the Zoological Gardens where we saw English cattle. We met*
*with a nice English party, two gentlemen and two ladies. Ghent is so*
*intersected by water as to form 26 islands, there are 80 bridges .*

Statistics appealed to Susanna. Contemporary magazines and
newspapers often contained columns of 'Curiosities' or 'Varieties' many of
which consisted of strange statistics. One of my favourites concerns the
time it would take a railway engine travelling at thirty miles per hour to
reach the moon! Victorian administrators gathered statistical data as a
prelude to - or instead of - redressing social ills. Recording obscure details
like the numbers of islands and bridges in Ghent was very much the thing
to do and Susanna was nothing if not conventional.

Her account of their travels is strictly factual, a long list of sights seen
and churches visited, with no real description or commentary. They were
conscientious - if uncritical - sightseers. At the back of her diary, together
with translations of the French and German names for various garments,
Susanna made herself a little note *'Best pictures by Rubens, Van Dyck, Van*
*Eyck, Teniers, Quentin Matsys, Hans Hemling*[sic]*, A Carver, Verbruggen'!*

Marion was getting fidgety. 'Do we really want to keep all this in?'
she asked, 'people will be bored to death.'

'I think we should quote some of it - it gives a flavour of her style.
And in its way it's quite interesting.'

'If you say so.'

'And I won't quote her anything like so much in the other chapters.'

'Good...'

I added another entry that seemed typical of Susanna's style. It
seemed a shame to have transcribed all this detail from her diaries and not
to be able to use it.

*June 2nd (Antwerp) We all started out together but soon separated. Emily*
*and I had a Commissioner to ourselves who took us to the Cathedral of*
*Notre Dame and St Paul where there is a representation of Mount Calvary,*
*the Crucifixion and the Orders of Purgatory and a great many very good*
*pictures - Emily and I went together to see the Rubens pictures in the*
*Cathedral, we had to pay a franc each to see the four. We afterward went*
*up the tower of the Cathedral, we first went up a big way and as we came*
*to a door we could not open we went down again and afterward went up*

*about 600 steps which is as far as we may go for a franc. In the evening we went a very pretty drive to a garden through plantations. Table d'Hote at 5 o'clock at Antwerp'.*

Mealtimes feature largely in Susanna's accounts. Back in England it was unacceptable for ladies to dine in public. If they stayed in a hotel they were expected to eat in their rooms, and most restaurants were for men only. Within a few years tearooms would open in the new department stores where ladies could go, alone or in company, and by the end of the century cafés and restaurants were happy to serve both sexes. But in 1858 dining at the *table d'hote* was a novelty for women like Susanna and Emily Jane Sneyd.

'It is interesting to see how John Sneyd organised their journey,' I said. 'Nothing seems to have been booked in advance, they simply arrived in a new city, found someone who spoke English and asked them to recommend lodgings. And it always worked - they never found themselves stranded without a bed for the night. If they liked the place, or the lodgings, or both, they extended their stay accordingly, if not they moved on. It's not even clear whether they had any idea of their ultimate destination or whether they simply took advice from other travellers en route.'

Both Susanna's, and her father's, diaries make it sound a very haphazard sort of journey. But clearly a structure of sorts existed to help independent travellers. Lodgings seem to have been readily available, and presumably there were people on hand who could translate the Sneyd's requirements into a language their landlords could understand. There also seems to have been a network of guides, *'valets de place'*, in Belgium who showed tourists round.

Churches and pictures featured large in their lists of things to see. Susanna and Emily seem to have visited virtually every church in Brussels.

'Listen to this,' I said, 'St Jacques, Notre Dame des Victoires, St Nicolas, St Catherine, St Joseph, St Marie, St Boniface, the Church of the Naissance, St Anne's Chapel, the Church des Finisteres, Bon Secours, Riches Claires and dozens of others. They even tried to visit the Jewish Synagogue.'

Marion had switched off and was filling a page with doodles.

'I do wish she told us a bit more about her impressions of places,' I went on. 'Foreign travel must have been so much more exciting then - they wouldn't have been familiar with places from books and postcards and TV programmes in the way that we are. And places wouldn't have been so alike. And shops wouldn't all have sold the same things. But Susanna's accounts blur into one long list of beautiful churches, fine pictures, nice lodgings - no sense of the places at all. What's she missing? What would you describe as the essence of Brussels?'

Marion perked up, 'Well, certainly not the churches. Golden Square, I suppose, all those great mediaeval buildings, art nouveau - she was too early for that, of course. The wretched mannekin pis - she did see him - did you realise he was actually 17th century? Lace. Wonderful food, chocolate - do you suppose the chocolate shops were there in 1858? But I suppose that would have been too self-indulgent for Susanna.'

'Probably. I suppose this bit is a little more descriptive. I found her account of an excursion:

*18th. Papa, Mary, Emily, Miss Blunt, Ada, Blair and I all went to Waterloo - We went in comfortable carriages to the Meerdam and paid about 20 francs for it. Sergeant Munday showed us all over the fields, he is a very nice person, he was in the Battle of Waterloo, we had our dinner at the mission which is kept by a daughter of Sergeant Munday's and niece to Captain Colt who wrote a book on Waterloo '*

'I didn't realise that battlefields were a tourist attraction at that date, did you?'

'No - but my son would have approved,' said Marion. 'Simon bored us to tears as a little boy - setting up the Battle of Waterloo on the table in his bedroom, scattering sand, moss and twigs all over the floor. My mother and I painted his soldiers.'

The battlefield site was open to tourists. Susanna acquired a little printed card with a view of the battlefield on it as a souvenir of her visit. There were not, at that time, a great many such souvenirs available for tourists to buy. Picture postcards had not been invented though it was possible to buy mass-produced topographical engravings quite cheaply. And travellers made their own records. The diary collection at Keele contains a sketch book with several watercolour sketches of unidentified continental scenes which were probably painted by one of the family on this trip. But overall Susanna brought very little home with her to remind her of her year abroad.

The record of sightseeing goes on and on, and sometimes the tedium is palpable.

*July 5th Emily and I went to see a Synagogue, we could not get inside. There was a good deal of rain.*

*7th Papa, Mary, Emily and I went to the Porte de Hal to try to see the Armoury but we could not get in.*

*10th Emily and I went towards the Porte de Hal to try to find a church but we could not get to it.*

*13th Mary, Emily and I went to try to see a Lace Manufactory, but we were told it was not made in the town. We went to the Botanical Gardens & the House of Parliament but we were too early to see anything, we went again at 12 o'clock and got in to the House of Commons, it was very dull and the seats very hard'.*

'**Weren't** they having fun?' said Marion.

Day after day the Sneyds visited churches, museums and palaces, admired the grand carriages in the streets, walked in the parks and watched out for members of the royal family. Susanna was an ardent royalist. By chance Prince Albert had sailed for Belgium on the same day as they did, aboard the steam packet 'Vivid'. They had seen over his ship while they were in Dover and were delighted to see him again at the station being greeted by one of the Belgian princes. Susanna and Emily spent a good deal of time around the royal palace in Brussels hoping to catch sight of members of the royal family. They spent two and a half hours in the cathedral at a service commemorating the twenty-seventh anniversary of the king's coronation *'to see the King and his party'*. Even a sighting of the Duke and Duchess of Brabant in the park merited a mention.

They saw the mannekin pis on July 18th, festively dressed in the uniform of the Garde Civile. They had seen him naked on a previous occasion with none of the shock-horror that Victorian ladies are supposed to have felt at the sight of the naked male form.

Their stamina was phenomenal. On the twenty-third they left Brussels for the Ardennes. They enjoyed the countryside and were fascinated by the state-run casino at Spa. Emily and Susanna went for long, long walks almost every day.

*29th Emily and I walked to the Cascade of Coos on the Anbleve, it is a fall of water of about 60 feet, it took us just 6 hours to go there and come back, it being a walk of 18 miles. In the evening we all went to the Redoute to see the gambling, there were a great many gentlemen and some ladies playing*

*at the rouge et noir and at roulette, people play against the bank which
gains so much that it is able to give the clergymen £40 a year and a great
deal goes to the King'.*

'They weren't fragile Victorian misses, were they?' I said. 'That's
three miles an hour - a good pace to keep up without stopping. And a
couple of days later they did an even longer walk - over eight hours - into
Prussia.'

'Isn't it interesting that John Sneyd had no qualms about letting two
unmarried young women go off, un-chaperoned, on all-day hikes in a
foreign country?' added Marion, 'It doesn't fit the image of young women
lying on sofas having the vapours, does it? They were a lot tougher and
more independent than we imagine.'

After a week in the Ardennes the family set out again by rail to
Cologne and then by steamer down the Rhine. They genuinely seem to
have enjoyed the trip down the Rhine - this is the first point at which a note
of enthusiasm begins to creep into Susanna's descriptions.

She and Emily Jane spent much of the journey in third class where,
ostensibly, the views were better, though one does get the impression that
they may have been avoiding the rest of the party. There was no love lost
between Mary Sneyd and her step-daughters, though their father would
have insisted that they were perfectly polite to her. Nor do Susanna and
Emily Jane seem to have had much affection for their little half-sister.

This is particularly surprising in Susanna's case for she clearly loved
children - but throughout the year they spent abroad she seldom records any
outings or activities with Ada. Equally revealing is the fact that no
photographs of Ada survive amongst Susanna's possessions. Ada was just
nine in 1860 when cheap photographs became readily available. As her
mother's cherished only child it is likely that numerous photographs of little
Ada were taken and distributed, but if any were given to Susanna she chose
not to keep them.

At last they arrived in Heidelberg. They spent a few weeks staying at
Muller's family hotel which, together with another hotel, Schreiber's, seems
to have catered for a specifically English-speaking clientele. After a few
weeks they moved into lodgings, though they regularly returned to one or
other of the hotels for dances and social functions. Their new landlord was
Professor Brown, an Englishman, and the lodgings were at 33, Leopoldstrasse.

There was a large English-speaking community in Heidelberg at this time - it was very much a centre for the literary and scientific communities. The members lived their lives largely independently of their German hosts, visiting and entertaining each other much as they would have done at home. There was an English chaplain, Mr Saxby, and an English doctor, Dr Jones.

The only Germans with whom the Sneyds came into real contact were families like the De Weilers with whom they played whist, anglophiles with a fluent command of English; servants, who were usually unsatisfactory because they did not understand their employers' requirements; and, on November 5th, the police, who did not understand the significance of Guy Fawkes night and objected to fireworks being let off late in the evening.

Sightseeing continued, but at a more leisurely pace and often in the company of other tourists. They intended to stay in Heidelberg for some time.

We were increasingly bored by Susanna's account of their travels - so factual, so lacking in any feeling of excitement. From Susanna's diaries we could never have guessed that Heidelberg is one of Europe's most beautiful cities - she could equally well have been describing a holiday in Clacton. And as historians, we found it irritating that Susanna told us nothing about the political situation. Just nine years before the Sneyds arrived, Heidelberg had been at the heart of the Baden-Palatinate rebellion and there had been plans to establish a General National Assembly there. The rebels had been defeated by the Prussian army at the battle of Waghaeusel and Heidelberg had been occupied by the Prussians for a year. Ideas about German reunification were still in the air and would find expression in Bismarck's policies within a very few years.

Were the Sneyds aware of any of this? Probably not. They had little contact with local people and political news reached John Sneyd in the foreigners' reading room through the filter of the English press - just as it would have done at home.

'For heaven's sake let's put in some of the Reverend John's diary now,' said Marion. 'I like this bit - he must have composed it himself - and at least it shows some feeling, even if its only irritation!'

*Picnics of old were picnics of pleasure*
*Where folk met together could find prey and leisure*

*But the picnics of Heidelberg all Picnics surpass*
*They are held in a room and not on the grass*
*Where none are admitted save those deemed elect*
*Such as Carnwath and Gargan may choose to select*
*'Tis a hybrid diversion 'tween Picnic and Dance*
*Five francs you must pay and that in advance.*

There was a distinct social hierarchy amongst the expatriate community in Heidelberg. Lord and Lady Carnwath were at its head - a circumstance which John Sneyd found extremely irksome. They, together with a Madame Gargan, organised many activities for their fellow countrymen, and decided who was, and who was not, socially acceptable. Victorian society in England was rigid with a whole system of rules and etiquette designed to rule out social climbers and other undesirables. These rules were less easy to apply abroad where people were divorced from their social and family networks, but the Carnwaths and their ilk were determined to keep up their standards. Some of the events they organised were obviously rather odd.

'Don't you think he's more entertaining than Susanna?' asked Marion. 'You can see him, frustrated by all this socialising and sightseeing. What's more, he seems to have felt overshadowed by his titled fellow-travellers - and embarrassed because Mary and the girls didn't have enough dresses for all the balls they wanted to go to. The decline from wealthy, powerful, landed gentry, to impoverished gentle-folk was under way - however carefully they tried to hide it'. Look:

*If to a ball a girl might wish to go*
*Her crinoline and tarlatan to show*
*She has to pay for two - the thing's a bother*
*One dear sweet dress she has but not another.*

'He must have written that himself, too. And then there's all that stuff about going to watch duels - the Heidelberg students seem to have gone in for an awful lot of duelling. I don't know whether they expected it to be a spectator-sport - not that that would have worried John Sneyd and his friends.'

'They do seem to have seen the local population as anthropological specimens,' I agreed. 'The grape harvest was another entertainment they saw as being laid on for their benefit. The harvesters kept giving them grapes - perhaps hoping it would make them go away!  There they were, frantically trying to get the grapes picked before the weather broke or the fruit got too ripe and there was this flock of English tourists getting in the way.....'

'There are lots of nice details....'

'Do you remember the squirrel?'

'No?'

'John Sneyd bought it for Ada as a pet.  They had it for several weeks and then she trod on it and broke its leg!'

'Clumsy!'

'Well, she was only seven.  Anyway, Susanna, being all tender-hearted, took it to the vet, and to the English doctor, and sat up all night with it.'

'Lucky squirrel!  What happened to it?'

'It died.'

'They met Mrs Gaskell, didn't they?'

'Briefly.  I don't think they were particularly friendly.  But John Sneyd did get her autograph.'

*November 24th - Mary went to hear Shakespeare read in German (for the third time).  Papa got Mrs Gaskell and Mrs Crespigny to sign their names in some books he had bought of their writings.*

We were absolutely thrilled when a signed copy of Mrs Gaskell's *Life of Charlotte Bronte* surfaced amongst Averil's possessions.  Someone had valued it - it had been beautifully rebound in grey leather, tooled in gold, by Harrods' bookbinding department sometime around 1900.  We wondered what other treasures lay buried in Rock Cottage.

'How good was Mary's German?' asked Marion.  'Shakespeare in German must be quite demanding.'

'I don't know.  They all had lessons, of course.  Susanna religiously recorded them - *'our twentieth German lesson', 'our twenty-eighth German lesson'* - hard to tell if it reflected her boredom or was just part of her fascination with numbers.'

Christmas brought a round of entertainments, a brief respite from the interminable lessons, children's parties, a performance of *Beauty and the Beast* in which Ada played a fairy - and visitors from home.

*December 24th We had our 33rd German lesson.  Tavie arrived here by the*

*8 o'clock train, he had been travelling all night. Ada went to a German tree at the Phillipps.'*

Fourteen year-old Gustavus seems to have travelled alone from Rugby to spend Christmas with his family, taking four days over the journey.

'Would you have let Simon do that journey on his own at fourteen?' I asked Marion.

'No - maybe when he was sixteen,' she said, after a pause.

I agreed. I wouldn't have let my fourteen year-old sons loose on the Continent either.

Gustavus, too, had German lessons, sharing a teacher with his little half-sister. Prince Albert's influence had not yet reached Staffordshire and the Sneyds were new to the Christmas or 'German' trees which seem to have given their name to the numerous children's parties to which the two young Sneyds were invited.

'He travelled all that way alone and then when he arrived they treated him like a little boy again,' I said.

In the new year Frederick also set out to visit his family. He left his regiment in Ireland on January 17th, but he had miscalculated the cost of his journey and ran out of money at Cologne. Getting money to Frederick was not easy, and was only accomplished with the aid of a friend who presumably spoke better German than John Sneyd did. We imagined him shouting in his overbearing way at uncomprehending German officials and becoming more and more incensed as the days passed and Frederick failed to arrive. They tried to telegraph money to him but failed and in the end their friend, Mr Parish, telegraphed the innkeeper at the Hotel Bellevue with instructions to advance fifty thalers to the hapless young man.

He had come to look after the womenfolk while his father was away, because, after months of inactivity, John Sneyd was going home. On February 5th he took Gustavus to Paris where they spent a couple of days and then returned, via Calais, Dover and London, to Staffordshire. John Sneyd left his son at Rugby and returned to Cheddleton. He spent some time at Ashcombe, re-negotiating the Daglishes' lease, and then set out to meet his parishioners and his bishop. It sounds very much as if he had been summoned home to account for his long absence and to make proper arrangements for his parish.

*February 25th Met a considerable number of the Freeholders of Ipstones at the Red Lion and consulted them as to the sale of the Living and found them disinclined to sell*

*26th ....met with the Bishop at Norton Bridge and tendered my resignation of the Living of Ipstones which his Lordship was not inclined to accept. I then proposed to have Mr Goodacre nominated and licensed as Curate which appeared to give satisfaction - I also called on Mr Goodacre and told him of my proceedings.*

'So it was all signed and sealed before anyone thought to tell Mr Goodacre,' I said. 'Typical John Sneyd!'

Mr Goodacre remained John Sneyd's curate for several years and then took over the living. In 1887 he was succeeded by his son who was vicar of Ipstones until 1916.

One gets the impression John Sneyd was happy to be home. He socialised, attended Petty Sessions in Leek and a turnpike meeting, and oversaw workmen who he set on to excavate and plant an expensive and elaborate flight of pools and waterfalls in the grounds of Ashcombe Park - an extraordinary project to start when he was resident abroad. Over the next year or two, six ponds with bridges and waterfalls were built, the margins were planted with exotic trees and fancy waterfowl were acquired from a London dealer. In fact, John Sneyd never really lived at Ashcombe again, so he had little opportunity to enjoy his creation. Landscaping of this sort had been popular sixty years earlier. As so often happened, John Sneyd had caught the tail end of a craze, and squandered yet more money that he did not have on a grandiose scheme designed to impress his neighbours.

Having set the pools project in motion, by March 5th 1859 John Sneyd was back in Heidelberg and it was Susanna's and Emily's turn to return home with Freddy.

'Why do you suppose Susanna and Emily went home?'

'Goodness knows. Maybe they were homesick. Maybe relations with Mary and Ada were getting very strained. Maybe it was proving too expensive. Maybe potential husbands were thinner on the ground than John Sneyd had expected.' I really didn't know.

They spent two days sightseeing in Paris with Frederick, travelled to Boulogne and crossed to Folkestone on March 17th, arriving at quarter past six in the morning. They took the train to London and another to Rugby where they spent the night at the Golden Eagle. The following morning they breakfasted with Tavie - Rugby school seems to have been remarkably accommodating about allowing boys to spend time with visiting relations - then Freddy and Emily took the train to Cheddleton while Susanna stopped off at Uttoxeter to visit Aunt Mary.

A few days later she returned to Cheddleton. She, Freddy and Emily then moved up to Sharpcliffe for the summer. In the absence of their parents the three siblings seem to have enjoyed themselves hugely, entertaining their cousins and other family members. John William often came to see them, and for the first time in six years they were able to be at ease with him; he could stay the night and they all went to church together.

Meanwhile, the Reverend John, Mary and little Ada travelled to Baden Baden and thence to Switzerland. They moved from hotel to hotel, going on long trips to view glaciers and mountain scenery, taking boat trips on the lakes and making friends with numerous other travellers. It must have been exhausting for Mary with a bored small child in tow, but, away from the formality of Heidelberg, John Sneyd seems to have been much happier. He preached to groups of tourists on Sundays, revelled in long mountain walks while his wife and daughter rode in carriages or on mules, and visited various monasteries and other institutions.

'Listen to this,' said Marion, 'we **must** keep this bit in':

*May 25th We left home at 9 o'clock am to visit Dr Gugenbahl's Institution for Idiots. After looking through the Establishment - which appeared to me to be an institution for the delusion of the public and to promote the misery of Cretins by filth - we proceeded to the top of Abendborg, a very high mountain.*

'And there's the bit about seeing the monks and the St Bernards, how hospitable they were but how uncomfortable his bed was. He was tall, remember, and beds were often too short for him. And we must keep in the bit about the eagle.' In Switzerland John Sneyd had acquired a stuffed, fully-grown golden eagle.

'How on earth do you suppose they transported that?' I wondered.

'Don't ask!'

'They weren't exactly travelling light, were they? Don't forget John Sneyd's box.'

John Sneyd, for some inexplicable reason, was carrying with him *'my box of miscellaneous matter relating to Ipstones and Bradnop'*. John Sneyd was lord of the manor of Bradnop which consists of a hamlet and a wide tract of moorland. Ipstones was his parish. Keele University now houses a large collection of documents - mostly deeds dating back to the 16th and 17th centuries which relate to properties in the two districts. Many of them are annotated in John Sneyd's handwriting. He records that he lent them to antiquarians he met on his travels, quite confident that papers relating to 17th century farmhouses in obscure parts of North Staffordshire were of international interest.

It was true - there is a lot of entertaining stuff in John Sneyd's travel diary. But I didn't feel this was the right place to use it.

'This is supposed to be a book about Susanna,' I objected, 'do we really want to know what her father was doing all the time?'

'Well, it's a sight more interesting than her diary,' retorted Marion, 'and you were the one who wanted to write this chapter as the story of an English family abroad. Besides, we need to explain why the romance with Charles Ingleby got so far without her father's intervention.'

'Well, I think the readers must have got the picture by now.'

On November 9th the Reverend John Sneyd and his wife and daughter returned to England. They had no real home to come back to and it looks as though the decision to return was taken on the spur of the moment. Perhaps Mary was weary of the incessant travelling.

For a few days they stayed in Dover, then John Sneyd hurried home to Staffordshire to sort out his affairs. By early December he had taken lodgings for his family in Leamington and that was where they were when they received Susanna's letter saying that Charles Ingleby had proposed to her.

'At last,' said Marion with some satisfaction, 'now we are getting to the really interesting bit!'

Basford Hall 1880.

Ashcombe Park.

Ipstones church.

Ipstones church.

Water-logged fields near Basford Hall.

The remains of the Bath Houses with Rock Cottage in the background.

# Ashcombe Park Estate

comprising

## THE IMPOSING GEORGIAN RESIDENCE

containing about 10 Bed Rooms and 4 Reception Rooms, and situated in

*Very Charming Old Gardens and Grounds, and a Beautifully Timbered Park*

CHAIN OF FISH PONDS surrounded by Rhododendron Clumps and Woodlands
of great charm

**STABLING, LODGE, GARDENER'S COTTAGE and FARMERY,**

## FOUR EXCELLENT SMALL DAIRY FARMS

Cheddleton Grange, 57 Acres :        Basford Bridge, 78 Acres ;
Felthouse, 27 Acres ; and            Holly House, 32 Acres.

**Two Small Holdings and Cottages,**

TWO SMALL PARCELS OF WOODLAND,

the whole extending to about

## 552 ACRES.

The Fishponds 1926

# "SHARPCLIFFE HALL"

comprising the

## *Charming Elizabethan Residence*

containing

**Lounge Hall, 5 Reception, 16 Bed and Dressing and Two Bath Rooms.
Modern Conveniences and Offices.     Electric Light and Central Heating.**

### Beautiful Tudor Gardens

Sloping to a Lake, with Squash, Hard and Grass Tennis Courts, and

## *Magnificent Views for 40 miles over Delightful Rural Country*

with about **50 Acres,** or

Lots 1, 2, 2a and 3, together, about **367 Acres**

or with **The Model Home Farm,** Lots 2 and 2a, of about **157 Acres.**

Also in Lots.

## Three Good Dairying & Sheep Farms from 103 to 137 Acres

THREE SMALL HOLDINGS          WOODLANDS

and

## A Fine Sporting Woodland Property of 158 Acres

The whole Estate extending to about

## 876 Acres

---

## *Most Beautiful and Romantic Country*
## *with Heavily Timbered Steep and Winding Valleys*

sloping to streams, which join to form a

SMALL  BROOK  WHICH  HOLDS  TROUT

and with attention could be made to give good sport.

Huge rocks outcrop, and the well-known Sharpcliffe Rocks, rising nearly 100-ft., are a feature of the property, as are also the

## *The Beautiful Woodland Walks and Drives*

are very attractive, especially the Drive up to the House from Basford, which winds up through meadows and hanging woodlands, rising 400-ft. in about 1 mile, affording charming vistas of hill and dale.

The higher land chiefly comprises some

## Fine Dairying and Sheep-rearing Grassland

There is also, by way of variety, a small piece of

Moorland, where the Heather and Bilberry flourish.

## The Estate affords some fine Shooting
## with particularly high birds.

The Woods lie splendidly for holding game and driving, and, besides reared game, a mixed bag of natural birds is obtained, including Snipe, Woodcock and Duck, and about 1,000 Rabbits are killed in an average season.

Sharpcliffe Hall.

Sharpcliffe Hall in the 1920s

Ashcombe Park. Pam with John and Jean Haig.

Souvenir of Waterloo.

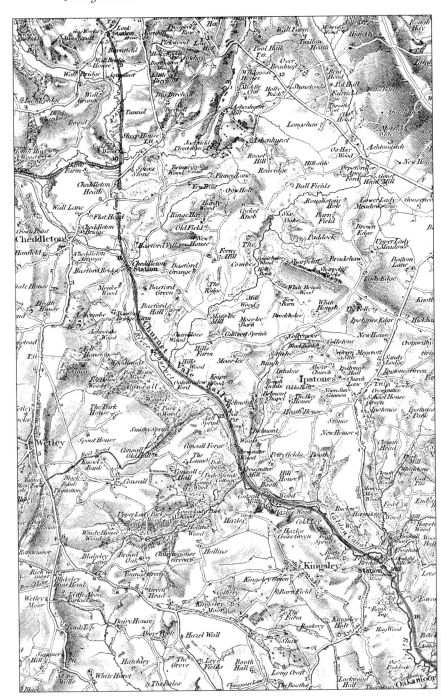

Chapter 5

# Ipstones

But it would be a while before we could write the wedding chapter. We kept getting side tracked.

'I'm beginning to think that this whole project is like trying to read a Dicken's novel - masses of strange people constantly leaping into the story and so many extraordinary happenings that you lose track of the plot,' said Marion happily, as we sat having lunch in our favourite cafe in Leek. 'And the pages are all out of sequence - people and facts are just appearing at random,' she went on, through a mouthful of rich, sticky date and walnut cake.

I paused, swallowing a spoonful of clotted cream crème caramel. She was right, I supposed. We had by this point read all the diaries so we had a broad picture of Susanna's life, but the way we were filling in the detail was certainly confusing. We would follow up what seemed a perfectly simple lead, then we would meet someone who would set us off on a completely different tack. And some of these encounters were truly bizarre - we never knew what would happen next. It was great fun!

We had by then made numerous visits to Staffordshire and felt very much at home. Greystones cafe in Leek was definitely our sort of place - a fine 17th century house set back from the road behind a pretty cottagey front garden. The Nicholson Institute - Leek's library-cum-museum-cum-art-school - had been built uncomfortably close to it in the 1880s, a truly hideous building with an acid-green copper roof and ugly tower.

But inside Greystones it was peaceful, despite the traffic thundering past the mullioned windows along what had become the A53. The room was crammed with a motley collection of antique tables and chairs - but we had missed the lunchtime rush and most of the tables were empty. A fire burned in the huge inglenook fireplace, pictures lined the walls and pamphlets jostled each other on the broad mantlepiece and along the low oak beams.

The proprietors' sideline was selling the work of local artists and writers. They were a middle-aged couple, he a dapper, courteous, agile waiter threading his way deftly through the crowded room and she a brilliant cook producing an endless variety of soups and pies, salads and savouries and a wide range of truly sinful cakes and puddings.

'So now its time to go up to Ipstones, respected colleague,' Marion said cheerfully, draining the last drop from her pot of extra strong tea.

On a previous trip to Staffordshire we had met the incumbent of Ipstones, the Reverend Stanley Price. He happened to mention that Ipstones church was hoping to restore the Sneyd memorial - the strange broken slate and enamel family tree that we had struggled to interpret on our first visit. Rather uncertainly we asked if there was anything we could do to help - we had had a great deal of support from people in Ipstones village and we thought this might be a way of repaying their kindness. Stanley had suggested we contact the lady who was co-ordinating the fund raising effort - an energetic American called Jodi Peck who had once lived in Belmont Hall. We had made an appointment to see her.

We were total strangers and she was a little uncertain at first - but soon agreed that Susanna's diary would make a fascinating evening's entertainment!

We had already discussed at length what we might do. Marion had a longstanding interest in amateur theatricals and had dismissed my suggestion of giving a lecture about our researches as 'deeply boring'. She wanted to do something much more dramatic.

Gradually the idea took shape. Marion would be Susanna and would read extracts from the diaries. I would be the narrator and fill in the background to the entries. Marion would be in costume. Now it was my turn to be difficult! The 'olde time music hall' look, long skirt, Eliza Dolittle hat and shawl, that usually passed for Victorian dress, offended my sensibilities. The whole point of the reading was that we were telling a real story in Susanna's own words. If Marion was going to wear period costume we would get it right (besides, I was in the middle of a PhD on Victorian dressmakers! Making a suitable outfit from a contemporary magazine pattern, would double as a useful time and motion experiment. There was plenty of evidence that nineteenth century dressmakers worked appallingly long hours but none that told me how much one woman could achieve in the fifteen or sixteen hour working day many recorded working).

Marion groaned as we set aside a weekend to make her dress. She did not see herself as a downtrodden Victorian seamstress and sixteen hour days were not to her liking.

On my way to Northampton a few weeks later I stopped off at the National Newspaper Library in Colindale and selected my pattern. It came from the *Milliner's and Dressmaker's Gazette of Fashion* for April 1874. Eighteen-seventy-four fell roughly in the middle of the period covered by Susanna's surviving diaries. She was then forty three - Marion was a youngish fifty six; it was a plausible date to choose. Besides, the style was attractive and interestingly cut. Half-sized tissue paper pattern pieces were issued with the magazine and these had been pasted on to a long, fold-out strip of blue paper by some well-intentioned librarian many years previously - the paper and glue, even to my inexpert eyes, would not meet current conservation requirements!

My plan was to sketch the pattern shapes and do measurements which could later be scaled up to fit Marion's rather-more-than-standard-size figure. It was just my luck that the Newspaper Library was full to capacity on the day of my visit. Unfolding and measuring the pattern pieces in a confined space was a nightmare and my neighbours - and the staff - glared at me with undisguised hostility, wishing they could find a reason to ask me to leave. Was I using pencil rather than ink? Yes. Was I resting my tape measure on the tissue paper itself? No. Was I straining the spine of the volume I was working from? Not really. Reluctantly they let me get on with it.

We had already acquired the fabric, a heavy, black, silky synthetic, the chief merit of which was that it was sixty inches wide and cost £1 a yard. Susanna was in mourning in 1874 and besides, ladies of her age and era wore a lot of black.

'Good. I like wearing black - its very slimming,' Marion said, cheerfully oblivious to what an 1870s dress really looked like.

I spent the evening measuring Marion, scaling up my pattern pieces on to pages of *The Times* (large, but not always large enough so sheets had to be sellotaped together) and tacking together a half-toile cut from an old floral chintz curtain - no expense was to be spared in the execution of this project! I have been dressmaking since I was thirteen, but pattern-cutting is a skilled process and I was beginning to doubt my own competence as Marion bustled about, making dinner, studiously ignoring the increasing pile of discarded sheets of mangled newsprint. But to my utter amazement the toile needed only a few minor adjustments before we could unpick it and use it as a pattern.

'Susanna must have been helping.'

'Didn't you think she would?'

The full skirt, worn over a crinolette, and the bodice, with its 'back interest' detailing, did not flatter Marion, even when executed in supposedly-slimming black; the banana-shaped sleeves with their two rows of seams were uncomfortably tight and constricting, and she complained bitterly.

'I look like Queen Victoria at her dumpiest!' she wailed. 'The diet starts tomorrow.....'

But I was delighted. The dress was surprisingly convincing; Victorian ladies had no choice of styles - if full skirts were in, that is what you wore, even if, like Marion, you were short and plump and they did nothing for you. Now I had to find a solution to the problem of her short, thick, fair hair....

It was to be a hectic weekend. As well as making the dress (thirty-three woman hours using a sewing machine - and by 1874 dressmakers would have used sewing machines) we had to finalise the script (my shorthand for cut in half and then some) and try it out on Marion's long-suffering husband.

For some reason I was convinced that this reading was to be very, very important. We **had** to get it right.

Susanna's 1859 diary is not at Keele. We had only her father's diary to tell us about what happened to her between the end of 1858 when she was still with him in Heidelberg and January 1860 when she was living with him in Leamington and preparing for her marriage. It was from John Sneyd's diary that we learnt that Susanna and Emily Jane returned home with Frederick in the spring of 1859. He himself remained abroad until November and apparently knew nothing of Susanna's courtship until the two letters arrived.

*December 8th Received a letter from Susan informing me that she had received a proposal of marriage from Mr Chas Ingleby. I also got a letter from Mr Ingleby and I wrote to both of them by return of post and requested an early interview with the Gentleman.*

John Sneyd was willing enough to consent to Susanna's marriage. Whatever it was that caused the marriage break up was not obvious on first acquaintance.

We had fantasised at length about the separation. Averil's story about Charles being a hermaphrodite did not convince us. We tried to find another explanation but our offerings were equally far-fetched. Susanna, we discovered, had had two operations for piles in the course of her life, the first shortly after she left Charles Ingleby. This was quite sufficient to lead me to a diagnosis of violent anal rape!

Marion's preferred explanation was even more fantastic. Having realised in a flash of inspiration that the little crosses that appeared at intervals throughout the diaries related to Susanna's menstrual cycle it was a simple leap of imagination for her to decide that the entry *'both x'* meant that Charles and Susanna were menstruating simultaneously and that Charles Ingleby was therefore actually a woman masquerading as a man!

'What is all this intellectual pretence?' I asked her. 'Serious historians? Rubbish! We're both *Sun* readers at heart - actually *The Sunday Sport* is probably nearer the mark!'

Of course we already knew quite a lot about the Victorians' attitudes towards women. We were both old enough to remember when some of the ideas were still current, and we were feminist enough to find them offensive. Victorian women were both the 'angels in the home' who inspired man's better nature, and temptresses who might ensnare him. They were weak and in need of protection but at the same time capable of much greater self control and self sacrifice than their menfolk.

Nearly everyone agreed they were incapable of reasoning like men - though some families, including the Sneyds, were more enlightened than others in their attitudes to girls' education. Women's activities were restricted and had to be approved by the men in their lives. Women had no political rights, and after marriage they and all they possessed became the property of their husbands. Girls and women were expected to be demure, obedient and deferential. Cleverness was discouraged. As respectable women did not work, marriage was the only career open to girls like Susanna Sneyd. Parents and daughters alike spent much time, money and effort in pursuit of a 'good' husband. A girl's entire future depended on it.

'Pam, 'Marion broke in, 'did I ever tell you about that article I found? I've got several bound volumes of a Victorian magazine called *Leisure*

*Hours*. There's a lovely article in one of them called *A Recipe for Happiness in Marriage*. We should quote it —-'

She rummaged through her bookcase. 'Here, look:

...good housewifery is a great ingredient in domestic felicity. Accomplishments in their bearing on domestic happiness must, of course, be viewed in reference to the position of the parties in life. ...In the middle classes music, and a moderate taste for reading will be found to answer pretty well every purpose. For a country clergyman's wife, Dr Miller has given us the standard "an ability to make a good apple dumpling and sufficient intellectual cultivation to relish Butler's Analogy." In the higher classes, where there is more time to be filled up, the range of accomplishments may be higher. ....Beauty, whether in form or face, is an element which, though not ranking as essential, is yet a more important part than might at first sight appear in domestic happiness.

That was written in May 1872 - twelve years after Susanna and Charles married. Then it goes on to say that women care less about their husbands' appearance than men do about their wives'.'

'What's new?'

'And then it says that as there are so many different standards of beauty it 'happily gives a wide choice in this matter'!'

'Poor Susanna! Still, she was reasonably attractive, she could play the piano and she read a lot - how do you think she was on apple dumplings!?'

'And look at this bit! 'In the course of life, beauty perishes, money is lost, but a principle of rectitude will remain like a strong cable enabling the marriage to ride out every storm. .....To have been born of a family whose principles have been tested is no small advantage.' That could have been Susanna's motto, couldn't it? Not that it helped when push came to shove.'

However angry such attitudes made us, it is unlikely that either Susanna or John Sneyd questioned the mores of their day and Susanna must have been painfully aware of the disadvantages of spinsterhood. At twenty-eight she was on the shelf alongside her thirty-five year-old sister, Emily Jane. Not that Susanna was an unattractive young woman. She was no beauty - her face was too strong and her jaw rather too heavy - but she had a pleasant, serene expression. She was also docile, conventional and anxious to please, all qualities prized by Victorian husbands.  She loved children - and she seems to have liked men; Charles Ingleby was by no means her first love.

We know that Susanna broke off an engagement to a Mr Leek in 1856. None of her diaries for that period survive, and her father's only contains the occasional cryptic reference to her *'sweetheart'*.  Leek is a common enough name in the area and we know nothing more about him, but a letter to Susanna from her cousin, Harriet Blunt, survives, praising her for her selflessness in breaking off the engagement to go and care for her sister (another Harriet - Harriet Bamford) and her four tiny children.

The letter begins with a sovereign remedy to help Harriet Bamford's condition - a nauseating concoction of mutton suet in boiled milk - then Harriet Blunt turned her attention to Susanna:

*...I earnestly hope and pray that the time may come that you will see that even this was well for you - but it is impossible that you can feel it yet - or that you can find any comfort except in the conviction that you are following the finding of God's Will - that you are doing what is most right in breaking off your engagement, at whatever sacrifice to yourself, as soon as you perceive that it is your duty to do so - and that instead of selfishly burying yourself in your own grief you are striving to bring comfort to your sister and to relieve her and her husband from anxiety about their children by taking the care of them so much upon yourself.....*

Harriet's letter went on for several pages in this heavy, moralising tone.

'How comforting would you find that?' asked Marion.

'About as helpful as the suet-and-milk mixture.  But it's the stuff of Victorian novels, isn't it?  Susanna's sacrifice was seen as the height of a Christian woman's  duty.  Not that I'm convinced - I think  she had a different agenda.'

'What was that?'

'Well, Harriet's missive goes on to suggest that all was not well between Susanna and Mr Leek.  She says Susanna could not have married him without having - where is it now?  *'......the slightest doubt of the entire affections of your husband'*.  I suspect Harriet Bamford's illness gave Susanna a good excuse to break off the engagement **and** be seen as selfless into the bargain.  And being at Mickleton was no great hardship to her.

Dora, the eldest Bamford child, was her god-daughter, and she seems to have been very fond of her brother-in-law. Yet when her sister died there was no talk of her moving in as his housekeeper - that really would have been self sacrifice. No, Susanna came home and he re-married!'

Nor we concluded, was Susanna's continental journey entirely without romance. At the front of the Reverend John's diary for 1859, along with his poems about Heidelberg balls and picnics and verses copied from other sources, there are some lines entitled *"The Younger Brother's Claim"*. Whether he penned them himself, or copied them because they seemed appropriate, we do not know.

> *'When e'er in rapturous praise I speak*
> *Of Susan's eye, of Susan's cheek,*
> *And vow my ardent flame;*
>
> *They tell me that I praise in vain,*
> *For Susan proudly will disdain*
> *A younger brother's claim*
>
> *Yet my fond heart will not resign*
> *The hope it formed to call her mine,*
> *When first my eyes beheld her;*
>
> *I still believe my Bible true*
> *For there 'tis clearly proved that you*
> *Susanna hate an elder'.*

'Who do you suppose the younger brother was?' asked Marion.

'The only brothers I remember them meeting were the Trotters - not Del-Boy and Rodney! What were their names?' 'Yes, here it is, Henry, Edward and Mowbray Trotter. They went walking on the Mannheim Road and then went home and played cards.'

'Very romantic!'

'Well, it might have been.'

It also seems that, while Susanna, Emily and Freddy were living up at Sharpcliffe in the summer of 1859, Susanna had a brief, but ultimately unsatisfactory, fling with their cousin William Sneyd-Kynnersley.

Charles Ingleby, therefore, had not been her only suitor. She had chosen to be with him and expected that he would make her happier than Mr Leek or Mowbray Trotter or Cousin William would have done.

'I was sadly mistaken,' murmured Susanna.

On a cold November evening we made our way up to Ipstones to give the reading that we had planned so carefully. Stanley Price was there to greet us with Mr Blore, the caretaker. Was he, we wondered, a relative of Mrs Blore, Susanna's whisky-drinking cook, the one who broke so much of the family's crockery? Better not to ask.

The doors at the end of the hall burst open and like a minor whirlwind Jodi Peck filled the hall, putting the props she had brought on the stage. Barley-sugar legged table, chenille cover, balloon-backed chair, leather-bound books, aspidistra, lamp with bead-fringed shade. Men arrived to install the sound system. Others set out chairs. We had not expected such sophistication - Jodi was working miracles.

It all took on a dream-like quality. All this feverish activity on our behalf, and nobody - especially us - really knowing whether we could deliver what we had promised.

'They'll arrive at seven,' Jodi warned. 'I'll put reservations on the front seats - lots of the family are coming. Michael and Seiko from Cambridge, John and Sue from Nottingham.....'

We had envisaged a village audience and expected Judy, Humphrey and Averil. To have people driving the width of the country to hear us was pretty daunting!

We were already nervous and Marion was getting panicky - I had learnt by now of course that she tended to panic when we got lost (heaven knows why, she should have been used to it), or when she thought we were going to be late, - but this was the worst I'd seen.

'Great,' I thought, putting on a show of icy calm to conceal my own nerves. 'This performance with all the paraphernalia was her idea! I'd have been quite happy with a simple lecture. I give lots of lectures. I'm even quite good at it. But all this business of scripts and costumes - I don't do acting!'

After she had changed, Marion stayed out of sight, resplendent in the black dress but complaining loudly that the strings on the bonnet I had constructed (very effectively, I thought, with £3's worth of ribbons and flowers from Stevenage market) were uncomfortable, impeded her hearing and were slipping off.

Humphrey came backstage. He was to assist 'Susanna', his relative, to her seat, thus, we fondly hoped, making a connection for the audience between the present day family at Basford Hall and the ancestor whose diary we were about to read.

I could see that the hall was full.

'Not a lot to do of a November evening round here!' I told myself firmly.

It was time to begin. I could see Marion was literally shaking as Humphrey ushered her into her chair and handed her her glasses. I wondered whether Susanna was nervous, too, at having her story told, in her father's old parish to an audience many of whom were the descendants of people she had known - then scolded myself for being fanciful.

But none of us need have worried. The audience was flatteringly uncritical. The names and places were familiar, the story of one woman's steadfast good sense in the face of difficulty was one everyone could identify with.

In the interval we were submerged in people with stories to tell and congratulations to give. It was the same at the end. We took names, addresses, notes. But as the audience drifted away it became obvious that one family group had hung back, determined to see us. At last the wife approached Marion. She was a tall, statuesque woman with a strong face and a great halo of frizzy, dark hair. She spoke quietly with a trace of the soft Staffordshire accent.

'We've something we think you ought to see.'

Her husband and daughter hovered behind her.

Dr Sneyd had earlier introduced her to Marion as Joyce, the wife of his cousin, Colin. He and Colin were both grandsons of Ralph De Tunstall Sneyd, the nephew who Susanna had brought up after her marriage failed. We hadn't known of Colin's existence before that evening.

'I've got these papers, she said, and we've never shown them to anyone.'

'Then are you sure you want to let us see them now?' asked Marion carefully, feeling that it was important not to seem too eager - not to put Joyce under any pressure. We could almost hear Susanna's prompting voice - 'Yes. Now. Don't stop now.'

There was a pause.

'Yes,' said Joyce at last, fingering a locket which hung on a gold chain round her neck. 'We've talked about it and we think you are the right people. This is the right time. We'd like you to see them.'

'What exactly have you got?' asked Marion gently.

'Lots of things, mainly letters - Charles Ingleby's courtship letters to Susanna,' Joyce said quietly, 'and other things too.' She opened the little locket. Susanna smiled out from the little gold frame.

Marion had been right. By presenting Susanna's story dramatically we had touched chords and tugged heart-strings.

And I had been right too. This encounter would open the most important door we could ever have hoped to find.

Chapter 6
# 'Oh, how I wish I were worthy of his love'

It was three months, with Christmas in between, before we could go back to Staffordshire. The weather was icy; I was recovering from a vicious bout of flu and arrived in Stoke-on-Trent feeling far from well and with a graveyard cough which could be heard  half a mile away. Marion was concerned for me. To cap it all, as we arrived I had a message that my eldest son had been arrested on a charge of burglary (false, but at the time deeply worrying).

We had been booked to give two talks to the Keele Local History Society; one on Susanna's clothes, which I had researched, the other on the medical evidence in the diaries, in which Marion had immersed herself with ghoulish relish!

Since the librarian at Keele had been so accommodating to us with the diaries we felt under an obligation to give the talks, but the timing was worse than unfortunate.  Upset, feeling ill and with Marion nervous and twitchy, we made our way to Keele.  Marion had offered to do both talks by herself so that I could go home - but I felt that my husband could sort out what I prayed was a mistake.  Having struggled up to Staffordshire I was determined to stay!

Under the circumstances the talks went better than we could have hoped, and over tea and biscuits afterwards, we met someone who was to become a close friend and adviser on all things medical, Dr Alun Davies. Nonetheless, we were glad when the meeting finished and we were able to get on with what, for us, was the main purpose of the visit - meeting the Shentons and seeing Susanna's letters.

Joyce and Colin Shenton welcomed us to their bungalow on the edge of the moors.  Although a modern bungalow, the inside was beamed, low and cosy like an old farmhouse kitchen and a solid fuel range in an inglenook warmed the room, a kettle permanently singing on the hob. Tea flowed.  Cats viewed us disdainfully from the window ledge and a small, noisy terrier demanded our attention.  Horse brasses and china filled every ledge and hung from the beams. The room glowed with warmth and reflected light, and spread on the circular pine table in the middle were the letters. Piles of them.

We sat down - Joyce at the table with us, Colin nearby in a Windsor chair, listening intently and asking questions. It was a pattern that would be repeated often in the future.

Susanna looked at the little oiled silk pouch she had made for the letters and wondered why she had kept them. She now hoped the two women would make good use of their opportunity. Dear Ralphy had understood the importance of her little archive after all - she was pleased that he had managed to get that right. And he had impressed its importance on his children.

'I wish I had known Ralphy's children,' murmured Susanna sadly. 'John William was so difficult as he got old. What do they call that disease today - Alzheimer's? - we just described it as childishness. He was so horrid to poor dear Ralphy, not leaving him Basford, refusing to meet his wife, not wanting to see his children. Yet the marriage turned out well. Not many people could have coped with Ralphy but Harriet seemed to manage him all right,' she thought gratefully, 'and this grandson and his wife still seem to understand the value of discretion.'

She watched us all carefully. Ralphy's grandson was a gentleman, she could see that. Strong - she liked that in a man - but very dependent on his wife, just as dear John William had been so dependent on her. Colin was compact, not quite as tall as his wife, but muscular. Unlike dear Ralphy, this grandson had had to work hard in his life. But still he took a pride in his appearance, he was fine-featured, his hair was still thick. She wasn't so sure about the little goatee beard...

Our voices interrupted Susanna's scrutiny of her great-grand-nephew.

'We think you ought to look at this first,' said Joyce pushing a little bundle of pages across the table to us. 'So that you understand the full story of Aunt Susan's marriage.'

It was obvious that, to Colin and Joyce, Susanna was still a member of their family. We started to read the cramped, painfully-written pages. It was an account, written on scraps of paper, almost a secret diary, that we later decided Susanna had made for her father, or her lawyer, detailing the abuse she had received at the Ingleby's hands. Even after a century and a half it made harrowing reading.

We moved on to the letters, skimming through Charles's crabby writing. These could scarcely be called love letters - he came across as a dreadful old woman! And, unbelievably, amongst these papers which documented the most miserable few months of Susanna's life, there was her missing 1859 diary! Later we would find many other letters and we would learn everything we could possibly want to know about the affair.

'I don't believe it!' we said to each other as document after document surfaced. 'I don't believe it. If this was a novel people would say it was too contrived to be true!'

There was no time to read all the papers that evening and we needed to get to know Joyce and Colin. They had so much to tell us about Ralph De Tunstall and his family, and so many other treasures to show us; some of Susanna's wedding presents, Susanna's mother's medical chest, drawings done by her father as a schoolboy, a table that had belonged to Emily Jane, Ralph De Tunstall's hunting horn which Colin blew to earsplitting effect, photographs, and then, as night fell, almost as an afterthought, another wooden box of letters.

'These are all Susanna's letters to Ralph and his to her,' said Joyce.

Year after year, from the time he went away to school at the age of eight until he was a young man in his twenties travelling on the Continent, Susanna and Ralph kept each other's letters. Susanna put them in date order and stitched them into books. We marvelled at her energy.

We made arrangements to come again .....and again .....and again. Eventually we would hire a photocopier to be delivered to the bungalow so we could copy the precious documents without taking them away. But at this stage we were content just to have solved the mystery of the marriage breakdown and were blithely unaware of how much was left to do!

'Right,' Marion said. 'The readers need to know the whole story now. We've dropped enough hints.'

'I think we need to quote from the documents as much as possible - let the past tell its story in its own words,' I answered, 'even if it does mean lots of passages in italics ..... and we'll let Susanna describe what happened.'

This time Marion agreed. 'Of course. Why else would she have found all this material for us?'

Susanna smiled.

'I rather enjoyed living up at Sharpcliffe with Emily Jane and my brothers,' she began. 'You've seen the house haven't you? Very isolated, the ground falling away in all directions, with the shadows of the clouds scudding across the moor on a clear bright day. Without Papa's restricting presence John William was able to visit and stay with us whenever he wanted to. It was a happy time.

Freddy was always so amenable to everyone, and poor dear Wettie so uncomplaining and grateful for all that we did for him. He longed to walk on the moors with the rest of us or go shooting with John William - but he was never able to, crippled as he was with that dreadful rheumatoid arthritis. He longed to write fluently - but even holding a pen was such a struggle for him, so very painful. Such a gentle uncomplaining person though, and Freddy was his constant companion - they loved each other's company.

Gustavus could be very trying - so much younger than the rest of us, so wilful and always wanting his own way, but he was charming and it was difficult to deny him anything.'

'I don't even remember the first time I saw Charles Ingleby. I knew of him - one knew everyone by sight in a community such as ours - but we did not visit. His father had been assistant to old Mr Bourne the doctor. Then he went to Birmingham and made quite a name for himself; he specialised in ladies' complaints. Of course, I never met him, he died in 1845 when Charles was just twenty-three. Charles said he scarcely saw him, he was always so busy with his patients. It was Mrs Ingleby who was the most important person in Charles's life. I wish I'd realised just how important......

Charles styled himself curate of Cauldon Low. There was a small community of quarrymen's families up there - very rough - and a bare little hut where they used to hold services - but it wasn't part of any parish. I believe Sir Christopher Leighton suggested he take charge of the district - Sir Christopher was vicar of Ellastone. Without Papa present Charles could not call on us at Sharpcliffe, of course, even had he so wished, and I now think he would probably not have approved of the games we played if he had called - the charades, the cards, the silly giggling.'

Marion's voice cut across Susanna's thoughts. 'Pam - do you remember the letter that Christopher Armstrong sent us from Cumbria? He was a distant descendant of Charles's and we had quite a lengthy correspondence with him. He sent us a copy of a letter from one female cousin of Charles's to another - didn't she describe him as *'somewhat namby-pamby'?'*

I nodded. 'And as *'a poor thing, very evangelical'.'*

We'd found Christopher's address amongst the correspondence in Averil's trunk. He'd been researching the Ingleby family history and come across the story of Charles's marriage. He, too, realised that for a marriage to fail in 1860 something pretty dramatic had to have happened, so he had tracked down Susanna's descendants and written to Averil. She had replied with the hermaphrodite story. Their letters were twenty years or more out of date when we found them and we had not expected Christopher to be at the same address - or even still alive - but we'd written anyway. He was, and well over ninety but very alert. He'd sent us a great deal of information about the Ingleby family, including a photograph of Charles, a tall gangling figure, slightly stooped.

'He wasn't exactly a heart throb was he?' said Marion.

'Anything but. He was rather as I imagine Dickens's Uriah Heap; sort of oily and mock-obsequious. It's the posture I think.'

'I had arranged to go to Devon in the late autumn, to Sidbury Manor,' Susanna continued, ignoring our assessment of Charles's appearance, 'to visit my Aunt and Uncle, Papa's younger brother Tom and his wife. I was very fond of them and was looking forward to the long train journey. I very much enjoyed travelling by myself.'

'I thought young women had to be chaperoned?' said Marion.

'Obviously not.'

'I was twenty-eight,' murmured Susanna - 'they do have some peculiar notions! Well, you can imagine my utter amazement when I arrived and discovered that Charles Ingleby was in Devonshire. I was all but speechless when I discovered why. It seems that he contacted Mama's brother, Uncle John Holley - who incidentally was once Papa's curate - and told him that he had fallen desperately in love with me having seen me leaving church one day.

With Papa away my relatives took control. Uncle John had written to Uncle Tom and so the meeting had been arranged. They were anxious I should be married. I was dreadfully old as far as finding a suitable husband was concerned - and Papa needed to get Emily Jane and me married so that he no longer had to support us. I'd had other offers, of course, and I was beginning to regret that I had refused them. The idea of remaining unmarried troubled me greatly. I wanted children of my own you see; then, quite unexpectedly, came Charles Ingleby. I remember recording it in my diary:

*November 30th Mr Charles Ingleby came to call and stayed to dinner. Mr Charles Ingleby came to Devonshire to see me. He sat by me at dinner. December 1st Mr Ingleby dined here. I sat a great while with him alone as I thought because the rest were too busy to come downstairs.*

'In fact Aunt Tom and cousin Emma had contracted scarlet fever and were too poorly to come down. My cousin Carrie and I were sent the next day to stay at lodgings in Sidmouth so that we should not catch the disease. Mr Ingleby immediately moved to Sidmouth to be near us and paid me a great deal of attention. However, when I received his letter containing a proposal of marriage I was beside myself with anxiety. I had only just met the gentleman, I hardly knew him - he seemed to have made his offer with unseemly haste. Without thinking very clearly I wrote and refused him, saying that I could not agree to his wishes. I sent the letter at once and then spent a completely sleepless night, feeling very unhappy and sure that I had done an extremely foolish thing of which I should all my life repent.

But Charles Ingleby was not inclined to be so easily dismissed and at once contacted my aunt. Even though she was ill she wrote to me the same day urging me to reconsider. She explained how Uncle John had recommended him, how she understood what a shock it must have been to me and how she had already told Mr Ingleby that she did not in the least know what my response would be. She suggested that I might write to John William for advice and promised me that if I decided to refuse Mr Ingleby the matter would be kept very quiet - no-one in Staffordshire need ever know. That she thought, would be the least disagreeable outcome for us both. But she also urged me to think hard - I remember her very words: *'After I saw Mr Ingleby I was so very pleased with him that I was doubly anxious that he should succeed with you, dear Susie - He is the most perfect gentleman and so amiable and so gentle and good in every sentiment that he possesses that I think he would make any woman happy.'*

Certainly he seemed very insistent, and I suppose I thought it might be my last chance of marriage so, when he wrote again, a very, very kind letter, I was carried along by the romance of my situation and Aunt Tom's advice. So I accepted.

I vowed to make myself worthy of his love and asked for help from 'above' to make him happy. And I was happy myself then, happy and excited. I was to be married. I would have my own home and children. Almost in a daze I wrote to Papa to tell him the news, sure that he would approve a fellow clergyman, and a wealthy one at that, as my future husband. Charles wrote as well, and we waited for Papa's reply.

Papa wrote to say that he wanted to meet Charles and it was arranged that we would both go to Leamington at the beginning of December. My father and Mary were lodging there, in the best part of town, by the park and Pump Room and near the main shopping street. Charles paid for me to travel first class from Devon - an unusual luxury for me - and stayed with us for two days, accompanying us to church.

As I had expected, Papa was only too happy to consent to our marriage and the spring of the following year, 1860, was set for our wedding. I suppose I should have realised at once that Mrs Ingleby was not pleased about Charles's impending marriage. She raised objections to every date he suggested but eventually we fixed upon April 11th.

I stayed in Leamington with Papa, Mary and Ada. The first few weeks of January were happy and busy with shopping and preparations - that is what first made you interested in my diary I think. Papa bought an ornament for the neck as his wedding present to me. It cost £8-10s.

Aunt Mary gave me £3-5s to buy a dress and I chose a blue silk, one of the bright blue ones made using the new dyes invented by Mr Perkins - 'aniline dyes' we called them. I always liked vivid colours but most of them were not suitable for ladies' dresses. My wedding dress was a lovely pale lilac silk which cost five guineas and I had a Honiton lace wedding veil and a wreath of orange blossom, wax, of course, but very realistic. The bridesmaids' bonnets were so pretty; they cost 1 guinea each. Lots of friends and family called to congratulate me. Cousin Rosie came, she was to be one of my bridesmaids. Dear Robert and his four children came for four days; Freddy came before he went to Ireland with his regiment and we all had such fun together.

Many of my other presents were lovely things made by friends and relations. As women we had very little money of our own you see, many presents were home-made and I greatly treasured the ones I received: sofa cushions, pocket handkerchiefs, a kettle holder, an antimacassar and so much more. Of course, you have seen the list at the end of my diary.'

'Strange how things have changed,' I said to Marion. 'Obviously you wouldn't expect a Victorian bride to be given things like microwaves and toasters but I would have thought she would get some household stuff. I couldn't find anything much written about wedding presents - there's a good thesis topic for somebody - but I did look in some of the nineteenth century women's magazines we have at work. Useful presents were apparently only for the servants and even then they should be decorative - teapots, bedspreads, that sort of thing. But for ladies, presents should be personal - clothes and jewellery as Susanna had - or ornamental. Sets of silver cutlery and porcelain vases were said to be *'particularly suitable'*, as were books on how to be a good wife. Susanna had *The Wife's Demand* if you remember. People got a lot of jewellery - I found a letter from Carrie, one of the Sidmouth cousins, telling Susanna about her sister Emma's wedding. She was the one who married Captain Gale and went out to India. Almost all Emma's presents were jewellery. It seems Susanna and John William sent Carrie money to buy something she thought Emma would like and she bought a ring set with an amethyst and opals from Susanna and a gold and blue enamel bracelet and a locket from John William.'

'A bit like the one dear Mrs Bradshaw sent me,' thought Susanna. 'Mrs Ingleby gave me jewellery too - a lovely set in pearls and amethysts.'

Joyce Shenton pushed a little blue leather-covered jewellery box across the table to us. We opened it carefully and there it was, the very bracelet that Mrs Bradshaw had given Susanna, silver, set with blue enamel and monogrammed with the initials S I. A beautiful piece - and just in case there was any doubt, the case contained a little note in Susanna's handwriting *'from Mrs Bradshaw'*.

'The weather was dreadful that year right into the spring,' Susanna continued, 'cold, so cold, thick snow and ice and my chilblains were very bad. There were many days when they were so painful that I could not put my boots on. In January Charles wrote to me *'I scarce remember the roads in a worse state: an inch or two deep in snow, partially frozen and with ice below. It would have been very bad walking but it was even worse riding.'*

We wrote to each other almost every day because it was so difficult for us to meet and I suppose I should have begun to see the difficulties that lay ahead from his letters. Looking at them now I can see how fussy he was - obsessed with health: his health, my health, his mother's health. I don't recall Papa or any of my brothers being like that. Almost as soon as we had fixed to marry he started to send me long letters on how I should look after myself - he even sent me bottles of liniment for my chilblains:

*December 19th 1859. I much fear, that being desirous to see your friends again after a long absence, you will venture out into this severe cold more than is prudent. You may not feel the ill effects at the time but it tells afterwards. I can speak from experience on this point and I am quite persuaded of the desirableness of an abundance of warm clothing. I was as little particular about these things as any one until a few years ago.....*

*I am very glad that the liniment has done good. If it does not remove the chilblains, you could then, by and by, try Mr Sutton's, which he says, has proved efficacious. I have no doubt that the pills also did good, as the chilblains proceed from a defective circulation and are therefore benefited by internal as well as external remedies.*

Marion was starting to seethe. I recognised the symptoms.

'Talk about passion killers - I'd have ditched him there and then if all he could send me was letters like that, bottles of liniment and homilies on staying indoors. I love you? I cannot live without you? Not a word! And what about this:

*December 31st 1859. Of course you have heard of Mrs Mather's bad accident owing to her dress taking fire the other night in taking a piece of coal off the fire. One arm appears to be burnt badly, and other parts of the upper part of the body in a less degree. She was better yesterday. The pain must have been great as even a small burn is very painful. How very very dangerous are ladies light spreading dresses to come near fire. It will be necessary dear Susie never to forget this.'*

'Actually,' I said, 'quite a lot of ladies got badly burned wearing crinolines - they could be anything up to four feet in diameter, you know, so your skirt could catch fire when you thought you were still some way away from the grate. Then, of course, there was so much air trapped underneath that you went up like a chimney!'

Susanna nodded. 'I remember that dreadful accident well - I kept many newspaper reports of such incidents. Poor Caroline Mather - she was Papa's cousin, you know, she married the vicar of Oakamoor. She died from her burns. I was always very careful myself. And Charles did not scold all the time - he also wrote to me about other things he thought would improve my mind:

*.....There is an interesting article and notice on the late Lord Macauley in The Times of December 31st... there is small prospect now of a History of England like his being completed....*

*The Picture of Eastwood Ho is an able and interesting one; Mother and I saw it in September at Scarborough at Sarony's Photographic Rooms.*

But mainly we wrote to each other about our forthcoming wedding and life together:

*I think you could not possible find anyone better than your cousin Rose* [as bridesmaid]; *by all means secure her. Should you at all like to ask your other cousin there, or anyone else instead of my asking, as I do not at all mind if there is anyone else you would like.*

'Rosie was Uncle Henry's daughter,' thought Susanna, 'she married Mr Mocatta. My other bridesmaid was her sister, Mary Anne. We were all very good friends.'

*I should fancy that with the ordinary license either Church, Cheddleton or Ipstones, would be available.*

*January 11th. With respect to a Bonnet or Veil, I believe that the latter is more usual but pray do as you like best. I shall like either quite well.'*

*January 16th. My mother thinks that Easter Tuesday is not a day to fix upon.*

*January 18th. Do you think your eldest brother* [John William] *will be present at our marriage? I hardly think that Mr Sneyd will wish for him to be so but I should be glad if he may as I think you would.*

There was no way in which John William could have attended, though of course I should have loved to have had him there. Charles did not understand the nature or depth of the quarrel between Papa and John William or how extremely difficult and unforgiving Papa could be. He was to find that out all too soon as it turned out.

Charles was quite awkward about the honeymoon.

*Where do you think you would like to go to?  It will hardly be the time of year to turn one's steps northwards.  Scotland is, I think, delightful in the month of August, but in April or May it is a different matter.  I have moved about a good deal and seen a good many places - so I think it ought to be left to you to fix.  Should you like the South of England or the Continent?  The Continent is not altogether in a very settled state though it might do well enough for a few weeks.  Italy is in a particularly uncertain state or there are parts of it which might have been desirable.  There is Switzerland though it is rather early in the season.  There is Pau and the Pyrenees....the climate* [there] *is beneficial to the chest....*

Charles did not like any of the suggestions I sent him and I think really he had already decided that we would go to Pau. He had spent some time there with his mother - many English people lived there - they even had a hunt with its own pack of fox hounds. Most importantly, Charles thought, there was a very good English chemist! I was excited at the prospect of being married and really not very concerned where we spent our honeymoon. It was what was to happen during it that was important. Anyway, I too had travelled extensively in Europe. So we decided on Pau. Even then he had some misgivings,

*I am a very poor hand at French, but I have no doubt that together we shall manage quite well......'*

Having decided on our honeymoon he then started to fret about the wedding invitations and we had some quite serious differences about who was to be his best man and more importantly who was to take the wedding service. He wanted his vicar, Sir Christopher Leighton. I wanted my dear brother-in-law Robert Bamford. In the end they both officiated. I managed to persuade him away from Mr Whieldon as his best man as I had heard he was unable to speak coherently in public and behaved rather peculiarly. In the end Charles acquiesced and asked his cousin and sent yet more letters about the wedding breakfast arrangement:

*I have not yet made out a list of persons to whom to send cards, but if confined to relations and a few of neighbours and intimate friends I should think that 35 or 40 might pretty nearly cover it.....*

And from his letters I did begin to get a much clearer picture of his mother - she never wrote to me once, you know, to congratulate me or welcome me as her future daughter-in-law - but I was sure that his love for me was strong and that he would smooth my path with her. I suppose I just didn't want to see that she would always be the most important person in his life or that I was the one who was going to have to fit in with her wishes in every way; that he would always side with her. And her rudeness and obstinacy were clear had I not been so blind:

.....[my Mother] *has had divers letters... I hardly know whether I can call them altogether of congratulation for some are as much of condolence but this is under the idea that having lived together for so long we are about to live separately.... It is quite possible and perhaps only natural, that my mother might have felt more heartily acquiescent had it been with one with whom she had been intimate for some years, but I am sure it will be your care to do everything which is right and good and considerate.'*

How dreadful it sounds now I read it again! - and so like her. She was always so stubborn. One day she slipped on some icy steps. Charles was frantic with worry:

*I wanted her to have Mr Sutton, but she says no. She has never had a Doctor in the 15 years nearly that we have been here. When she has had any little thing the matter with her I have never been able to persuade her to see anyone.*

She really was quite severely bruised - perhaps she had even cracked a rib. But by the time she did let Mr Sutton come and apply leeches to her it was too late to do any real good. I began to worry more and more about what our life would be like living with Mrs Ingleby. I half hinted that we should have our own home but this was greeted with absolute refusal. On Aunt's advice I then suggested that at least we should have our own sitting room where we could be private sometimes. You cannot imagine the fury that brought down on my head. I really should have seen what was coming!'

We leafed through the pile of Charles's letters which were strewn over Joyce Shenton's kitchen table - the little grey, oiled-silk pouch in which they had lain silently for the past century and a half, lying limp on the dresser. The more we read them the more sorry we felt for Susanna. Charles's mother prevented him accepting a living of his own at Ashbourne saying that it was too far away, though Susanna had written congratulating him on being offered his own parish, adding that she would love him to accept it.

Mrs Ingleby was outraged at the very thought that Susanna might want her own private sitting room and Charles was obviously having a very difficult time with his bossy, over-bearing and obsessively jealous mother. If his letters had not been so infuriating we might even have felt sorry for him too.

*You must remember that this is a small house, the rooms not only small but few in number..... My Mother is very touchy and sensitive on this matter; I have produced very considerable soreness of feeling when this matter has been raised. She spoke that perhaps she should 'be in the way'.... If she is sensitive about what she thinks may have the appearance of my separating or estranging my self from her you must bear in mind the length of time I have been with her........'*

*'Do not let your relations persuade you that the absence of any private room, specially set apart, will necessarily not be agreeable to you but first think for yourself what prospect there seems of the present accommodation here being satisfactory.... I know that a separate house is in most cases the usual and perhaps more eligible course, but in the poorer classes for instance the opposite is continually true.'*

'What on earth has that got to do with it?' spluttered Marion. 'And what had the experience of the 'poorer classes' to do with either of them? Poor Susanna. She was letting herself in for a prison sentence!'

'I capitulated, of course,' sighed Susanna, 'what else could I do? Charles was clearly so cross at my suggestion, he wrote two whole letters about it, full of underlinings and capital letters. So I said I was sorry and Charles was kind enough to send a letter immediately thanking me most warmly. I felt it was best not to antagonise his mother before we had to live together. She obviously hated the idea of my going there. She had decided that a very great deal of decorating needed to be done before I arrived and had workmen in. But they could do no right either and she insisted on taking down and putting up pictures and heavy curtains herself.

*My Mother's back was so very bad yesterday that she could not go out with me. She has done too much -she is as skilful in these things as I am unskilful - she said that if she had known there would have been so much work for her to do for your benefit she would have left some of it until you came....*

*Believe me, my dearest Susan, yours very affectionately,*

*Charles Ingleby'*

I felt so guilty. I'm sure Charles wanted us to live together harmoniously, and so did I. I'd known the difficulties of fitting into a new family at first hand. I'd had to get used to Papa's second wife Mary; she could be very unkind and Papa always took her part in any disagreement. Emily Jane and I were very much pushed out, especially as we both still felt warmly towards John William. I don't think Papa ever really forgave us for that. Charles knew that and he wrote to me:

*....you will not be disappointed in looking for more affection and kindness than you have met with of late - Mr Sneyd said he had always required 'obedience to the family' and I dare say Mrs Sneyd too may have felt that she was entitled to exercise it in a like manner, but never mind Dear Susan, if you should in this latter case at present have to be obedient to authority which perhaps may not always be over kind or considerate. In a little while you may hope that you will be considered and valued - I hope I shall never give you cause to feel that you are other than kindly and affectionately treated.*

'Oh, what awful cold letters,' burst out Marion again, 'even given the difference in written and spoken style'. *'Kind and affectionate!'* That sounds like an elderly uncle's letter to a wayward niece!'

'We met very few times before the wedding, Susanna continued. In fact altogether we only spent ten days together and then always in the company of other people. Charles and I played at chess sometimes. I found that we were exactly well matched, winning the same number of games each. Emily Jane and I spent one afternoon at Oakamoor with Mrs Ingleby and she visited us at Woodlands once before the wedding with Charles. So Charles and I did not really know each other at all well before we were married.

Then of course there was all the awful business of my marriage settlement. I think I'll leave that for you to explain. It was all so very tedious and difficult - something over which I had no control at all. I was entirely at the mercy of Papa, Charles and whoever they saw fit to oversee my finances. So very different from now. We were mere chattels really.'

'You'd better do that part,' said Marion to me, 'you're much better at setting out the factual bits accurately.'

'The boring bits you mean?' I responded. 'Well, it was like this.....'

Prior to the Married Woman's Property Act of 1882 married women could not own anything. Legally, a wife's property and money belonged to her husband as soon as the wedding ceremony was complete. Well-to-do families protected their daughters by setting up trust funds for them which usually consisted of a lump sum from the bride's parents matched by a similar amount from the husband's family. This money was for the woman's use if her husband could not, or would not, support her. However, by law, a married woman could not act for herself in financial matters - though she could do so before she was married or after she was widowed.

Her 'marriage settlement' was therefore managed by trustees who had to be approved by the men of both families. It was to these trustees that the wife would apply if she wanted to realise any of her capital. The choice of trustees was a delicate matter; they had to be impartial, diplomatic and trusted by both families - so the selection of the trustees for Susanna's settlement caused endless problems. Charles did at least keep her informed of the negotiations - presumably her father did not.

*Mr Sneyd said he should propose to settle £3000, as he had done upon his other daughters who married; and he allowed he said £150 a year during his life. I asked him to suggest what sum he would think fitting for me to settle. He asked if £5000 would be satisfactory - to which I at once assented.'*

'Wow!' said Marion. 'She was going to be wealthy wasn't she? £150 a year, if Papa paid up, and a nest egg of nearly £8000 (£362,000). Even if she couldn't manage it herself.'

'Charles got that bit wrong,' I said. 'John Sneyd only offered £50 a year - and the settlement money wasn't going to come from him anyway though of course he never made that public. It was Susanna's grandmother's money that she was given - Jane Debank set up a trust fund to make sure all her granddaughters had proper dowries.'

By March, perilously close to the wedding, the business of the settlement had still not been sorted out and Charles was becoming irritable. He was beginning to see just how difficult it was going to be to do business with his future father-in-law and how very insecure John Sneyd's finances were. Beset as he was by a mother who did not want him married and was obviously not going to make life easy when he was, and an intractable and litigious father-in-law, poor Charles was between a rock and a hard place.

John Sneyd was well known and no-one wanted to have to deal with him. Charles struggled to find someone who would act as his trustee.

*March 21st - Mr Challinor* [John Sneyd's solicitor] *has suggested two alterations which he said would be preferred. Both were quite unnecessary - one a very trifling matter but not within Mr Challinor's province to decide upon. The other I dare say was well meant, but rather gratuitous - perhaps I might also say a rather impertinent suggestion...... I have instructed Mr Wragge* [Charles's solicitor uncle] *to reply to these suggested alterations in the negative. I may, just between ourselves, mention one hindrance which is in my way. It was said to me the other day by a relative, in confidence, and I repeat it to you in confidence also, "Mr Sneyd is of a litigious spirit and this will increase your difficulty in meeting with a trustee".*

However, by the 26th of March Charles had persuaded his friend, the Reverend G.A. Perryn of Trafford Hall in Cheshire, to act for him. The wedding could go ahead.

'I saw so many people in the days before my wedding,' Susanna remembered. 'My cousins Emma and Carrie from Sidmouth arrived. Papa, Mary and little Ada met them in Birmingham. Friends called to give me their good wishes. And my wedding bouquet arrived, a gift from Charles's uncle, Mr Wragge, with a note from Charles:

*It should be taken out of the box tonight and covered with cotton wool.*

Charles was always so meticulous. Of course I did not have to arrange any of the food - that was all taken care of by the servants. I suppose it was really rather a simple wedding. No arches of flowers on the road to the church as Ada had when she married, no tea for the servants....

Emily Jane and I stayed at Woodlands with cousin Rosie for several days before the wedding. During that time I went to say goodbye to some of the cottagers and spent a day at Heath House with Mrs Boucher - Emily and Rose were with me. And I packed my things of course - all the new clothes that I had bought for my honeymoon. On the evening of the 10th my Uncle John and cousins William, Henry and Clement and my brother Gustavus came to visit, and Mrs Boucher and Mrs Galbraith. I was glad of their support and company since I had little from Papa and Mary - they chose to go to Lord Shrewsbury's Ball at Newcastle that night with William and did not get back until between four and five the next morning.

The 11th of April dawned - my wedding day. I was so excited. I was married from Woodlands at Cheddleton Church. Papa rode with me in the carriage. Charles and I did not stay for long at the wedding breakfast. We caught the train at Cheddleton station a little before one o'clock - Mrs Wragge was with us. Sir Christopher Leighton went with us on the first part of our journey to Leek, then Mrs Ward accompanied us to Stoke. They were all very kind to me. We arrived at London at 9.50 pm and stayed the night at the Victoria Hotel. We had a private sitting room. I suppose we were both very tired and nervous.'

'I do get the feeling that the Reverend John and Mary are conspicuous by their absence,' I put in. 'You'd have thought they could have stayed at home on the eve of their daughter's wedding and seen her off at the station afterwards.'

'You were not impressed, were you, by my description of my honeymoon?' Susanna went on. 'Lists of towns and places: churches and monuments; a castle with a fine tapestry and the tortoiseshell cradle of Henry IV.... I remember hearing you laugh over my description of the Pyrenees as *'very white'*. I was hurt, you have no idea, no idea at all, what a huge effort it was to write down anything and make it all seem normal - only my calendar at the front alerted you to the fact that anything was wrong. It was perceptive of you to notice the tiny entries of *'two beds'* and *'very unhappy'*.

And yes, as you surmised, something was wrong, very, very wrong. The weather was dreadful - bleak and snowy and the carriages we spent such long hours in were cold and uncomfortable - jolting us over interminable rutted roads. Needless to say my chilblains were dreadfully painful as well.

When did I realise? Almost immediately really.

I knew what marriage was about. I had older married sisters, nephews and nieces. I had married friends. We talked about such things of course. Your idea that Victorian women were entirely ignorant of the facts of life is nonsense - and we lived in the country don't forget. So I had a very good idea of what to expect on my honeymoon and that, with God's blessing, it would lead to children. For two nights Charles came nowhere near me - he had never been particularly amorous, but I had put that down to shyness or perhaps the fact that he thought he ought not to be too familiar before the wedding. I tried to encourage him.

After three nights I asked, very gently, if something was amiss. I cannot begin to describe to you what ensued. Charles became violent and completely unreasonable. He screamed at me, accusing me of knowing things which no pure, unmarried, Christian lady should know. He accused me of being almost a harlot. I was bewildered and in despair. I was as gentle and loving as I could be and for the next six nights Charles did his best but he was unable to.....

I thought I was to blame - but now I suppose for him it must have been as if his mother was watching from the corner of the room - she was never far from his thoughts and he constantly mouthed her opinions on everything. After those few embarrassing and futile attempts Charles would not even share a room with me.

On April 27th he frightened me by shrieking and shaking all over and saying that he was ready to commit suicide. I tried to put my arms round him begging to be told what I had done wrong, but he would not tell me and said I ought to know. And I did not in the least know having done all in my power to please him.

We spent the days walking endlessly in the bitter cold looking at buildings and churches but seeing nothing, and the evenings in hotel lounges; anything to avoid being alone together. Then Charles decided that we should cut short our honeymoon and return to England. Can you imagine my mental torment?

On May 2nd we arrived back at Folkestone and left at once for Oakamoor, arriving at Woodbank by the five o'clock train. They were not expecting us of course - our room was not ready. Not that it mattered. Charles at once asked his mother to have two rooms prepared. We each had our own bedroom. I spent a sleepless night as you may imagine, friendless in that cold, austere house. Outside the sky was lit red by the brass works in the valley below. I could smell the fumes and hear the clanging of trucks carrying coal and ore, the shouts of the workmen. I thought I would never sleep again.

After a night or so of separate rooms I pleaded with Charles for us to share a room, and for the next few nights we had one bed - but it was to no avail. Charles had another bed brought into the room. He complained my heavy breathing kept him awake. Then he moved into the spare room - which he found uncomfortable so he moved back. With small ceremony he then turned me and all my belongings in there - and there I stayed until I left.

It was dreadfully noisy from the foundry, the air was gritty, and everywhere there was an acrid, metallic, sulphurous smell which mingled with the gassy fumes from the coke they used for smelting. It burnt my nostrils and coated the back of my throat. And it was so dirty. The floor of the works was coated with about an inch of coal dust - that was to catch the molten metal if it spilt. They told me that was usual in brass works. But of course it spread everywhere. It was on the men's clothes, on their feet - and it blew about. The grass and hedges around the works were black with it, all the buildings round about were blackened, it came into the house - you could even taste it in the food. The hems of our long dresses were soon marked and some of my petticoats and drawers were quite spoilt - they never came clean however many times they were washed.

Of course, outside Woodbank we tried to present as fair a face to the world as possible. As Charles's new bride I accompanied him to church, took walks with Mrs Ingleby, called on his relations, visited the local school and attended a tea there where we were given a silver tray by the children as a wedding gift. It was heartbreaking - if they had only known the sham that was our marriage.

Mrs Ingleby made it clear I was unwelcome and she and I spent as little time together as was seemly. Until the beginning of June my friends and relations were able to call on me and I was able to go to Cheddleton to visit them. I was careful not to say too much - such intimate details are not for public discussion - but of course they knew I was not happy. I suppose I still clung to the thought that in the end all would be resolved.

But as the days turned into weeks it became intolerable. When I asked to be allowed to visit my cousin Minnie - her husband was Dr Fraser, vicar of Alton, just down the road from Oakamoor - I endured several hours of scolding for wishing to visit in an *'improper manner'*. I did not at all know what they meant. Minnie and I had grown up together, she was like a sister to me, I did not need a formal invitation to go and see her.

Eventually I was not allowed to see anyone, and when Charles found out that I had written to my family hinting at my unhappiness he was beside himself with anger. I cannot describe his rages to you. Mrs Ingleby was as unpleasant as it was possible to be, saying that she thought there was no good in me. Charles became almost deranged - screaming at me for hours on end, banging my bedroom furniture violently with his fists and turning from me if I tried to look at him or reason with him, shouting 'those eyes, those eyes.' I was told by them both that my eyes showed my badness.

I begged to be allowed to visit Woodlands and eventually was given permission, but at the last minute Charles rushed wildly to the front door, barring my way. I at once said that if it was not liked I would not go, but he screamed at me, 'Go, yes go, get out of my sight.' Mrs Ingleby told me to return upstairs to my room and there I stayed for hours and hours, without so much as a cup of tea, not daring to come down. At last, in the evening, she came up and said it was as well that I had stayed there as it had taken her all that time to calm him. That night I was kept up very late, they were both so very violent.'

'Remember Woodbank?' I asked Marion.

She nodded.

We'd looked at Woodbank from the outside on our first trip to Staffordshire, but eventually we wrote to the owner and made an appointment to visit. We called there one damp October morning. It is a large villa, now divided into two substantial houses, so Charles' protestations about the small size and paucity of rooms were nonsense. Old Mrs Ingleby was related to the Wragges, who part-owned the Cheadle Brass Works. Charles and his mother rented what was, in fact, a modern company house.

We admired the views over the wooded valley - yellow and brown leaves still clinging to the trees in the warm autumn rain, bright wet grass, dark glistening evergreens. To our surprise, the present owner produced an illustration of the view from the dining room window as it was in the 1870s. The brass works was effectively in the Ingleby's front garden.

Standing on the stairs, looking along the hallway, now painted a crisp white but then probably dark grey or green with varnished brown woodwork (so as not to show the dirt) it was possible to envisage the scene - Charles barring the door with his body, Susanna hesitating on the stairs in her outdoor garments and Mrs Ingleby, cold and hard in her widow's weeds, standing gesticulating between them.

'By this time I was almost bereft of reason myself,' Susanna continued. 'I still did not understand why Charles was so very angry. I had only wanted to obey God's will and celebrate our marriage by the procreation of children - the very reason the church gives its blessing to marriage. Charles, having calmed down a little by the next morning, said that I must write and confess all my faults to those I had told of my unhappiness. He would read all my letters and if he approved of them he might, eventually, forgive me. If I did not do this he would brand me as a harlot and spread word, through his solicitor, of my lewd behaviour. Lewd behaviour! I was mortified. I had no choice but to comply - I had to find some way of reaching Papa - but how, with Charles reading all my letters?

I decided to write to Mrs Boucher first. Dear, wise Mrs Boucher who knew me so well and to whom I had already confided most of my troubles. I hoped she would be able to read in my letter what I had **not** written.

*Dear Mrs Boucher,*
*Mr Ingleby asked me on Friday morning who I had told I was not happy and so with several others I had to name Mrs Bradshaw and you. I am very sorry I mentioned anything to you as I know that sort of thing ought to be kept quiet as the fault is most likely to be on both sides that causes them. When I wrote to you I think I told you what I had done wrong, such as making too light of my chilblains and other ailments; not talking sufficiently and to be thought not to take an interest in what I read, and being sleepy sometimes in the day - I committed one fault which I would not explain before. This was a short time before our marriage. I put my hand on a part of Charles that I ought not to have touched. I did not intend the least harm by this and I am very sorry I did it. I think I have now told you all my great sins -*

'Why ever did Charles let her send that?' I asked. 'Even if you didn't know the story it sounds very tongue-in-cheek.'

'No sense of irony, I suppose.'

'And what part of your husband are you not supposed to touch?!'

'But she and my other friends had already guessed my distress,' Susanna went on. 'I managed to send another letter to Rosie and either she or Mrs Boucher alerted Papa to my situation and to my plan. Knowing that on the 11th of June Mrs Ingleby was to go by the 8.25 train to Birmingham I grasped my opportunity and, running to the station with no luggage, took the 12 train to Highfields. Dear Rosie was waiting at Oakamoor station for me and we travelled together. A great many of my friends joined the train

- Rosie and Mrs Boucher had made sure there would be plenty of people there in case Charles or Mrs Ingleby tried to stop me.

Papa arrived at Highfields by the evening train to help me. I had never in my life seen him so utterly beside himself with rage when he knew how I had been treated. I had left Woodbank, never to return.'

We sat silently at the table for some time, unable to speak. Marion had tears in her eyes.

'I'll make some more tea,' said Joyce. 'You'll have a bit of supper with us won't you?'

Deftly she made chicken sandwiches with stuffing, and ham sandwiches with mustard, garnishing the dish with parsley and tomato wedges, set chocolate cake and home-made biscuits on plates covered with paper doileys and poured strong tea into pretty porcelain mugs - even the most impromptu of Joyce's meals was beautifully served. As we ate, Colin and Joyce revealed that the papers and letters that they had shown us that evening were only part of a very much larger collection.

'You'd better come again,' said Colin finishing his tea. 'It's been interesting this evening.'

Over the next few months we were able to piece together the aftermath of Susanna's flight. For a few days immediately after her escape she was comforted by her beloved Aunt Mary in the familiar surroundings of Highfields. During that time her father interrogated her at length, gradually drawing from her all the painful, intimate details of the failed marriage - perhaps that was when she wrote the account we had read.

John Sneyd had to be sure of his facts before he began his assault on Charles Ingleby. He consulted brother clergymen, instructed the invaluable Mr Joseph Challinor - and then whisked Susanna off to Scotland where Mary and little Ada were holidaying. For several weeks they toured Scotland by train, coach and steamer. Susanna's diary reads like an account of a normal holiday with no hint of the distress and embarrassment she must have been feeling.

'She had iron self control,' I said.

'Didn't she just.'

'I wonder if she took anything in on that Scottish tour. I think it was the first time she'd been to Scotland and they went to some wonderful places - Fingal's Cave, Oban, the Trossachs, up Ben Nevis, through the Caledonian Canal. It would be nice to think she found the grandeur of the scenery soothing; that it helped put her problems into perspective.'

'I'm not sure she cared for scenery all that much. She probably just appreciated being kept busy.'

Meanwhile back in Staffordshire the lawyers were thrashing out a solution. Much of the correspondence survives. Loyally, Mr Ward, Charles's solicitor, expressed the view that the couple stood a chance of having a happy marriage if Susanna would agree to a reconciliation. Mr Ingleby, he argued, was a mild man, no physical violence had taken place, Mr Ingleby had little knowledge of the world and his behaviour had proceeded from simple ignorance; he now understood he had been unreasonable and hoped Susanna would return to him. Nonetheless Mr Ward advised his client to go to London to be examined by Michael Partridge MRS, surgeon to King's College Hospital and Professor of Anatomy at King's College, to prove that he was physically normal and thus refute the more damaging personal slights that John Sneyd was taking pains to publicise. A copy of the certificate was sent to Susanna by Mr Challinor. It was probably the most unlikely piece of evidence that we could have ever hoped to uncover!

*I have this day examined the Rev Chas Ingleby and I do not find that there is anything in his physical formation to prevent him from having sexual connexion. I may add that from various circumstances I believe he is capable of prolific sexual connection so far as he is concerned.*

'So he wasn't a 'Will-Jill' then?' said Colin, using the colourful Staffordshire vernacular. He had been raised on the story of Charles's infirmity.

'What a dreadful thing to be labelled all those years. Poor chap, poor, poor chap.'

Colin was clearly distressed at the injustice that his family had perpetrated on Charles Ingleby. We were less sympathetic. Whatever Charles's sexual situation his behaviour had been cruel and abusive.

'Perhaps Charles was actually gay?' suggested Marion. 'Or impotent?'

'Or simply repelled by the very idea of sexual activity?' I said. 'We shall never know.'

But I was wrong. While this book was being written Marion took a holiday in Portugal leaving me slaving over a hot computer - an unfair division of labour if ever there was one. One morning a postcard arrived. 'Am reading V. Glendinning's biography of Swift at present (which is excellent). I quote 'Hermaphrodite, just to add another strand to the pattern of linguistic shift, was the contemporary term for queer.'

Of course! John Sneyd was using the idiom of his youth. It was as simple as that. His words had been quoted and misunderstood - new and more graphic terms had come into use to describe men of Charles's sexual persuasion. Homosexuality was illegal in 1860 and, like many others, Charles had sought to hide his sexual orientation behind the convenient skirts of a wife. He may even have believed Susanna would be quite happy with the situation. Victorian men were actually encouraged to believe that their wives had no sexual feelings. In *The Functions and Disorders of the Reproductive System*, published in 1859, William Acton wrote:

> As a general rule, a modest woman seldom desires any sexual gratification for herself. She submits to her husband, but only to please him; but for the desire of maternity she would far rather be relieved of his attentions. No nervous or feeble young man need, therefore, be deterred from marriage by an exaggerated notion of the duties required of him.

Charles seems to have been just such a young man. Indeed he had hinted as much in one of his letters to Susanna. *'You will not, I am sure, expect too much, and that being so I am quite sure we shall be very happy together'*.

Susanna did not expect *'too much'* for a normal marriage - but for Charles Ingleby it was far too much. And by Acton's standards, she was not a modest woman. She was anxious for her marriage to be consummated and was distressed and bewildered by Charles's failure to do so. He was shocked by her desires. She was not the innocent undemanding bride he thought he had married. To naive Charles this made Susanna little better than a whore.

Charles was almost certainly sexually inexperienced. He was an only child and he had been brought up by a mother who had allowed him little contact with the outside world. As a schoolboy at Rugby he had not been allowed to board but had lodged with a local clergyman; as an undergraduate his mother had moved to Oxford to keep house for him; as a young man travelling on the Continent mother had come too. Perhaps Anna Maria Ingleby knew better than her son that a heterosexual relationship would be a disaster for him or perhaps she was simply jealous. Whatever her reasoning it seems unlikely that she would have welcomed Susanna back had there been a reconciliation.

And regardless of Charles's protestations, John Sneyd had no intention of allowing his daughter to return to her abusive husband and his witch of a mother. He set about recovering her clothes and other possessions from Woodbank. Only a small box was returned and John Sneyd despatched a scorching letter to Mr Joseph Challinor denouncing his son-in-law as a thief and a liar.

Charles's accusations about Susanna's immodesty and the slur on the way she had been brought up reflected on her father - and John Sneyd was not a man to let an insult pass. He made sure that everyone knew about Charles's behaviour - letter after intemperate letter survives. To his brother-in-law John Holley, one of the family who had been instrumental in brokering the match, John Sneyd wrote:

*....I am sure that your disgust will rise to intense loathing at the additional information I am about to convey to you of the Evangelical Oakamoor sinner. Just before Susan left that den of iniquity her tormentor induced her to write to Mrs Boucher a statement of every circumstance of her life and conversation that had given him offence and to express her deep sorrow for these offences and imperfections of her mind and conduct; she lamented her incapacity to please him, her chilblains, her sleeping during his sermons in church - and more specifically her want of delicacy before and after marriage, particularly she had to say that she had once, before marriage, placed her hand on one of his thighs......*

'So **that's t**he part you shouldn't touch!' said Marion in disbelief.

*....this piece of freedom he received at the time with a smile, but a little while ago it was remembered as a great offence against morality.... The reports circulated of his behaviour towards his victim have created great consternation and have generally been ascribed to insanity, but the cause of the malady seems first to have crept into the minds of a few ladies of our acquaintance.... He was booked by them as wanting in virility. When I in my innocence gave it as my opinion that such an infirmity would cause a*

*greater degree of tenderness I was told that was not the case.*

'That's interesting,' said Marion, 'imagine the sort of conversation John Sneyd and his friends must have had. '*A few ladies of our acquaintance*' means friends rather than family, doesn't it? Not the decorous sort of small talk that we are led to believe went on at Victorian dinner parties.'

'Yet another myth exploded.'

*I told Susan of my suspicions,* continued John Sneyd's letter, *and in the course of my examination I learnt that he had never attempted to consummate the marriage for 3 nights and when some hint was given that some more active measures were expected he abused her as indelicate in the extreme and wondered where she had gained such knowledge and exclaimed about the way she had been brought up. Nevertheless he made the customary attempts, without effect, and to do him justice he did his best for 6 nights leaving her just as he found her excepting in the mortification of her mind. After these six attempts he seems to have given it up as useless. I was not aware of the beast's infirmity when he called upon me or I should have been driven upon him..... Mr Boucher intends next Tuesday to move for his removal from the Clerical Book Society, and there is no doubt of him being excluded from it. Mr Frazer means to eject him from doing duty at Cauldon. I have threatened him with obtaining on Susan's behalf articles of the peace against him and I have also instructed Mr Challinor to institute proceedings against him to dissolve the marriage on the grounds of impotence. I have likewise sent Mr Sleigh to beg as a favour that he will give him and his amiable mother notice to quit their house.... May God forgive me but I do truly hate and despise the knife-backed mule. What right has he to think of matrimony - his abstinence for three nights shows his knowledge of his own unfitnes...... My friends seem to think that just removing Susan will not be punishment enough I have therefore authorised Challinor to demand some pecuniary compensation..... some think that the fear of such a disgusting exposure will operate on his sordid mind - doubtless his Mother will not wish to part with much of the mammon of Unrighteousness.....*

And so it went on, page after page. Today the letter shocks by its lack of compassion. With wiser counsel on both sides the marriage might even have been saved, but the Victorians saw impotence - and homosexuality -

as moral rather than physical issues.

Unfortunately for Susanna her father's intervention could never restore her reputation. Wild rumours began to circulate. The Sneyds were well-known in Staffordshire and for them to be involved in a scandal of this proportion was too good for the gossips to resist. The tales improved with telling. Charles Ingleby was not a complete man. The Reverend John Sneyd had driven to Oakamoor and horsewhipped the Reverend Charles Ingleby. John William Sneyd had also been to Oakamoor and horsewhipped Charles Ingleby. Of these happenings we found no evidence whatsoever.

But Charles was forced to resign his curacy and was dismissed from the local Clerical Society. Nonetheless, he and his mother remained at Oakamoor for the rest of their days. The shame must have been almost intolerable. At least one poison pen letter addressed to *'Master Charlie'* survives. But Charles Ingleby was a wealthy man and so the lawyers came to an agreement - a legal separation under which Charles was to pay Susanna £100 a year, to rise to £150 when his mother died and he no longer had her to support.

On reflection, John Sneyd must have seen that this was the best solution. Technically the marriage could have been annulled, but Susanna would have had to undergo an embarrassing physical examination to prove she was still virgo intacta. She would always have been tainted by the affair and her chances of her finding another suitor would have been slim indeed.

Her best hope was to stay away for as long as possible and allow the dust to settle. On August 23d when the rest of the family returned to Staffordshire Susanna remained in Scotland with her married sister Penelope Brodie. Penelope had married in 1848. By this point she had seven children aged between two and eleven, and when Susanna arrived the whole family was staying at Baberton House just outside Edinburgh.

Susanna, photographed by Josiah Spode in 1863.

The Reverend Charles Ingleby.

Mrs Ingleby, Susanna's mother-in-law.

Woodbank, Oakamoor.

The brass works at Oakamoor. This was the view from Woodbank.

Cheddleton Church.

| No. | When Married. | Name and Surname. | Age. | Condition. | Rank |
|---|---|---|---|---|---|
| 335 | April 11th | Charles Ingleby<br>Susanna Sneyd | full age | Bachelor<br>Spinster | Cler<br>O |

18ỏ0. Marriage solemnized _in the Parish Church_ in the _Parish_

Married in the _Parish Church_ ____according to the Rites and Ceremonies of th

This Marriage was solemnized between us,　*Charles Ingleby*　*Susanna Sneyd*　in the Presence of us,

Susanna's marriage certificate.

Woodlands.

168.

sh    of _Cheddleton_    in the County   of _Stafford_

| ank or Profession. | Residence at the Time of Marriage. | Father's Name and Surname. | Rank or Profession of Father. |
|---|---|---|---|
| Lerk in Holy Orders | Woodbank . in the Parish of Cheadle | John Tomlinson Ingleby _deceased_ | Physician |
| ___ | Woodlands | John Sneyd | Clerk in Holy Orders |

of the _Established Church by Licence_ by me,
                                            _Robert Bamford_
                                                _Offg Min:_

{ _George W Wragge_
{ _Emily J Sneyd_   _Kate Mary Sneyd_

John William, photographed by Josiah Spode in 1863.

Leek Market Place seen here about 1900.

Looking over Cheddleton towards Morridge.

Mr Joseph Challinor of Leek, the family solicitor.

Cheddleton Station at Basford Bridge.

Chapter 7
# 'I went alone to the daffodil fields'

Susanna's position as an estranged wife should have been acutely embarrassing, but in Edinburgh, amongst strangers, she almost seems to have relished being the focus of attention. Wealthy women's lives were dull and restricted.  Servants did the housework and cared for the children. Ladies sewed, sketched, shopped, and attended a stifling round of social events at which they met and re-met the same people.  Not only was Susanna a new and agreeable member of the Edinburgh circle but she was also the heroine of an extraordinary tragedy. No doubt a carefully-told version of her story earned her sympathy and admiration.

'Her diary suggests that she was quite enjoying herself,' I said, 'and perhaps, temporarily, she was.'

The Brodies were wealthy.  Baberton House, near Edinburgh was grand, even by Sneyd standards.  It was a three-storeyed, 17th century house and its main claim to fame was that the exiled Charles X of France lived there for some time after his abdication in 1830.  The family owned another, larger, property, Idvies, in Forfarshire, and a town house in fashionable Moray Place in Edinburgh. Penelope Brodie had married well.

But Susanna's stay with the Brodies had its downside.  She entertained the children - Effie, the eldest, Johnnie, Annie, James, David, Alexander and little Frederick - and Penelope's husband and mother-in-law made much of her, but it seems Penelope was less welcoming.  She may also have been very unwell - shortly before Susanna's arrival she had given birth to a stillborn child. Childbirth was a hazardous process in 1860: a stillbirth could well have been the result of a prolonged and painful labour or of unskilled medical intervention.

'I've got this book,' said Marion, 'about a Scottish gynaecologist - *Simpson the Obstetrician,* by his granddaughter, Myrtle Simpson.  You should look at it.'

I did. The blood-curdling account of the career of the famous James Yates Simpson in Edinburgh in the middle years of the 19th century made me feel quite queasy.  He championed the use of chloroform and forceps and developed an instrument for extracting breach babies.  His intentions were good but his case studies made disturbing reading.

The woman had a contracted pelvis. Her first labour had been long and difficult and had lasted for four days. The child had eventually been drawn out in pieces, the operation taking more than an hour..... Jane Carstair's last baby had been born dead after a terrible labour lasting three days that ended in the baby's head being broken up before it could be extracted...

I had given birth to three children myself and had been extremely ill with the second one - when I turned up at my doctor's sixteen months later, unexpectedly and unintentionally pregnant with my third son I had been offered a termination on the spot. I'd refused - but I really felt for poor Penelope who had no such options. She had produced nine sickly babies in quick succession, only to see most of them die before they grew up.

*1860 August 19th Penelope was moved to a sofa and in the evening she was carried into the drawing room. She is allowed to eat anything,'* wrote Susanna.

*25th Mrs Brodie and I went a walk in the woods near here. The Dr called. Mrs Brodie, Effie, Annie and I went to Edinburgh. I bought one mohair dress from the dressmaker.*

Susanna had left her clothes and most of her belongings at Woodbank, and as yet they had not been returned. She must have been sorely in need of a change of dress.

*28th Mrs Brodie, Effie, Johnnie and I went in the carriage to Banelaw, we from there walked to Habbie's How, a walk of about 10 miles.*

*29th We went to Moray Place. I found my law deeds had arrived there, I signed them before Mrs Brodie. I am to have my first £50 on the 12th December and the next on the 13th June.*

*31st Mr Brodie began his work again in Thistle Street - he left here by the 9 train. Effie, Johnnie, Annie and I walked with him to the station.*

'You said that we weren't going to quote much more from her diaries,' said Marion reproachfully. 'You said they were tedious in the extreme, readers would never wade through them and stay awake - and then you go and quote another great chunk. Yes.... I know,' she went on before I could say anything, 'it gives a flavour.'

*September 1st Penelope went out for her first drive*
*6th I took the 4 eldest children a walk.*

*October 18th I called at Hazel Bank to wish Miss Souter "good bye".*
*Penelope was very unkind indeed. Mr Brodie had a long talk with us  he*
*was very kind.*

'What on earth do you think she said?' asked Marion.

I couldn't imagine, but given Susanna's gift for understatement it was probably very cruel.

'Perhaps she was jealous because Susanna got on so well with all her Edinburgh friends. Or because the children and in-laws liked her so much,' I hazarded. 'Or perhaps she was still feeling very ill after the stillbirth. After all her own difficulties she might have felt that a marriage without sex wouldn't be such a bad thing and Susanna should have stuck it out.'

'Penelope went mad - well a bit peculiar, anyway - as she got older,' Marion went on. 'It's in her father's diaries - he went up to Edinburgh and talked to his son-in-law about *'poor Penelope's mental state'*. Maybe this was the beginning of it - or perhaps it was post-natal depression.'

Susanna shuddered. There was no way, after all this time, that she could let us know what Penelope had said. It had been so very unkind - deeply, deeply hurtful - but it didn't really matter now. We didn't need to know.

The sisters never saw each other again. Susanna kept in touch with the children and met some of them again as adults. She recorded their deaths and the birth of the youngest Brodie child, Phoebe, in 1861, but the rift with Penelope was permanent. The Sneyds were a family that bore grudges!

Nonetheless, her life in Edinburgh had been a good deal more interesting than it was to be back home at Woodlands. She shared that house with her sister Emily and cousin Mary Anne, daughter of her Uncle Henry, the former vicar of Wetley Rocks. Susanna paid her father £50 (£2,300) a year rent.

'Typical John Sneyd,' I said. 'give her a £50 a year allowance with one hand and take it back in rent with the other.'

For months Susanna's diary is full of other people's doings and household trivia - with particular emphasis on a new lamp and its consumption of oil! She also did a good deal of sewing for her male cousins Clement and William Sneyd-Kynnersley. She seldom ventured out. Tongues must have wagged and rumours spread - it did not pay to flout convention in Victorian England.

'It must have been dreadful for her,' Marion said, 'so embarrassing, knowing people were gossiping about you.'

'She seems to have socialised happily enough in Edinburgh,' I said, 'but certainly once she got back to Staffordshire she seems to have gone into a sort of depression. Her family tried hard to engage her in activities but after her first Sunday at home she seems even to have given up attending church for a time, recording how she *'finished unpacking'* or *'walked in the garden'* while the others went to the service.'

'I suppose I did,' thought Susanna. 'People tried to be kind, of course.'

She remembered how she had written to Dryden that January *'I do not go out visiting at all'* and had admitted to him that she would still like to hear something of Charles - *'people don't like to talk to me about him - I think he must feel very sorry he was so unkind to me, he must be so very dull now, as I think hardly anybody goes to see them'*.

Gradually she had come to realise the enormity of what had happened. An unbearably bleak future stretched out before her, but in the secluded gardens at Woodlands, hidden by trees from prying eyes, Susanna felt safe.

Family and friends visited. The Bouchers from Heath House, the Bradshaws who were now the tenants at Basford and the Daglishes from Ashcombe, were all regular visitors.

On November 23rd Mary Anne persuaded Susanna to visit some of the cottagers in Wetley Rocks with her and on the 29th John William walked with her to call at Heath House, a few hundred yards from the end of Woodlands driveway. On December 20th Emily managed to get her to go to Wetley Rocks to see prizes given to the schoolchildren.

Mr Boucher was vicar of Cheddleton, and the Sneyds and Bouchers had known each other for years. Mrs Boucher had befriended the young Miss Sneyds, Susanna was godmother to one of her sons, and she had been the first person in whom Susanna confided when her marriage ran into trouble. Susanna saw her almost daily at Woodlands - but still she was reluctant to venture to Heath House. This refusal to visit her most trusted friend gives some indication of the depth of Susanna's depression.

John and Mary Sneyd were absent, and the children, including John William and several cousins, all gathered at Woodlands for Christmas. If Susanna would not go out then her family would come to her.

*December 24th Wm, Henry and Clement went to Leek. John Wm, Freddy, Wettie and Tavie came to stay here. Rosie returned here from Derby. Mrs Leigh called. Games were played in the evening.*

'I did my best' thought Susanna, 'you don't realise how difficult it was. It wasn't just the gossip. I knew I could never marry again, never have babies. I felt my life was over. I even wrote to Robert Bamford about adopting a child. He didn't think it a good idea. She looked again at her brother-in-law's letter: '....there are four here who would be only too happy to be adopted by their Aunt Susan so spare your superabundant sympathy for them...' Dear Robert, he meant it kindly, but of course he remarried soon after that. Then the children had a stepmother. She was good to them, they didn't need me. But you can see from my diary entries for 1861 that I did try harder in the New Year.'

*January 2nd - I went to see old Mrs Morton*

*5th  Emily and I called on the Charles Halcombs we had dinner with them*

*10th  I went to the school for the first time for a very long time.*

*11th  Mary Anne and I called at Heath House*

But it was still some time before she felt able to accept more formal invitations.

*March 6th Emily, Mary Anne and I spent the evening at Heath House. We met Mrs Galbraith, this is the first tea party I have been out to in the neighbourhood since I returned home. A windy evening.*

She began to visit cottagers in Wetley Rocks on a more regular basis, walking along the muddy lanes to spend uncomfortable afternoons sitting on hard chairs, in cold, stone-floored cottages, making improving conversation with the old and the sick. But she was less happy about going to Cheddleton and for some reason could not face the shopkeepers in Leek.

Not until May 24th did she visit the town and then only to go through it on the way to see John William at the Harracles, near Horton. It was a long, long walk. It was August 5th before she visited Leek properly, in the pony carriage with her stepmother. She did not enjoy it and it was months before she ventured into town again. Yet when she lived at Basford she had gone to Leek almost every week.

Recovery was a slow process and there were anniversaries to cope with.

*March 11th  This day last year I went with Mr Ingleby to Cauldon Low for the first time.*

*April 11th  One year. In the morning I painted numbers for the bells here. Papa went to Sharpcliffe. Emily went to the infant school. Mrs Downman, Mrs Henry Sneyd and Miss Stagg called and also Mrs and Laura Worthington.  I went alone to the daffodil fields, the flowers were at their best, the anemones are now quite out in this wood.*

'I think the use of the word 'alone' is important here,' said Marion. 'Susanna seldom did anything alone. And what **was** it about daffodil fields? Almost every year, whether they were in Armitage, Abbots Bromley or Cheddleton, she went to the daffodil fields on her anniversary.'

I didn't know.

'Maybe she found that the flowers helped her cope with the bad memories?' I hazarded. 'Or maybe the church was decorated with daffodils when she got married and it seemed an appropriate reminder? Interesting that there were so many daffodil fields about - were they being grown for sale, do you suppose?'

The diaries threw up so many questions; we would never be able to answer them all.

Marion was becoming intrigued by Susanna's use of language. There were odd constructions - *'I began rheumatism'* - and occasional, incongruous, slang expressions. We puzzled over the *'severe tea'* that she had at a friend's house, only to discover that 'severe' was a slang term for 'excellent', much in the same vein as schoolchildren today use 'wicked'. But when her father wrote her a *'severe letter'* in October 1860 we couldn't be sure whether he was scolding her or being kind and supportive.

In 1865, on holiday in Dover, she went and had her ears pierced *'alone'*. Was she being particularly brave or daring? Or were the people she was staying with being unfriendly and leaving her to her own devices? She certainly did a lot of things alone when she was at home without stressing the fact that she was by herself. Perhaps we were reading too much into her entries - but they were so formulaic that even the slightest change of words was noticeable.

On another occasion Marion got excessively excited to discover that in the 1880s Susanna used the expression *'members of the working class'*.

'How interesting - don't you remember Dr Snell saying it was 20th century term?' she said.

'Really?'

I was unimpressed. I was the one transcribing the wretched texts and 'interesting' was definitely not a term I would have used to describe Susanna's literary style. Yet just occasionally she would come up with a particularly telling or evocative sentence. Marion's favourite was *'I put away my coloured dresses'* - a perfectly straightforward statement recorded in February 1873. Her father had died, she would be in mourning for two years and by the time the period of mourning was over those coloured dresses would probably no longer be fashionable. But it was also a moving way of describing her sadness, and, though she didn't know it, the beginning of the end of the happiest part of her life. For a time we even toyed with the idea of using it as the title for this book.

Another idea for a title was *'Beyond Description'* which was the way she described herself in a letter to her solicitor. The letter to Mr Challinor thanked him for helping her invest her marriage settlement - something she could not do for herself because, technically, she was a married woman and unable to manage her own money. As a separated wife she had no legal status; she was, quite literally, beyond description. But somehow the phrase (which she had underlined) seemed to encapsulate an almost 20th century, tongue-in-cheek, sense of the injustice of her situation.

Many of her other surviving letters were quite intemperate; long ungrammatical rants to her friends about her problems and sorrows, very different from her restrained, almost austere, diary style. It made us wonder what her spoken language was like. Sometimes we felt we knew her so very well; at other times she seemed to elude us altogether.

'I don't think she ever got over her broken marriage,' said Marion. 'She always recorded her wedding anniversary, you know, even celebrated it with John William. Underneath the iron self discipline I think she was a very sad lady.'

John and Mary Sneyd and little Ada had spent some time in Herefordshire at Hoarwithy in a property belonging to Robert Bamford, but at the end of March, 1861 they arrived home and shared Woodlands with the girls. Susanna had to move to a smaller room to make room for them. Their arrival provided Susanna with a more active social life and a wider range of visitors. Her father and stepmother seem to have been much less sympathetic to her desire for privacy than were her siblings and cousins.

John Sneyd divided his time between the girls at Woodlands and his sons up at Sharpcliffe. The way the Sneyds expected their children to run their own establishments seems very strange to modern eyes. Freddy and Wettie were twenty-two and twenty, Tavie was eighteen, and they had lived on their own for several years, with occasional help from their sisters.

As the year went on Susanna spent some time with her cousins at Stockport, some with Minnie Fraser at Alton and was with the Bamfords at Mickleton for six weeks in the autumn. She spent her time caring for the children there and visiting neighbours. She remained close to Robert and there are hints that, had it not been for the law of affinity which forbade a man to marry his deceased wife's sister, and her own unresolved marriage, he might have asked her to take Harriet's place.

*September 28th  I sat a good while with Robert in his study.*

*October 1st  Made a promise to Robert.*

'What do you suppose that was?' we asked each other.

Susanna smiled to herself; Robert had been such a delightful man. Poor dear Harriet was so very, very lucky.....

But by Christmas she was back at Cheddleton.

*December 25th Xmas day.  Mary Anne, Tavie and I went to Wetley Rocks in the morning, the rest all went to Cheddleton, in the afternoon we all went to Cheddleton.  We played at quiet games.*

Christmas was primarily a religious festival and Susanna at this date makes no mention of Christmas presents given or received. That year, when the remaining Sneyd children gathered at Woodlands their eldest brother was not with them - and not just because their parents were in the neighbourhood.

In July 1861 John William Sneyd had married Agnes Cotton of Etwall Hall in Derbyshire. He had told Susanna of his intentions in November 1860. Susanna wrote excitedly to Dryden in New Zealand:

*January 15th*

*John William* [is engaged] *to Miss Cotton, she is a very nice person, she is 13 months older than I am which makes her about 8 years younger than him, he says she is as near perfection as anyone can be...*

John William and his father were still estranged and he seems to have visited his sisters only when their father was away. In the autumn of 1860, with John Sneyd safely in Herefordshire, Susanna recorded, *'October 28th John Wm sat in the Ashcomb pew.'* It was obviously an unusual occurrence.

John William's impending marriage was an additional difficulty. Though the Reverend John could not bring himself to settle the quarrel with his eldest son, he was not indifferent to his welfare. In June he was persuaded to meet Agnes and her mother. The Bradshaws, who were the tenants of Basford Hall, were close friends of the Sneyds. Mr Bradshaw was vicar of Grindon, and Mrs Cotton had been a Bradshaw before her marriage.

*June 10th  Mrs Bradshaw brought Mrs Cotton and Agnes to call here to see Papa...*

*11th  Mrs Bradshaw brought Mrs Cotton and Agnes again to call.*

*27th  Papa, Mary and Ada went by train to Etwall and stayed two nights there.*

At one of these meetings the Reverend John arranged with the Cottons that he would pay Agnes an allowance of £40 (£1,800) a year after her marriage - so long as she kept it secret from John William! It was a loaded gesture that could well have driven a wedge between husband and wife. It was also totally unnecessary. John William was marrying a young woman of very considerable fortune. Agnes's marriage settlement from her parents was more than £12,000 (£550,000). John William was a close friend of Agnes's father, which no doubt smoothed his path, but he himself had little to offer. He seems to have wooed and won Agnes on the strength of his personality alone.

John William's sisters greeted the wedding with unrestrained enthusiasm.

*'July 11th Mr Boucher drove Emily and me to Stoke in our pony carriage. I bought John Wm and Agnes a dinner service £8. Emily bought them a breakfast tea service £4.'*

'They were very generous presents' I said. 'Do you think the Reverend John subsidised his daughters? Where else would Emily Jane have got £4? When Susanna married she gave her a Honiton lace veil that she worked herself.'

The Reverend John and Mary did not got to the wedding, though they allowed ten year-old Ada to attend and be a train bearer.

*Tuesday July 16th John William's wedding day. Emily, Bertha and Fanny Cotton, the young twin Miss Bradshaws & Miss Sitwell were bridesmaids. We arrived at the church at 11. Mr Paget Morley & Mr Morley married them. There were about 50 for the breakfast. Ada & the 3 little Ashworths were the train bearers, about 100 schoolchildren and some old people had tea in front of the house. The bride and bridegroom went that night to Chester on their way to Ireland.*

Susanna and Emily visited their brother and sister-in-law at Etwall in February 1862.

*19th Emily and I left Cheddleton by the 3.59 train and went to Sudbury and from there we had a fly to Etwall which cost me 16s. Miss Bill, Mrs Wright, Mrs Whathall, Mrs Milne and Mrs G Wedgwood were staying there. Mr and Mrs Baker and Mrs Monsley dined there. I wore my wedding dress for the first time since my wedding.*

Victorian wedding dresses followed the prevailing fashion and were re-used for day or evening wear, as appropriate. Susanna's husband and his mother had not socialised much so her trousseau had not contained evening dresses. Her wedding gown was the most appropriate garment she had for the grand dinner with John William's in-laws. It must have revived bitter memories, but Susanna was too sensible - or too controlled - to give in to them.

'We weren't so sentimental then,' thought Susanna. 'I didn't really mind. It was a beautiful dress; it would have been foolish not to get some wear out of it. My chief problem then was that I was so unwell - and such an embarrassing complaint!'

Susanna was already suffering from a condition that would plague her for the rest of her life. In March 1862 she and Emily went to see their cousin Mary Anne who had moved to Derby. Clearly there was an agenda to this visit and one gets the impression that Emily and Mary Anne were worried about Susanna and were urging her to see the doctor.

*March 8th We all called at Mr Evans to consult him about my complaint. Mr Evans called at Oriel Terrace* [Mary Anne lived at number 6] *to examine me.'*

Having finally persuaded her sister to take medical advice Emily hurried home to Woodlands to explain matters to their father. They arrived back in Derby by the first train on the 10th and John Sneyd immediately went to discuss Susanna's condition with Mr Evans.

On the 13th *'Papa - called on Mr Evans at the College & brought him & his assistant here at about 11 o'clock, I had a Surgical Operation performed on me for piles. I took Chloroform & felt nothing of it...'*

Presumably the operation was performed at Mary Anne's house. It was quite normal for surgeons to operate in private homes; indeed, they were usually safer than hospitals as there was much less risk of infection. The following day Susanna admitted to feeling very poorly but she made no further complaints to her diary. Mr Evans visited daily and Emily nursed her, sat with her and read to her day after day.

Susanna winced at the memory. After a week she had been well enough to get up to wash herself, but it was nine days before she could actually sit. A day or two later she began to come downstairs and on the twenty-sixth she took her first walk. On the 31st she saw Mr Evans for the last time and paid his bill of £7-12s-6d.

'Expensive,' I said, 'and it didn't work. Just left her with scar tissue that made matters worse.'

'But I wasn't to know that,' thought Susanna. 'Mr Evans was so persuasive, so sure it would help.'

Despite her operation, 1862 was a good year for Susanna. Agnes gave birth to John William's son at the beginning of May. Susanna knitted and sewed for the baby.

*May 3rd John Wm & Agnes's son and heir born at Etwall at about 3 o'clock in the morning. John Wm has taken a house at Armitage for 3 years at £30 a year.'*

But childbirth was a risky business and poor Agnes developed complications. John William wrote to Susanna on June 23rd. He was distraught.

*I am afraid that my dearest dearest Agnes is as ill as she can possibly be - I do not believe there is such a girl in the world, high and low, rich and poor all send to enquire after her, she is so universally beloved. The church bells are not to be rung, and I am sure the prayers of the parishioners, both in church and out are most fervent for her. Thank God our child is everything we could wish. A very fine boy, & very healthy. If it is God's will to take my dearest, dearest wife, will you dear Susan, be so good as to live with me? It is dearest Agnes's wish as well as my own.*

Agnes had contracted puerperal fever, an agonising and usually fatal illness involving infection of the torn perineal tissues. It was often passed to the patient by the poor hygiene of doctors or nurses who had recently attended another birth - the condition was rife in lying-in hospitals. Etwall Hall was demolished in 1959, but it lay behind the church - hence the need to silence the bells so Agnes could get some rest. On June 25th John William wrote again; Agnes was beyond hope: *'Poor dearest, dearest girl she has been the perfection of a wife to me.'*

Within days Agnes was dead. Susanna had been given a new role. She was to be the baby's foster mother. No doubt she grieved for her sister-in-law - but she must have been excited too.

*July 3rd I worked at my black dress. Poor dear Agnes was buried.*

*24th I was packing & straightening - I was so busy I sat up all night. Emily helped me with my packing.*

*August 5th I left home by the 9.44 train & came to Etwall.*

*8th John Wm's baby was christened by the Rev Paget Morley "Ralph De Tunstall".*

*9th I was with Baby most of the day.*

In fact, she was to be with him for the rest of her life.

'It was a new beginning for me,' she thought, 'the best thing that could possibly have happened. Well, at least to begin with.....'

Chapter 8
# 'John William and I went to Armitage'

'I don't remember this at all,' I said as we drove through Armitage. It had been our first port of call when we made our original research trip to Staffordshire but that time we had come in from Lichfield, down a lane lined with attractive houses and bungalows. My memory was of a pleasant, if undistinguished, little town.

We had only been back once, after dark, but now that we were embarking on Susanna's book, I felt I needed to refresh my memories of the place. Six years had passed since our last visit, in which time we had published John William's 1844 diary; an edited and annotated version of the Reverend John Sneyd's diaries; a booklet for Oxfordshire Record Office about Susanna's youngest brother, the ghastly Gustavus Sneyd; an esoteric booklet for our university department analysing a private census of Ipstones taken by John Sneyd in 1839; another for Ipstones church about a carpet made by Susanna in 1877, and papers for various local history journals. We had actually been pretty busy. But none of it had required us to revisit Armitage.

For some reason we had fought shy of writing about Susanna. Her diary was the least publishable of them all, her style was tedious and repetitive, yet of all the diarists she was the one we empathised with the most. We felt we wanted to do her justice but did not know how.

Armitage is much larger now than it was in Susanna's day (the census showed the population as just 250 in 1861), and this time we thought it a depressing place, an overgrown industrial village with no real centre, dominated by the canal and its embankment, and swamped by modern housing estates.

In Susanna's time it was still an agricultural village of widely spread houses and cottages with fields in between, but there would have been a good deal of heavy traffic on the canal and Armitage had industry in the shape of two potteries which produced sanitary ware. Indeed, one of the potteries was almost in the back garden of Armitage Cottage. Susanna never referred to it but little Ralphy found it fascinating and made numerous childish drawings of the smoking kilns which dominated the skyline from his bedroom window.

'He was only a child,' thought Susanna, 'but I did tell him it wasn't a very nice place. The owners weren't at all our sort of people. Not like Mr Spode; he was a gentleman. And they made - well, it wouldn't have been so bad if they'd made cups and plates. Of course Ralphy didn't understand....'

Armitage church was then relatively modern, rebuilt in the 1840s, in the Norman style to replace a genuine Norman church. Bob and Bridget's Rectory was completely new in 1862 and had been built by the incumbent, Mr Wilson, partly at his own expense. It was a rambling, red brick, gabled house with gothic doorways and windows.

The grandest houses in the village then were Armitage Lodge, next door to the Rectory, home to Mr and Mrs Birch and their children, and Hawkesyard, the seat of young Mr Spode (Josiah Spode IV, the great grandson of the potter) and his wife. Old Mrs Spode, his mother, had acquired the house in 1839 and made various alterations. Hawkesyard was a strange, quirky building, some way out of the village, five bays of honey-coloured stone and faced brick, with 'gothick' windows, turrets, crenellations and tall chimneys (demolished for safety reasons many years ago), standing in acres of carefully planted gardens. The gardens were famous for their rare ferns and the subterranean tunnels carved into the soft sandstone beneath them.

Armitage cottage, where Susanna, John William and little Ralphy were to settle, was a comparatively modest property, a child's drawing of a house with a central front door surrounded by five symmetrically-placed windows, of which one of the ground floor ones had been converted to a bay. It stood, surrounded by trees, on the corner of Boathouse Lane on land that now belongs to Armitage Shanks.

Rugeley, the nearest town, has also grown out of all recognition. It was where Susanna went to shop and had the nearest station. It also had a rather unfortunate reputation. In 1856, just six years before Susanna and John William arrived, the local doctor had been hanged as a serial killer. Rugeley had attracted a good deal of unwelcome attention and the town fathers had even considered changing its name. William Palmer, the Rugeley poisoner, had been a racing man and had got heavily into debt. He killed his wife and several of his children to claim on their life insurance and poisoned at least one of the friends to whom he owed money. Palmer was believed to have killed a total of fourteen people; the case was a cause celèbre - two inch lengths of the rope that hung him changed hands for the enormous sum of 2s 6d (£6) each. Journalists flocked to Rugeley, and it is from the account of one of them in a February issue of the *Illustrated Times* that we get some idea of the Rugeley that Susanna would have known:

It was a long straggling town, 'very clean' and home to many 'persons extremely well-to-do in the world'. The streets were paved and lit by gas. The Shoulder of Mutton public house, kept by 'the eccentric Mr Clewly' was described, as was the bookseller's shop with its mahogany frontage and plate glass windows where Susanna went to have copies of Ralphy's *Chatterbox* magazine bound. Ben Thirlby's chemist's shop where Palmer bought his poisons was described in detail - no doubt that is where Susanna shopped for the *'grey powders'* - a mixture of mercury and chalk used for colic in children. Brook Street, wide and tree-lined, was the best residential street, but was also home, for several days each June, to the Rugeley horse fair which attracted buyers and sellers from all over the United Kingdom and Ireland. There was a new post office and a brash new church as well as one that dated from the 13th century (both dedicated to St Augustine). The house for the headmaster of the grammar school, gothic red brick, surrounded by trees, home to Susanna and John William's friends, the Bonneys, was also modern.

What the journalist barely mentioned was the industry. Some two hundred and fifty of Rugeley's four thousand inhabitants were employed in foundries. There were two large iron foundries that also made agricultural machinery, a large sheet iron and tin plate mill and Bladen's brassworks which specialised in plumbers' brass fittings. There were also three corn mills, a brewery and a tannery, and, within the parish, a number of coal mines owned by Earl Talbot and the Marquis of Anglesey. It seems unlikely that Rugeley was such a pristine town after all - tanneries and breweries are notoriously smelly, foundries are noisy and dirty, miners tramping home through the back streets in those days before pithead baths would have brought their pit dirt with them.

The neighbouring hamlets, Pipe Ridware, Mavesyn Ridware and Hamstall Ridware, to which Susanna walked - to buy eggs, visit her dressmaker or take visitors to see their quaint little churches - have changed much less than Armitage and Rugeley. The flat, muddy tracks Susanna walked have become flat, muddy tarmac. Hedges have been grubbed up and replaced by barbed wire; many of the cottages have been gentrified and one of the churches is now a tiny theatre, but she would still recognise them. The countryside is pleasant but flat, typical mid-Staffordshire agricultural land with no outstanding features. It must have seemed very pedestrian after the dramatic landscapes of north Staffordshire; the change in the scenery was very apparent to us as we drove south from Stoke-on-Trent. The weather that day was grey, cloudy and mild, not one of the extremes of heat, cold, wind and wet that usually characterised our Staffordshire excursions. Even the hawthorn bushes, covered in blossom like poured cream, did little to enliven the dull, flat fields.

'An uneventful landscape, that's the word,' said Marion at last. 'But perhaps that suited John William and Susanna, they'd had enough of drama. Do you think there is any link between landscape and personality? Do people who live in dramatic landscapes feel a need for drama in their personal lives?'

'I doubt whether the landscape had anything to do with it,' sighed Susanna. 'I was happy in Armitage.'

*1862 July 12th John Wm, Mrs Howe,* [the housekeeper] *Caroline Botham* [the nursemaid], *Baby & I left Etwall soon after 11 o'clock, we arrived* [to lodge] *at Mrs G Myatt's, Rugeley, 20/-* (£46) *a week. John Wm & I called on the Birches at Armitage Lodge.*

'That is how it all began. It was wonderful; there was no gossip, no-one knew my story - though of course I did tell some people eventually. In Armitage I was respectable again. Keeping house for John William was thought to be almost the same as keeping house for a husband. I had dear Baby to care for - he was like my own son. And we had such good friends in Armitage; we were invited out often, dinners, dances, concerts, plays and charades at the Birch's, picnics, croquet and archery parties. I had to have so many new dresses that first year - my old ones seemed drab and ordinary, not at all suitable for the jolly life we were leading. It had been such a long time since I had enjoyed myself.'

The sort of houses that the Sneyds and their friends lived in seem to have been let fully or partly furnished. When the Sneyds let Ashcombe and Woodlands in 1858 Susanna, Emily and Mary spent a good deal of time making inventories, especially of things like books which tenants could easily purloin, but they left their furniture, linen, plate and all manner of personal goods in situ. It is difficult to know just what furnishings Susanna and John William found at Armitage Cottage but clearly they were insufficient. They did a good deal of shopping, Susanna made blinds, altered *'carpets'* and Mrs Howe the housekeeper washed them.

John William and Agnes had for a time lived at a rented house called The Green, at Ashbourne, but had moved back into her parents' home for the birth of their baby. They would have had a few household possessions with which to furnish their new home. John William had some items from Etwall delivered by Astor's on the 29th - Agnes's share of her late father's possessions. A box of linen came from Ashbourne on August 8th and a further van load of items arrived on the 15th.

'It must have been very difficult and sad for him going back to the house he had lived in with Agnes and packing up their things to take to Armitage,' said Marion.

'Heartbreaking. But very different for Susanna - real excitement, I should think. Her own home - and a baby to look after.'

'There was that huge kitchen garden' thought Susanna 'and we arrived just as all the produce needed picking and preserving. We got one of the Carthy's in to do it - the postmaster's wife if I remember rightly. And that first night somebody got into the garden and took our beans - I suppose they thought the cottage was still empty and it would be a pity to let all that good food go to waste. We were so cross! Then a few days later the washerwoman's little girl stole what was left of our gooseberries. I don't know why we minded so much - there was always plenty, we used to give it away.'

By July 21st Susanna and John William had the house straight enough to move in but there was still a great deal to do - between July 29th and 31st John William and Mrs Howe went to a house sale at Cannock and bought a removal van full of things and over the next year or so sales would furnish other household goods. They waited until December before acquiring a dining table, for example. Buying new does not seem to have been an option John William considered.

'Why not, do you suppose?' Marion asked. 'Couldn't he afford it? Were there any furniture shops nearby? How common was it for people like the Sneyds to buy household goods at sales?'

We were finding so many aspects of 19th century life that we knew nothing about. Nor, it seemed, did anyone else. And there were so many little details that seemed to us to be interesting.

'How many people would know the cost of moving furniture in 1862?' I asked Marion. 'But here it is, *'all the things came in Astor's removal van, charge 1s a mile'*. That's £2 to us.'

Susanna listened to us with amusement, remembering their first few weeks in Armitage. 'Mrs Howe left after a few weeks, on August 18th. She only came to help us settle in. Then I had to find a new housekeeper and learn to run my own household. First of all I employed Mrs Braithwaite - she had £12 (£553) a year. Caroline Botham, the nursemaid who had come with us from Etwall stayed on and from time to time we employed Jackson as gardener - and Mrs Peate from the village used to come to do the weekly wash. Ours was a very modest household - Mama would have been quite shocked. John William found it difficult, I think. But it didn't matter to me.'

Their little household revolved around baby Ralphy. Susanna recorded all the milestones of his childhood; his first tooth, when he took his first steps; even when he began to use a knife and fork. The first marker came very early.

*1862 July 17th Baby began short clothes.'*

'What does that mean?' asked Marion. 'You know about dress.'

'Well,' I answered, 'Ralphy was just over three months old, wasn't he? Victorian babies wore long clothes until they began to become active. Then they wore dresses that allowed them to kick and wriggle - quite often they literally were long baby robes that had had the bottom foot or so cut off - you find quite a few like that in museum collections.'

'How can you tell?'

'Different stitching, different type of cotton, that sort of thing, and sometimes embroidery that looks unbalanced - lots on the bodice and none where you'd expect it at the hem.'

Marion looked doubtful

'Why did little boys wear dresses though? They did, didn't they, until they were quite big?'

It was amazing how often people asked that when they looked at

Victorian baby clothes, I thought. And it was so obvious.

'Potty training. Imagine a little boy in trousers - lots of buttons and tapes, towelling nappies and cloth pilches.....'

'What?'

'Sort of fabric over nappies. No plastic pants - you know what little boys are like, don't tell you they need to pee until it's too late. In fact, I remember my friend Val who moved to Edinburgh when her youngest was at that stage - mine were a bit younger - wrote to pass on her latest piece of maternal wisdom -"put them in kilts, nothing underneath, until they're in control of themselves!" '

'Ralphy had a kilt, didn't he?' interrupted Marion. 'So what about this bit? *'1865 October 4th  I worked at Ralphy's high dresses.  28th Ralphy began his high dress & knickerbockers.'*

'Well - that was the next stage. Once he was potty trained Ralphy would have worn outfits that looked a bit more masculine - short smocks with baggy trousers in washable fabrics - Susanna obviously made them for him. Then when he was eight he progressed to knickerbocker suits. She proudly recorded the address for Mr Lamb of Derby as that of *'Ralphy's tailor';* though actually, of course, he was John William's.'

'Ralphy looked so sweet,' thought Susanna tenderly. 'He was such a good little boy, affectionate, precociously bright and confident in the company of adults. He did everything with us. I suppose John William and I were quite elderly to have a first child  - he was forty when Ralphy was born and I was thirty-one. We had both been sorely disappointed in our marriages - our future as a family unit depended on Ralphy. Without him I would have had no role, and John William would have had nothing to hope for. Our friends understood that, I think, they made much of Baby and gave him presents. It is not altogether surprising that he grew up thoroughly spoilt.....'

For a moment she was back at Basford, hearing John William's croaky voice scolding her after one of Ralph's many misdemeanours.

'You've ruined that child, ruined him!'

But that was many years later.

'Would it have been any different if I'd been stricter?' She didn't know. 'I wanted him to love me,' she thought. 'I couldn't bear to see his face when I was cross, couldn't smack him. And he did love me, I'm sure.'

She remembered the letter she'd had from John William when she was staying at Titsey Court with Gustavus; when would it have been? She could see herself sitting in the window reading the letter, the trees outside were golden yellow, the gardener was raking up leaves....

'October,' she decided, 'October 1868. He'd have been six.' She remembered the letter clearly, she'd kept it with her treasures, re-read it when Ralphy was being difficult to remind herself of how things used to be. She could quote it from memory....

*I enclose a letter from Ralphy, you will see he sends you kisses in every way he can think of, he is very anxious to send kind Aunty kisses. We all want kind Aunty to come home again very much'*

'She set great store by kisses, didn't she?' I said, 'remember those awful hand-drawn hearts in the scrapbooks, *'22 kisses RDTS', '28 kisses today', 'Kisses like Aunty's peas',* and so on.'

'She was smothering him,' agreed Marion. 'Was that sort of sentimentality usual then?'

'Well, if you read Mrs Warren - and Susanna did - there's an awful lot of stuff about naughty children weeping tears of contrition and kissing Mama tenderly as they promise to be good from now to eternity!'

*How I Managed My Children From Birth To Marriage,* written in 1865 by Mrs Warren, editor of various 19th century women's magazines and writer of numerous tracts on household management, was Susanna's childcare bible. She had an alarmist style that probably appealed to Susanna and laid great stress on safeguarding children from every possible source of infection. Regular bowel movements ensured health, but if they failed, castor oil and Gregory's Powders were her sovereign remedies, with boiled onion for worms. Children should have at least one 'diet day' a week when no meat was eaten, and bread and butter or bread and milk formed a large part of their daily fare. Fruit was considered too acid for childish stomachs and lemonade should not be drunk more than twice a week however hot the weather. Babies should be encouraged to walk, not crawl as she believed crawling weakened the ankles. Nursemaids should be carefully supervised and not given too much responsibility. Mrs Warren had an answer for everything!

Her fictional children were too good to be true, relishing the various improving tasks she gave them, positively enjoying plain, nourishing nursery food, happily giving their pocket money to the poor, studying assiduously at home with Mama (to avoid having their minds polluted by contact with 'rude ungovernable' schoolfellows) and always learning from Mama's wise and lovingly administered punishments.

'Reality must have come as a shock to Susanna,' observed Marion. 'Ralphy wasn't like that at all. He didn't do anything he didn't want to, spent all his pocket money and then asked for more, skipped lessons whenever he could get away with it, and never learnt from Susanna's punishments.'

'That's because she didn't give him any,' I interrupted. 'Read the letters. She nagged and scolded and threatened and bribed; but at the end of the day he got his bribe, regardless of whether he had earned it or not. I guess it was much the same when he was little. At the end of the day he only had to lisp 'Dear Aunty Susan I do love you' and he got away with murder.'

'But he was such a lovely baby,' sighed Susanna, remembering Ralphy's first birthday in May 1863. 'We were all so relieved that he was healthy. So many children died in their first year - not just the cottagers' children. We gave him birthday presents. Not like when we were children - by the 1860s children were more indulged. I gave him a box of wooden bricks. John William came home from Stafford where he was on manoeuvres with the Yeomanry and he brought a toy water cart,' she smiled to herself. 'Dear John William was so proud of his little son. Papa would never have left what he was doing to be there for one of our birthdays. Then Alice and Ada Birch came bringing a box of letters and a ball that they'd all outgrown....'

She thought back to Ralphy's other birthdays. Strangely she couldn't remember anything about his second birthday, but she remembered his third clearly. They'd given him a toy wheelbarrow to play with in the garden but it was a wet day and she couldn't let him take it outside. He'd made such a fuss - they were thankful when Catherine put him to bed. Toys should teach the child something, she believed. When he was four she'd given Ralphy a rake and fork so that he could pretend to work in the garden like Jackson. That was the first year he'd had buns and plum pudding on his birthday, which had become a family tradition - better than those sad, bony, little corpses of hedgerow birds that Papa and the boys had liked at home.

She'd never really enjoyed eating blackbirds and thrushes herself.

What other presents had Ralphy had? Later birthdays blurred into each other. Of course his most important present ever had been Jennetta, early in 1866. Susanna remembered the scene. They'd gone to a Christmas tree party at Hawkesyard with three year old Ralphy. There were lots of grown ups and children there. Mrs Gardner had called him outside - she and John William knew what was coming, of course, it had all been arranged in advance - and got him to pat her stout little Shetland pony. Then she lifted the little boy up on to the pony's back. It was getting dark and there was a bitter wind. Susanna wanted to get Ralphy back indoors into the warm.

'She's called Jennetta, dear,' Mrs Gardner had told him. 'Can you say Jennetta?'

'Jin Ett A,' whispered Ralphy obediently.

'Well done,' said Mrs Gardner. 'Now, would you like to take her home with you? She needs a little boy to ride her.' Ralphy had been a bit uncertain at first but she and John William had encouraged him.

Ralphy was a gentleman's son and the sooner he learnt to ride the better. Day after day one of the household led him round the lanes on his pony. Once, when he was six, his nursemaid let go the leading rein and Jennetta *'galloped away with Ralphy'* - Susanna had been so alarmed and she remembered her hand shaking as she made the entry in her diary. She had scolded Betsy severely, but with hindsight she realised that, given the length of Jennetta's legs and her age - she was eighteen by then, and overweight - Ralphy would not have come to much harm. But not until he was nine and had almost outgrown the little Shetland did she allow him to ride alone. Eventually the pony was given away and she was never replaced. It would seem Ralphy did not much care for riding.

Susanna was conscientious and practical and determined that Ralphy should have the best care she could provide. 'Look,' I said to Marion, 'here she is, in July 1862, in the middle of the chaos of moving to Armitage and setting up home, making sure that Ralphy has the first of the three vaccinations that would protect him against smallpox - even though it made him *'very poorly and sick'*.'

'Do you remember that list of instructions we found. Ralphy's daily routine?'

We looked at it again. 'It's entitled *'Ann's rule'*,' I said. 'Ann was with them in the summer of 1866. He was four. But I imagine the rules were the same for all the nursemaids. They must have thought Susanna intolerably fussy - and she didn't pay at all well.'

*Prayers $^1$/2 past 8. Servants' breakfast soon after 9. Take Master Ralphy out at 10 come in at 11, then give Master Ralphy his lunch and put him to bed, now clean off his boots etc., and help the other servants if required or do sewing. Have your gown changed and Master Ralphy dressed before 1 o'clock then bring us dinner. Directly after both dinners take Master Ralphy out, bring him in not later than $^1$/4 to 5, then give him his tea and sit down to sewing. Master Ralphy is to be ready to come down when the bell rings for the tea things to go out, he is to go up to bed at 7 o'clock after which empty everything then sit down for sewing for an hour, after which do your own work. Evening prayers $^1$/4 to 10, go to bed at 10.*

*Always wash everything you use for Master Ralphy's meals directly you can leave him. On the wash day help Mrs Peate only when Master Ralphy is in bed (in the morning and evening) On the ironing day from an hour before dinner and in the afternoon if Mrs Ingleby is able to attend to Master Ralphy, and after tea. Saturday evening do your own sewing. One afternoon each month to go to see friends, without some good reason requires some extra duty.'*

Susanna's nursemaids certainly were underpaid. Caroline Botham received just £6 (£290) a year. Mrs Beeton writing in 1859 recommended £8 (£390) to £12 (£550) a year for a nursemaid or £5 (£245) to £10 (£490) if they were also given an allowance for tea, sugar and beer. They weren't.

In August 1863 Caroline gave notice to leave - perhaps she had found an employer who would pay something rather nearer the going rate. She was replaced by Catherine Goodall, again at £6 a year. Catherine stayed for two and a half years, until June 1866 when Mary Ann Webb (Ann) took over. Ann only stayed a few months despite rather better pay - £8 a year - and a family holiday in Llandudno.

But in the end Susanna found a girl who suited. Betsy Leigh arrived in October 1866 when Ralphy was nearly four and a half. In January 1867 Susanna recorded paying her her first full quarter's wages - £1-10s. She recognised that in Betsy she had found a 'treasure' and agreed to pay her a pound on top of her wages for each full year she stayed - and Betsy did stay until Ralphy was old enough to go to school.

'Do you remember the valentines?' I asked.  Betsy instituted the custom of giving family valentines.

'Poor Ralphy,' laughed Marion, 'even when he was away at school Susanna and Betsy still religiously despatched their valentines to him every February, even though he told her that none of the other boys received them.

Susanna continued to uphold the custom until he was well into his teens, though eventually she did give him money instead.  In 1873, in his first term at a new school mind, eleven year-old Ralphy had to remember to send valentines to his father, aunt **and** the housemaid.  And then he got into trouble for having put the stamp on the back of one of the envelopes for a joke.  The card was delayed and Susanna had to pay twopence extra.  She was not amused; listen:

*Thank you for your letter, Papa and Catherine join me in many thanks for the very pretty Valentines you sent us.  Catherine was surprised that you remembered her surname.  Yours was the only valentine she got on the right day, but she had 4 the next day.  I thought you were considering that as you wrote to me that would serve instead of a Valentine as mine did not come until the 15th, owing to the stamp being put on the back of the letter; I suppose you or some other boy had put it there for "fun", but it was no good there.*

Betsy also made much of his birthdays, one of her early birthday cards to him is in one of the scrapbooks at Keele, she made it herself, its beautifully neat.  And do you remember this bit?

*1867 May 3rd  Fine.  Ralphy's birthday.  Betsy dressed his hat with flowers & took him to the school, he got a good many presents.'*

Today it seems deeply unjust that five year-old Ralphy, the only child of a gentry household, should have received gifts from the impoverished children of the local cottagers, but in the 1860s it would have been seen as a way of paying respect and evening up the score.  The Armitage gentry, Susanna and John William among them, were generous and charitable to the poor of the village in times of need.  That little Ralphy was fêted by the village children showed their families' gratitude.  And no doubt Ralphy's 'gifts' were mostly produce from the local gardens and hedgerows.

The relationship with Betsy lasted a lifetime.  She married and had two sons of her own to whom Susanna gave many of Ralphy's cast-off toys.

She continued to visit the family regularly and as an adult Ralphy often used to go and stay with Betsy, by then Betsy Cliff, and her husband in Newcastle-under-Lyme. Ralphy kept the letter she wrote thanking him for her wedding presents.

*Armitage. May 6th 1879*
*My dear master Ralphy,*

*I am very much obliged to you for the very handsome present please to thank Dear Aunty and Papa for the present from them both. I was so surprised when I opened your letter to find such a gift enclosed therein, really I do think I am very fortunate in receiving so many tokens of respect. I hope it will be a nice fine day for my wedding. I am sorry that Dear Aunty and Papa are not strong, you must take every care of them both does Papa's throat fail him now as it used to do? ...... I suppose you are nearly as tall as Papa. I saw the Yeomanry in Lichfield today and it made me think of your Papa and wonder if you would ever be a soldier, but I suppose you would never be strong enough for that. Are you being tutored anywhere now under a clergyman or at a school? I suppose you will soon be going to college..... Many people in the village ask me how you all are and if I ever hear from you for you must know my Dear that Dear Good Aunty was beloved by all who knew her or who came in her way. Truly I can say those were the happiest days of my life when she was my mistress and you my daily care. Thank you all very much for your good kind wishes, please give my duty to your Papa and Dear Aunty and love and every blessing for you my Dear Master Ralphy,*

*Your affectionate and faithful nurse*

'She sounds as if she means it,' I commented, 'of course you'd expect her to be deferential, but the *'beloved by all who knew her'* and *'happiest days of my life'* bits are more than polite, if you see what I mean.'

'Well, she wouldn't have accepted their invitations to visit Basford if she hadn't been fond of Ralphy, would she?' said Marion, 'she didn't have to, she could have found some excuse.'

Betsy cared for him but it was Susanna who educated Ralphy, teaching him to read and write and do simple sums. First he wrote his name - page after page of 'Ralph De Tunstall Sneyd' - the 'De' always had a capital - in careful, childish copperplate. She encouraged his interest in history and natural history and even as a little boy he collected stones and birds' eggs, fungi and flowers. Friends and family contributed coins and curiosities and Susanna encouraged him to make lists of his 'treasures' as handwriting exercises. He excelled at drawing - his scrapbooks are full of pictures he and Susanna drew.

'He was much better than she was,' observed Marion, the ex-art teacher. 'Ralphy's drawings show real flair, even if the subject matter is a bit odd. He had that rare ability of knowing instinctively how to compose a picture, where to place objects.'

When we looked carefully at Ralphy's artistic efforts we realised that 'a bit odd' was an understatement.

'No wonder Susanna didn't like him drawing from imagination,' said Marion. 'You remember all those letters urging him to copy things out of books? I think a child psychologist would find these interesting.'

There were drawings of strange mythological creatures, angels with heavy black wings looking like bluebottles, houses surrounded by bugs and snakes.

'The poor child felt he was besieged on every side,' said Marion, 'look there's not a square inch of space in this one that doesn't have something threatening in it!'

Battlefield scenes in which the sky was full of arrows, and worse, were a popular theme, as were views of machinery in heavy black.

'There's the pottery again,' I said, 'if Susanna was constantly telling him what a bad place it was maybe that explains the colour - though I suppose it actually was very sooty.'

'And he's signed all the drawings,' said Marion, 'but that's his grown-up handwriting.'

'Why would he have bothered to do that? One eye on posterity again?'

'Well perhaps, but his drawings are so much better than Susanna's, that maybe he was making sure no-one thought he drew so badly?'

Susanna had done her best to arouse Ralphy's interest. One of his favourite spots was the Trinity Aisle in Mavesyn Ridware church. We'd thought that rather strange at first but then Bob and Bridget took us there and we saw that the aisle contains the tombs of crusaders, rows of upright stones carved with outlines of knights in full armour, roughly half (or child) size; to an imaginative little boy they must have seemed magical. And

Ralphy was an imaginative little boy.

'Too imaginative by half,' grumbled Susanna.

Ralphy was the most important person in her life but Susanna made many friends in Armitage. The village had its share of gentry families, notably the Spodes, the Birches and the Wilsons. Josiah Spode at Hawkesyard was the great-grandson of the potter and though he was not himself much interested in the family firm it continued to provide him with a generous income. Josiah Spode IV had moved up the social scale and lived the life of a gentleman. The Spodes were childless and when Helen Spode died in 1868, Miss Gulson, a niece, moved in with her uncle as his companion. He used his considerable wealth to finance concerts and entertainments and to indulge his hobbies. He was a keen amateur photographer - the pictures he took of Susanna and John William still survive. He was also an able musician and between 1871 and 1885 was organist at Armitage church, but in 1885 he and Miss Gulson converted to Roman Catholicism and Mr Spode's money went to finance the building of a Dominican priory on his estate.

The Birches at Armitage Lodge had a large family of daughters and one son, Lightwood, who at this stage was still a schoolboy. Mr Birch was a businessman with interests in London and the family seem to have lived in some style. Mrs Birch became Susanna's friend and confidante and in her turn Susanna became particularly friendly with young Louie Birch, collecting ferns with her and going with her to practice the organ in Armitage church. Mrs Birch had a conservatory full of rare ferns; Susanna was given cuttings and sent off sample leaves for her friends and relatives to admire. Ferns and fern gardens were a Victorian obsession. The younger girls, Alice, Ada and Constance, and Lightwood, when he was at home, often visited Armitage Cottage and Susanna taught them archery. They played with little Ralphy, entertained him to tea, when he was old enough, and gave him presents.

The third family with whom John William and Susanna socialised was the Wilson family at the Rectory. Mr Wilson was a gentleman clergyman, like their father, and had a large family including an unmarried daughter who befriended Susanna, and four little boys aged between five and ten.

Other Armitage families like the Wetheralls (the Reverend Wetherall

was vicar of nearby Brereton), the Landors of Lea Hall and the Coyneys of
Selwood House, were part of their circle, as were Miss Pennington, Miss
Oldham, and the Bonneys, Levetts, Gardners and Jellicorses in Rugeley,
and numerous other families in the surrounding area. Susanna's 1863 diary
lists at least thirty local families with whom they were on visiting terms.

'Do you remember Selwood House?' Marion asked.

I giggled.

On our second trip to Armitage we had found a café - Marion was
desperate for her afternoon cup of tea - in Selwood House, the Coyneys' old
home, now a guest house. There was nothing wrong with the tea, but the
rest of the menu had caused us a good deal of mirth, particularly the section
headed 'Chip Meals': sausage and chips, egg and chips, fish and chips,
beans and chips, sausage, egg, fish and beans with chips - we earmarked the
cafe for our 'Alternative Britain' tours. We shared a Kit-kat, unwilling to
risk anything else from the menu. 'It even provides an introduction to the
British sense of humour!' Marion pointed to the poster on the wall which
proclaimed "If you can't smell burning it must be salad".

John William's acrimonious relationship with his father apparently
carried no social stigma in Armitage - perhaps he and Susanna were sparing
with the truth or more likely, away from the Reverend John Sneyd and his
spiteful young wife, they were accepted on their own merits. Certainly they
continued to socialise with the County families, and old family friends in North
Staffordshire like the Wedgwoods and the Crusos still invited them to stay.

Their social round sounds exhausting. In 1863, for example, a fairly
typical year, the couple went to three 'grand' New Year's parties, dined out
fourteen times, went to three concerts, one picnic, two archery meetings, six
croquet parties, two formal lectures and two performances of amateur
theatricals, all in and around Armitage. John William went to the Stafford
Ball and he and Susanna went to another ball when they were staying with
friends. Susanna made two visits to Cheddleton, one in the spring and one
in the autumn.

They spent five days in Wales staying with the Spodes and various
other house guests in October and stayed overnight with the Hinckleys of
Stowe Hall, the Cottons in Derbyshire, the Wedgwoods at Barlaston,
Colonel and Mrs Dyott at Freeford, Lord Hatherton, friends at Brocton Hall
and at Bentley, and they spent Christmas, as they would do for the next five

years, with the Maynes of Tixall Lodge. They went to yet more dinners and social gatherings when they were away from home.

At home in Armitage Susanna paid and received calls or walked with the young Miss Birches or young Miss Wilson two or three times a week. Members of the family came to stay; 1863 brought visits from Emily, Freddy and Gustavus, their cousins William Kynnersley, Carry and Mary Anne Sneyd, Frank Hand and Clement Sneyd, their friend Ernest Worthington and John William's brother-in-law, Rowland Cotton.

They went several times to Stafford and Lichfield, and made excursions to view Ingestre and Shugborough as well as making regular trips to visit and shop in Rugeley.

'We're very different, aren't we?' Marion said on the phone after reading this bit. 'I wouldn't have written it like that at all. Couldn't you have described some of the events - the rustle of the ladies' silk skirts, the thwack of mallet on croquet ball on a hot summer's afternoon in the Rectory Garden, the sour, prickly taste of the ginger beer they served.....?'

'I could if I'd been there,' I answered, rather sharply. 'As you well know, Susanna doesn't give us that sort of detail and this is supposed to be true, remember? I can't just make it up. I keep telling you, it would be different if I was a novelist!'

Susanna sighed. Of course she hadn't gone into detail. Her diaries only allowed her a few lines a day and the bare entries she had made were quite enough to remind her of what had happened. 1863 had been such a happy year. Dreamily she remembered waltzing with John William at one of Mr Spode's parties, wearing the new white tulle dress she had had from Mrs Dinsdale in Rugeley; the skirt was full, tightly gathered at the back, closely pleated at the front, worn over a wide crinoline. The room was warm and lit by dozens of twinkling candles, the band played sweetly, and she was happy, floating......

'Poor Charles would have considered it foolish and dangerous,' she realised. She thought about the charade she had acted with the Birch girls that New Year of 1863; 'Mat-Rye-Money' (matrimony). They had ordered their costumes from London; she couldn't remember which firm they had used - Marie Schild? Debenham and Freebody? She had painted the sign, *"Corn And Rye Sold Here"* and the backdrop for the shop which was the basis of the middle scene. Alice and Ada were so keen on acting - she'd always felt conspicuous herself. After that first year she'd been happy to let the girls get on with it while she sat in the audience. But she'd enjoyed being part of it all, able to lend extra spoons and teapots to Mrs Birch to serve the refreshments.

Marion's thoughts about hot summer afternoons in the Wilsons' garden stirred other memories. 'Croquet was a newfangled game. I always preferred archery,' she thought, remembering the target she and John William set up in the cottage garden. 'But I always had to hunt for the arrows that got lost in the shrubbery. John William didn't have the patience.' They'd had a wonderful time that summer, and she had been so grateful after the humiliation of the previous two years. But each season had its high points....

Christmases with the Maynes at Tixall had been enjoyable, too. Tixall Lodge was enormous, the gatehouse to a long demolished Elizabethan mansion built for one of the Ansons. They had built Shugborough to replace it in the 18th century but for some reason the Lodge had remained standing. The Maynes only rented it, but they loved the old place and were so upset when they were asked to leave. That was in the early 1870s, Susanna remembered. The rooms with their dark oak panelling and huge log fires would be hung with garlands of evergreens - there was always lots of ivy in them - Tixall Lodge was smothered in ivy. And Mrs Mayne thought the world of Ralphy. They'd gone to church in Milford, it was always interesting to hear a new preacher, then back to the Lodge for roast beef and plum pudding, sour little tangerines, mince pies and rich, brandy laced Christmas cake.

Gentry families in Susanna's day had a great deal of leisure to indulge themselves. John William spent time with the Yeomanry, attended Petty Sessions, gave advice and witnessed signatures in his capacity as a magistrate, but, again to take 1863 as a sample year, these activities took up just twenty three days of his time by Susanna's account. No doubt Josiah Spode occasionally visited his factory; Mr Birch was a JP like John William and attended Petty Sessions, had business interests in London and owned various properties; Mr Wilson preached and attended to his parish. But none of them had anything approximating to a full time 'job'. Susanna looked after Ralphy, Mrs Birch and Mrs Wilson both had big families of children and Mrs Spode had a large staff to oversee, but all four had servants and time on their hands. Socialising was the accepted way of filling this time and it was not all about pleasure.

Social networking was an important activity and was a key means of transacting business and making contacts. In theory at least, people of your own social class were reliable advisers, trustworthy business colleagues and appropriate partners. They would sell you property at a fair price, lend you money or borrow yours at a fair rate of interest (banks were still suspect and many people still favoured the old methods of managing money); they would recommend a good solicitor or doctor, they would circulate information about vacant church livings and available commissions in the armed services, keep you abreast of investment opportunities and provide introductions if you were travelling in a part of the country where you knew no-one.

It was a system that worked well. The concepts that a gentleman's word was his bond and that a gentleman's agreement was binding were still accepted and those who bucked the system soon found they were social outcasts. Mothers of marriageable daughters networked as a way of finding suitable sons-in-law; mothers of younger children collaborated in finding reliable nursemaids and acceptable schools.

Susanna nodded agreement. 'Dear Mrs Challinor was so kind in helping me find the Miss Cranes' school in Leamington and dear Uncle John told us about Mr Cornish - how would we have managed to find schools for Ralphy without their advice?'

But, in country districts there was a serious flaw - the social network was small and relatively static. This was partly because in the days before the car it was not possible to travel far in a day, even if you had your own transport or lived near a railway. The Spodes, Birches and Wilsons all had carriages - Hawkesyard was some way out of Armitage village and the Sneyds were often grateful for lifts to and from functions there. Sometimes they hired a fly, a sort of horse drawn taxi, and returned the favour of giving lifts to their friends.

But in March 1868 John William went to a sale at Mr Chadwick's and bought a wagonette, £20 (£922). At the end of May he bought a horse from a local gentleman farmer, Mr Pallett for £27-10s (£1,268) and on May 30th Susanna recorded delightedly that they had been for their first drive.

'I really thought we were moving up in the world. Indeed, our relationship with the other Armitage families was scarcely an equal one.

We had neither the money nor the staff to give parties and although our new friends called, we could only entertain informally; it was only the neighbourhood children who stayed for meals and learnt archery in the garden. Unfortunately Mr Pallett's horse did not like carriage work; sometimes it wouldn't go!

For a time we lent it to a farmer for ploughing as part of a team to get it used to pulling,' Susanna went on, 'but it was too stupid.'

Because people saw each other so often topics of conversation must have been painfully limited. Visitors were much fêted - as Susanna had been in Edinburgh. They brought news from different parts of the country and might provide useful introductions. The women swopped recipes, exchanged needlework patterns, gave each other seeds and cuttings from their gardens, read novels, sketched and gossiped. Parties which had some purpose, croquet, archery, a picnic, went some way to alleviating the boredom but even they became repetitive.

But the good thing about Armitage was that both Josiah Spode and the Birches laid on extremely lavish entertainments. Susanna recorded that seventy or eighty people went to a concert there in January 1863, for example. Even the Bishop of Lichfield was invited.

The Sneyds and their friends were intelligent people. No doubt they read the newspapers and were awed at news of the successful laying of the Atlantic cable, laughed at pictures of the newly invented bicycle, marvelled at the discovery of diamonds in South Africa and admired engravings of the Albert Memorial. They must have been shocked by President Lincoln's assassination and concerned when the Franco-Prussian War broke out.

They were all involved with the village school in Armitage and probably approved of Forster's education act. The incorporation of Bedford College for women must have seemed a revolutionary step, a great opportunity for clever girls - though of course it didn't do for a girl to be too clever! They would have remarked when the army abolished flogging or when debt ceased to be an imprisonable offence or when Trade Unions were legalised, but these things made little impact on their everyday lives.

The Reform Act of 1867 extended the franchise to 938,000 voters, some of whom must have been people they knew, and they probably questioned whether it was a good idea to allow so many to vote. Susanna and her women friends must have welcomed the first Married Women's

Property Act which gave married women some rights over their own money - although John William and his cronies probably disapproved. By contrast, the introduction of Bank Holidays was probably seen as an inconvenience - the shops would be shut and the servants would expect a day off. But none of it made any deep impression on the little world of Armitage.

One of the few outside events that merited a mention in Susanna's diary was the Prince of Wales's marriage, and that only because the village celebrated it.

*1863, March 10th  We did not go out. Mrs Birch called here. The Prince of Wales was married to the Princess Alexandra Caroline Maria Charlotte Louisa Julia at Windsor, there were very great rejoicings everywhere. Mr Spode gave more than 120 men roast beef and plum pudding in a tent in his park and afterwards gave tea to about 70 women. Mrs Wilson and Mrs Birch gave tea to about 160 children in the School room, rosettes were given to all. A beautiful day.*

Such celebrations were funded by the gentry and it was usual to segregate the sexes and give the menfolk a rather better meal. The thinking was that because men worked harder they needed more meat.

At local level, Victorian society was compassionate and humanitarian in ways that would have been incomprehensible to Susanna's mother and grandmother who had grown up in a harsher, more self-reliant age. Penelope Sneyd never involved herself with her husband's poor parishioners in the way that her daughters did. But by the mid 19th century, clergymen's wives and daughters, and any other local ladies they might choose to involve, saw it as part of their role to attend the village school, at their own convenience of course, to help teach the girls needlework.

Within a few months of Susanna's arrival Mrs Wilson invited her to help out in this way at Armitage school. It was an invitation she would have expected. Susanna chose to go to Armitage school on a weekly basis. Each December she  awarded prizes to the girls for the needlework they had done for her, keeping a little notebook to record their attendance and work. To gain a prize girls had to earn at least two marks per lesson and Susanna's system of penalties ended with the dire warning, '*Work done so badly that it has to be unpicked loses 3 marks*'. But, as with Ralphy, Susanna seldom deducted any marks and nearly all her charges got a prize. She even gave one of the least able of them a job. Sebina Condé was housemaid at

Armitage Cottage for a few months in 1870.

'Do you remember that article I found in *The Penny Magazine*? asked Marion. The article, illustrated with engravings, described a village school established and endowed by the Reverend William Gilpin in the New Forest. It catered for twenty girls and twenty boys 'as far as possible from the day labouring part of the parish' who were to be 'clothed and educated; the boys taught reading, writing and the first four rules of arithmetic and the girls to read, knit or spin, sew, or mend their own clothes.'

That was in 1835. Nice to see the distinction between the genders spelled out like that. I guess it was much the same when Susanna and Emily Jane were helping out at Wetley Rocks in the 1850s. Girls were getting rather more formal education by the time she was at Armitage - and certainly after 1870 - but sewing was always pretty important.'

Village schoolteachers could expect a good deal of other help and interference from the local gentry. They provided regular 'feasts' - parties with food and games - for the schoolchildren, and turned up in force to watch their protègés enjoy the largesse bestowed on them. For their part the schoolchildren were expected to wear clean clothes, be grateful and put on a show of polite deference to their patrons. Naturally Susanna and John William were soon invited along to view these exercises in local charity, which in Armitage usually took place in September. One wonders whether such events were entirely enjoyable for either the children or the teachers.

'I would never have thought of it like that,' murmured Susanna, reading another of her diary entries from those first, heady months in Armitage.

*1862, September 30th The grand school feast at Hawkesyard. The Wilsons, Birches & Mrs Green & the young Miss Wetheralls were there. Of the schoolchildren there were 80 girls & 76 boys'.*

Susanna was soon involved in other forms of local charity. She attended missionary meetings, gave donations to good causes and visited poor cottagers. Mr Wilson instituted a system of 'districts' by which each member of the gentry who was so inclined had a particular set of poor people for whose welfare they were responsible and who they were expected to visit every week or two. Susanna was a conscientious visitor - the little calendars at the front of her Armitage diaries are peppered with entries for '*dis*', her regular perambulations of the district allotted to her.

At a local level charitable activity was extremely highly organised, especially in rural districts. Numerous schemes existed which entitled a particular parish or committee to 'tickets' for the local hospital, the spa at Buxton, the lunatic asylum or some more local operation like the provision of a loan box of first-size baby clothes for poor mothers. The parish paid a subscription - it was these subscriptions that supported the institution - and received a number of tickets based on the amount paid. This parish subscription was raised by donations from the gentry and they in their turn were allotted the tickets according to the sums they had donated. When a deserving case presented itself, Susanna, or Mrs Birch, or whoever had an appropriate ticket gave it to the person in need who was then entitled to a place in the hospital, the loan of the baby clothes box for a month, or whatever provision was deemed necessary. This ensured that charity remained a personal matter between patron and supplicant; subscribers knew exactly who benefited from the money they had donated and therefore they were often also prepared to offer additional help at the point of need - paying for a fly to take a sick person to hospital, for example. Susanna was a willing subscriber.

She also gave of her time to help other causes. Most districts held an annual bazaar at which items made by local ladies were on sale. These consisted of more-or-less-useless items like pen wipers and poker work - ladies' magazines were full of instructions for making such things - and more useable items like baby clothes and under-linen. The whole process was really rather pointless; ladies like Susanna spent substantial sums of money on materials and weeks of time to make items for the bazaar. They then gave more of their time as saleswomen - bazaars usually ran for several days - and spent yet more money on buying items donated by other people. The useless ones were recycled as presents while garments were donated to the poor. Usually the proceeds were given to some missionary fund or church building programme. It was a typically Victorian way of finding work for the supposedly idle hands of women and girls at the same time as raising funds. Needless to say, Susanna was a tireless maker of bazaar goods.

'Bazaar organisers were recognised as a particular social type,' I told Marion one day. 'I found this advertisement in one of the magazines I was using to look for dressmakers' advertisements......'

Marion was not entirely sure about my preoccupation with 19th century dressmakers. Getting a PhD was all very well but if it interfered with my work on the Sneyd project.....

'It was for Southall's sanitary towels.'

Marion pricked up her ears.

'Really? What sort of date? I often wondered how they managed. Does it come into costume studies? I don't suppose anyone has ever asked you this before!'

'Only a couple of million times. When I worked at Leicestershire Museums I used to give this talk on Victorian underwear - actually, my friend Jane still does. We worked it out the other day; she's the fourth generation of costume curator to be landed with it.

I had a suitcase full of Victorian underclothes and I used to describe how a ninteenth century lady got dressed in the morning - it was enormously popular with Women's Institutes and church groups. You'd find yourself in a chapel, they'd say prayers, then it was over to you to entertain the troops with a collection of corsets and divided drawers.....'

'Divided drawers?'

'Can we come back to them? I'm losing the thread.'

'OK.'

'Well, at almost every lecture someone would ask how Victorian women managed their periods, and they **always** started off by saying 'I don't suppose anyone has ever asked you this before!''

'Sorry to be so unoriginal - but presumably it means you know the answer?'

'Well, there's nothing particularly odd about it. People used to make their own sanitary pads out of old sheets or whatever they had to hand. They fastened them in place with a belt and some sort of sling - actually there was a patent for one of those sometime in the 1840s. It was made out of kid, I think, but I guess they were usually home-made.'

'Mine of useless information, aren't you?'

'Do you **want** me to go on? And of course they washed the pads and reused them for as long as possible.'

'Oh, the joys of womanhood!'

'People were still doing that well into the 1940s of course. When I gave the underwear talk there was usually some old girl in the audience who remembered odd things hanging on her mother's washing line. But the interesting thing about the Southall's advert - which dates from the 1870s, by the way - was that they were offering free samples of their purpose-made cotton wool towels to ladies who organised bazaars - presumably that way they were targeting women who could actually afford disposable towels.'

'Did Susanna buy them?'

'Not if we believe her account books. I imagine she would have thought them an unnecessary expense.'

'Back to the divided drawers,' said Marion, 'and, respected colleague, I really think we ought to include this conversation in the book.'

'I don't think Susanna would approve. So now you want to know about under-garments? Well, the first thing the respectable Victorian lady put on in the morning was her chemise - that was a shapeless sort of garment like a loose, knee-length, short-sleeved nightie. You have to understand that the shape of most of the underclothes changed a bit as the century went on, but for most of Susanna's lifetime the complement of garments would have been the same. Her mother and grandmother would have worn rather less when they were young.'

'Really?'

'Yes. The obsession with underwear was down to the Victorians. Right, we've got the chemise. Then, over the top she puts on her drawers.'

'Divided?'

'Yes; that means,' I saw Marion preparing to frame a question and I hurried on, 'wide-legged knee-length cotton trousers but with the crotch seam left open.'

'Why?'

'Well, over the top of those, scrunching them up into uncomfortable folds and ridges, you wore your corset.'

'So?'

'Have you ever tried taking your corset off when you've got a dress and other under-garments on top? That's what you'd have had to do to get your drawers down.'

'So the split seam made it possible for you to..? But why didn't they put the corset on first - that would seem the obvious solution?'

'So that it stayed clean. Corsets were very difficult to wash and dry - people did, of course, but as infrequently as possible. Another myth is that people didn't wash much in the past. Actually they were at least as clean as we would be without hot and cold running water and plumbed-in washing machines. By wearing your chemise and drawers of washable cotton next to the skin they absorbed perspiration and other body dirt. OK? Then, over the top of the corset went whatever sub-structure the dress needed.'

'Pardon?'

'Crinoline, crinolette, bustle.'

'Crinolette?'

'It was a sort of half-crinoline - an intermediary stage between the crinoline and the bustle. Then on top of that you wore a petticoat bodice, or chemisette - I think Susanna just called them bodies - that was like a little fitted blouse, on your upper half, and at least one petticoat, or what we would call an underskirt to smooth out the line of the foundation. Then the dress went on top.'

'Heavens. Did Susanna have all that?'

'Yes, she probably made most of them - she was forever buying calico and white cotton - but she certainly bought petticoats, crinolines and stays. She'd have had lots; a respectable lady's trousseau would have included at least a dozen of everything washable.'

'For goodness' sake,' murmured Susanna, blushing, 'talk about something else! I did other things besides sewing, you know.'

It was true. She was painstaking and would go to endless trouble for friends. In 1863 she made a set of 'Family Game' cards - what we now call Happy Families - for Alice Birch's fifteenth birthday present. Drawing and painting Mr, Mrs, Master and Miss and their accoutrements for each of the various sets must have taken ages. The cards were a success and she promptly set to to make another set for the young Wilson boys. Yet hand-painted cards cannot have been very durable; the colours would have smudged and the backing papers peeled after a very few games.

Some years later she found another outlet for her meticulous art work. She drew and painted a number of copies of the Sneyd coat-of-arms. We do not know how large they were but each one took several weeks of her free time. One was for her younger brother Gustavus, one for Lizzie Sneyd, her cousin William's widow, one for her cousin Henry and one for John William.

John William also tried to occupy his time usefully by joining the Stafford branch of the Staffordshire Yeomanry. However, the Volunteer Yeomanry was less important than it had been when he had first joined up back home in Leek. There was no longer any threat of invasion and the Volunteers' role as a peace-keeping force at home was diminishing with the increasing numbers of paid police and the more settled economic climate. As a twenty year-old John William had ridden with his father as part of the force which went into Stoke-on-Trent to deal with a mob rioting about the price of bread in 1842.

Those 'Chartist' riots were, in part, responsible for the setting up of a local police force - a move which John Sneyd had opposed vociferously. He enjoyed his roles as Yeomanry officer and Justice of the Peace and did not want to cede any of his authority to paid officials, men of a different social class whom he did not respect and whose values he did not share. John William may well have agreed with his father on this point. Like his father and grandfather, he was a keen supporter of the Staffordshire Yeomanry, relishing the opportunity to dress up and drill with guns and swords. Susanna took Ralphy to see the Volunteers if their manoeuvres brought them anywhere near Armitage and occasionally she was her brother's guest and dined with the officers.

As a young man John William had his portrait painted in his Yeomanry uniform, and as a middle aged father he wore a somewhat larger version of the same uniform to be photographed with his sister and little Ralphy. But the men he and his brother officers commanded took a dimmer view of service with the Volunteers. They were, for the most part, farmers and tradesmen, with stock and crops to tend and livings to earn. Drill for them was a chore, and one in which they could see less and less point. The Yeomanry gradually declined in the face of their indifference, but in the 1860s it was still active enough to occupy John William's attention.

'Don't forget what happened in February 1868,' murmured Susanna. 'We heard that there was a threat to blow up Rugeley gasworks. We were so worried for our friends in the town. John William and the others arranged for a hundred-and-seventy special constables to be drafted into Rugeley.'

Not surprisingly, the attack never materialised.

Rural society was fairly peaceful but there would always be malcontents and petty criminals. Like his father, John William had been sworn in as a Justice of the Peace and attended local 'justice meetings' as Susanna always called Petty Sessions, and the Assizes at Stafford. There was no obligation to attend, and the number of magistrates who turned up to the sessions was very variable - sometimes only one or two attended and had to do all the work, sometimes there were too many for the amount of cases to be heard.

Only occasionally did Susanna record the cases John William heard. In 1863, for example, he attended a meeting about *'bad meat'* - Susanna does not tell us who was selling it - and heard a bigamy case. In 1865 he dealt with a local housebreaker, eighteen cases of poaching and on August 17th *'Jaggard's case for cruelty to a pony.....'* But for the most part she is remarkably uninformative about what John William did in his capacity as a JP. *'January 16th 1865 Mrs Fiennes and a Lady called and got John William to sign a paper'* is a typically meaningless entry.

'He didn't discuss it with me,' thought Susanna. 'It was men's business. But he liked me to keep a record of the meetings he attended - so he could claim his expenses, you know. He wasn't very good at keeping accounts. He didn't like writing.'

In the autumn, winter and spring of 1865-6 John William was unusually busy. The 'Cattle Plague' - a particularly virulent form of cattle disease believed to have come from Russia - was raging in the country. It was first identified in August 1865 and Alfred Proctor MRCVS described it for *The Coventry Standard:*

> The animal first appears to be affected by the common cold, the coat staring, a little running from the eyes and nose; secondly the eyes seem a little bloodshot and anxious in expression, general excitement seems to pervade the whole system, and the animal is frequently urinating and voiding its faeces in small quantities. This is followed by swelling of the lips, eyes, and under the throat. At this stage blood and mucus is generally seen oozing from the nostrils and the brain frequently becomes much affected. It is at this stage the animal succumbs.

Strict measures were introduced to limit the spread of the disease by preventing the movement of cattle but initially these were the result of local, not national, legislation. As a magistrate John William was one of the people who had to create the rules and see they were enforced. No doubt he did so conscientiously - he was an active, practical man who understood farming and livestock. But he and his fellow magistrates were hampered by government incompetence.

On Sunday March 7th 1866, a 'day of humilation' was held for the cattle plague. Victorian society still hoped for divine intervention in times of crisis - both Susanna's and her father's diaries record government-decreed days of prayer for national disasters like smallpox epidemics and in 1870 she copied out in full the new prayer that had been introduced in response to the outbreak of the Franco-Prussian war:

*O Almighty God, King of all Kings, whose power no creature is able to resist, to whom it belongeth justly to punish sinners, & to be merciful to them that truly repent, assuage we beseech Thee the horrors of this war, which Thou hast permitted to break forth in Europe, restrain the passions of the combattants, inspire the conquerors with mercy, and the vanquished with submission to Thy will.....*

But few people really expected their prayers to be answered and on Monday, March 8th John William went to Stafford for a meeting about measures to be introduced to halt the plague - but *'there was no meeting as the Government had not settled about the Cattle Plague'* - though in fact the Cattle Diseases Prevention Act had received the royal assent on February 24th. It was just that no-one had thought to send a copy of the Act to the mid-Staffordshire magistrates. There were more meetings, sales of livestock were stopped, and by September 1866 the epidemic had blown itself out. 124,294 cattle had died nationwide; just 2,339 of them were in Staffordshire.

By temperament John William Sneyd was more like his grandfather than his father. He had loved the family estate and remained bitter about his disinheritance for the rest of his life, but he was a traditionalist and it is unlikely that there would have been much that was innovative about John William's stewardship of the Ashcombe lands. His greatest pleasure in life was shooting. Each year he spent a few days with his friend, Sir John Crewe, at Warslow Hall, up on the moors above Leek. They bagged enormous quantities of game:

*'October 28th 1866 Fine & bright. John Wm returned home from Sir John Crewe's by the 7.7 train, they shot 400 head of game one day & 300 the next & several woodcocks,'* wrote Susanna, proud of her brother's contribution to the carnage. A man who was a good shot never lacked for invitations. Susanna's diary mentions his more unusual victims - owls, cats

and the occasional dog - and she recorded whenever his hosts sent grouse or venison or hares for the table.

In Armitage John William was doing the things he had done all his adult life but in a different environment. Susanna, on the other hand, was having to learn a great many new skills. She had never been in sole charge of a house before. She had to learn to keep house, look after a child and manage on a relatively tight budget. John William had his £100 (£4,495) a year from the mortgaged lands at Consall. She had £100 a year from her husband, and, when it was paid, £50 a year as part of her marriage settlement from her father. Unfortunately John Sneyd was very dilatory in making his payments. In March 1871 Susanna wrote to him asking whether he ever intended to pay her annuity and he replied, apologetically:

*I want you to be assured that it has not been caused by any want of parental affection towards you but purely from a want of money, occasioned by a heavy debt left me as a legacy by my father, by being much in debt myself on the death of my father, and by a very large amount of money spent in buildings. I have had a large family to maintain and educate and have acted injudiciously in purchasing estates which I now find it difficult to dispose of.*

'It was to his credit that he could admit as much,' said Marion.

'But it didn't help Susanna pay the bills, did it?' I answered. 'And read the next sentence. *'There are very few people who expend personally less on themselves than I do'*. That's John Sneyd for you, nothing was ever his fault, circumstances just couldn't help conspiring against him.'

In addition to the annuities from her husband and father Susanna had a lump sum of £3000 (£136,000) which had been her father's contribution to her marriage settlement and which was administered by trustees.

'Actually she **should** have been able to manage her own money,' I told Marion. 'Lawrence Stone's book talks about mid-19th century legal separations which gave a wife the right to deal with her own financial affairs.'

'In *The Road to Divorce*?'

'Yes - but obviously Mr Joseph Challinor didn't recommend it. Perhaps it was just too modern an approach for North Staffordshire.'

'If only I'd known,' thought Susanna, 'I was at their mercy, all those men advising me, telling me what was best.'

John William paid £30 a year for Armitage Cottage and Susanna paid him £50 a year, in two installments, for her board and lodging. They lived comfortably but they were certainly not rich. They had a cook and a nursemaid, usually paid £12 (£553) and £7 (£322) a year.

Susanna and her friends had endless servant problems. Her parents and grandparents had employed large numbers of staff who knew their places. Servants then were sacked if they infringed the rules, there were plenty of others ready and willing to replace them. But by the mid-19th century fewer and fewer girls wanted to go into service. There were plenty of other opportunities in factories and workshops where, although hours were long and pay was poor, what a girl did out of working hours was her own business.

The general servants Susanna employed were near the bottom of the servant's hierarchy and they had to be able to cook as well as keep house for their kind, but exceptionally pernickety, mistress. It was a tall order. In the eight years they were at Armitage Susanna employed seven general servants in quick succession and there were four other women from the village who filled in (for 6s a week) when one servant left and Susanna had yet to find a replacement. Some came to her by recommendation, the way her parents had expected to find staff, but usually she had to resort to the local employment agencies or *'servant's registry offices'* run by the Misses Wile and Ward in Burton-on-Trent and Mr Palmer in Hanley.

Susanna kept meticulous household accounts, itemising every penny she spent on lemon drops or gave to a beggar woman. John William seems to have been responsible for his own and his child's clothes for these do not feature in Susanna's lists - though occasionally she bought knitting wool to make baby clothes or small items for Ralphy out of her own pocket. She kept separate books for her own personal expenditure on clothes, books, presents and charitable donations, others for what she spent on travel and others for expenditure on coal for the household and plants for the garden. They make fascinating reading.

In the Armitage account books, coal, washing, mangling and payments for mending boots and shoes appear at least once a month; in winter up to three lots of coal a month (about six shillings worth at a time - £14) would be delivered to Armitage Cottage, presumably because there was nowhere to store larger amounts. Victorian tradesmen were obliging about supplying small quantities. Regular largish payments were made to Rugeley shopkeepers; Wentworth's man, Hawkins' man - the groceries and meats she had from them were not itemised. Susanna made regular separate purchases of lard, eggs, butter and cheese, herrings, oatmeal, pikelets, teacakes, bread, buns and gingerbread and occasionally bought oranges, lemons, chickens and rabbits. Once or twice she bought a goose for seven shillings (£17) and once she bought a whole ham for seventeen shillings (£41). Towards the end of their stay in Armitage she began to buy tinned sardines and 'Liebig's Essence'.

'Liebig invented both Bovril and Marmite,' I told Marion. 'It could have been either.'

She looked suitably impressed.

In the 1860s and 70s oatmeal was twopence-halfpenny a pound (50p). A penny - 1d - then was worth around 20p in today's money and twelve of them made a shilling - 1s. Cheese was about 9d a pound (£2) and enough soda to do three month's worth of washes cost 6d. The cost of washing varied between 12s (£28) and £1 a month (£48) according to quantity; the average price for a day's mangling was 5d (£1). Mops cost 3d apiece but didn't last very long, a blackleading brush was 1s and a new broom handle cost 3$^{1}$/2d. The sweep charged 1s a chimney and it was 2d to have a pair of scissors sharpened.

Susanna was a careful housewife and paid to have household items repaired. An itinerant tinker got 3d for soldering the handle back on to her dustpan in July 1866, for example. The account books tell us not only what she bought but show us the repetitive nature of her purchases and reinforce what we know about her meticulous nature. One suspects that the diet at Armitage Cottage was fairly boring.

'She's forever buying herrings,' commented Marion. 'Rugeley's a fair way from the sea - how fresh do you suppose they were?'

I didn't know. Presumably they came by train from the coast, but without refrigeration at the fishmonger's their shelf life must have been pretty limited. No doubt he used ice from an ice-house but I wasn't sure how effective it would have been.

'Do you remember the ice-house at Basford?' asked Marion.

Halfway down the track from Basford Hall to Averil's cottage there was a door in the bank. It opened into a sloping passage which led to a vast, brick-lined, egg-shaped chamber built deep into the hillside. Each winter it would have been filled with ice from the Churnet, stacked on planks to allow for drainage and wrapped in straw and sacking to insulate it. This ice would have been used in hot weather to keep food fresh or to make iced puddings. When the hall was full of people it had been a useful resource but by Susanna and John William's time it seems to have fallen into disuse. But maybe the Rugeley fishmonger had access to a similar store.

Susanna discovered herrings in oatmeal sometime in 1866 and from then on, each member of the household seems to have eaten at least one herring a week to judge by the numbers she bought. By the time they returned to Basford in 1874 the average was more like three herrings a week apiece.

Fruit and vegetables would only have been available in season and the cottage had its own large kitchen garden. In late summer the account books detail numerous purchases of bilberries and occasional purchases of mushrooms.

'I imagine she bought them from people selling them door to door,' I said. 'I expect she would have been unwilling to turn anyone away who came to her door with goods to sell - buying from them was a form of charity, helping those who were trying to help themselves.'

Though she employed a cook-housekeeper as well as a nursemaid for Ralphy, Susanna did take charge of some aspects of the housekeeping. *April 6th 1864 I went to Ridware and Mrs Brassington's for eggs and put 100 in lime.*

Susanna preserved eggs in lime water, a hundred or two at a time. Her recipe for lime water survives in a letter sent to her by her sister Emily Jane. It consisted of two ounces of fresh lime to every three pints of cold, boiled water. First a little water was added to the lime, then the slaked lime was added to the rest of the water and stirred into a solution. *'Then immediately cover the vessel with some folds of linen and a weight upon the top.'*

Preserving eggs in lime was a technique that had been in use for at least a hundred years and some recipes claim that eggs preserved in this way would keep for up to two years. Mrs Beeton was less optimistic and herself preferred simply to lay eggs down in bran, first waxing or oiling the shells - a thoroughly fiddly process that had to be done in two stages to ensure that the entire surface of the shell was coated. Preserved eggs, she felt, should only be kept for two or three months and were best used in cooking as the whites tended to get rather tough with keeping. In the days before factory farming it was often difficult to acquire a large quantity of eggs at a time and Susanna's diary is full of references to the numbers of farms she visited and the various prices she was charged. She was indignant if she ever had to pay as much as 1s a dozen.

Sometimes Susanna helped with making jam, sometimes she sowed seeds in the garden, but her main practical contribution to the household was repairing linen, mending soft furnishings and making or mending clothes. She set herself to learn about other aspects of housekeeping as conscientiously as she set out to learn about childcare, by buying books and manuals - *The Book That Every Family Needs*, *Beeton's All About Everything*, *Everyday Work in the Household* by Cathleen Moss and the relentlessly optimistic *How We Managed Without Servants by A Lady Who Can Help* and Mrs Warren's *How They Managed Their House on £200 a Year*. She had classics like Mrs Randall's *Domestic Cookery*, Mrs Beeton's *Household Management* and *Modern Cookery* by Eliza Acton, but she also acquired titles like *Cookery and Other Practical Matters for Working Men's Wives*, *How to Hash Curry and Stew* and Mrs Bentley's *What to do with Cold Mutton*.

'I got that out at the British Library,' I told Marion. 'Couldn't resist the title. It was disappointing though, just an ordinary cookery book with recipes for everything from lemonade to leeks. Only sixteen out of two-hundred-and-eleven pages were devoted to mutton and none of the recipes were particularly economical. Clever titles are nothing new!'

'Like *Thinking About Fishcakes*?'

I laughed. Marion was writing a cookery book based on Susanna's recipes and this was working title number two. She had already discarded *Frumenty, Fried Leeks and Figgy Pudding*. Never content to do things the easy way, Marion had conscripted a wide range of people - descendants of the Sneyd family, and people who lived in places where Susanna had lived, to make up the recipes, photograph them, comment on them and interview elderly people about similar things they remembered eating when they were young. It had the makings of a fascinating book. The people of Abbots Bromley had been particularly helpful. The schoolchildren had made

Abbots Bromley soup and oatcakes as served to the poor of the village from the soup kitchen Susanna had helped to run in the bitter winter of 1873-4. Not to be outdone, the local ladies' club had organised 'The Great Abbots Bromley Pudding Evening' to serve and taste a series of Susanna's pudding recipes.

I'd missed the school soup day, but had been there for the puddings. One of the tasters, Mr Grundy, was quite probably the descendant of the old Mrs Grundy who Susanna used to visit. His little grandson, Joseph, had helped make the soup at the school. Unwittingly, Mr Grundy provided Marion with her new title. As the Pudding Evening progressed conversation turned to memories of different foodstuffs and we were asked all sorts of questions. 'I've been thinking about fishcakes,' announced Mr Grundy suddenly. The incongruity of the statement was irresistible.

Susanna collected recipes from friends and family for medicines and ointments, as well as for food, and she cut articles she considered useful out of newspapers and magazines. Several of these related to the convenience of using the new canned mutton and beef that was becoming available. Even the manufacturers recommended it for use in institutions and the armed forces rather than in gentlemen's kitchens but Susanna was ever willing to try a new way of economising. Besides, tinned meat was soft and both she and John William had problems with their teeth.

The recipes she collected were a mixed bag ranging from a perfectly delicious way of pot roasting lamb, through a deeply unappetising vegetarian recipe for Christmas pudding which substituted tapioca for suet, and recipes for cakes and biscuits many of which are leaden and not sweet enough for modern tastes, to a time-consuming method of candying the stalks of lettuces to make a substitute for angelica.

Medical recipes form almost half the collection. There are no fewer than twenty seven cures for chilblains. Susanna suffered from crippling chilblains on her hands and feet every winter; sometimes they were so bad she could not put shoes on, sometimes she could not dress herself and often she was unable to hold a needle. It was one of the many things about her that angered Charles Ingleby. The suggested remedies included turnip poultices, egg white, brine and chicken fat, but none of them worked for Susanna. She also suffered from neuralgia - it was a common complaint in the 19th century and there was no effective cure, but amateur pharmacists offered brown paper soaked in vinegar and sprinkled with ginger or an oatmeal poultice covered with linen which has been soaked in spirits of turpentine, to alleviate the pain. Rather more exciting remedies were a concoction of henbane, opium and chloroform (all readily available from the local chemist) or drops of gelsemene (a deadly poison distilled from aconite root) taken in wine. One day Susanna recorded that she had taken too much gelsemane and frightened herself badly.

There was a remedy for the quinsy throat John William developed while at Armitage and another for piles from which Susanna suffered all her life. Neither worked. John William's throat deteriorated to the point where he could no longer speak and Susanna had two operations. There were cures for coughs, earache, boils, styes and diarrhoea. They were all stored in a part-used 18th century commonplace book. We found a photocopy of it at Keele on one of our early visits - another example, we felt, of Susanna coming to our rescue.

It happened quite soon after another research trip when we had spent a good deal of time up at Keele and been heavily dependent on the student's union cafeteria - then a typical student botulism-with-chips-a-speciality type of place. A couple of weeks after that we found ourselves, for reasons too complicated to explain, late one Saturday night in Nottingham trying to find somewhere that would provide us with a quick snack before driving south. The pubs had stopped serving and the only fast food place we passed was, without a shadow of doubt, the worst fish and chip shop in the United Kingdom.

'We **must** bring the 'Alternative Britain' tour here!' I said.

Sitting in the car toying with the inedible fat-soaked chips and grey cardboard-flavoured fish we had misguidedly purchased, we invoked our unseen colleague. Another Staffordshire visit was looming and enough we felt was enough.

'Come on, Susanna. The research is fine - but do you think you could pay a bit of attention to our creature comforts? Please?'

Two weeks later we arrived in Staffordshire for a weekend of invitations to wonderful meals from people we barely knew. Averil provided us with an amazing home-made soup; Jodi Peck gave us afternoon tea with raspberry jam made from Belmont raspberries - descendants of the ones planted by Susanna's great grandfather; Christine Chester gave us a farmhouse high tea. It went on and on.

Do you really think she was listening?' we asked each other incredulously.

On the Monday, at Keele, we were given a document we had not asked for - the librarian had got the wrong folder off the shelf - we had wanted the next one along, we could tell by the reference numbers. The folder we had contained photocopied pages of what we recognised as an 18th century commonplace book. The original owner - another Susanna Sneyd - had filled it with poems, paragraphs of information that interested her, prayers, drawings, riddles and proverbs. Her name appeared on the front together with an 18th century date, followed by our Susanna's name and *'given to her by her Aunt Mary'*.

'It must originally have belonged to old William's sister Susanna,' I said, consulting the family tree. 'She was a year younger than him, married Alexander Day Broughton - that's the connection with the Broughton family - and she died in 1808 aged.....' I did a rapid calculation - 'forty. Then it must have been given to Aunt Mary who gave it to our Susanna, probably because she was the namesake of the first owner. Interesting, but its certainly not what we asked for.'

There was no-one there to change it for us; the librarian was away and the items we had asked for had been left out for us. We put it to one side and got on with the other documents we had asked to see.

Or rather, I did. Marion was feeling very strange that morning; for no apparent reason she felt utterly exhausted. I was quite worried about her, she was pale, clearly not herself and totally unable to concentrate. In fact, at one point she fell asleep in her chair to the amusement of the other researchers in the Special Collections.

'It was quite extraordinary,' she told me later. 'I can only remember feeling like that once before.'

She went on to tell me how she had taken a friend to see a healer who was supposed to be good at helping people with arthritis.

'He lived in a council house on a scruffy estate near Nottingham,' she told me, 'and he had a dusty old shed at the bottom of the garden. It was full of spades and flower pots and there was this strange looking electrical contraption in the corner. There was a strip of frayed coconut matting on the floor. He sat you down in a broken-down Windsor chair and his old collie used to come and lie underneath it - apparently the dog had arthritis too and used to benefit from other people's treatments...!'

'How on earth did you hear about him?' I asked. Visiting strange men in garden sheds didn't tally with the practical, sensible Marion I thought I knew.

'One of the girls who worked in my pottery recommended him. My neck was so stiff I couldn't work and he'd really helped me so I hoped he'd be able to do something for Joan. Anyway, after she'd seen him she was a lot better, but on the way back I could hardly drive I was so tired. That evening his wife rang up, asked how I was, said they were worried about me because they'd tapped into my energy to help Joan. I didn't like that, they should have asked me. I never went back - I was out of my depth.'

'And that was how you felt in the library? Weird!'

Certainly someone had used Marion's energy for something. She was still a limp rag when she woke but was just about able to go and do some photocopying we needed.

Meanwhile I finished what I was doing and thumbed again through the pages of the 18th century commonplace book. Halfway through the entries were upside down. Someone had obviously turned the book the other way up and started again from the back - paper was expensive in the 19th century and books and ledgers were often re-used - this time I looked more carefully. There was no mistaking the handwriting. Or the subject matter. Not only had Susanna attended to our creature comforts - she had given us her cookery book!

Chapter 9
# Do you remember Bradnop?

'We need another chapter about us, respected colleague,' Marion insisted. 'Remember this is our story as well as Susanna's and there's so much you haven't told them.'

I sighed. We worked very differently. Marion was the one who enjoyed writing fiction. I had published quite a lot, but it was all factual stuff, museum catalogues, reviews, papers about obscure artefacts - I wasn't finding it easy to write this sort of book. We had decided I should write *the Susanna book* as we called it, while Marion would do *Thinking About Fishcakes*. She was convinced that something very peculiar had occurred, channelled through her, when we found Susanna's recipes, so it was up to her to use them to best advantage.

She was right, of course; we had had so much fun on our research trips, encountered so many delightful people, had so many strange experiences - but they didn't all fit neatly into the chronology of Susanna's story.

Snippets of information turned up all over the place - like when we'd been in the Nicholson Institute and we'd found those photographs of John Sneyd and Mary.

'What did she see in him?' I wondered. 'She was a lovely young woman, he aging, his waistcoat straining over his expanding stomach and a black eye patch over his injured eye. And he wasn't even a nice person.'

'Don't forget the poem,' giggled Marion.

The Nicholson Institute has a poem written by Dr Darwin in 1791 to Susanna Sneyd, sadly not our Susanna, but her great-aunt, owner of the commonplace book that our Susanna re-cycled as a recipe book:

> Now with light bound she mounts the wreathed car,
> Rolls her blue eyes and wreaths her golden hair,
> Fond youths bow homage as the wheels proceed,
> Sigh as they gaze and call the goddess Sneyd.

'Worthy of the great McGonagall himself,' we'd said delightedly, 'who else could have thought of a goddess called **Sneyd**!'

But it was difficult to include many of the things that happened to us because, for the most part, our trips were a patchwork of experiences that happened in no particular order. Usually our visits were built around a fixed point - a lecture to give, an appointment with Bruce.....

'You see, you haven't even told them about Bruce,' Marion scolded gently.

Bruce was a local GP with a passion for books who was gradually easing himself out of the NHS and into publishing. He had gone into partnership with Ray, the lovely gentleman who ran a secondhand bookshop in Leek. Bruce, a spiky-haired entrepreneur, and Ray, a calm and staid fount of local knowledge, were an odd pairing but they seemed to get things done.

Their rambling bookshop was on a corner of a main road in the town and you were straight into the first room through the shop door, then off in to many other rooms, one of which was an office, cash desk, copier room and general store all in one. We were to have many meetings here with Bruce or his assistant Chris, while Ray hovered agreeably in the background, dealing with the odd book sale or call on his vast knowledge of local history and books.

Ray was also the accepted senior statesman of the Leek Local Historical Society.

'**They** were a difficult bunch, weren't they?' I said, remembering the reading we had given in the Nicholson Institute to a largely unresponsive audience. The acoustics in the big room were dreadful - it was high and echoing.

'I wonder how dear Ralphy got on singing his songs - unless he had a powerful voice, a soloist would be all but lost in there. I don't see RDTS as a baritone, do you? More a tenor - counter tenor even....'

'Talk about a grasshopper mind,' said Marion in mock exasperation, 'they don't know about Ralphy's concerts yet, and you're **supposed** to be writing about Bruce and Ray.'

I could barely remember how we first met. 'Through Jodi Peck,' prompted Marion - but he had been a tremendous find. He only published books that related to North Staffordshire and surrounding areas, in short runs but at surprisingly reasonable prices.

'There really can't be many areas that are so well served for local history publications,' said Marion, 'weren't we lucky?'

When we had first met Bruce we had no real idea what to do with the wealth of material we were uncovering. In the cramped little office of his Bath Street shop, perched on stools, tottering piles of dusty books at our feet and more perched precariously on shelves above our heads, constantly interrupted by customers and people wanting to use the photocopier, he listened, assessed, and suggested we try something easy to start with. He had a deceptively laid-back manner. 'John William's diary,' he said decisively, 'there's not too much of it, give it an introduction - make it into a picture book, local pictures sell.'

We had already told him that there were lots of family portraits and that we had taken reels of film. I remembered how elated we'd been as we left his shop, punching the air like football supporters as we walked down the street - not for nothing were we both the mothers of sport-mad sons. Susanna had watched our unseemly behaviour with distaste. We had gone on to a celebratory lunch at Greystones. Coffee and cake, lunch, or tea and cake at Greystones would usually complement our visits to Bruce from then on.

It had been a steep learning curve, that first book, not easy at all, disciplining ourselves to find the right number of illustrations, caption them appropriately, get all the permissions in place for use of other peoples' materials, write an interesting, coherent introduction, supervise the layout. We were neither of us at this stage particularly computer-literate and stood transfixed as Chris, Bruce's assistant, adapted our photographs for publication. Marion's husband, George, in shorts and a sun hat, was deftly removed from a photograph of Welsh mine wagons, groups of cattle were moved to more picturesque locations, faded prints enhanced.

'We've come a long way,' I thought, 'we could do all that ourselves now.'

And in 1996 the book had come out! We quickly dubbed it 'That incredibly good book by those two frightfully clever women' as we discussed it over the phone. We knew we were being childish but we didn't care.

The experience had stood us in good stead when Bruce accepted our second book - a much more ambitious publication, the edited diaries of John Sneyd, Susanna's father. This time the problem was not layout, but footnotes, index and glossaries. We were learning fast. Bruce allowed us to have our heads - and the resulting publication was a dense 264 pages long. But it was well received, our university department was impressed, and it was followed by a string of smaller publications for various organisations.

We were making use of our research, I thought, even if it wasn't reaching a very wide audience. Our books were in university libraries, other students could read John Sneyd's farming accounts, say, or his accounts of Petty Sessions, or of the family's foreign excursion.

'It would be nice to do something different with the Susanna book though,' said Marion. 'There's something that all women can relate to in her story. Think how people react to the reading.'

Susanna certainly seemed to attract people's sympathy. Back home in Hertfordshire I had taught various courses with Victorian themes and I usually managed to use some of the Sneyd material - Susanna's account book, her medical recipes, details of how she fed her family, her wedding preparations, her clothes - she was becoming quite well-known, and, yes, people did seem to warm to her. And there was that lady up at Ipstones - I found this story frankly creepy, though it had delighted Judy Scott-Moncrieff. The Ipstones church ladies had tried out Susanna's biscuit recipes - for Marion's cookery book of course - and decided on a Biscuit Tasting morning. Judy had gone to it. Out of the blue this lady, who had heard Susanna's story, went up to her.

'May I stroke you,' she said to Judy, 'you're the nearest I can ever get to Susanna!'

'And it's a proper story with a plot,' Marion continued, ignoring my digression, 'well, a theme, anyway; riches to rags, the decline of a gentry family. And a cast of extraordinary characters - the Reverend John, the ghastly Gustavus, Ralphy the would-be-Druid. You couldn't make it up.'

Food had played a big part in our trips I thought, even before Marion had got started on *Thinking About Fishcakes*; whether it was delicious home-made pies and salad at Greystones, Averil's soups, or one of our impromptu picnics.

I fondly remembered a picnic on the lawn at Basford. We had hoped to be able to take Averil out to repay her for her many kindnesses, but she was old, becoming frail and was increasingly reluctant to leave her cottage.

Instead, one glorious summer's evening we had taken salads, fruit and wine to Basford; Humphrey and Judy had contributed more wine, Averil had brought jellies she had made for the three year-old twins, and Edward brought himself. We had sat outside as the sun set across the valley, the scent of newly-cut grass in the air, drinking, laughing, telling stories. It was the first meal we had eaten at the hall, and, ferrying plates and glasses from the kitchen, through the library, on to the lawn, pottering round the greenhouse looking at her vine, we felt closer to Susanna than ever.

'To Susanna!' Judy had said, emotionally, raising her glass.

'To Susanna!' we had all echoed.

'This may be the first time anyone has raised a glass here to Susanna, don't you think?' said Marion.'

'Don't be so foolish,' thought Susanna, 'what do you think John William said when we celebrated our wedding anniversaries with cake and wine? These people have an impossibly romantic view of me!'

There had been other memorable picnics in all sorts of strange places. Marion had an optimistic belief that carbohydrates were good for the brain - though in my case they never seemed to get further than the waistline. Lunches of chocolate-spread sandwiches, banana sandwiches, peanut-butter-and-marmite sandwiches enlivened many a visit.

'You had to be there,' I thought, as I remembered one such meal in a layby at Bradnop during which we had tried to devise a menu for an imaginary picnic with some of our stuffier university colleagues. We had begun by congratulating ourselves, as we so often did, on finding the project in the first place. So many other people had glanced at the diaries and dismissed them as valueless - **we** were the ones who had seen the story they had to tell. It was a well-worn theme but it reinforced our partnership, enabled us to express our gratitude to each other for all the fun we were having without actually saying it in so many words. The meal for which the menu was planned would never take place. None of our colleagues would have been entertained by the prospect of eating chocolate-spread sandwiches in a layby. Our suggestions ranged from the obvious kippers-and-custard through brawn-and-baked-beans, peanut-butter-and-Campari - lunatic, fourth-form humour. From then on 'Do you remember Bradnop?' was a catch phrase calculated to send us both into paroxysms of laughter at the most unsuitable moments.

'I remember my aunt saying at her eightieth birthday party, "The trouble is that my body doesn't realise there's a sixteen year-old inside trying to get out"' said Marion. 'But in our case it's more like a couple of fourteen year-olds!'

By any standards Bradnop is a silly name and for us it had another ludicrous connotation. Amongst the boxes of Sneyd papers at Keele were numerous letters relating to first the Reverend John, then Dryden Sneyd and the collection of heriots at Bradnop.

Heriots, for the uninitiated, are a sort of mediaeval death duty to be paid to the Lord of the Manor when a tenant died and his heir took over. In Bradnop they consisted of 'the second best beast or good' or its equivalent in money. The Sneyds were Lords of the Manor of Bradnop and intent on claiming their rights to heriots even when these were being abandoned elsewhere. The value varied, but it was seldom more than £5 (£300). In the nature of things it was unlikely that more than two or three tenants would die in any one year. Often no-one did. Nonetheless, John Sneyd pursued his heriots avidly, sending in his bailiffs to 'distrain' a widow's mirror, a bed, a bull - this last much to the astonishment of its owner. It was an old bull worth considerably less than any one of his in-calf cows in the field next door. He assumed it was being stolen - it never occurred to him that John Sneyd's bailiff thought it was his second best beast!

Meanwhile the Reverend John Sneyd paid several hundred pounds to Counsel in London for opinions about the legality of his claims. After a day reading these ridiculous documents, I suggested to Marion that we drive out to Bradnop; it was a pleasant evening and the clean country air would make a nice change from the stuffy library. As we drove up the muddy lane towards the village the craziness of John Sneyd's quest became apparent. We passed one impoverished farm after another, their yards littered with rusty machinery, dirty straw, bent sheets of corrugated iron and dispirited chickens. Eventually we stopped the car in a gateway. Marion was giggling too much to drive.

'He was as mad as a pit-full of snakes,' we spluttered, 'what on earth must his London lawyer have thought!' Even today, we were sure the value of the second best beast on a Bradnop farm would scarcely be worth suing for.

Sometimes our visits had a definite agenda. As we read John Sneyd's

1859 diary and his account of pond building at Ashcombe we realised that we had never seen his pools. We contacted John Haig. Did they survive? If so, could we come and see them?

He replied that the ponds were still there 'but a bit overgrown'; unfortunately he and Jean would be away at the time of our visit, but their son, Quentin, would be at home and would be delighted to show them to us.

We arrived in Staffordshire in the middle of a heat wave. It had been baking hot for weeks, a hosepipe ban was in operation across the entire country and the weather forecasters could predict no end to the drought. Naturally we did not pack wellingtons and raincoats. It was a foolish mistake. When we awoke the following morning the sky was dark and distant rumbles of thunder suggested that the rain was not far off. We dressed as appropriately as we could, borrowing jackets and shoes from Barbie, and arming ourselves with umbrellas, but we knew we were ill equipped for exploring the countryside in the pouring rain.

By the time we reached Ashcombe the heavens had opened and the rain was coming down in stair rods. Quentin met us at the door, a short, thickset man in his forties, he was clearly ill at ease in the company of two older women. After a few pleasantries we set off across the fields accompanied by Angus, one of the family's Newfoundlands (the other took one look at the weather and wisely declined the offer of a walk) with Quentin in anorak and boots silently leading the way, the only one of us properly dressed for the weather.

The grass was long and wet and the valley was filled with a sickly, chemical-sweet smell. We knew what it was but this was the first time we had encountered it at first hand. The BSE crisis was at its height, herds were being slaughtered and the carcasses had to be disposed of. One technique that was being used was rendering - incinerating the animal at a temperature thought to be high enough to destroy the prion that was believed to cause the disease. There were only a handful of rendering plants in the country and one of them was nearby.

The key defect of rendering as a method of disposal was that it produced large quantities of a greasy, stinking fluid euphemistically called 'condensate'. This had to be disposed of somehow, and, we were told, the Staffordshire firm paid local farmers to spread it on their fields at the rate of £100 per tanker load. MAFF claimed it was safe but no-one believed them. The stench made people ill, the fluid killed the grass in the fields and there were fears that it might contaminate the water supply.

We had heard horror stories from several sources about the greed of a handful of local farmers who were taking several tanker loads of condensate a **day**, and of the tactics the owners of the plant employed to stifle local opposition. We heard that one protester had had a lorry full of infected cattle carcasses parked on the land next to her house for several hot summer days; another had had her house and garden 'accidentally' sprayed with condensate. The Environmental Health Department seemed unable or unwilling to take action and there was a climate of fear and despair throughout the area.

We slipped and slithered across the field, over a stile and through a gate into what appeared to be a wood. The rain intensified. In the course of a hundred and forty years John Sneyd's trees had grown and multiplied, forming a dense canopy which absorbed the rain, and at close quarters we could see the rhododendrons and other ornamental shrubs he had planted. Foliage had encroached on the pools, some of them were so choked as to be little more than bogs, and the waterfalls had long since ceased to flow, but here and there we could see evidence of the fine stonework that had made them. It was an even more grandiose project than we had imagined.

Angus, meanwhile, being a creature of habit, was stubbornly refusing to return the way we had come. 'I usually take him the full circuit,' said Quentin, apologetically, clearly unable to control the enormous, gentle animal.

We followed them, up the slippery stone path that edged the pools, branches snapping in our faces, water dripping down our necks, to the top of the flight. What an incongruous trio we were, I thought. Quentin showed us the channels that fed the pools - it was an ingenious arrangement. He was more relaxed now, relieved that we were genuinely interested in what he had to show us. The rain pelted down even harder. I was wearing an ankle length denim skirt and laced leather boots - the least inappropriate garments that I had been able to find. My feet were soaked and the hem of my skirt flapped clammily round my ankles. Susanna would have been familiar with the sensation!

The sheer lunacy of the situation suddenly hit us. Sheltering behind a dripping laurel we clamped our hands to our mouths and rocked in silent mirth. Quentin and Angus were way up ahead - but we felt it would be discourteous if Quentin saw us laughing. He was doing far more than we could have expected of him and we had no wish to hurt his feelings.

Quentin led us back through the stable yard and outbuildings - Angus had to be helped through a rather high, tight doorway - and back to the hall, now talking quite animatedly about his job on the railways and his plans for the estate. Back inside he offered us a cup of tea. The kitchens at Ashcombe have changed little since Jane Debank's day. A gas cooker c.1960, and a small formica topped table, were the only concessions to modernity; ancient pine kitchen cupboards and dressers were still in place and the wall tiles were at least a century old. In the warm, confined space the smell of wet, condensate-impregnated Angus was overpowering.

Quentin bustled about, making industrial strength tea in thick mugs, quite chatty now, discussing how he would have to clean up as he was giving a dinner party for his aunt and uncle the next day - his parents had clearly been away for some weeks. As we were about to make our excuses and leave he offered to show us his trains. Quentin's model railway is legendary in the area and it would have been churlish to refuse so we headed through to the main part of the house, followed by Angus.

'Wet boots, Angus, wet boots!' said Quentin ineffectually, presumably using the family argot for dogs with huge wet paws.

Angus ignored him and added an overlay pattern of muddy paw prints to the chequered stone hall floor. He had found friends - albeit ones who were unwilling to pat his sodden coat and who moved with great rapidity when he attempted to shake himself dry!

In a small windowless room (butler's pantry?) Quentin had an amazing model railway layout.

'I've set it in the 1950s,' he said, 'my favourite period.'

He was particularly proud of the way he had designed the roads and signing at the level crossings. Old road signs were another of his passions - he pointed to a stack of rusting enamel.

'So much more sensible than modern ones. You could read a sign by its shape even when it was covered in snow.'

Once inside he proceeded to run his railway. A stationmaster's peaked cap hung on the wall by his head. His knowledge was encyclopaedic and his enthusiasm boundless; Quentin was passionate about his hobby. I was fascinated; one of my sons had had a model railway and I had always enjoyed helping him with his layout - I was quite sad when his enthusiasm waned and he took up mountaineering instead. But Marion was beginning to fidget - we needed to get home to change out of our steaming wet clothes and we were already running late for our next appointment. Gently we eased ourselves away.

The BSE crisis hung like a stinking, lowering cloud over our visits that year. Up at Basford, Humphrey's tenant in Basford Hall Farm was one of those taking daily deliveries of tanker loads of condensate and was spreading it on the fields around Averil's cottage. The hill was steep, the drivers drove fast, Judy feared for the twins' health and safety. Sitting outside, or even having the windows open of a summer evening had become impossible. But the farmer's lease was secure. 'That was down to my father,' said Humphrey ruefully, 'hopeless at business.'

Joyce and Colin were also worried. There were plans to build another rendering plant just behind their bungalow. If that happened a stream of lorries carrying the carcasses of slaughtered cattle would go up the lane past their bungalow - and a stream of condensate lorries would come out. The stench and the traffic would make their lives a misery - and they, too feared for their health and that of Nina, their little grand-daughter who lived with them for part of each week. They were heading a protest against the establishment of the plant - but they lived in a small village and even if everybody signed their petition the protest would probably be ignored. The photocopier we had hired to copy the Sneyd documents was a godsend for them then, they had been using it to copy protest leaflets. At one level we were pleased - at least housing the copier was not the imposition we had feared it might be.

One afternoon that autumn we decided to try to find Rownall Hall, the home of a Captain Powys - the Sneyds had visited there regularly. Gradually we were getting to know the area. We got lost less frequently now - except in Stoke-on-Trent itself.

Marion had a theory that Stoke was the home of the road gremlins - they moved streets and buildings about each night to confuse the unwary. And they didn't come much more unwary than us. Visit after visit found us lost somewhere in the six towns - en route to the library, the museum, Keele, Stafford or one of the other places we needed to visit. After a while we knew every street in Stoke. We had been down them all, both ways, several times. The trouble was we could never remember where we'd been going the last time. 'This looks familiar,' ceased to be a helpful comment. It **all** looked familiar.

We had begun to build some slack into our visits - there was always something we would find we wanted to do. Looking at the notes we had made on our first few trips we were staggered by the amount we had managed to fit in - appointment after appointment with people who had answered our appeals in the local press, trips to Keele, trips to Stafford Record Office, visits to Basford, Ashcombe and the bungalow. But as time went on we learnt to leave ourselves space, the opportunity to go and look at places mentioned in the diaries that just might be interesting, like Warslow, where John William had shot with his friend Sir John Crewe; the Harracles, the large, isolated farmhouse where he had lived after the quarrel with his father; Horton, where old William had pulled down illegal enclosures; and Ash Hall, Wetley Abbey, Westwood and Basford Hurst; grand 19th century houses where John and Penelope Sneyd had been entertained. It gave us an idea of the distances they had travelled, the terrain they had covered and the wealth and status of their friends.

So we set out for Rownall Hall. It was raining heavily, the sky was dark with every promise of the rain continuing for hours. We had been hoping to take photographs for the John Sneyd book but the weather gods were against us. There was a convenient signpost to Rownall from Wetley Rocks. Soon we knew we were in the right area - we could 'read' the land - planted park land with non-indigenous trees, signs on gates for Lodge Farm and Home Farm - there had been a large house somewhere nearby. A board on a gate proclaimed Rownall Farm.

'Let's go up there and ask,' said Marion, turning up the short narrow drive which had a heap of rocks in the middle leaving a space barely wide enough for the car.

Across the entrance to the farm yard was a huge, new, reinforced-wire gate. As we got out of the car a sickly-sweet smell hit us. Condensate. Two German Shepherd dogs, incarcerated in a tiny pen by the side of the gate, savaged the wire, barking hysterically.

'I get the impression they don't welcome visitors,' I said.

From a large black Mercedes in the yard an elderly man in a Russian fur hat eyed us with antagonism. A workman pushing a wheelbarrow hurried out of sight. The dogs became even more frantic. We stood rooted to the spot. A man wearing a breathing mask came out of a low building and headed towards us, his body stiff with suspicion.

'We're doing some research into 19th century houses,' I said sweetly, 'we're looking for Rownall Hall.'

The man relaxed visibly.

'It was pulled down a while back - used to be over there,' he pointed.

The man in the Mercedes got out of his car and glared at us coldly. The only thing missing was a Kalashnikov.

'**So** sorry to have troubled you,' said Marion retreating rapidly to her car.

The labourer almost smiled.

'I'll open the gate so you can turn round,' he offered.

The man in the fur hat scowled and the dogs attacked the wire with greater ferocity.

We were both shaken.

'I felt evil there,' I said 'tangible, frightening.'

'He was like something out of a Bond film,' said Marion, still shivering, 'but I think I know who he is - that's the owner of the condensate plant.'

'We need some lunch,' I said, 'let's go back to the 'Captain Powys' in Wetley Rocks.'

The pub was warm, muzak played in the background and the family at the next table ordered burger and chips. BSE was not high on their agenda. We sat by the fire, ordered sandwiches and sipped our drinks. Normality was beginning to return. But we should have known better - this was Staffordshire.

On the wall in front of us were two framed accounts of strange events that had happened at Wetley Rocks. We read them with a growing sense of disbelief. Both ended in death and the destruction of land - and both had happened at Rownall. Both concerned Captain Powyses. One of them had been sitting astride his horse watching his men harvesting. At the end of the day one of the labourers noticed he had not moved and asked him if he was unwell. He replied that he felt strange and asked to be helped from his horse and taken home. So they laid him on the ground while they went to get a hurdle on which to carry him home. He died in the night.

Nothing odd in that, perhaps, but the next day the labourers noticed that the grass where Captain Powys's hands and feet had rested had withered. It did not grow again for many months. Even stranger was the fact that his body never became stiff, and the undertaker was fond of telling - no doubt in return for many pints in the very pub we were in - how it was still pliable when he put it in its coffin.

More was to come. The next two men to rent Rownall also died suddenly without having been ill, the ground where their bodies had rested also became barren, they did not stiffen in death, either. Was this just a tale invented by an undertaker who had found a good way to get a free pint, or was there a curse on Rownall?

If there was, the next account told us why.

A wise woman had once rented a cottage on the Rownall estate. She gathered herbs for her medicines and ointments from the village common, but - sometime in the late 18th century, so the story went - Captain Powys's tenant at Rownall enclosed the village common including the patch from which the wise woman's most potent herbs came. She put a curse on that part of his land and from that day forward crops could not be harvested from it - they would grow, but then wither and die before they ripened.

The villagers were unnerved by this and when Captain Powys returned from the Napoleonic Wars they petitioned him to get rid of the 'Witch of Rownall'. A man of action, he sallied forth with a posse of villagers and hurled a flaming torch through her cottage window. It burnt to the ground with her inside, she made no sound as she burnt - and the patch of land that had been enclosed remained unfruitful.

'That sounds like a mediaeval story to me,' I said, 'or at least one related to Elizabethan enclosures - curses and witch-burning don't sound very 19th century to me. And remember, the Sneyd diaries cover almost the whole of the post-Napoleonic War period - surely they'd have mentioned something as dramatic as that happening just down the road.'

Marion was not listening. 'That land is still cursed. What have we just seen?' she shuddered.

Later that day we visited Colin and Joyce and described our experience. We were right, we had seen the owner of the processing plant - they recognised the description. Yes, they knew the story of the Witch of Rownall - and they had heard there really was a patch of land where nothing would grow.....

Nearly all our trips to Staffordshire included a visit to the warm, comfortable bungalow on the edge of the moors. Joyce and Colin were always pleased to see us, always entertained us royally. We were very priveleged.

It took us many, many visits to sort through all their documents. There were multiple copies of Ralph's various tracts, his own notebooks and diaries, books of the poems he wrote and published, Susanna's 'treasures', share documents, insurance policies, all the letters she had thought important enough to keep, copies of important letters she had sent, copies of John William's letters detailing the quarrel with his father. In the days before carbon paper or photocopiers all copy-letters had to be written out longhand by the sender. There were three trunks full of memorabilia. Without them, this book would have been impossible.

'And just think,' I said, 'they very nearly didn't come to Ipstones. Joyce only read about it in *The Sentinel* that afternoon and they just happened to be free.'

'Susanna was helping us again.'

'And you didn't believe me when I said how important I thought the Ipstones performance was going to be!'

Visits to Basford and to Rock Cottage were almost as frequent as visits to the bungalow. Like Colin and Joyce, Averil, Humphrey and Judy were always anxious to hear how our research was progressing.

'I always thought the Sneyds were a dull lot,' said Humphrey, 'until you two came along!'

But gradually our visits became more social, a way of keeping in touch with people who had resources we continued to use, yes, but who were now our friends, friends of us in our role as 'Pam'n'Marion' rather than in our roles as wives and mothers, lecturer and businesswoman. They really made Staffordshire a place where we had alternative lives.

Soon we added another couple to our circle - Alun and Angela Davies. They were both retired doctors, Alun was doing an MA in Local History at Keele and was much involved with the North Staffordshire Medical History Trust. He answered all sorts of queries for us from the Trust's medical library. It was Alun who discovered Acton's dictum about modest women not requiring sex with their husbands 'but for the desire of maternity'; it was Alun who unearthed a description of the surgical procedure for piles operations in an 1850s surgery text book to help us understand what Susanna suffered and why the operations didn't work; it was Alun who painstakingly explained to us the pathology of TB and the workings of the North Staffordshire Infirmary ticket system - and many, many other things.

'Yes, Susanna was in the London nursing home for six weeks - nothing odd about that,' he told us, 'the average length of stay in hospital was thirty-six days then - you see people picked up cross-infection after cross-infection.'

He was scathing about the plethora of modern medical history books - written by laymen with too little understanding of the practice of medicine.

'They complain that surgeons were too willing to amputate,' he would say, 'and argue that patients died unnecessarily from post-operative problems. Now, imagine this; you have a man with a broken thigh - he's been run over by an iron-rimmed cart wheel on a cobbled road - lots of lacerations, lots of manure in them - well, think of all those horses - how are you ever going to get that clean and prevent infection without antibiotics? Better amputate immediately than watch him get gangrene and have to cut his leg off later when he's weak and feverish. Mind, once anaesthesia became available maybe they did operate more than was sensible given the state of knowledge about asepsis.'

And he was well read. 'I think I know what Margaret Hale's mother died of, you know in Mrs Gaskell's *North and South*?' he said during one of our discussions. 'Mrs G was good on medicine, she used to go out with her doctor uncle on his rounds. I reckon old Mrs Hale died of uterine cancer. She was ashamed to let Margaret see her because of the foul smell - remember? We can't cure cancer yet but we do alleviate some of the worst side effects. Untreated internal tumours suppurate and stink. We forget that - radiation stops it. What you are seeing there is how an illness progresses without modern medical intervention. Just like in Susanna's diaries. And then there was Squire Hamley's son in *Wives and Daughters*,' he went on, warming to his theme, 'his death is a classic description of the progress of syphilis.'

Soon a visit to Angela and Alun also became a regular feature of our Staffordshire excursions.

'Poor Angela,' I said, 'she cooks us wonderful meals and tries to talk to me about 18th century embroidery.' In retirement Angela had begun to study embroidery seriously.

'And all we can do is talk about the Sneyd family's ailments.'

'And she is a wonderful cook,' said Marion reflectively 'do you remember that dish of potatoes-and-celeriac-baked-in-cream?'

'And the citrus tart, the Chinese fruit salad......'

'The lamb casserole, those delicious root-vegetables-in-olive-oil....'

Our mouths watered. Research into medical history could be so enjoyable!

Chapter 10
# Not all plain sailing

'So where are we now in Susanna's story?' asked Marion.

'Still in Armitage,' I answered, 'that's where we were when you decided I needed to include a chapter about us, just to confuse the readers!'

'I'll ignore that. Susanna had a pretty good time in Armitage, didn't she?'

'Yes, it was probably the happiest time of her life - not that that was saying much. But it was different for John William. I don't think he ever really got over his disinheritance and Agnes's death. To his Armitage friends he probably seemed friendly enough, easy going, a man's man, I suppose, happiest when he was out shooting or drilling with the Yeomanry, but gentle and kind with Susanna and Ralphy. Think of his letters. But underneath he was bitter, disappointed; that came out later. And even for Susanna it was not all plain sailing.'

Despite the tension between father and son Susanna and John William did not lose touch with their family and friends. Susanna was a tireless correspondent. And most of the events that upset the even tenor of life at Armitage Cottage were related to their family. As far as we can tell Susanna had broken off all contact with Penelope Brodie in Edinburgh and contact with Ada seems to have been minimal. Ada was much younger than her brothers and sisters and she spent a great deal of time in her parents' company. The quarrel with John William had taken place when she was a baby, and though she was a train bearer at his wedding - perhaps an attempt by Agnes to heal the rift in the family - she would have been heavily influenced by her father's view of her eldest half-brother. But Susanna and John William remained close to all their other siblings.

Susanna carried on a regular correspondence with Dryden in New Zealand as she had done from the time he first left home. There seem to have been a good number of people with Staffordshire connections in his circle. Relatives of the Armitage Birches were solicitors in Christchurch, a number of the Broughton cousins were in New Zealand and visited from time to time, even Mr Travis the local watchmaker had once lived in Leek.

But Dryden was having a difficult time - labour was scarce and expensive as men went off to seek their fortunes in the goldfields, his land flooded regularly leaving him with ruined crops - and though his letters are cheerful enough, with talk of entertainments laid on for the local children, the new cathedral being built in Christchurch and visits from the English National Opera Company, Dryden was homesick.

In 1867 he returned home. It is possible that John Sneyd summoned him back; with John William disinherited Dryden was now heir to the Ashcombe estate. Whether either of the brothers knew this is unclear but certainly it did not affect their relationship at the outset and Dryden was a welcome visitor to Armitage Cottage between 1867 and 1870.

Susanna also wrote often to Emily, now a confirmed spinster living alone in genteel poverty, and in return Emily sent her news of the rest of the family. She, Freddy and Tavie paid regular visits to Armitage. Sometimes Susanna tore herself away from baby Ralphy long enough to pay short visits to the Bamfords who moved to Little Dewchurch in Herefordshire from Mickleton in Gloucestershire in 1865, and from time to time she took little Ralphy to stay with his Cotton relations. In February 1865, for example, she took Ralphy and his nursemaid to Dover to see his Cotton grandmother and aunts.

John William did not go with them. His relationship with his wife's family had grown strained, as they accused him of owing them money and not paying the doctors' bills for Agnes's confinement back in 1862. It is quite possible that he simply could not afford to do so - the bills for her treatment could have run to hundreds of pounds and John William had no capital. Agnes was ill for weeks; the local doctors called several times a day and towards the end two doctors were summoned from London to attend her. No doubt John William wished, and was under pressure from his in-laws, to do everything humanly possible as they watched Agnes's slow, agonising death.

At the time, the doctors' bills were probably the least of John William's worries, but whether Agnes had lived or died they still had to be paid and now, Rowland Cotton, her brother, was making it clear that he thought this was John William's responsibility. There was also a dispute about some money Agnes's sisters, Fanny and Bertha had lent her to buy her trousseau and which Agnes had not repaid before she died. John William professed ignorance of this £160 (£7,040) and was grudging about reimbursing them. Less understandably, he was discourteous to old Mrs Cotton when she refused to continue to pay him the £12 (£530) a year allowance that had been part of Agnes's marriage settlement. Some acrimonious correspondence survives in which Rowland accuses John William of being stingy, rude, ungentlemanly and a liar.

With all this in the background the visit to Dover did not bode well. It was also wet and snowy and Ralphy caught a cold. No doubt Susanna and John William's sisters-in-law were perfectly polite to each other, the Victorians had a strict code of etiquette, and if pressed, the women of both families would have expressed total ignorance of their brothers' financial affairs, but at the same time Bertha, Fanny and old Mrs Cotton probably made Susanna feel deeply uncomfortable. She did not visit them again and by the time old Mrs Cotton died in 1868, the families had all but lost touch. Not until he was an adult did Ralph re-establish close contact with his Cotton relations.

But the problems John William had with his in-laws paled into insignificance alongside his difficulties with his father. Cheddleton is only thirty-one miles from Armitage, but in 1862 it was a good half-day's journey; three miles in a hired fly or on foot into Rugeley, by train from Rugeley to Stoke and from Stoke along the Churnet Valley line to Leek, Cheddleton or Wall Grange and then about a mile on foot or by carriage to wherever they were staying. Susanna usually visited for a week or so twice a year. Sometimes she stayed with her father and step-mother, sometimes with Emily, sometimes with the Crusos in Leek.

Ashcombe and Basford, Sharpcliffe and Belmont were all let, all gradually deteriorating in the hands of their various tenants. Woodlands, the least grand of all the estate properties was now home to John and Mary Sneyd and Ada. Parts of the estate had been sold, much of it was still mortgaged. Visiting at intervals, Susanna must have been painfully aware of the decline in her family's fortunes.

Often she went alone but sometimes Ralphy and his nursemaid came too, but only if they were able to avoid the Reverend John. Just once, in March 1864, Susanna took twenty-two month-old Ralphy to meet his grandfather, perhaps hoping that her father would be as charmed by the child as she was.

'It was quite dreadful,' thought Susanna, 'it was foolish of me, of course, but Papa was so cruel, barely looked at Ralphy, refused to allow him to kiss him. I couldn't bear to see Ralphy's expression - he was bewildered, no-one had ever treated him like that before. He cried and cried. I didn't record it in my diary. It was too painful to think about and I didn't want John William to know. I never felt quite the same about Papa after that.'

John Sneyd did record the visit *'Emily and Susan and John William's child called here'*. Perhaps he was not quite so indifferent as he wanted her to believe, though even in his diary he could not bring himself to admit he knew his grandson's name.

While in Cheddleton Susanna paid calls on old friends, visited Basford and Ashcombe - both still let to tenants - and attended the schools and church. Curiously, John William sometimes joined her. He still had friends in the area and it held many memories for him. He never got over the loss of the Ashcombe estate, but painful as it must have been, he enjoyed visiting his old haunts. It must have been difficult to make sure that he did not meet his father by accident and no doubt the family's friends found his visits somewhat stressful. John Sneyd made a bad enemy and anyone he knew who harboured his eldest son would incur his wrath. The visits home only served to make John William sadder and more bitter.

In March 1863 Susanna and John William received news that distressed them both. Their younger brother, Wettenhall, had died. Richard Wettenhall was twenty-two and had been an invalid for most of his short life. The family bible says he suffered from rheumatoid arthritis and we have no other evidence of what was wrong with him. John Sneyd bought Wettie a pony carriage to enable him to get about which would suggest that he was crippled. Nonetheless, Wettenhall lived up at Sharpcliffe for much of the time with his brothers Freddy and Tavie, so presumably he was not in need of constant nursing.

In the autumn of 1864, Susanna returned to Cheddleton for a holiday. This year she was probably looking forward to her visit, for Cheddleton church had been renovated and she was going to be at home for the grand re-opening. Her father had been heavily involved with the restoration work even though it was Mr Boucher's church - the Reverend John was not a man to stand back when an exciting project was under way in his locality. There was to be a village feast with two bands, games and fireworks and the Sneyds were entertaining numerous house guests including the bishop.

But on September 9th her brother Frederick was taken ill with an infection in his mouth and throat. He got weaker and weaker, Dr Heaton pronounced him seriously ill and got his colleague, Mr Sutton, to come to see him. Day after day the two doctors visited and pronounced '*dear Freddy*' a little better or a little worse but they do not seem to have prescribed any medication. Without antibiotics there was little they could do and Freddy died. The family bible records that the cause of death was consumption. Consumption is highly contagious and three of the Sneyd children had already died of it.

John Sneyd was frantic with worry and sat up night after night with his dying son. Freddy was the Reverend John's favourite child, and the outpouring of grief in his diary when the young man finally died is still painful to read:

*October 2nd My darling son Frederick expired about $1/4$ before 3 o'clock this morning. O my son Frederick. My son, my son, dearest Fred. Would God I had died for thee. Oh Darling Fred, my son, my son.*

In fact, of course, this is a pastiche of the Song of Solomon, but for all that, John Sneyd's grief was very real. The stiff upper lip is a modern phenomenon - Victorian men were not afraid to show their emotions. Interestingly, the Reverend John's account of Freddy's illness and death makes no reference to Susanna's presence even though she sat with her brother for hours on end, day and night

'Papa barely acknowledged me,' thought Susanna sadly, 'after I went to live with John William he almost seemed to disown me too. And of course, when I saw him I could tell him nothing of my life, nothing about what we did, or about Ralphy, or the cottage. So we were like strangers, exchanging politenesses, talking about the weather.'

If Cheddleton had mixed memories for John William there were places that had equally difficult resonances for Susanna. In November 1865, they all went to see their relations in Sidmouth - their choice of dates for seaside holidays seems somewhat unwise.

'It was a gruelling journey with a three year old child,' thought Susanna, 'but Ralphy was as good as he could be. Fourteen hours it took us. He sat on my knee nearly all the way and we made up stories and sang nursery rhymes. We left home at seven in the morning to go to Lichfield to catch the train to Birmingham. From Birmingham we caught the Bristol train; we changed trains there and got one for Exeter. That was where the problems started - the train was late and we missed the connection for Honiton. We had to wait three whole hours in Exeter for the next one. Of course we went for a walk - down Queen Street to Cathedral Close where we looked round the cathedral. But it was already getting dark and the shops began to shut. Uncle Tom met us at Honiton but it was nine o'clock before we got to Sidbury. Ralphy found the drive in the dark very exciting.

We visited Sidmouth on December 2nd. It was six years to the day since Mr Ingleby, Carrie and I went to stay there,' she went on unhappily. 'I tried not to be sentimental but it did revive bitter-sweet memories of walks on the sands with Charles in the icy wind with the grey wintry sea boiling round the rocky points that enclose Sidmouth bay. He was the perfect gentleman then, polite, attentive and solicitous about my cracked, itching chilblains. And then it all went so very, very wrong. It must have been awkward for Uncle and Aunt too. After all, they urged me to accept him. And I hadn't seen them since, though we'd corresponded. Of course, there was no unpleasantness, none of us mentioned it.'

To show she bore them no ill will Susanna, John William, Ralphy and his nursemaid stayed with Tom and Emma Sneyd for a full month. They left Sidbury on December 12th and decided to make their journey home rather easier than the outward trip had been.

'We spent the night at the Queen's Hotel in Birmingham,' remembered Susanna. 'In the morning John William set off for Rugeley - it was the time of the cattle plague and he had a meeting to go to. Catherine and Ralphy went with him, they were to go on home. I stayed in Birmingham - I'd been plagued with toothache while I was in Devon and I'd written to Mr English to make an appointment. He had premises in Colmore Row, just near Snow's Hill station. He used chloroform to dull the pain when he drilled my teeth - I was not unconscious, but it made me feel dizzy and sick.

While I was recovering in the waiting room - the chloroform could make you feel very unwell - I saw,' Susanna shuddered violently, 'Charles's mother! What could I do? I still wasn't myself, my head felt strange. There she was in her widow's black with the white cap - she never left off her mourning for Charles's father even though he'd been dead for thirty years by then. Those dreadful hooded eyes of hers, the beaked nose, she looked right through me. I summoned up all the dignity I could and gave a little bow in her direction. 'Mrs Ingl—' I muttered, scarcely able to pronounce her name. She **ignored** me! Turned her head away so there could be no mistake. The shame. The humiliation. My cheeks were burning and my legs were trembling but somehow I got out of that room, out into the street, and I walked and walked. Of course, I could never go back to Mr English's after that.'

'Poor Susanna,' I said. 'How ironic that she should encounter old Mrs Ingleby again just as she returned from a place that had happy memories of Charles.'

'It was a truly appalling insult, wasn't it?' answered Marion. 'The Victorians were hypocritically polite so much of the time; it must have been terrible.'

'Yes, indeed,' thought Susanna, 'yes, **indeed**. When in October 1869 I heard Mrs Ingleby had died, I felt nothing but relief. She was seventy two. I know it was very wicked of me - and I did feel sorry for Charles. My chief problem was one of etiquette. I felt it would be wrong of me to pretend to the world that I mourned her when I did not, yet I did not wish to insult her memory. I wrote to Papa for advice.'

'What is that all about?' asked Marion. 'Mrs Ingleby never wanted Charles to marry and treated Susanna abominably. What's more, Susanna's allowance was set to rise by, £50 a year, wasn't it on her death? I'd have thought Susanna would be jumping for joy.'

'Maybe she was, inside,' I said, 'but the Victorians were great on mourning. Whole books were published telling you what grades of mourning you should wear for who and for how long.'

'Grades?'

'Yes. First mourning meant lots of crêpe on matt black - they liked something called paramatta because it was such a dense black. Second mourning meant you wore rather less crêpe and could wear jewellery so long as it was jet - that's what Susanna is wearing in the Elliot and Fry photo Dr Sneyd has. Third mourning meant black without the crepe. Then the fourth stage was known as half-mourning - that could be white, grey or purple, all with black trimmings. So if your husband died you had a year and a day in full mourning, nine months in second mourning, three in black and six in half-mourning - minimum. It was proper to linger a little longer than etiquette demanded over each one. For a brother or sister it was three months in crepe, two in black and one in half-mourning, for a cousin three weeks in black and three in half-mourning and so on - though different books interpreted the rules slightly differently.'

'And for your mother-in-law?'

'Well, that was the problem. The marriage service implied that you and your husband became one flesh - so you treated your in-laws as your own family and mourned them accordingly. But Susanna's marriage was never consummated, she and Charles remained very separate flesh!'

'I think I'm getting the picture. So what did Papa recommend?'

'He advised her to act conventionally - eighteen months in crepe, three months in black and three more in half....'

'Two **years**? Poor Susanna!'

Susanna did have some problems that were unconnected with her relatives. It was not just toothache that troubled her. Her general health was not good and her old problem had reappeared. In the summer of 1867, after much dithering, she decided something must be done.

'I'd been unwell for so long,' thought Susanna, 'but only those closest to me knew what I suffered. I was so sore, and there was a burning pain all the time - and when I.... well, I bled and bled. So I tried to eat as little as possible to limit my difficulties; I'd read about the Home in my magazine *The Ladies' Treasury* and I wrote for details. They sent me an appointment. Then for a day or two I felt better - you know how it is. And I remembered how it had been when Mr Evans operated on me in Derby. So I wrote to say I would not, after all, go. Then I changed my mind!'

On July 9th Susanna and John William went to London. Her diary entries are factual and discreet.

*July 9th  John Wm & I left Armitage by the 11.45 train, we got into the quick train at Lichfield & arrived Euston Square at 3.50, we directly drove to 90 Harley St, 8 ladies at supper, 18 in the home, my room no 15, size 18 feet by 7 feet 9.*

'Statistics again!' laughed Marion.

I was anxious not to be sidetracked into a discussion about Susanna's very 19th century passion for odd 'facts'.  At this point the details of Susanna's operation seemed much more interesting.

*10th Fine. Mr Stewart saw me to ask questions. - I walked with John Wm in the afternoon & went to Mrs Dinsdale's.*
*11th Mr Stewart examined me & also Mr Lawson.*

90 Harley Street was Florence Nightingale's old hospital, and was by then a home for 'gentlewomen in times of sickness'.  Mr Lawson was noted for his bedside manner and his particular interest in the wellbeing of his patients. John William was there to support her - not many brothers, one suspects would have been quite so solicitous of a younger sister having a somewhat embarrassing operation - and Cousin Lizzie and various other London friends visited regularly.  Susanna was to have the best care available - but in 1867  a visit to hospital was still an ordeal.

So, probably, was being in London.  Numerous accounts survive of the dirt, the noise and the smells.

'Listen to this,' said Marion, 'this is Jane Carlyle - wife of Thomas, the celebrated author - on London.  'I have an everlasting sound in my ears, of men, women, children, omnibuses, carriages, glass coaches, street coaches, wagons, carts, dog-carts, steeple bells, door-bells, gentlemen-raps, two-penny-post raps, footmen-showers-of-raps, of the whole devil to pay.' Doesn't sound as if it would be a restful place to recover from an operation!'

'They used to put straw on the streets to muffle the sound of the traffic when there was an invalid in the house, didn't they?' I answered. 'I wonder if there was a permanent bed of straw outside the hospital?  And remember, Jane Carlyle was a miserable woman - someone-or-other said that the only good thing about her marriage to Thomas was that if they hadn't married each other they'd have made two other people miserable! But yes, after Lea Fields I imagine London seemed incredibly noisy to Susanna.  Though she does seem to have enjoyed being in the capital - all that shopping, even when she was ill.'

*12th  I called on Mrs Dinsdale & left my dress.'*

Mrs Dinsdale was Susanna's dressmaker.  She had first patronised her in Rugeley, but sometime in 1865 Mrs Dinsdale had left Staffordshire and taken premises in Wigmore Street. Given the uncertainty of surviving even minor surgery at this date Susanna's visit to her dressmaker immediately beforehand was a brave act of faith.

*13th Fine. I had my operation, under chloroform, performed on me for piles by Geo Lawson, Esq, 5, Harley Street & W G Stewart Esq, 12 Weymouth St, Portland Place. Both Drs came twice. John Wm came to enquire after me in the morning & sat $^{1}$/4 of an hour with me in the afternoon. I had only brandy & ice. The matron & nurse were in the room with me with the drs. The nurse Gillies sat up with me.*

*17th Both drs at once. John Wm & Lizzie came to see me. Great pain. Beef tea all week.*

*19th Wet. Both drs once. Lizzie called. Castor oil & enemas twice but no good, the nurse sat up with me. I was very faint. I wrote to Emily.*

*20th Wet. Both Drs at once. Castor oil of use. Helen called. Mutton for dinner. I wrote to John Wm.*

*21st Outside of my bed. Mr Lawson once. Miss Alexander called & read to me. I had a very bad night. Fine.*

*27th Fine. Mr Stewart once. I called on Miss Trappe, she was very ill at night with hiccups. I <u>sat</u> on my bed for the first time.*

*30th Fine. Mr Stewart twice. I went out for 10 minutes & had tea in the drawing room with Miss Wood. Mrs Dinsdale called to try on my dress.*

*31st I saw Mr Lawson & Mr Stewart. I dined downstairs for the first time.*

*August 5th Fine. Mr Stewart saw me. I spoke to Mr Lawson. I did a little shopping & wished the ladies in the home goodbye & packed.'*

'I think we need to go and see Alun,' I said.

Marion agreed - I noticed that she had stopped complaining about the blocks of quotations from Susanna's diaries.

Alun was delighted to see us.

'We must be favoured by the Historical gods,' he said. 'I've just found a *Textbook on Surgery* by F.C. Skey (1850) in a secondhand bookshop - and it has a section on 'Operations about the Anus''.

Marion and I exchanged glances. We were back in Staffordshire - we expected no less.

'Interestingly half of it is occupied by procedures to ease the piles without recourse to an operation,' he went on, 'they used a rectum bougie.'

'**What**?' we chorused.

'Skey tells us, see? A metallic instrument about two inches in length which should be introduced into the rectum while the person was in a sitting position and retained there for an hour or two at a time - they were applying pressure, you see, to reduce the swelling. Then they used cold alum solution as an astringent that they hoped would dry the discharge from the inflamed skin and mucous membrane - but if that didn't work, surgery became necessary. I was very interested to see the emphasis given to the dangers due to bleeding given the 'irritable nature of the disease', even sometimes causing the patient's death - no resuscitative measures were available you see.'

'Like?'

'Blood transfusions, intravenous fluids - I take him to mean that the more inflamed the part the greater the blood flow - like a boil or a septic finger. So he suggests using methods to calm the inflammation.'

'They don't seem to have done that for Susanna,' I put in, 'or at least she doesn't mention it.'

'No? Well then he suggests a controlled strangulation of the piles by tying a fine thread around them. The bulk of the pile will clot off and die, and by the time the thread comes away, perhaps days later, the blood vessels will have sealed themselves so no bleeding will occur.'

'Is that why she had *'great pain'*?'

'Possibly. But he goes on to say that that method is inconvenient and suggests using a fine wire, and after an hour when clotting can be supposed to have begun, cutting the pile away with a knife or scissors.'

'So she'd have been under chloroform for quite some time?'

'Yes. It was in regular use by 1855 except in cases where the patient was virtually unconscious from shock or blood loss - it wasn't that they were barbarous, but if the patient was in a very poor condition anaesthesia was an added danger - the North Staffs Infirmary notebooks are usually at pains to record that the patients who recovered had no memory of their surgery.'

We tried hard not to think about it.

'I notice that Susanna's first proper meal after the operation was *'mutton for dinner'*,' Alun continued. 'Mutton seems to have been the usual reward for progress. In the Infirmary notebooks you often find, 'Doing well. Mutton chop'. I see that for the first week she only had beef tea. The absence of solids, with opium for the pain, would have produced constipation, excellent for healing, but explaining the castor oil and enemas. The fact that this was the second operation would not have made it any easier.'

'Would it actually have helped?'

'A bit. I suspect that the piles suffered by our ancestors before turning to surgery were enormously larger and more distressing than most that we see today - there was a natural reluctance to operate before it became essential.'

'**Poor** Susanna!'

Chapter 11

# 'We had to unpack by candlelight'

*1870 September 27th Lea Fields, rent £45. Fine. We expected Astor's three vans at six o'clock but they did not come until nine, we left Armitage Cottage about four o'clock, the vans did not arrive here, Lea Fields, until half past seven. We had to unpack by candlelight. Mr Palmer called on his way to and from Rugeley.*

'Why do you suppose they moved?' Marion asked. 'Was John William afraid that Mr Palmer was compromising Susanna?

'I doubt it; they all seem to have been quite good friends and anyway Abbots Bromley was only about five miles away - he still visited.'

'Was the lease up on Armitage Cottage then? They seem to have been so settled in Armitage, I wouldn't have thought they'd have moved unless they had to.'

But she was wrong - sometime later we found a letter that explained the decision. Somehow it was always possible - eventually - to answer the questions we asked ourselves; it was part of what made the whole project so fascinating. Armitage Cottage had been damp, and John William thought it had affected their health. We remembered the diary entry Susanna had made about the smell from the cottage drains. On one occasion they had had to move upstairs to her bedroom to escape it. Then a little later on they had someone take up the boards in the drawing room to try to locate the source of the stench - Susanna does not record whether they succeeded.

'A dead rat under the floorboards?' guessed Marion. 'We had one when I was a child. Dreadful - I'd recognise it from half-a-mile away!'

Whatever the cause, the landlord was unwilling to rectify the problem, so John William had taken a lease on a new house, Lea Fields, after viewing several properties. Lea Fields was comparatively modern. It had been built in red brick with white stucco detailing in the classical style in the 1830s, and stood at the end of a long drive, on the side of a hill just to the north of Abbots Bromley.

'Do you remember the account books?' I asked Marion as we drove out to visit it. 'They had to pay the milk girl an extra 6d (about £1) a week

- she had such a long walk to deliver to them. They paid the postman extra too.'

Lea Fields is a pleasant unpretentious house with views over rolling farmland. Like nearly all the other owners we met, Peter and Susan Brandreth were happy to show us over their immaculate home and we were surprised to find that it was actually quite small. The house has been much modernised, but nonetheless we could see that there were only four bedrooms and no servants' quarters. How, we wondered, did the Sneyds fit into it? Susanna, John William and Ralphy would, surely, have had a bedroom apiece, which left one spare room for visitors. But where, we wondered did the two women servants sleep? Surely not in one of the main bedrooms? Were there, perhaps sleeping quarters over the stables?

'How come all these people are so **tidy**?' I asked Marion as we drove away after accepting an unexpected invitation to stay to lunch.

'Weren't they kind?' she said, ignoring me, 'and wasn't that home-made lemonade wonderful?'

'Mmm,' I was still musing on the tidiness question. The Brandreths ran a business from home which no doubt explained why the downstairs was so neat, but upstairs too? I thought of my sons' chaotic bedrooms with their unmade beds, piles of dirty clothing, used cups and glasses, soggy towels, full ashtrays and dog-eared folders of college work. Not to mention my husband's study with its teetering piles of papers on every surface including the floor. Then, of course, there was my sewing on the dining room table, boxes of computer equipment in the corner and yet more piles of books and papers in the living room and the bedrooms. I could not imagine displaying our slovenly abode to strangers researching previous occupants of our home - if indeed, anyone interesting had ever lived there, which I doubted.

Abbots Bromley is a long straggling place strung out along the road from Burton-on-Trent to Uttoxeter. It is full of pretty, picturesque cottages and posh 18th century houses and was an agricultural village, with fields, farms and barns lying just behind the main street. The church had recently been modernised when Susanna and John William arrived in the village, though a 13th century door and a late 17th century tower (a replacement for one that crashed to the ground dramatically in 1688) told of an earlier origin.

In the tower were stored a collection of reindeer horns and other paraphernalia relating to the Abbots Bromley horn dance, a pagan ritual that is still performed every September. Susanna regularly took visitors to see the horns in the church, but she never mentioned the dance in her diary, although the Brandreths told us that today Lea Fields is one of the stopping places on the performers' route. But she did describe it in a letter to Ralphy at his boarding school in Leamington:

*.....September 17th   About a week ago about 12 people came here and danced in the Hobby Horse show. It is an old performance which used to take place in this town 3 times a year and then the money gained went to some charity, one boy rides a wooden horse and several men carry horns which ought to have the arms of the chief families of the place painted on them, but now the men keep for themselves all the money they get...*

'I still believe they should have given it to charity,' muttered Susanna, 'they didn't need it themselves, they only spent it in the Goat.'

On our first visit, Marion and I did not take to Abbots Bromley despite its chocolate box prettiness. We visited one summer afternoon and were disappointed not to find a teashop - or even a teashoppe, olde worlde or otherwise. There are several excellent pubs but Marion requires tea, lots of it, at around four o'clock; all our expeditions had to take this into account. I always felt it wasted the last useful hour of the afternoon when shops, libraries and the like would still be open, but we had to accommodate each other. She found my inability to function in the early morning equally frustrating.

Abbots Bromley's main street was empty, almost eerily so, on that pleasant summer afternoon, but it was the church that we found truly creepy. It was open, but shrouded in dust sheets and heavily scaffolded. Only the horns, some of them now known to be from reindeer that roamed the area in the reign of King Offa, were readily visible, attached to sinister little wooden heads, pre-Christian and strangely evil in the deserted church.

'Let's get out of here,' said Marion after a few minutes, tea withdrawal symptoms adding to her unease. The atmosphere had disturbed me too and we shivered in the summer sun as we made our way back to the car.

'Not a nice place,' we agreed. 'No wonder Susanna was unhappy here.'

For some reason we had convinced ourselves that Susanna did not enjoy her stay in Abbots Bromley but it was difficult to pinpoint exactly why. The tone of her diary entries does not change, she still socialised, but with different people, still went to church, visited the poor, taught in the schools, sewed for bazaars, wrote letters and visited her family. But she was getting older - she was 39 in 1870, middle-aged by Victorian standards. There were fewer young people amongst her acquaintances and those that visited had usually come to play with Ralphy. Lea Fields proved to be just as damp as Armitage Cottage and worst of all, Ralphy was sent away to school.

Admittedly the social scene at Abbots Bromley was much quieter than Susanna had been used to. Her childhood acquaintance, Harriet Pickering (nee Gillett), wife of Thomas Pickering, Lord Bagot's land agent, lived at Abbots Bromley. She befriended Susanna, and her children, Eddie and Katie, became playmates for Ralphy. The Sneyds were sometimes invited to Blithfield by Lord and Lady Bagot, but the Pickerings, the Lowes at the Vicarage and a relative of theirs, a Miss Connell, Dr Day the curate and his new wife, and Dr Earlam and his wife, were their main companions.

'Mrs Day was a dreadful woman,' Susanna shuddered. 'She **drank**. Twice I and a great many other people saw her tipsy. I did my best to avoid her, she was not our sort of person - I was pleased when Dr Day moved away and Mr Horton came as Mr Lowe's curate.'

Miss Connell was also a strange woman. In February 1872 she moved out of lodgings in the village into Ilay Cottage. A few days later her *'Scotch servant'* arrived and on March 31st Miss Connell gave a house warming party, but within three weeks the servant had given in her notice and left without working out her month. Various people, including Susanna's servant, then took it in turns to sleep at Ilay Cottage.

'Was she an invalid, do you think?' Marion asked.

'I don't know - it sounds more like mental illness to me,' I said. 'Listen.

*April 27th I called on Miss Connell and took a message from Mrs Rock, she having kicked her dog the evening before.'*

'Perhaps she just didn't like dogs? Some people don't.'

'They don't usually kick them though. Wait, it goes on -

*May 3rd  John Wm called on Mr Lowe about Miss Connell.*

*7th  Miss Connell sent a man to ask me to call and see her as she wished me to order a Fly for me to go with her to Rugeley the next day to see about a servant. I called at the Vicarage to hear what Mr Lowe thought about us getting a servant. I ordered the Fly....'*

'Why might Mr Lowe have objected to her getting a new servant? Surely that was what you would expect her to do when a servant left?'

'I don't know; it's just rather odd that Susanna had to help so much.'

'Well, perhaps Miss Connell was quite old.'

'OK then - explain this:

*9th  The Policeman came in the evening to say Miss Connell had been talking in the street.'*

'Oh.'

*'18th  John Wm went to Rugeley about Miss Connell's case, he and Mr Horsfall went to see Miss Connell with Dr Lowe.*

*20th  John Wm, Mr Horsfall and Dr Gibbets went to see Miss Connell. Dr Lowe went to Stafford Asylum to make enquiries on Sunday.*

*21st  Poor Miss Connell left here at 11 o'clock with Dr Lowe to go to Edinburgh.'*

'So was she being shipped off to an asylum in Edinburgh, then?'

'Looks like it. Or maybe there were relatives there. Susanna's being very discreet as usual; I'm sure there's a lot more to it than she tells us. She didn't say much more in her letters to Ralphy - just that poor Miss Connell had become ill and had to go away and she didn't expect to see her again. Miss Connell seems to have been fond of Ralphy though, she kept sending Susanna presents for him.'

The understated description of Miss Connell's decline into apparent insanity is interspersed with details of Susanna's other day to day activities and makes slightly surreal reading. It would seem that she and John William took a good deal of responsibility for the poor lady. They saw her almost every day while she was in Abbots Bromley, and after she left, Susanna finished making three nightdresses that she had been working on and had them washed and sent off. Later in the year Miss Connell sent Susanna money and instructions as to how it was to be distributed amongst the poor of the village.

As soon as they had finished with poor Miss Connell John William and Susanna had another problem to contend with.

*June 18th   The sale at Miss Connell's.   John Wm and I were there nearly all day.   My dear father was attacked with partial paralysis.*

'So was this when the Reverend John had his stroke and they were summoned to Cheddleton, and the deathbed reading of the will that finally confirmed John William's disinheritance?' said Marion, hopeful that we were reaching another of the turning points in the story.

'No, not yet.   John Sneyd lived on until 1873, remember - but he did die of a stroke - I guess this was a sort of early warning.   Perhaps it was brought on by all the palaver over Ada's wedding - remember his 1871 diary?'

Marion nodded.   She had transcribed it.   Mary Sneyd was determined that her only child should have the best wedding money could buy.   Ada was making an extremely good match; her husband-to-be was Robert Ponsonby Hunt, the son of a wealthy Devonshire family.   John Sneyd's financial position had improved but the expense of this wedding was clearly a strain.   He was seventy two and his 1871 diary contains tetchy entries about *'Ada's paraphernalia'* and *'gowns and frippery for the bridesmaids'*.

Her trousseau cost £149-19s-8d (£6,800) of which £8-13s (£390) went on the wedding dress. Other expenses - including Mary and Emily's gowns at four guineas each and the wedding breakfast at £27-12s-3d (£1,250), but excluding the cost of entertaining the tenants at Basford - added up to £77-1s-4d (£3,400).   The road from Woodlands to Cheddleton church was lined with floral arches and wreaths and thirteen carriages carrying the wedding party drove the route.   Mr Boucher and the Archdeacon of Stafford conducted the service to a packed church with more guests waiting outside.

Ada's wedding present from her parents was a silver tea and coffee service priced at £50-7s-6d (£2,270).   Susanna went to the wedding and must have compared this lavish display with her own modest ceremony and equally modest wedding present, but she gives no indication of whether she envied or resented her little half-sister.

'So John William and Ralphy weren't on the guest list?' asked Marion.

'Apparently not.'

'Must have made things a bit difficult up at Lea Fields when the wedding cards arrived, I would have thought. I wonder how she explained it all to little Ralphy?'

' "Your Papa and Grandpapa quarrelled before you were born. Of course it wasn't either of their faults but consequently you have an aunt and grandparents you've never met. And it's your aunt - your Aunty Ada - who is getting married. But she doesn't like your Papa because your Grandpapa told her not to. Well no, she doesn't like kind Aunty Susan that much either. Oh, and while we're talking of such things, you have an aunt, uncle and cousins in Edinburgh who were very good to your Papa but your kind Aunty Susan doesn't get on with that Aunty so you've never met them either - and you mustn't talk about them or ask questions." Sounds like my family! Like me, I expect Ralphy learnt that mentioning people he wasn't supposed to talk about created the sort of atmosphere that went on for weeks.'

Marion looked sympathetic. 'Actually I do remember that in one of his letters home; well it must have been February 1873, the poor child dutifully writes something like, *"I am sorry poor Grandpapa is dead"* - and he never even knew him.'

'Families!'

'Mmm.'

In Armitage the household had revolved around little Ralphy but shortly after they moved to Abbots Bromley he went away to school. He was eight and a half. Betsy left then - Ralphy would have no more need of a nursemaid - but they continued to send each other birthday cards and valentines.

Up to this point Susanna had taught Ralphy. He could read and write, she had done sums with him, he was good at drawing and she had taught him to be interested in natural history and simple science. Susanna was enormously proud of him. Just before he left home she reported in her diary that Ralphy *'for his own pleasure wrote out part of the solar system'*. Now it was time to hand him over to the professionals and she had every reason to believe that her little nephew would do her credit.

*1871 January 26th. Fine. John William took Ralphy to Miss Cranes' school, Boxwood House, Beauchamp Square, Leamington.'*

The school was recommended by Mrs Joseph Challinor; two of her sons went there as did young Gilbert Wardle from Leek. It was run by six spinster sisters, there were between twenty and twenty-five little boys, and the regime seems to have been fairly gentle. The Miss Cranes often took their little charges on outings. On March 9th Ralphy reported that *'Miss Caroline kindly took us to see a stuffed crocodile, it was a very small one.'*

Over the two years he was with them he described visits to see a hot air balloon; Warwick museum (with considerable detail about the exhibits); the tight rope walker, Blondin; a conjuror; Warwick Castle (he was much impressed by an inlaid table said to be worth £10,000 then); Kenilworth Castle; a magic lantern show, and *'demonstrations of the different look of colours by common gas and by limelight'*. It was quite a varied programme for a small boy.

Family friends visited, took him out and gave him presents. Susanna seems to have been quite embarrassed by the Challinors' generosity; on several occasions Joseph Challinor gave the little boy 5s, the equivalent of about £20 today. When the Miss Landors of Rugeley went to Leamington they gave him a book on eggs and nests and a cake and when he left them they filled his pockets full of apples and pears. The Maynes from Tixall also visited him and gave him cakes and oranges as did Mrs Birch of Armitage Lodge.

It all seems to have been quite relaxed and he may well have meant it when, in the first letter home each term, he assured Susanna that he was *'very happy at school'*.

Science appealed to him. He reported to Susanna in 1871 that his Aunt Emily had sent him a shilling for his ninth birthday with which he had bought a *'magnete - it attracts well'*. Someone showed him a microscope and he was so impressed that he spent a shilling of his pocket money on a small one; he later replaced it with a better one at twice the price. The Miss Cranes encouraged him to press flowers and grasses and he built up a collection of fossils. One of the other boys - Harrison - taught him to play cricket and for a time he became quite keen. Susanna allowed him to buy himself a bat for three shillings.

She and Ralphy wrote to each other weekly.

'How curious that they kept all the letters,' I said. 'I suppose it was like the diaries. One eye on posterity all the time. Delusions of grandeur!'

Marion thought differently. 'I think she was trying to hold on to him,' she said. 'Trying to preserve his childhood in aspic because she knew, one day, she would lose him.'

'Perhaps. But think of the trouble she went to - putting all the letters in order and stitching them into books. The time it must have taken - though I suppose she had plenty of that.'

'Not that she always got the order right, especially not at the end,' Marion added grimly. Dealing with the Ralphy letters, as we called them, had been Marion's job. We hoped to publish them one day.

'*My Dear Aunty* would be a good title,' Marion suggested. 'That was how he always started his letters.'

But Ralphy was never very good at dates - in fact, as he got older the dates at the head of his letters became ever more unreliable. And he was quite capable of heading a letter home from school '*Lea Fields*' or later '*Basford Hall*'. Latterly Susanna had lost patience and the last few year's worth of letters were not in books. She'd obviously tried to put them in order and sometimes she'd corrected the dates Ralphy had given - and sometimes she, too, had got it wrong. Marion was having terrible trouble getting them in the right sequence, especially as these were long letters, written by Ralphy as a young teenager with lots of news and ideas. *My Dear Aunty* had been on hold for some time!

Both Susanna and Ralphy were keen on astronomy and exchanged news about seeing meteors, comets, shooting stars and eclipses of the moon. The Miss Cranes cannot have insisted on early bed times. At least once Susanna wrote to them asking them to allow Ralphy to stay up:

'*November 8th 1871*

*.....Our Stafford papers say that from the 12th to the 15th of this month there will most probably be meteors to be seen in Leo and I shall be much obliged if the Miss Cranes will allow you to stay up to see them as you have such a surprising taste for Astronomy...*'

Both she and John William fostered his interest in curiosities.

'Really they only had themselves to blame for how he turned out,' we agreed.

Susanna sighed. It was easy to see that **now**.

John William wrote only occasionally. He freely admitted that he hated letter writing, but even he could not resist telling his little son about their visit to Lichfield museum. '*There are a great many things there that would please you. There were 7 tiny sharks preserved in a bottle and there is the jaw of a large shark and several snakes. And lots of tortoise shells all of which I think would suit your taste ....'* He also got out his pen to describe the rare Camberwell Beauty butterflies he found on the moors when out shooting with his friend, Sir John Crewe, and took the trouble to catch and preserve some Red Admirals Susanna found in the garden.

Susanna wrote about curious events in the locality; when the church at Stone was struck by lightning or when the Blithfield gamekeeper, coming in from shooting with a raging thirst, drained what he took to be a glass of beer. It turned out to be cleaning fluid - enough potassium cyanide to kill forty men - and he died an agonising death. She wrote of curious things she had read in the newspapers; the birth of a hippopotamus called Guy Fawkes at London zoo; the elephant from Wombwell's menagerie that was being taken to Manchester by train in a horse box and demolished it so that it had to be walked there by road; a dreadful fire in Chicago; a hurricane in Sicily which left a thousand people homeless; a projected new law to prohibit the shooting of elephants.

She missed Ralphy horribly and consoled herself by playing with the Pickering children to whom she lent Jennetta. Katie rode her a lot.

'And do you remember this bit,' I said. 'I don't suppose Eddie and Katie were in the least interested. I'm sure it was Susanna who wanted an excuse to linger over Ralphy's things:

*March 28th Fine. Eddie and Katie came here about 3 o'clock, we went to gather violets and afterwards they looked at Ralphy's playthings.*

'An early case of empty nest syndrome,' agreed Marion. 'We all have our own ways of dealing with it. Remember that's how we first met. I decided to do an MA because my two children were having so much fun at university.'

'Chance would be a fine thing,' I grumbled. My nest was still much too full.

John William seems to have had a better time in Abbots Bromley than Susanna. Though he and Susanna still visited together in the village, John William seems to have had quite an active and independent social life. He went shooting, returned to Armitage to stay with Josiah Spode at Hawkesyard, spent time with Lord Bagot at Blithfield and, in March 1871, was invited to stay with his illustrious distant relations at Keele.

'Reverend John, eat your heart out!' laughed Marion, remembering how sycophantic John Sneyd had always been to the family at Keele, recording delightedly on one occasion that *'Mr Sneyd spoke to me'*. Had he known of John William's invitation to Keele Hall he would have been beside himself with envy and rage.

Valentine's day, Easter and Ralphy's birthday came and went. Susanna despatched a valentine to him, ordered some photos to remind herself of how he was growing up and sent him *'a nice book of birds'* for his birthday. Ralphy's school did not have an Easter break and it would be the end of June before he came home for his first holiday.

*May 3rd I - wrote to Miss Crane having heard that Ralphy had the Measles.*

'So the poor little thing couldn't even come home when he was ill?'

'Seemingly not. But the Miss Cranes do seem to have been quite kind.'

*15th   Ralphy and the rest of the boys who had had measles went to Kenilworth for a little change.*

But term ended at last.

*June 21st  Showery.  John Wm took Jennetta to Rugeley to meet Ralphy who was coming home for his first holidays.  A Miss Crane brought him to Birmingham and a friend of hers came with him to Walsall, the rest of the way he travelled alone.*

Ralphy was just nine and she had not seen him for six months. It had been difficult for both of them and Susanna never really got used to it. For the last night or two before he returned to school she would sit up most of the night mending his clothes and sewing on name tapes.

It would be many years before Ralphy lived at home again. That first summer holiday lasted for just six weeks.

Though Susanna and John William had heard from Ralphy regularly they did not really know how he was getting on until the end of his first term. Ralphy's letters were usually short, after all he was still only a little boy, but when something interested him he would go into considerable detail. His handwriting varied but he was capable of a quite respectable copperplate when he tried.

However, it seems that the Miss Cranes supervised his letters home and usually corrected his spelling. Susanna and John William received fair copies which carefully masked how little Ralphy was actually learning.

Not until they got his end of term report (in the form of a letter from the eldest Miss Crane) did they have any real cause for concern. The report does not survive but Susanna's first letter of the new term gives some indication of what it contained.

*Lea Fields*
*August 7th 1871*
*My dearest Ralphy,*
*....I was very glad to hear you had arrived at school alright. I thought it very kind of the Miss Cranes letting you write so soon. I wonder if you took a look at our old house as you passed Armitage... I hope you will have as pleasant companions in your bedroom as you had last half year..... I hope you will be a good boy, and work very hard at your lessons, you know I was very sorry you should have been obliged to be kept to the first 2 rules in sums, because if you pay attention you are not backward at figures and I do hope you will say the church catechism without one mistake, as you can easily do that, if you think of what you are about, and mind you say your prayers slowly, as it is impossible to think of what you are saying when you seem to get them over as soon as possible, do not let Miss Crane have to tell you once about being too quick over them, or your voice being too low to be heard. I was pleased with the way you have got on with nearly all your studies and I think the Miss Cranes have taken great pains with you. If you work hard till Xmas I will give you a book called 'Flowers of the Fields'. I think it is as easy to understand as any book on botany. It has about half as many pictures as there are pages and is a 7 shilling book.*

*Did you remember to tell the Miss Cranes that I had made your old suit of clothes large enough for you and that I wished you to wear them until they are too shabby with an old collar buttoned onto the jacket as they are not large enough to button onto your shirt. In the two suits that are alike, the set which has been worn the most has a large C on them and the other has B. I should like them worn as marked....*

*Your Uncle Gustavus won the first prize at the Archery match which was held at Uttoxeter last Thursday, it was a silver toast rack....*

*All your pets are going on well and Jennetta is staying at the Pickerings.*
*With much love,*
*I am your loving Aunty*
*Susanna Ingleby.*

It is typical of many letters he would receive over the years; bribes and exhortations to work hard, concentrate and keep up with the other boys, meticulous instructions about his clothing, family news and news about his pets. Susanna also took it upon herself to guard his collections while he was away and to add the items he sent her - crests, coins, odd botanical specimens and the increasing number of items donated by family and friends.

*August 14th 1871*
*....I have put all your treasure safely away and I have finished your account about bones, and covered the book with yellow paper.....*

His bribe for good work at the end of 1873 was a cabinet to keep his curiosities in. In fact Susanna never had the heart to deprive him of his end-of-term reward no matter how badly he had done.

Ralphy stayed with the Miss Cranes until midsummer 1873. They seem to have become very fond of him and continued to write to him after he moved on to other schools but they had spoilt him thoroughly and taught him very little.

In the autumn of 1873 he transferred to the Reverend Walsh's, Waterloo House, Waterloo Place, Leamington. As Susanna told him *'Mrs Joseph Challinor very kindly recommended that school so very highly to us and said she quite thought it would not do for you to go to where you would have no lady to see to you. At that school there is a Governess who teaches the younger boys'*. Susanna was very concerned that he should make friends with *'gentle boys'* and worried about him playing football with older children who might be rough.

The Reverend Walsh employed three masters as well as the governess; Ralphy does not tell us how many children there were in the school but it sounds as if it was quite a sizeable establishment; they had first and second eleven cricket teams and a football team that played, and beat, Rugby school.

His first letters home were obviously not as carefully checked as the ones he had sent from the Miss Cranes' and they are full of spelling mistakes. However on September 1st after he had been at school for several weeks he sent what looks like a copy letter. The Walshes seem to have been anxious to impress parents with the way the boys were fed.

*My dear Aunty,*

    *Thank you very much for your nice letter. I am very glad that papa's throat is better. I hope you are getting on very well in London and I am glad you like the rooms you are in now. We get up at a $1/4$ past 7 have breakfast at 8 and begin lessons at $1/2$ past and go out at 12, dinner at $1/2$ past 1 and begin work again at $1/2$ past 3, tea at $1/2$ past 5 and lessons at $1/2$ past 6 and have prayers and go to bed at 8. We have for breakfast bacon, ham, brawn, rolled beef and some of the boys have Australian beef which they bring themselves. We have square blocks of bread some of the largest being 4 inches and coffee in mugs, - for dinner we generally have mutton, beef, veal, ham, pork and sometimes hash and curry and large treacle or jam tarts. We began our table napkins last Sunday week; at tea we have cups for tea - we play an hour in between dinner and work, there is a large gymnasium with tan on the ground so if the boys fall from the ladders they may not hurt themselves. I like school very much; the 4th class boys go out with Miss Scott to buy grub every Saturday. Give my love to Papa and tell him I will write to him the next time.*

    *I remain,*
    *Your loving Nephew*
    *Ralph De Tunstall Sneyd*

'Why would they bring Australian beef if there was all that other stuff on offer?' asked Marion.

'He probably added that himself - and its probably the only true bit! Remember, later in the term, he wrote saying that he had sausages every Tuesday and an awful lot of soup and porridge. He also complained several times to Susanna that his bedclothes were too short and did not cover his feet - Ralphy was tall for his age - but nothing was done about it.'

Towards the end of term there was a flurry of correspondence between Susanna, John William and Mr Walsh, but none of it survives. Much later, Susanna was to write to her friend Mrs Cruso that they had been advised never to send Ralph to a public school because of *'his weak brain'*. There is nothing to modern eyes to suggest that Ralph had any learning disability though he does seem to have been rather immature; he was an original thinker with wide ranging interests, an enquiring mind, a talent for drawing and a good deal of personal charm, but not much self discipline.

Victorian schools set much store by rote learning of facts and neat handwriting, and it is probably true that he would have been made very unhappy at a public school. It is likely that Mr Walsh had been entrusted with preparing him for entrance examinations and feared he would not succeed.

John William and Susanna then sent him to Mr Mills at Hockerton Rectory. They seem to have known very little about Hockerton but the selling point for Susanna was that Mr Mills was *'a gentleman'*. There were four other pupils and Mr Mills had three small children of his own. The tuition must have been almost one to one and Mr Mills operated a three term year so Ralphy came home for Easter and was with Susanna and John William when they moved to Basford.

One school project survives from his time at Hockerton - a neatly drawn and painted map of the Rectory and grounds pasted into one of Ralphy's scrapbooks. Mr Mills reported that Ralphy tried to please but knew nothing whatsoever about Latin - but instead of doing lessons Ralphy and the other pupils spent a good deal of time in Hockerton church, chipping the plaster off the walls to prepare it for renovation. Susanna worried that he would spoil his clothes and wrote that she would not like to see the mess he got into with such work, but it does not seem to have occurred to her to complain to Mr Mills.

The Ralphy letters were a lot more interesting than Susanna's Abbots Bromley diaries, we decided.

'Get on with the story,' Marion urged. 'Tell them about John Sneyd being taken ill.'

She could be very bossy.

'All right.'

*June 19th 1872   One of Mr Joseph Challinor's clerks came to tell us our father was very ill. John Wm received a telegram; we started off directly - & arrived at Woodlands about 6.30. We both saw our father.*

*20th  Mr Joseph Challinor was here nearly all day.*

*21st  Fine. My dear father had a better night & day - we were all called up about 1 o'clock as Mary thought my dear father so ill. Dr Heaton came & stayed the rest of the night.*

*24th Dreadful thunderstorms. Dr Heaton came alone. Mr Joseph Challinor was sent for as my dear father had wished to have his keys, will, etc.*

*25th Wet, thunder. Mr Sutton & Dr Heaton came. Mr J Challinor came in*
*the evening & found the will. I saw my dear father, we all went into his*
*room.*
*26th Showery. John Wm & I left Woodlands.....'*

'It reads like Dickens, doesn't it?' said Marion. 'The thunder sets the
scene like the fog at the beginning of *Bleak House.* I wonder if she saw it
as an omen?'

'Perhaps. I hadn't thought of it like that. Of course it was a false
alarm, he got better and went to see Sir William Gulls, the Prince of Wales's
doctor, in London. Nothing but the best for John Sneyd. That was where
he actually died a few months later.'

Obviously something in the will had upset John William. We tracked
down a copy. It was a grandiose document which carefully disguised the
reality of the Reverend John's financial situation and hurled a final,
calculated insult at his eldest son. All John William was to receive was *'the*
*silver plate that was presented to me on account of and soon after my*
*prosecution of Charles Carus Wilson for a libel on my conduct as a County*
*Magistrate.'*

'That isn't even true,' I said. 'John Sneyd behaved so badly over the
Carus Wilson affair in 1838 that he had to resign from the Bench and the
silver was presented on his resignation. Of course he got himself reinstated
a few years later.'

'I'd forgotten about that,' said Marion, 'didn't he get Carus Wilson
put in prison?'

'Yes. This was the sort of thing John Sneyd was capable of when
crossed. Carus Wilson was a clergyman who lived in Leek for a while and
was a passionate advocate of teetotalism. John Sneyd wasn't; he thought
working men could get drunk if they wanted to. Nothing to do with his
selling his barley to brewers, of course! Well, various of the local publicans
tried to interrupt Carus Wilson's temperance meetings because they thought
he was threatening their livelihood. There was a scuffle at one of these and
a local pub owner accused the Reverend Carus Wilson of assault. The case
came before John Sneyd and he refused to hear Carus Wilson's defence and
fined him a pound (£44).

Very unwisely the Reverend then published a pamphlet denouncing
John Sneyd's high-handed treatment of him; John Sneyd sued for libel and

the case went to Quarter Sessions at Stafford. Carus Wilson got three months in prison! There was a lot of gossip, the Archdeacon became involved and begged John Sneyd to withdraw the case because it brought the church into disrepute. But he wouldn't. Magistrates did abuse the law for their own ends then, but some people thought he'd overstepped the mark and put pressure on him to resign.'

'So why did they make him a presentation?'

'I think it was a sort of acknowledgement that they understood, but thought he'd gone too far.'

'Poor John William,' thought Susanna. 'Of course both he and Papa knew their bible. Judas received thirty pieces of silver for betraying Christ. How could Papa have been so vindictive?'

'John Sneyd was a nasty piece of work,' Marion added.

In fact when the Reverend John Sneyd died he did not actually have enough money to cover all the bequests he made. His widow, Mary, lived out her life supported by her son-in-law with an allowance of just £100 (£4100) a year from her late husband. Gustavus, the youngest son, received £5000 (£207,000). Penelope Brodie and Susanna were left just £100 each. £1000 (£41,000) was to be divided between Harriet Bamford's four young children, but neither Ralph De Tunstall nor the Brodie grandchildren received anything. Emily Jane, the only surviving daughter not to have married, received £3100 (£130,000), equivalent to the £3000 marriage settlements and £100 legacies her married sisters received. Ada received £1100 (£46,000) to add to £2000 she had already had. £50 went to Mr Boucher '..*a token of my gratitude for many acts of kindness received from him*'. And Dryden got Ashcombe and everything else.

At the end of his life when he must have realised just how grave his financial position was, John Sneyd added a codicil to his will to the effect that Ada's and Emily Jane's legacies must be paid in full before any of the others. Everyone else had to wait for their shares until Dryden was able to realise enough money from the estate to pay them. It was a sad end to all John Sneyd's hopes and pretensions.

Nonetheless, Susanna grieved his passing.

*1873 February 17th My dear father died at 10pm at 63, Gloucester Terrace, Hyde Park, London, aged 74.*

*22nd ....My dear father's body was brought to Woodlands from London.*

*Mary, Emily, Dryden, Gustavus, Uncle Tom, Henry, tall Clement & Mr Hunt*
*came with it.*
*24th Fine. Snow on the ground. My dear father was buried in the vault at*
*Cheddleton. John Wm was too poorly to be there. Dryden, Gustavus,*
*Uncle Tom, Mr Brodie, Mr Bamford, Mr Hunt, Cousin Tom, Henry, tall*
*Clement, Mr Mather, Mr Sutton, Dr Heaton, Mr Joseph Challinor & 40*
*tenants, also Cousin C Broughton & Mr Geo Humphreys attended the*
*funeral.*

'Too poorly?' queried Marion

'If you believe that you'll believe anything. Too angry, more like.
Susanna is just being discreet.'

'In her **diary**?'

'Well, remember these diaries were all kept in the library at
Ashcombe. Averil remembers them there. So presumably visitors might
have read them and Susanna didn't want posterity knowing just how John
William felt about his father. Very concerned with keeping up appearances
she was.'

'Positively hypocritical, I'd say.'

Marion had worked on John Sneyd's diaries and felt he deserved to
be exposed for the unpleasant individual he was. She had come to dislike
him intensely.

It may have been anger rather than illness that kept John William
from his father's funeral but his health was not good. He suffered from
neuralgia and what Susanna describes as a quinsy throat. In the summer of
1873 he decided to go to London to consult **the** throat specialist of the day,
a Staffordshire man, Dr [later Sir] Morell MacKenzie. Susanna went with
him for a holiday and Ralphy joined them at the end of term.

John William had already had one batch of treatments from Dr
Mackenzie in the spring and now he decided to go for a rather more
intensive course. Dr Mackenzie practised galvanism which was a form of
electric shock treatment. It was fashionable, expensive and painful. There
is no evidence that it did any good whatsoever. He had developed a set of
brushes that were inserted into the patient's throat and the current was
somehow passed through them - it sounds excruciating. He also seems to
have perfected a system for extracting the maximum fees from his patients
by insisting on extra treatments if the weather became unseasonably hot or

if the patients became unwell. In the six weeks they were in London John William made thirty-seven visits to Dr Mackenzie.

He convinced himself that the treatment was helpful and even returned to London for some top-up treatments, but in reality Dr Mackenzie made no impression on John William's throat. Susanna reported on his progress to Ralphy and it is clear that she was unable to see any improvement. Dr Mackenzie insisted that once the throat was healed - by the magic of his box of electrical tricks - John William's voice would gradually become stronger and more audible, helped by healthy living and clean country air. He was wrong. Within a few years, John William could barely speak.

But even without the medical treatments this was an eventful visit. Susanna shopped and went sightseeing; they visited Crystal Palace, the South Kensington museums, the zoo (where Susanna had her purse stolen with 23s (£50) in it) and Madame Tussaud's, the botanic gardens and the Albert Memorial. They called on friends and family, travelled all over the city by omnibus and underground.

'I've read quite a lot on 19th century London recently.' said Marion. We said before that it was noisy but had you realised just how dirty it was? Listen to this - it's from *Leisure Hours*. I like it partly because of the language and partly because of the fascination with statistics - you begin to see where Susanna got it from:

The 300,000 houses of London are interspaced with a street surface of about forty-four square miles and therefore measuring collectively about thirteen and a quarter million square yards of which a large proportion is paved with granite. Upwards of 200,000 pairs of wheels aided by a considerably larger number of iron shod horses' feet are constantly grinding this granite to powder, which powder is mixed with between two and ten tons of horse dropping per mile of street per diem.

'Delightful!'

'Wait, there's more -

.........besides an unknown quantity of soot deposits discharged from half a million smoking chimneys. In wet weather these several materials are beaten up into a thin gruel like compound known as London mud.

Do you want me to go on?'

'I can't wait!'

'.......of which the watery and gaseous parts are evaporated during sunshine into the air we breathe. The close, stable-like smell...'

'Oh **lovely**!'

'.....and flavour of the London air, the rapid soiling of our hands, our linen and the hangings of our rooms bear ample witness to the reality of this evil. To state the matter plainly and without mincing words - there is not at this moment a man in London, however scrupulously cleanly, nor a woman, however sensitively delicate, whose skin and clothes and nostrils are, of necessity, loaded with a compound of powdered granite, soot and still more nauseous substances.

That was published in October 1854. Graphic, isn't it?'

'Mmm. Of course London's pea-soup fogs were famous - think of Sherlock Holmes.'

'Then I found *Notes on England* by a Frenchman, Hippolyte Taine.' Marion had got the bit between her teeth now. 'There are whole chapters on London; some descriptions are really vivid. How about:

Sunday in London in the rain: the shops are shut, the streets almost deserted; the aspect is that of a vast and well-ordered cemetery...

Or this:

The rain is small, compact, pitiless.... There is water everywhere, filthy water impregnated with an odour of soot....

And look at this description:

But what offends the eye most are the colonnades, peristyles, Grecian ornaments, mouldings and wreaths on the houses, all bathed in soot; poor antique architecture, what is it doing in such a climate? The flutings and columns in front of the British Museum are begrimed as if liquid mud had been poured over them. St Paul's, a kind of Parthenon, has two ranges of columns, the lower range is entirely black, the upper range, recently scraped, is white, but the white is offensive, coal smoke has already plastered it with its leprosy.'

'But he was French. And I'm pretty sure Taine was known for being Anglophobic. It's not necessarily how Susanna saw it.'

'I don't know. What about the 'stifling lanes, encrusted with human exhalations' off Oxford Street, and the number of harlots offering themselves in return for a glass of gin....'

'Well, plenty of people wrote that sort of thing - remember Mayhew and Charles Booth; I doubt if any of that impinged on Susanna. She probably just noted that there was more poverty than she was used to back home, in much the same way we react to the numbers of homeless people and beggars. And remember, we've already worked out that Rugeley must have pretty dirty with all the foundries and mines, and Oakamoor had all that soot coming out of the brassworks, and I doubt if Leek was all that clean, either. All the silk mills would have been powered by steam, let alone the house fires, so there'd have been a lot of coal dust in the air there too.'

'I suppose so. Victorian prints always make places look so clean and sanitised. I think it's worth describing though. Think of all those excursions they made. And there were hardly any public loos for ladies - those at the Great Exhibition were quite exceptional - so there'd have been nowhere to wash your hands.'

'She was a lady; she'd have worn gloves all the time she was out. I guess being in mourning was almost an advantage - smuts wouldn't have shown on the black.'

John William and Susanna had their photographs taken; the Elliott and Fry portraits now in Dr Sneyd's possession date from this visit, and Susanna visited her dressmaker - several times. And on June 11th she received momentous news:

*11th Poor Mr Ingleby died aged 51. I had left him just 13 years.*
*18th Wet part of the day. John Wm's 27th visit to the Dr, he also went to the hospital for the throat bazaar. I went to Mrs Dinsdale to order widow's mourning. I wrote to Emily, Ada & Mr Palmer.*

'The **throat** bazaar?'

'That's what it says.'

Susanna was determined to behave correctly. Her widow's mourning cost her £19-10s, a good deal more than her wedding outfit, and on June 19th she ordered *'deep black visiting cards at £3-10s.'*

Things were changing rapidly. Their father was dead, John William was planning to move the family back to Basford when the lease on Lea Fields expired and now Susanna was free of her husband.

'Basford wasn't mentioned in the will - how come John William got it?' asked Marion.

'An entail dating back to old William's day - and no, don't ask me about entails - I really don't understand them.'

'I was quite pleased to leave Lea Fields,' thought Susanna. 'The house was in poor repair and we could not persuade the owners to do anything. And the view from our window was very much spoilt with Mr Pickering having cut down so many trees. Then he cut down a high hedge and planted a new one between us and the road and put up wooden palings to guard it. It was very ugly, and that disagreeable family, the Adies, could see in. But Basford was not at all as I remembered it.'

Charles Ingleby's death would have far reaching consequences. Susanna inherited a small sum, but the most important effect would be that Mr Challinor had to let her manage her own money again. Unlike wives, adult single women and widows could handle their own financial affairs, though in fact this was to prove a mixed blessing for Susanna. Unprotected by husband, trustee or lawyer she was easy prey for the more unscrupulous members of her increasingly impecunious family.

Chapter 12
# 'John Wm, Ralphy and I came to live at Basford'

In the spring of 1874 John William took up his inheritance and moved back
with Susanna and twelve year old Ralphy to his childhood home, Basford
Hall. This necessitated a trip to London to order carpets and furniture from
Maples. Basford was far larger than either Lea Fields or Armitage Cottage
and as this was to be their permanent home they would need much more in
the way of furnishings than they already possessed. There was to be no
buying secondhand for Basford. They paid a man 1s-2d a day for packing
their breakables and on March 31st set off with four vans *'and a trussel'*
from Astor's removal company. Either they didn't remember how
unreliable Astors had been when they moved from Armitage or the firm had
the local monopoly.

'They must still have been in touch with Miss Connell,' I told
Marion, 'do you remember that little drawing we found at Colin and
Joyce's?' Miss Connell had drawn - and signed and dated - a charming little
picture of removal wagons and horses on a strip of card to commemorate
their move from Abbots Bromley; perhaps it had been intended for Ralphy's
scrapbook.

Their cousins, the Broughtons, had lived at Basford for many years,
but were soon to move out. For a week John William, Susanna and Ralphy
had to stay at Woodlands while the Broughtons got themselves ready to go.

'They must have known when John William would be arriving,' I
said. 'Do you think they were delaying on purpose.'

'Why would they?'

'Perhaps they felt they were being pushed out? Or they knew they
hadn't kept Basford in good repair?'

Clearly they hadn't. Over the next few weeks John William
consulted surveyors; Mr Griffiths, the county surveyor and a Mr Hamilton.
Cousin Clement Broughton consulted his surveyor, Mr Okeden, and there
were numerous, increasingly acrimonious, meetings at Basford. Susanna
confided to Ralphy in one of her letters that she had gone out for the day
*'not liking to be in the house with so many gentlemen'* namely, John

William, Cousin Clement, three surveyors and, for some unfathomable reason, Cousin Clement's coachman. She probably really wanted to avoid witnessing yet another family quarrel. Eventually the whole matter went to court and John William got his money, but for months he and Susanna lived in a house with peeling paint, broken window frames and a leaking roof, camping in the housekeeper's room which was the least damp. It was not a good start.

The return home also brought them into closer contact with their relatives than they had been for many years. Emily lived in Cheddleton and Dryden was just down the hill at Ashcombe. It must have been galling for John William to watch his younger brother lording it over the estate that should have been his, but for a time relations were cordial. Dryden lent them his gardener and sent plants from the Ashcombe gardens and he and John William even went to meetings together. And at least John William had the Basford estate to manage. He had six tenant farmers, Harrison, Clowes, Alcock, Tatton, Tudor and Turner, and their annual rents added up to £254-4s-6d (£12,600), a fairly substantial increase on the family's annual income.

There was also shooting and fishing on his land. The Broughtons had neglected to look after these rights and for the first few months of their occupancy John William was much troubled with poachers setting lines for his fish. Day after day he would go down to the river, destroy the night lines and bring home trout which he and Susanna ate. On one occasion he confiscated rods from a group of poachers and Susanna saw nothing wrong in earmarking the nicest of these for Ralphy.

Susanna, and Mr Blore the gardener, planted flowers in the exposed front garden; like her successors she found that geraniums grew well and made a cheerful show. The greenhouse supplied cucumbers and grapes. These were sold to friends and to the greengrocer in Leek for a few shillings a pound.

*1875 September 15th Fine. Blore took 10lbs of grapes to Leek for which he only got 2s-6d.*

The vine is still in the Basford greenhouse and still fruits copiously. Susanna kept ducks and chickens as pets and for their eggs, but even with her own poultry she still made her regular forays round the local farms to collect eggs for preserving. They grew fruit and she and the cook made pots and pots of blackcurrant jam, redcurrant jelly and rhubarb and strawberry preserves. Blore won numerous prizes at local shows for everything from cauliflowers to white currants. He died, suddenly, in November 1875 and was replaced in the garden by Harrison who seems to have been much less able when it came to winning prizes.

Mrs Blore, the gardener's wife, helped out in the kitchen. Susanna still had terrible difficulty keeping staff and when Mr Blore died she moved into Basford Hall as full time cook at £14 (£636) a year. It was a poor salary for a trained cook but clearly the position suited her - she stayed twelve years.

'Do you remember the canary?' I asked Marion.

'No.'

'Well, apparently Mrs Blore brought her canary with her when she moved into Basford and Snow - or was it Lily - caught and ate it.'

'Snow? Lily?'

'One of the family's white cats - don't you remember how Susanna was always giving away white kittens?' I am a cat person and I was amused by the descriptions. Marion is not and the references had passed her by. Snow and Lily were apparently exceptionally clever cats; Ralphy had taught them to beg and do tricks and they produced a series of white kittens which were much sought after by the Sneyd's friends and relations for their prettiness and inherited intelligence.

'Mrs Blore was stoical about the canary,' I went on, 'assuring Susanna that she had only cared for the bird because it had been her husband's and refusing the offer of a replacement. She probably knew it was only a matter of time before one of the wretched animals repeated the performance. Kitchen canaries stood no chance against Snow and Lily's progeny.'

Mrs Blore was fond of Ralphy and did not complain about the strange things she had to do on his behalf. We had giggled over the passage we found in one of Susanna's letters to Ralphy in May 1878:

*While Mrs Blore was washing the slow worm she cut off the parts you did not like & then rolled it up & put it in a French Mustard bottle & we put the spirits over it & it looks very well, the sore place has broken out a little again. Mrs Blore was very kind in doing it very nicely for you & I said I would tell you she seemed to be getting quite fond of such things...'

'Do you think she saw the funny side?' we asked each other. It was impossible to tell.

'Strange that Mrs Blore was happy to pickle Ralphy's slow worm but flew off the handle when Susanna told her what pudding to make for dinner,' I said, remembering another batch of entries.

'Well, she drank didn't she?'

After 1875 the household account books show frequent purchases of replacement china and a much increased consumption of whisky. On 15th December, 1885, the entry actually reads *'Whisky for Mrs Blore'*.

Mrs Blore was not the only servant to find herself doing bizarre chores for Master Ralph. In November 1879, aged seventeen, Ralph wrote home, *'Please ask Harrison to stuff the hedgehog and clean Linda's skull.'*

Linda had been one of the family's St Bernards!

Harrison and Mrs Blore may not have been the perfect servants but at least they stayed. Susanna had many more problems with her housemaids. Basford was large, isolated, cold and damp; keeping the rooms clean and the fires lit was a daunting task for one person, even if, for most of the time, only three other people lived there. Susanna's young maids were overworked, underpaid and bored, there were no other young servants to chat and giggle with, only opinionated, whisky-drinking Mrs Blore, the deaf master, strict, fussy Susanna, and, in the holidays, the young master with his outlandish hobbies. Eerily quiet rooms full of pickled sea-horses, stuffed hedgehogs, snake skins and skulls did nothing to persuade young women to stay.

Consequently Susanna found herself with a long sequence of problem servants. She took on girls with family problems, girls who were slightly backward, girls who were anxious to be instructed in the Christian faith. Few stayed more than a year.

There was Mary Docksey who went home with a bad leg and never came back; Rose Bettany who was a relative of Mrs Blore's and was so unhappy that after six weeks her mother and aunt came to beg Susanna to release her; bad-tempered Annie Lomas who kept giving in her notice and retracting it; Nelly Turner who only stayed for twenty-two days; Edith Campion who was sacked after a few days, reinstated, and gave in her notice the following month.

Annie Starkey was probably Susanna's most troublesome

appointment. Much correspondence survives between Susanna and Mrs Hopper, manageress of the agency which sent Starkey. Annie received a proposal of marriage from the carrier who gave her a lift on her journey to Basford and who she had only just met. She took it seriously and spent money on items for her bottom drawer. The man was never seen again. She spent much time and energy pursuing him and both Susanna and Mrs Hopper became embroiled in the search although it is clear neither of them expected him to be found. Starkey then gave notice, took a new post, disliked it and returned to Basford. Her story points clearly the way employers' relationships with their servants changed over the period covered by the diaries. There is nothing to suggest that Susanna's grandparents were bad employers - quite the reverse - but neither they nor her parents became involved with the personal lives of their staff other than providing the occasional wedding present.

As if living in a semi-derelict house was not bad enough, Ralphy became very ill. John William brought him home from Hockerton at the end of July and he was already sick and feverish. On August 3rd Dr Heaton diagnosed typhoid fever. Typhoid was a killer disease and Susanna must have been crazy with worry. Day after day Dr Heaton and Mr Sutton visited, took his pulse and prescribed medicines.

'Why pulse?' we asked Alun. 'We'd use temperature wouldn't we?'

'Most doctors didn't have any way of measuring temperature,' he replied. 'There were thermometers that were accurate enough - but it could take up to five minutes to take a patient's temperature and most GPs wouldn't have had them. Pulse rate would be a perfectly good measurement of his condition. How high did it go?'

'140 - is that bad?'

'Pretty bad - he wouldn't have lasted long with it at that level - 80 would be about average for a twelve year-old boy.'

Susanna, John William and Catherine, the housemaid, took it in turns to sit up with Ralphy through the night. Gradually his pulse returned to normal, he was able to sit up and then to come downstairs for a few hours.

A holiday in Wales in September, presumably intended to help him convalesce, brought on a relapse. At first Dr Heaton thought he had scarlet fever but eventually decided that it was a second bout of typhoid. For five months Ralphy was very ill. They had a quiet Christmas with him still confined to his room, but at last, on December 30th Susanna reported that he had dined downstairs for the first time. The crisis was over.

On April 8th, 1875, after a long period of recuperation, Ralphy returned to school at Hockerton Rectory.

The stress told on Susanna. She succumbed to bouts of something she called 'tic doloreux'.

'Whatever is it?' we asked Alun. 'Susanna had it a lot, so did her mother and there are references to other people suffering from it too.'

'It's a type of neuralgia,' he explained.

'Well, I've heard of neuralgia,' I said, 'but I don't really know what it is.'

'It means pain from the nerves; but this is a special sort of neuralgia, called trigeminal neuralgia, an inflammation of the nerves of the face and neck. It's not uncommon and is excruciatingly painful and debilitating. These days we can relieve it. Left untreated its horribly painful.'

'Susanna took to her bed when it was at its worst,' Marion volunteered.

'I'm not surprised. At one time, not that long ago, in really severe cases, we used to sever the nerves to reduce the pain. It was a pretty drastic solution because the patient would lose mobility in that side of the face. The key's in the word doloreux - very painful.'

We had concentrated on the 'tic' part and envisaged some sort of mild facial twitch. Apparently this related to the sudden onset of pain and the spasms that the face went into with it.'

'Poor Susanna,' we thought.

She also suffered from bronchitis, rheumatism and worse chilblains than ever. It is scarcely surprising - they could not afford to heat Basford properly and the oases of warmth that would have been the kitchen and living rooms were separated from each other by long, icy passageways. The roof leaked, so the top floor was always damp, and no doubt this affected the bedrooms below despite the fires they lit in them throughout the winter. The onset of cold weather or illness saw much moving of bedrooms as the family exchanged large rooms with beautiful views for ones that were comparatively cosy.

Although Basford stands on a hill the soil is clay and the ground soon becomes waterlogged - Susanna's father had spent a good deal of money on unsuccessful attempts to drain it. Any excursion meant a walk of several miles along muddy tracks or through wet grass. Waterproof footwear was not yet available - all her life Susanna wore tightly laced leather boots which would gradually have become saturated. Staffordshire weather, we know, can be extreme, and Victorian winters were severe. It was not a healthy place for her to live.

John William seems to have been fitter than she, though his throat was deteriorating and years of shooting without ear protectors rendered him increasingly deaf, but in the damp and cold of Basford he developed lumbago for which he was prescribed a fearsomely pungent *'burning lotion'*.

'What on earth do you think that contained?' asked Marion. 'Lucky Susannna had to rub it into his back and she believed the fumes damaged her eyesight. Certainly by 1875 she was wearing blue tinted glasses provided by her Manchester oculist.'

'It would have been something like horse liniment,' said Alun, 'a rubifacient - makes the area red. The fumes might have made her eyes water but I doubt if they'd have done any permanent damage. It was probably just a coincidence that she found her sight deteriorating soon after John William had had his lumbago treatment.'

Ralphy had one more term at Hockerton after his illness but Mr Mills was not happy with his progress and in September Ralphy went to a new school, this time as a pupil of Mr Cornish, vicar of Debenham in Suffolk. Debenham was a comparatively poor living, worth £282 a year, and like many other clergymen in his position, teaching gentlemens' sons brought in extra income.

This time Susanna and John William had found a suitable place for Ralphy. Mr Cornish took boys to prepare them for public school or university, and others, like Ralph who were unlikely to progress far. He was not particularly impressed by young Master Sneyd and within weeks had written to John William.

Susanna told Ralphy:

*...he found you very backward in everything and said that he thought sums were the thing you could do the best. I said I always think you did things nearly as well before you ever went to any schools so you must work hard whilst you are at your lessons. Do not think of anything else except*

*them and try to do as well as the other boys, never mind thinking about coins.*

She had no compunction in letting Ralphy know his shortcomings.

It was a long and complicated journey to Debenham. First the walk to Cheddleton station to catch the train to London, then the long journey south and finding a cab at Euston to go to Liverpool Street. The cab driver would pick his way through the congested London streets bustling with horse-drawn carriages of every size: smart private carriages, their owners taking the air, with high-stepping, pretty bays; brewers' drays hauled by majestic Suffolk Punches; omnibuses with two or four in hand; donkey carts piled high with goods for market. It would probably have been the most interesting part of the journey for the young teenager from rural Staffordshire. At Liverpool Street Ralphy boarded the train for Ipswich, several tedious hours away. Then it was a fly for the ten miles from Ipswich to Debenham. The journey took a full day. Richmond Gale, son of Susanna's cousin Emma, also became a pupil of Mr Cornish's - his journey to school from his home at Bardsea in Lancashire was even longer than Ralphy's.

From Ipswich they would have driven along the twisting road that is now the B1077. Through a flat agricultural landscape with few woods and no hills, Ralphy might have noticed Westerfield House and the little village of Witnesham, and caught a fleeting glimpse of Helmingham Hall.

How different it was from the countryside he had been used to, the hills and wooded valleys around Basford; the busy canals, the potteries and the railway track that ran through the centre of Armitage village; the impressive black-and-white half-timbered houses in Abbots Bromley. Here the thatched cottages were plastered and painted white or pastel colours. Some were decorated with the pretty Suffolk pargeting - raised plasterwork of intricate floral or scroll patterns which may have appealed to his artistic sensibilities. It was a different world. Regional characteristics were much more marked in the 19th century and, to begin with, even the slow Suffolk burr spoken by the locals, must have been as incomprehensible to him as Dutch or Swedish.

The Cornishes only had three or four pupils at a time and school, for Ralphy, meant adapting to the ways of another household and living as part of a large family, rather than learning the impersonal rules of an institution.

He had been too indulged at home to find it easy.

Mr Cornish was a keen antiquarian and natural historian and encouraged his pupils in the same pursuits. But in Ralphy's letters home it would appear that Mr Cornish was frequently ill, or absent. Often his eldest son, Charles, came home and taught the boys. Only in his final year at school did Ralph mention that there was a new schoolmaster and a school mistress. Evening 'lessons' consisted of the boys drawing while Mrs Cornish read to them, all by candlelight.

It was an undemanding life, and Ralphy remained Mr Cornish's pupil for six years.

Like Ralphy, Vaughan, the youngest of the Cornish sons, was a passionate collector of curiosities. They quickly became friends.

*Debenham October 9th 1875*

*My dear Aunty,*

*Thank you very much for your nice letter. I hope Papa will enjoy his birthday I have lirnt to walk on stilts I have bought a pair for myself for 2 shillings I went a mile and a half on a pair that was lent me. I have subscribed a shilling to get some fireworks on Guy Fox day. Please look in my duplicate box and send me all my best duplicats please put them in a small box and pad them with cotton wool and they will come for 2 pence I will pay you the money when I come back. I have a very good change with Vaugne he sais he cannot wait till cristmas. I am sending a peace of lace bark from Jamaica It is very prity. There are a great many very old pieces of pipes about here some of them about the date of Queen Elizabeth I have got a good many of them. The boy who ought to have joined me at Ipswich came on the following Thursday. His name is Manners the son of Lord John Manners the Post Master General....'*

At this point Ralphy remembered to answer some of the questions his aunt had asked in her last letter.

*I see that my tin box is not sat upon. We have Wednesdays and Saturdays for our half holidays. This house stands up a nice drive a tolerable distance from the town. The church is about 5 minutes walk from here I am very glad you are both better. I am glad the pets are well. Thank you for taking care of the rabbit....*

This was fairly typical of Ralphy's letters to Susanna. His spelling was abysmal and she scolded him for it in nearly every letter, reminding him time after time that he was *'so very backward'* - modern child educationalists would no doubt be horrified by her negative approach. She constantly asked how his school work was getting on - for the first year or so of his sojourn at Mr Cornish's she was preoccupied with him starting the *'rule of three'*.

'She can't mean his three times table, can she?' I said. 'He was thirteen!'

'No,' said Marion, 'it's those sums where you give three bits of information and expect the pupil to calculate a fourth.' She looked at her notes. 'I copied some examples from some 19th century arithmetic text books in the Education Library. Of course, they're complicated because they use pre-simplification Imperial measures - nails and ells, pipes of wine, furlongs and seconds and thirds, halfpennies and farthings, pennyweights and so on. Look, these are from a book published in 1827: 'Bought 12 Pockets of Hops each weighing 1cwt 2qrs 17lbs. What do they come to at 5l 1s 4d a cwt?' l means £ of course.'

'I haven't a clue.'

'£100-8s-63/4d,' Marion answered. 'The book gave the answers, too! Then there was, 'If I buy 61/2 yards of Irish cloth for 1l-3s-10d, how much must I pay for 8 pieces each containing 26yds?' That's £38-2s-8d in case you hadn't worked it out.'

'I hadn't. So what were the rules of one and two that Susanna was so cross that he was still doing?'

'Much less clear. All the books talk about the Rule of Three but not the rules of one and two. But in the same book the sums you did immediately before you got on to the Rule of Three were Compound Addition, Compound Subtraction, Compound Multiplication, Compound Division, Doudecimals....'

'What?'

'Well, that's what it says but I guess it means 'Duodecimals' and Reduction.'

'I'm none the wiser'

'I copied examples - see, here:'

'I'm not sure I even understand the answers,' I said. 'Where do the 11 seconds come from in 4?

Marion shrugged.

We concluded that Ralphy's grasp of arithmetic was more sophisticated than ours if he could cope with sums like that!

Sometimes, to please Susanna, Ralphy remembered to tell her that he had *'begun Ovid'* or started learning the letters of the Greek alphabet, but for the most part he told her about coins he had swapped, the wild life in the local stream and the plants and *'foscils'* he had collected. In fact all the boys bought fossils at a penny or two a time from the girls who worked at stone picking on the neighbouring farms or from the men who dug clay for the local brickworks - no doubt they saw it as a lucrative sideline.

For Ralphy the fact that the Cornish's latest litter of puppies had been left out on the lawn on a hot day and had almost died of sunstroke was much more interesting than his lack of progress in maths; the diet of the hedgehog the boys were keeping was fascinating in a way that French could never be; details of the dish of lettuce with brown sugar and milk that was the food craze at Debenham Vicarage in the summer of 1876 was of much more immediate interest than Latin. A few years later Ralph would meet and become friendly with Oscar Wilde. Wilde's dictum on education -' a marvellous thing, but it is as well to remember from time to time that nothing that is worth knowing can be taught' - would have applied well to this young schoolboy. When Ralph reported progress at school it was usually that his drawing was improving or he was enjoying a particular book that was being read, or *'getting on swell'* at football.

'Football was such a horrid, rough sport,' thought Susanna, 'and some of the boys were so much older than Ralphy, I was afraid he would get hurt. And 'getting on swell' was such a coarse expression - I preferred it when he played cricket - such a nice, gentlemanly game.'

Ralphy and various of his school friends paid regular visits to old Uncle John at Barton Bendish where they stayed for days at a time, shooting, riding, collecting fossils and driving Uncle John's carriage at breakneck speed through the flat Norfolk countryside. Mr Cornish was no doubt glad to see the back of them - the reader is left with the distinct impression that he took the education of his charges extremely lightly, especially those who, like Ralphy, were never going to sit entrance examinations.

'I had hoped he would be able to earn his own living,' Susanna went on sadly, 'and I tried to encourage him with tales of other people's successes. Alicks Fraser, Cousin Minnie's son, was going to sea; a Fraser cousin from Australia was the best pupil his schoolmaster had ever known; one of the Wilson boys from Armitage was going into a solicitor's office; even cousin Dora Bamford was going to art classes which she paid for herself.'

'So Dora was an independent woman, was she?' said Marion. 'Very modern.'

'Averil didn't mention that, did she?' I said, 'she remembered Dora and Harriet Bamford as little old ladies when she was a child. That portrait of their mother, Susanna's sister Harriet, used to hang in their drawing room, over the fireplace, she said.'

'Did they give it to her?'

'No, her mother, Phoebe, bought it. Don't you remember Humphrey telling us that she bought up all the family memorabilia that she could lay her hands on after Averil inherited Basford. Another Sneyd with an eye on posterity. She wrote a diary, too!'

Susanna worried about many of the things Ralph told her. The news that as a fourteen year old he had chosen to travel from London to Ipswich in the guard's van of the train distressed her enormously and for a variety of reasons.

*We were pleased to get your letter yesterday and to hear that you had arrived at school safely, but we were very sorry that you went in the Guard's van as you ought to have known that after your Papa had taken the great trouble in putting you into a comfortable carriage that you ought to have remained there until you arrived at Ipswich, instead of getting out and going to the Guard's van which is not a 'Lawful place' to travel in besides being very draughty, and you know what a great deal of money has been spent to try and keep you in better health....*

'Well, it was cold and draughty which might have given him a chill,' reasoned Susanna, 'and the guard would have expected a tip for allowing him to travel there - I don't suppose Ralphy thought to give him one. They were not suitable people for a gentleman's son to spend time with - so rough,' she shuddered. 'By choosing to travel in the Guard's Van he had disobeyed his father and broken the law! And the servant of the train might have got into trouble.'

'Revealing choice of words,' observed Marion, *'servant of the train'*.

'Yes. I suppose it was beyond her to understand that a young teenager on a long boring train journey might find travelling in the guard's van a bit of an adventure.'

The scolding went on for several letters and Ralphy was forced to apologise profusely. Ralph was a bit of a handful sometimes but Susanna's response did seem disproportionate.

'The Cornishes seem to have got fed up with him too,' I continued, 'there was that letter where he tells Susanna that Mrs Cornish will no longer let him use her natural history books.....'

Marion rummaged through her transcripts of the Ralphy letters. 'This one?

*.....There are a very pleasing varity of creatures in this river here, there are neuts, horse leaches, cadicis, minows and many other things. When I get home I shall have to look at the natural history of Belmont for I am in a hurry to see them more particularly as Mrs Cornish has put a stop to me reading hir books on the subject, and partly because she thinks some of the things are ugly, in fact I think that none of the family care very much for natural history....'*

'That was rather silly of her,' I said. 'I suppose she hoped it would make him concentrate harder on his studies. She should have known it wouldn't work.'

'He actually had quite a lot of trouble with Mrs Cornish,' said Marion. 'Remember the oatcakes? *'Mrs Cornish thought they were like a sort of leather flavered with butter and gruil.'!'*

Susanna had sent him back to school with a supply of oatcakes, a traditional Staffordshire dish, usually eaten hot, rolled up like a pancake, with butter or cheese, or at breakfast with egg and bacon.

'They serve them at the university,' I said, 'I quite like them.'

'Mrs Cornish didn't - and I think I agree with her. And do you remember the coat-of-arms?'

'Well, even Susanna warned him about that,' I laughed.

In the Christmas holidays of 1877 Ralphy had made a copy of the Sneyd coat-of-arms.

Secure in her belief that copying was a good exercise, Susanna had encouraged him.

'It was good for the child to understand that he was a member of an ancient family,' she mused. 'I'd copied the arms myself for relatives. Ralphy was so anxious to take his piece back to school to show them - and he had drawn it beautifully - but I wasn't at all sure it was a good idea.'

'It wasn't,' said Marion. 'Listen: *'When I showed the shield to Mrs Cornish she laughed it to scorn, she said she did not believe we were related to the Welsh Kings.'*

Then in her next letter Susanna wrote, *'We told you we thought it a pity to take the Sneyd Arms to school as Arms are not cared for there.'*

'Wonderful turn of phrase!'

'Then she obviously thought she ought to defend them: *'....your Uncle Gustavus could easily prove how every quartering there belongs to the Sneyds'.'*

'We know all about that, don't we?'

Dr Sneyd had showed us an article in *Staffordshire Notes And Queries*. It proved that in the 1890s Gustavus, abetted, if not aided, by John William and Walter Sneyd of Keele, was party to the forgery of documents that 'proved' the Sneyds' descent from the kings of Mercia.

We had been amused by the account of how Gustavus, supposedly the scholar of the family, was approached by a man in the British Library. One of the building blocks in the Sneyd pedigree was their supposed appearance amongst the donors of land to Hulton Abbey in the long lost Hulton Abbey cartularies. The monks had promised to pray for their benefactors and their relations in perpetuity, and just so that no mistakes were made, cartularies -documents which detailed the donors and their ancestors - were prepared and given to the Abbey.

'I suppose you couldn't risk great uncle Charlie coming back to haunt you because the monks had accidentally left him off their list,' I said, unable to take the idea seriously.

Gustavus's contact just happened to have the relevant pieces of the missing cartularies which he handed over and then disappeared as mysteriously as he had come, leaving no address. The story was the more piquant to us because Abbey Hulton, the area of Stoke-on-Trent in which the abbey once stood, featured in our 'Alternative Britain' game every time we missed the turning on the way back to my house from Leek.

Susanna's well-intentioned offer of a remedy for Vaughan's sore throat added fuel to the Cornish's flames and provoked an alarmed and rather tactless letter from Ralphy.

> *....It also turns out that Vaughans cough was not quinsee. Mrs C thought it very stupid & made a great fuss about me telling you about it she neaver means to use the salve, she says there are plenty of doctors in this village. There has also been a great fuss made about my coat of arms, saying that I ought to take out a lisence for it.....*

Susanna's reply was huffy. Ralphy does not tell us how Mrs Cornish responded to her suggestions for cures for his worms and chilblains. Her sovereign remedy for worms involved carrots, plenty of them, raw, boiled, in soup. In the chilblain season she urged him *'... wear your mitts in the house if your hands are cold and perhaps Mrs Cornish will let you have a little alum and water in a small basin ....to put them in but it must be warm. I do my hands in front of the library fire....'*

Her instructions about his personal hygiene must have been equally annoying to his teachers. In October 1878 sixteen year-old Ralph was admonished: *'I hope you have asked the servants to let you have a bath every Saturday & mind and cut your nails and never button your trousers with your left hand as it wears holes at the top & do your exercises...'*

'I suppose part of the reason for Mrs Cornish's antagonism was that Susanna was so parsimonious,' said Marion. 'While Ralphy was boasting of his ancient lineage his aunt was insisting on getting the last ounce of wear out of his school clothes and refusing to make £50 donations to Mr Cornish's church.'

'It would have been Mrs Cornish who had to find a needlewoman to do the alterations,' I agreed, 'and she would have been able to see just how ill-fitting and uncomfortable his clothes were becoming.'

'Nonsense,' breathed Susanna, 'she was needlessly extravagant.'

She remembered writing to Ralph - he'd have been fifteen and would soon be coming home for Christmas and she knew she would have to buy him some new trousers. She'd have to give him a prize, too, as she always did at the end of term, and Christmas was always so expensive, what with extra food, Christmas boxes for the servants and the paper boy - and it cost so much to run Basford. She was constantly worried about money.

*'Mrs Cornish says your trousers are too tight,'* she had written, *'but as the same trousers were thought not to fit before last holidays we must be*

*content that you have been allowed to wear them this term, but be careful with your new ones, as three pairs of new trousers a year cost a great deal & if you only came home twice a year 2 pairs of new would be enough, that is one plague of the three term plan.'*

'She seems to be implying that Ralph would have grown less if he only had two holidays a year rather than three!' I laughed.

'No, no, no,' grumbled Susanna. 'But Mrs Cornish thought us so very wealthy - and really I had to watch every penny I spent.'

Poor Ralph, with his untidy handwriting, poor grammar and shaky spelling, had to mediate between the two of them, only to be castigated by Susanna.

'His writing was dreadful,' she thought, 'I always tried to make sure that any thank you letters he wrote were written at home so I could check his spelling. I never even dared show his letters to Emily - she would have been so shocked. She'd have taken great pleasure in telling me we were wasting our money sending him away to school.' She looked again at another letter she had sent him:

*'You spell "doors" "doars" & "Michaelmas" "Micalmas" & your friend's name cannot be Priesly, it may be Priestly and you must know that "wrong" is not spelt "rong"...'*

'What do they think I should have said?' she wondered. 'He was nearly eighteen!'

But as an adult Ralphy wrote stories and poems, published pamphlets and wrote diaries and letters describing his travels and researches. Many of these survive - and for the most part his spelling was perfectly acceptable. Perhaps Susanna's constant scolding made him so nervous that he was incapable of writing properly when he was writing to her.

Even in his absence, Ralph was the chief focus of her attention. Susanna kept her diary religiously, never missing a day, but after their return to Basford the entries become briefer and briefer reflecting how dull her life was becoming. They had visitors occasionally; Mr Palmer, not yet re-married, came to stay several times; and Susanna's friend Fanny Cowell with her vast brood of children visited most summers and divided her time between Susanna and Emily. But increasingly, family visiting the area stayed at Ashcombe with Dryden or at Belmont with Aunt Mary and called for a courtesy visit or two at Basford. One gets the impression that Basford was a fairly uncomfortable place to be. Susanna and John William seem to have socialised with fewer and fewer people.

'We lived simply and regular invitations to dinners, concerts and croquet parties were a thing of the past,' Susanna was resolute, 'but we were both getting older, we didn't want to go gadding about like we did in Armitage. We were quite content as we were. I visited poor people and attended the local Dorcas meetings.'

These were sewing meetings at which ladies made clothes for the needy. These clothes were then sold - usually to other ladies who donated them to deserving poor people. Tea was provided on a rota basis, and one of the ladies read something improving aloud while the rest sewed. I had heard of the Dorcas Society but had never known quite what it did. 'Look, this is what she says about it', I said:

*November 8th 1875  Nearly fine. The Dorcas sale. Mr and Mrs Boucher, Emily, Miss P Wardle, Miss Goldstraw and I were there, we went at 5 o'clock. Mrs Bradshaw gave the tea, the customers came at 7 o'clock. I bought for Mrs Blore 1 petticoat, 3s-9d, a chemise 1s-2d, and bedgown 11d. I gave Mrs Alcock one of all three things. I gave Mrs Blore her things also. Dorcas things 19 chemises, 13 petticoats, 6 shirts, 8 bedgowns, 2 small petticoats, 2 nightgowns, 8 pairs socks.*

They were charging much the same as draper's shops - it would have been a lot less effort for them to buy the garments direct! It's interesting that Susanna saw her own cook as an object of charity.'

'Right up Susanna's street,' Marion commented dryly. 'And look at this.' For the most part Susanna's charitable cases make depressing reading; they were mostly old people who became ill and died or ended up in the workhouse - but just occasionally there were success stories. Marion had just found one.

*1878 February 20th Little Ernest Clowes broke both his legs in the Mill.*

Susanna remembered the accident clearly. The Clowes family had just moved into the mill. Naughty Ernest was just five and a half. He went into the mill and began playing and his pinafore got caught by an iron bar which was going round and he was wound round this until one of his legs was broken in two places and the other knee was crushed. His father was not far off and heard his calls and at once stopped the wheel before going to see what was the matter; he had told the child to stay at home and did not know he was there.

'I went to see him every other day to take him oranges and jellies and some of Ralphy's old books to look at - not that he could read, of course. He did not seem to suffer much pain but being fastened down so tight was awkward for a little child,' she recalled.

'Fastened down tight?' she heard Marion say.

'To prevent him moving the legs - they were splinted, of course, but because they were badly cut the doctor had to check that they did not become infected so he had to have his bandages removed each day. Of course, if an infection had set in, one or both legs would have been amputated. But there was no infection and a couple of weeks later Ernest was put in plaster. He was very cheerful - I suppose he liked all the attention he was getting. Someone gave him two pistols - larger than Ralphy's. They made a great noise and smell of powder. When I told John William he said they were very dangerous to use in bed. Mrs Clowes said she did not like them, and that he had already nearly finished one box of pink papers and she wasn't going to get him any more! But he got better,' Susanna glanced at the transcript on my desk: *'On April 22nd Ernest was dressed and walking about.'*

'He was lucky!' said Marion. 'A broken leg could easily have been a death sentence in 1878.'

'They do get interested in the most ordinary of things,' thought Susanna. 'But when they get their teeth into a subject they don't let go - look at the fuss they made over the carpet!'

Susanna was a capable needlewoman and spent much of her time making and mending. In 1876 she started on a new project. The diary entries were cryptic and for a long time I could not work out what was going on:

*July 17th Fine. I walked to Leek for shopping. I afterwards joined Emily & Dora at Mrs Wardle's to learn carpet work.*

I already knew about Thomas and Elizabeth Wardle - later Sir Thomas and Lady Elizabeth. I had in my time curated collections of William Morris fabrics and knew that Thomas Wardle rediscovered most of the natural plant dyes Morris made such a feature of using. But in his own day Thomas Wardle was best known for developing a method of dying tussore silk - it was for this that he received his knighthood. Tussore is wild silk and it has a coating which makes it semi-impervious to most dyes.

Mrs Wardle developed a style of embroidery to popularise her husband's new, brightly coloured, tussore silks. She taught other local ladies, and her band of needlewomen became known as the Leek Embroiderers. They received commissions from many local churches and from others as far afield as Khartoum and Zanzibar. In 1880-1 Mrs Wardle founded the Leek School of Embroidery to train local girls and because of her husband's connections in London the school was able to acquire designs from some of the foremost artists of the day - people like William Morris and Walter Crane. For a short period the school enjoyed minor celebrity.

Susanna was a close friend of Thomas Wardle's sister Phoebe, and she must have known many of Mrs Wardle's needlewomen, but thus far there had been no indication that she was ever formally associated with them. But the diary entries were beginning to tell a different story:

*1876 July 18th Fine. I got up at 3 o'clock to work at patterns for the carpet.*
*19th Fine. I got up at $^{1}/_{2}$ past 3 o'clock to do the carpet pattern. I took Emily's pattern back to her in the morning.*
*24th The carpet frame came so I began to work.*
*25th Fine. I began to work at the carpet at 6 o'clock in the morning & worked nearly all day.*

Susanna obviously spent a huge amount of time on this carpet. Entry after entry read, '*I worked at the carpet.....*'

'How **big** is this wretched carpet?' I scribbled in the margin of Marion's copy of my transcription of the 1876 diary. 'Hereafter, in boredom, I shall abbreviate it to 'IWATC',' I added a few pages later.

At last, in April 1877, I came across the final entries:

*April 30th Fine. I finished the carpet & packed it up.....*

'Hurrah!' I added,

*.....Miss Clowes, Miss Turner and Miss Tatton came to see it.*
*May 1st Fine. I took the carpet to Mrs Wardle's....*

Susanna had spent nine-and-a-half months working on the carpet - admittedly with some gaps when Fanny Cowell and her children came to visit and when Ralphy was at home - and I envisaged something pretty large. My mother had made carpets and rugs - I had sorted wools for her when I was a child - but they had seemed to be finished quite quickly. There had been a cream stair carpet with rust and green borders, I remembered, with matching rugs for the landing and hall. That had taken a long time, most of one winter if my memory served me. Mum had a little treadle machine, of course, but, unlike Susanna, she also had a full time job as a primary school teacher. Yes, I decided, Susanna's carpet must have been pretty big!

'*The Ipstones church carpet*', as Susanna was now calling it, was displayed at Mrs Wardle's for some weeks along with the new altar frontals that **had** been made by the Leek Embroiderers, and she recorded taking various people to see it - clearly she was proud of her handiwork. Then on August 9th she recorded that Ipstones church was re-opened:

*Miss P Wardle & I went to early Sacrament & stayed all day. Sir L Staines preached in the morning and Mr Grier in the afternoon.*

Ipstones church had been restored and extended by the architect, George Gilbert Scott, who was responsible for vandalising so many beautiful mediaeval churches in the name of 'modernisation'.

'The renovation cost £1,200 (£54,000) of which, no doubt, G.G.S. got a substantial proportion,' I said.

Susanna had commissioned an east window to be erected in memory of her father - we had seen it. It was in muted yellow and green, dull red and dark blue, and depicted four saints; we struggled with their names which appeared in complicated gothic script, St Augustine, St Leonard, St Erdda? Ordda? and St Alban.

'Odd choice of saints,' I commented.

'Well, St Augustine brought Christianity to Britain and it's St Leonard's church. Was he martyred using chains?' said Marion, looking at the length of chain St Leonard was holding.

I didn't know - I was no better on saints than she was.

St Erdda/Ordda was untraceable but clearly had something to do with building - he or she was holding the model of a cathedral.

'What about St Alban?' asked Marion. I shrugged.

Susanna looked on in disapproval. 'What has the world come to?' she wondered. These women with their amazing electronic toys - mobile phones, computers, things that she could never have imagined in a month of Sundays - were completely ignorant of the lives of saints who had been familiar to her since she was a girl.

Eventually a trawl of the internet produced some information. St Leonard had been released from prison in a miraculous manner which presumably explained the chain. A phone call to a friend in Ipstones turned St Erdda/Ordda into St Caedda or Chad, former bishop of Mercia. But nothing could explain why Susanna chose St Alban, a pagan who hid a priest fleeing from Roman persecution and was himself martyred because of it. It seemed unlike Susanna to have any sympathy for an unbeliever, however charitably he had behaved.

At the bottom of the window in the same gothic script was the dedication:

> To the memory of the Reverend John Sneyd given
> by his daughter Mrs Susanna Ingleby

I suppose,' said Marion thoughtfully, 'she was erecting her own memorial as well as honouring her debt to her father.'

The window was made by the firm of Burlison and Grylls, church furnishers most probably recommended by George Gilbert Scott. Burlison - or was it Grylls? - had been his father's right hand man and had then gone into business on his own account. Susanna's window would, we were told, have cost around £200 (£9,000) - a substantial sum for someone who claimed she had to watch every penny she spent!

'The rest of the family were notable by their absence at the opening ceremony, weren't they?' I said. 'Even if John William wanted nothing to do with his father's church you'd have thought he might have shown up to support Susanna. And where was Emily, for heaven's sake? Not to mention Dryden and Gustavus, Mary and Ada, the Bamfords.... Even Ralphy didn't go and he was home for his holidays, wasn't he? Poor Susanna!'

But we were still no wiser about the carpet.

'Have we ever actually seen it?' asked Marion, 'I don't remember a carpet in Ipstones church. Mind, we hadn't got to this bit of the diary when we went up there.'

I got out my photographs. Ipstones church had a plain red carpet in the chancel and down the aisle. It looked modern.

'Well, I suppose I could write to the vicar....'

But Susanna had got there before me again. Some years previously a local lady, Barbara Fishburn, had been in the vestry and tripped over a dirty piece of matting acting as a doormat. She bent to straighten it and realised that it was hand-made.

'I make tapestries myself,' she explained.

Susanna's carpet could not have fallen into better hands. Barbara Fishburn is a retired schoolteacher, a brisk, energetic, intelligent lady, keen on all things to do with her church. She picked the battered little rug up, took it home and washed it and then took it to the museum in Hanley to see if they could tell her any more about it. They couldn't, but suggested that it might be the work of the Leek Embroiderers.

She put it away, hoping one day to learn more.

'When Stanley Price (the vicar) first came to Ipstones I showed it to him,' she said. 'I told him I was keeping it in a box under my bed. You could see he thought that was the best place for it. That or the dustbin - then, of course, you wrote to him.'

Some weeks after I received Stanley's reply we went up to Staffordshire. Over cups of tea in the Vicarage we met Barbara, heard her story and saw the fragment of carpet. Even washed and wrapped in tissue paper it was a deeply unimpressive scrap of fabric. And there was a large rent in it. Hand-made or not, and despite my interest in textiles, I would have thrown it away and gone to Allied Carpets for a decent doormat! It was about sixteen inches by twelve with a scrolling floral design in soft green, dull orange and dusky pink on a cream ground and was tightly embroidered in a stitch that had been cut to make a pile. The back was an untidy tangle of loose ends and crossing threads and it was difficult to tell what stitch had been used. It was obviously part of the border of a much larger carpet but there was nothing remotely ecclesiastical about it. So this was what Susanna had spent so many hours working on....

But Marion and Barbara were handing it with great reverence and talking in hushed tones about how moving it was to see it, so I kept my opinion to myself.

'Do you know what happened to the rest of it?' I enquired.

Stanley had been asking around.

'Apparently it was dumped behind the organ when it began to wear out,' he said. 'The mice got at it and in the end it was burnt - oh, a good few years ago. Before my time.'

'Poor Susanna,' we thought, 'all those hours of work.'

The Ipstones reading, our meeting with Colin and Joyce, and our discovery of Susanna and Ralphy's correspondence were still some months in the future and for a while we thought we knew all there was to know about Susanna's carpet. So it came as something of a shock to discover, as we read Susanna's letters, that she had only worked part of the carpet. Fourteen other ladies also made sections and the resulting carpet was, we believe, intended to be five yards by three, so each of the participants made a piece a yard square.

'Nine-and-a-half months to do a square yard,' I said in disbelief. **'Why?'**

In her letters to Ralphy Susanna described her progress and that of his Aunt Emily who was making another section. She complained about delays in getting the right colours and that the wools were *'far from strong'*, but that didn't really answer the question.

Perhaps she had used a particularly slow and complicated stitch? We went and looked again at the fragment, took photographs, did sketches. We visited other churches supposed to have carpets made by the Leek Embroiderers. The carpet in St Edward's was glorious, I remembered, completely unlike the Ipstones fragment, a joyful, glowing blue studded with flowers and beautifully neat on the back. And we had been so excited when we found those kneelers at Meerbrook, too, made from scraps of hand-made carpet - though we never really knew if it was the right carpet - then the verger showed us those altar frontals Mrs Wardle's ladies had made. I remembered the sensual, glittering silks with a thrill of pleasure. Of course, that was one of our troubles; we kept getting sidetracked!

Eventually I went and talked to my friend Elaine in Potters Bar. She was a retired needlework teacher who had a huge collection of books about embroidery. Between us we decided that the carpet was worked in velvet or raised stitch, which is basically a loop held in place by a cross stitch, worked over a knitting needle or special piece of wood called a 'mesh' to give a pile. We experimented. Velvet stitch is not a particularly difficult stitch to do, though the carpet was quite tightly worked with thirty six stitches to the square inch.

'It was remarkably hard to work the stitches so close together,' chided

Susanna, 'and you must remember that my eyesight was not good and I could only work in daylight. It is very clever of you to have discovered so much - though I cannot imagine why you should care to do so. You must know that I was not much slower than the other ladies. In the end our completed carpet was only four yards by three yards. Dear Mrs Worthington died before her piece was finished and poor Miss Challinor worked her entire section on a piece of canvas of the wrong gauge, so her contribution was made into a separate mat. The completed sections were put together by a local tailor. And yes, I was rather proud of my effort.'

It was surprisingly satisfying to have built such a detailed analysis from such slender clues, I thought, but perhaps that was just because I was interested in textiles.

Marion was anxious to get on with the rest of the story. 'Let's get back to what happened at Basford,' she said, obviously relieved to be rid of the carpet.

John William and Dryden did not remain on good terms for long. Susanna does not make it clear when things began to go wrong - but the last reference to anyone from Ashcombe visiting Basford comes in 1875 during Ralphy's first attack of typhoid when Dryden sent to enquire how the boy was. Gradually Susanna ceases to mention Dryden, though for a while she and Ralphy continued to visit and even dine at Ashcombe. By 1876 the brothers were taking each other to court.

*1876 September 6th Showery. John Wm went to Leek to conduct his fence case against Dryden...*

*November 10th Fine. The Sneyd fence case was tried before Mr Spooner. Dryden won. I worked at the carpet.*

*December 8th  John Wm went to see Mr Spooner about the fence case but he would not hear it again.*

Even the judges had had enough of that one!

Over the next few years there were many many *'land case', 'road cases'* and *'fence cases'*. Indeed, on the same day that Susanna proudly took her piece of carpet into Mrs Wardle in Leek *'John Wm & Dryden, Mr J Challinor, Mr E Heaton & Mr Tennant met at Tatton's about the Land case'*.

The Ashcombe estate joined the Basford one. John Sneyd had, after all, run the two together and there seem to have been anomalies and inconsistencies in the way the boundaries were drawn. Touchy about the loss of his inheritance, John William was never going to give Dryden the benefit of the doubt if he seemed to be encroaching on the Basford lands. Dryden was equally difficult. In January 1879 he sent a summons because John William had *'burnt some wood he had on the canal island'*. The canal was the boundary but it was unclear which owned the island. Litigiousness, like diary keeping, is a Sneyd trait.

'They were so stubborn,' thought Susanna. 'But I loved them both. Dryden was just two years younger than me, we'd always been close, we wrote every month all the time he was in New Zealand. But I lived with John William and Ralphy. In the end I had to choose John William.'

She sometimes saw Dryden in church; there was a diary entry about him walking out one Sunday because of the way Mr Ridgeway read the lessons. Then in March 1888 she recorded that Dryden had started going to Cheddleton church again. Once she wrote that he had a cold. In December 1889 she mentioned that he had fallen into the canal at Cheddleton but that their cousin Tom had managed to pull him out. It seems that she was reluctant to sever her connection entirely.

'It was dreadfully difficult,' sighed Susanna, 'and very sad. Sneyd men can be so pig-headed.'

Only Ralph was immune. He visited Ashcombe regularly, dined with his uncle, received presents from him, all of which must have infuriated John William. For the rest of their friends and family the feud required the exercise of a good deal of diplomacy.

'Do you think they had a series of signals?' asked Marion. 'A towel hanging out of the upstairs window, say, to mean "Dryden's here, don't call"?'

'Goodness knows. It probably explains why they didn't have many visitors and got so few invitations.'

'Not much of a life for poor dear Ralphy, though, was it?'

'Probably not - though he was a menace as he got older. It's difficult to know which of them to pity most.'

Ralph made very little progress with his studies at Mr Cornish's. Susanna continued to berate him soundly. By 1877 even his cousin Richmond, who was four years younger than Ralph, was ahead of him in

French. *'Everyone but everyone,'* Susanna wrote, *'goes abroad these days and think how very terrible it will be if you cannot speak French'*. Ralph did think how very terrible it would be and concocted a plan to learn German as well. Susanna - wisely - treated that idea with contempt. However he did persuade her to allow him to have music lessons with a Miss Norris in Debenham at the cost of £4 a term, for two lessons a week, thus relieving the Cornishes of even more of their responsibility for his education.

'I did not consider music a suitable pastime for a boy,' thought Susanna, 'piano playing was for girls, but I agreed in the end. In the holidays we allowed him to practise his fingering - but we had no piano at Basford then so I painted a strip of paper to represent a keyboard and pasted it to a table.'

Marion was shaking with laughter. 'Oh **poor** Ralphy!'

'Why do they find that so amusing?' wondered Susanna. 'Then he wanted to learn dancing - that was a necessary skill for a young gentleman. I sent money for Mrs Cornish to purchase him a pair of pumps. Within a few weeks he reported *'I can dance quadrilles and walteys etc very well.'* Walteys! I ask you!'

While continuing to scold him for his poor work and insisting that he forget about his collections while he was at school, both she and John William continued to acquire items on his behalf. They were sending out very mixed messages.

'Look at these two letters,' said Marion, 'they really only had themselves to blame.'

*Basford Hall. June 13th 1876*
*My dear Ralphy,*
*Thank you for your letter. The Emu's egg* (from Beatrice Fraser) *is green in two shades, the darker making a pretty pattern on the lighter green, it is very perfect; the peach stones are quite different from the much forced and the slightly forced grown in England, the Australian are quite round & have no sharp edges & at a little distance they look so pretty as if they were carved, the piece of wood for throwing is not like any English wood....*

*Basford Hall. June 20th 1876*
*My dear Ralphy,*
*Thank you for your letter...... I am glad to hear you have been improving your drawing but it would give me greater pleasure hear sums, Latin and*

*French were going on well, you must work hard at them; the young Bouchers get on so very well Herbert has a 1st class and Charlie has won his 3rd scholarship. These two Mr Bouchers came home from Cambridge on their bicycles, they were three days in the journey...... if you get on with your lessons your Papa will let you have a few bones that were found at the Water House in some limestone rocks, the best parts were sent to the Manchester Museum, these your Papa has are quite small, they were a Mammoth and an Irish Elk. This Mammoth was found several years ago, the Irish Elk only about 1 year ago...*

But she was scornful and angry when Ralph tried to explain things to her. In June 1877 he described to her how James Cornish recommended blowing and keeping birds' eggs:

*I will now give you a bit of advice you should neaver blow an egg at both ends, like this, (sketch) but you should suck it, or blow it, like this (sketch) Some people like this  better but I do not (sketch) you should neaver hard boil eggs if you can help as if there is the least crack in them they will stink and get bread mites and even grubs, you should always have cotton wool, and neaver bran with eggs as bran breads both worms and mites.*

As Susanna had helped him form his collection and blown his eggs for him (from end to end) and had bought him bran on which to keep them, his tone was somewhat tactless, but her reply was quite unkind, to the effect that she wasn't in the least interested in eggs and *'doubt very much whether I shall ever blow another'*. Perhaps the fact that Ralph had got his *'idears'* from James Cornish contributed to her irritation.

'I was becoming very tired of the Cornishes by then,' agreed Susanna, 'they had such strange ideas. And when Ralph wrote that letter about rice being bad for the eyesight - I quite lost patience with him.' She looked again at the reply she had sent.

*I cannot think what has made you talk about rice, I do not suppose we have it oftener here than else where, we may have had it three times since you have returned to school, we have it oftener when you are at home as anything made with milk is so good for young people or indeed anybody, but as your Papa has egg & milk every day we have not much milk for puddings. Mr Boucher & Mrs Broughton have rice nearly every day & at any rate Mr Boucher's sight is very wonderfully good, he at his old age does not use glasses & I have never heard that Indians lose their sight with living on rice.*

'Perhaps I was a little harsh,' she admitted.

Eventually Mr Cornish began to question what his problem pupil might do for a living. Ralph decided he would like to farm and Mr Cornish gave him the name of a friend who might take him on as a pupil. Susanna pooh-poohed this apparently sensible suggestion. John William, it seemed, did not like farming and would be unlikely to agree, they would have to be very diplomatic, Ralph should let her broach the topic when she thought John William was in a good mood *'for if he once says 'no' nothing will make him change his mind.'* It may be that she was representing her brother fairly; perhaps he had indeed inherited their father's stubbornness, but reading between the lines it seems more likely that it was she who opposed Ralph's plan.

'I certainly had no intention of allowing him to leave school at sixteen,' sighed Susanna, 'he was a child. Mr Cornish did not seem to realise the sort of family Ralph came from.'

Ralph was not to be deflected and proposed a compromise:

*August 1878. If I leave Mr Cornishes in August 1880. When I shall be more than 18. Years old, & go to a farmer from September 1881. when I could go traveling till December & start farming in January 1882 when I should be between 19 & 20 years old. I think that would suit every one. During the time I am at Mr Cornishes I will work very hard at everything, & then I hope things will happen as I have told you or something like it.*

Susanna accepted it grudgingly:

*Oct 1878 If you take to farming in 3 or 4 years of course, as time goes on, you will have to do what good you can in the place, perhaps be a Magistrate when you are older, so you must get very clever or you will be passed over as not fit to help in doing good in the county. Captain Colvile both farms and works very hard for the good of this neighbourhood.*

However, she ignored Ralph's suggestion that he should spend time working with Captain Colvile in the holidays and gradually Ralph's enthusiasm for farming seems to have faded, or maybe his father did indeed forbid it.

'Then, as if farming wasn't bad enough Mr Cornish suggested Ralph become a pottery designer,' sniffed Susanna. 'I suppose he saw Ralph's talent for drawing and knew that he lived near Stoke-on-Trent. It may seem a sensible suggestion to you now,' she went on, 'but the whole idea was impossible then. Ralph was a gentleman.'

They might have done well to encourage Ralph to farm or design - it might have occupied his mind..... Another of his enthusiasms was to prove much more worrying. In the summer of 1878, aged sixteen, he was confirmed and began to think seriously about religion. In December 1878 he wrote to Susanna saying that he would like to visit the newly built Roman Catholic church in Cheadle, preferably on Christmas Eve, to see the ceremonies.

Susanna was horrified. 'I saw Catholicism as a dangerous, foreign creed which a foolish parliament had encouraged to spread by passing the Catholic Emancipation Bill in 1829,' she reasoned. 'The troubles in Ireland in the 1870s revived our fears about the influence of Rome. And I'd read that book *Plain Reasons Against Joining the Church of Rome*. Lots of people thought as I did. I told Ralph we would be too busy to go to Cheadle and that the weather might be bad. I suggested we might go at Easter, hoping that by then he would have forgotten all about it. How could I have known what he would do next?'

In the early summer of 1879 Ralph announced that he was thinking of becoming a Roman Catholic himself and that he had been in touch with a Catholic priest about taking instruction. The Cornishes and Miss Norris, the music teacher, were shocked to the core and Susanna was beside herself. She rallied friends and family to her cause. In letter after letter she poured out her fury and disgust - some of them must almost have singed Ralph's fingers as they came out of their envelopes:

*June 1879*

*I met Mrs Bradshaw coming out of Leek last Friday and she expressed great astonishment at your liking the Roman Catholics & that if you had seen all the folly of them that she had seen you would be sure to dislike them very much.*

*I am not at all surprised to hear that Mr & Mrs Cornish do not understand you when all your own relatives are so very much astonished at your once having thought of the Romanish faith, when you had been brought up a Protestant & from what you said when you wished me goodbye at Cheddleton Station I hoped you had given up all that FOLLY & meant to attend to your lessons & try to be of some use in this world, but you have not the slightest power to change your religion before you are 21, & I hope long before that your brains will be more able to understand what is right, I hope Miss Norris will forgive you & teach you music again but she will not stand any of your nonsense, & I hope next time you write you will be able to say you have given up all your foolishness....*

*I have heard from your cousin Dora, she is most sorry to hear of you ever having wished to be Roman Catholic & I think she thinks when you understand more about the Church of England & the Church of Rome you cannot possibly wish to leave the former & she cannot think how you could be so wicked as to write to a Roman Catholic priest without asking your relations, but I trust when you come home you will be able to tell me you have given up all such foolish ideas, or we shall not say a word about you beginning to shoot, or to take any interest in you. You must begin to be of some comfort to your Papa and try to please him then perhaps you will have a happy holiday, but we will not stand for any disobedience.*

*July 1879*

*I had hoped before this that you had got all your foolish notions out of your head, you know you have no powers to do anything before you are 21, & I should think long before that you will have gained the sense to know how very wicked it is to disobey a parent & it is worse in your case than in most people because of being an only child & your Papa a widower & how you could like to follow the directions of a Priest who to obey caused you to tell so many LIES is perfect madness. I should not think of asking Betsy* (his old nursemaid) *to meet you while you have any of that foolery about you, it would be the greatest grief to her to know how disobedient you had been, but if you directly give up this nonsense I will write and ask her if she can come for a few days - but I shall not invite her without you are getting some sense; nor ask for you to be taught shooting as I will have nothing to do with a disobedient child.  Mr Boucher called here one day and said if you felt you were properly prepared to receive the Holy Communion he had no objection to you receiving it - he is very much annoyed with you for ever thinking of changing your Baptismal Faith.  He tried to explain how it was a 4th Creed that was made by some old Pope - but as I dislike the whole thing so much I did not care to remember about it. All you have to do is forget this nonsense you have picked up & become a good member of the Church of England, your friends will then forgive this short time of foolery & be kind to you, but not a single person will put up with a disobedient child.*

If Ralphy had intended to shock he had succeeded beyond his wildest dreams. And Susanna had mishandled the situation grossly. Despite enforced promises to forget about Roman Catholicism, Ralphy secretly visited the Roman Catholic priests in Leek during the summer holidays. Leek is a small town and nothing remains a secret for long. Word soon reached Susanna who dispatched another scorching letter to Debenham. Ralphy was grovelling in his apologies and promised to remain *'a member of the Church of England'*.

'I suppose I should have been kinder, more supportive,' she whispered, re-reading the letters she had sent all those years ago, 'then perhaps it would never have happened. But I was so very, very angry.'

*Oct 1879  I am very glad to hear that you now intend to belong to the Church of England & in that way please all your relations and friends, who cannot understand how you could ever have liked the Romanish faith, with it's deceit and lying, & all the wickedness it led you to, with Mr Cornish being in Devonshire when we first knew your thought he was in such a fuss that he told the Devonshire Sneyds, taking in also your Cousin Henry and his wife so you see how soon it spreads, but if you behave right now you will soon be forgiven.*

Ralph had his own ideas about what was right - but decided to bide his time. Coming on top of all her other worries, the stress of the quarrel with Ralph took its toll on Susanna's health.

Ralphy's drawing of Armitage cottage.

Armitage cottage.

Susanna, John William and Ralphy in August 1868.

Mary Sneyd, Susanna's step-mother.    Agnes (née Cotton), John William's wife.

Mr Palmer, Susanna's admirer.    Aunt Mary.

Lea Fields, Abbots Bromley.

RUGELEY, FROM THE SOUTH, LOOKING TOWARDS THE RAILWAY.

Rugeley in 1860.

S.S.C.    Moving house.    on the road.

Miss Connell's drawing of the move.

The valentine letter to Susanna
with the lock of hair on the
opposite page.

Will you marry me?
We shall be so
happy I will love
you so much. We are
two sweethearts I will
do every thing for you

I send you a lock of
hair. I am your affectio-
-nate lover.
February 14th = 1869.

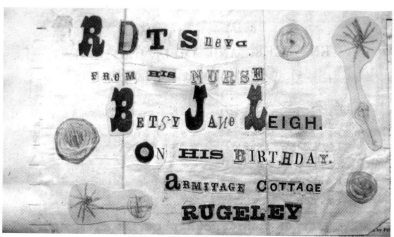

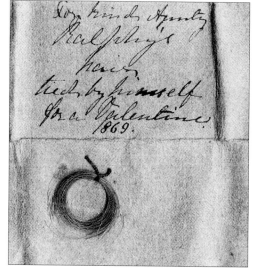

Card for Ralphy's 5th or 6th birthday from Betsy his nurse.

One of Ralphy's drawings.

Hawkesyard,
home of Josiah Spode IV.

The Trinity Aisle in
Mavesyn Ridware
church.

Illustration from *The Girls' Own Paper*, 1886, entitled 'Sewing for the Bazaar'.

Illustration from Ralphy's scrapbook. The family shopped at Whitworth's.

JENNETTE . 1866 .

Jennetta, drawn by Susanna in Ralphy's scrapbook.
Throughout her diaries she spells the pony's name with an 'a'.

Rough-haired St Bernard like Linda de Chamonix.

Ralphy aged about eight.

## Chapter 13
# Pam'n'Marion

'What about all our other visits?' asked Marion, 'there's an awful lot you still haven't told them about us.'

'As I keep saying, it won't all go in. It's a question of priorities!'

'But surely you're going to include the Norfolk and Suffolk visits? And what about our performance at the New Vic - you **can't** leave that out.'

'You really do like to be centre stage, don't you?'

'Yes, I'm a frustrated actress - I wanted to be one, you know!'

As far as Marion was concerned our performance of Susanna's story, based on the reading we had given at Ipstones, had been the highlight of the whole project.

It had been my idea that we should contact the New Victoria theatre in Newcastle-under-Lyme. I knew that Peter Cheeseman, the director, was interested in work with a local theme and had put on various drama documentaries. We wrote to him. To my surprise, and Marion's unfeigned delight, he made an appointment to see us - and agreed to put on a version of the Ipstones reading. We could have the Studio theatre for a night, the services of an actor, various technical staff and a child from the Young Vic society to play Ralphy. Peter would direct it. There was a slot the following September....

Over the next few months we worked at the script, adapting and using it for various other audiences; a local history group, an audience of Judy and Humphrey's friends at Basford. We incorporated extracts from the courtship letters and from Susanna's secret diary, and introduced other voices. We made another dress for Marion to wear in her incarnation as the young Susanna.

'Yes that horrible pink thing. It made me look even more elephantine than the black one,' she grumbled.

At last it was time to go to Stoke-on-Trent to perform *The Vicar's Daughter* for real. We spent a long day rehearsing in a small back room - the Studio was in use - and sorting out where we would add music and illustrations.

'You must tell them here about Maddy's music,' Marion broke in. Marion's daughter is a musician and a composer and had composed and recorded some theme music for us. Marion was proud and excited.

'It was overwhelming,' she said, 'to hear it blasting out, filling the theatre, fussy, insistent, plaintive at times for Susanna, slimy and insinuating when her ghastly brother Gustavus entered the story.'

Marion had studied Susanna's letters and diaries intently and tried to find her voice, the best way to interpret the bland, expressionless sentences. It was not easy. *'I went to the daffodil field alone.'* Just a statement of fact. *'I went to the daffodil field* (pause) *alone.'* More meaningful. This was the entry that commemorated Susanna's first wedding anniversary!

At the beginning of the entry about their father's funeral Susanna recorded, *'Our dear Father was buried in the vault at Cheddleton. John William was too poorly to be there.'* Statement of fact. Perhaps he really was ill. But if she read it: *'John William was too* (pause) *poorly* (pause) *to be there,'* it had a quite different meaning, implying that there was some doubt about both John William's illness and his motive for absence.

'I think the best bit was what Peter did to the Mr Palmer episode, as he directed us,' I said.

In August 1869, Mr and Mrs Palmer, of Armitage, separated - we do not know why - but over the next few months, Mr Palmer and Susanna became close friends. Perhaps their broken marriages made common ground between them. On December 1st Mr Palmer sent Susanna a pair of mittens. Over the next few weeks they met regularly at evening dinners and parties, but in January 1870 he began to pursue her in earnest. She seems to have encouraged him. He visited almost daily and sent her presents, the list reads rather like "A Partridge in a Pear Tree"!

Previous audiences had always found it amusing, but Peter found ways of making it even funnier. Marion started off by reading the various entries straight, and then gradually, as the list grew longer, I as narrator, intervened:

Marion: *January 4th Fine. Mr Palmer called here to have his army paper signed, he brought me 3 eggs & a camellia.*

*7th Fine. Mr Palmer called here, he brought me a flower & an antimacassar and...*

*27th Fine. Mr Palmer called and...*

Pam: The rest of these two sentences has been carefully erased, painted over in white and ruled through with ink lines. What was it that Mr Palmer gave Susanna that she was so hesitant to record? A kiss?

Marion: *January 31st Damp. I made a shade for Mr Palmer.*

*February 3rd Fine. Mr Palmer called. Ralphy rode his pony. Mr Palmer told me about his will.*

*10th Bright. Mr Palmer called in his chair drawn by a donkey.*

Pam: And then?

Marion: *23rd Mr Palmer brought an antimacassar & some flowers.*

Pam: And on the 28th?

*28th Mr Palmer called & brought several camellias.*

Pam: On March 2nd?

Marion: *Mr Palmer sent a hyacinth.*

Pam: Then?

*4th Mr Palmer called on his way to Rugeley, we had some cherry brandy.*

*9th Fine. Mr Palmer called here, he brought an antimacassar, some flowers & eggs.*

Pam: And the next day?

Marion: *Mr Palmer sent a matchbox.*

Pam: And on the 12th?

Marion: *A little snow. Mr Palmer sent Ralphy a tortoise.*

*14th Fine. Mr Palmer called here, he took home the neckties I worked.*

*18th Damp. Mr Palmer called on his way to Rugeley. I wrote to a Naples Bank for him. - Mr Palmer brought the striped antimacassar...*

Pam: Mr Palmer was going blind. He could no longer see to read or write and in later years he employed a young boy to lead him about and do errands for him. But at this stage he was still able to get about independently. The Sneyds went to Llandudno for a holiday in May but as soon as they returned Mr Palmer was visiting again.

Marion: *June 10th Mr Palmer sent potatoes, asparagus & gooseberries....*

And so on. It worked brilliantly, though perhaps it was a little unfair to Susanna to treat this episode so lightly. In fact this was a serious relationship. On June 13th she recorded that she and Mr Palmer had had a long talk about Charles Ingleby and their wills. But both he and Susanna were still, technically, married to other people and she had a responsibility to John William and Ralphy. Year by year Susanna recorded his birthday, June 28th, in the calendars at the front of her diaries; he was three years her junior. They exchanged photographs and Susanna kept Mr Palmer's carte de visite amongst her *'treasures'* for the rest of her life. It survives, faded almost beyond recognition.

But in September 1870 John William and his little family packed up and moved away from Armitage Cottage to Abbots Bromley. Abbots Bromley is only a few minutes away from Armitage by car but in 1870 it was sufficiently distant to prohibit frequent visits. Susanna and Mr Palmer corresponded regularly, but gradually the relationship withered and died.

Dramatically, the exchange added some much-needed light relief to Susanna's increasingly sombre story.

Not until the afternoon of the second day, the day of the performance, was the Studio ready for us. At last we could go through the script from beginning to end, with music, slides.... We finished rehearsing and flopped exhausted. The learning curve had been vertical.

Peter looked at us quizzically. 'Not bad,' he said, 'the only trouble is we need to cut it by an hour!'

We did! There was no time to go through it again before the performance - in fact the last cut was made just twenty minutes before the curtain rose. How the technicians got the sound and light cues to work after these last minute savage cuts we could not fathom - but somehow it all came together. Marion was elated, ecstatic.....

I had to admit it had been an interesting experience; exciting, hard work; and on stage I had felt confident enough. I really couldn't put my finger on why that evening left me feeling uneasy - afterwards I had felt uncomfortable, out of my depth, inadequate, a rank amateur. Perhaps it was because my sons had made no attempt to disguise their contempt for the whole episode or because my husband had been diplomatically silent about it. However complimentary other people had been, the memory of that evening is one I try hard to suppress.

'**My** family enjoyed it,' said Marion defensively, 'and the theatre was full.'

'Helps to have a lot of friends!' I answered sourly.

'I feel we did her justice. It's a pity your family couldn't have been a bit more enthusiastic. I suppose it's just their way. I thought your commentary was clear, compelling - scholarly even. We're very different, you know - I'm a glass half-full person. Your glass is always at least half empty. You always expect the worst of any given situation. And you always seem alarmingly controlled and unemotional to me. Even Peter thought it went well, he wouldn't have offered to work with us again if it had been disastrous, would he?'

But try as I would I could not convince myself.

Of course not all our expeditions were to Staffordshire. Descendants of the Sneyd family now lived in other parts of the country and some of them had pictures and other memorabilia we needed to see. But our funding was fast disappearing and overnight stays in places where we had to pay for our accommodation rather than trespassing on Barbie's good nature, not to mention her living space, had to be kept to a minimum.

One excursion we did make was to Norfolk and Suffolk to meet Roger Wykes Sneyd, a descendant of Susanna's Devonshire uncle and aunt. We also hoped to find out more about Susanna's mother's family, the Holleys, and to visit Debenham where Ralphy had been to school between 1875 and 1881. We had to make the maximum use of our time.

The trip started badly. Within twenty miles of home we found we were heading in totally the wrong direction in impossible traffic. Marion panicked. We stopped for coffee to calm her down and found ourselves in a seedy lorry drivers' pit stop drinking unrecognisable brown fluid - OK for 'Alternative Britain' tourists, but not for soothing Marion's jangled nerves.

'Oh **dear**,' I thought. Marion in a panic is hard work!

Consequently we were a little late arriving at Roger's, but fortunately his directions were excellent - and the winding Norfolk lanes ensured Marion was driving slowly enough to follow them. Once lost, she tends to speed up, an excellent recipe for getting as far away from your chosen destination as possible. And then she calls down curses on whoever designed the road signing system in that part of the world. Her daughter assures me that she has been doing this all her life. We think she enjoys the stress!

We knew Roger was an old naval man and somewhat eccentric. One

Christmas card he sent us included a lengthy note about an Aldis (Marion's surname) who designed some sort of lamp for the navy - with a long description of how much better it was than the design that replaced it.

'Different from the usual run of Christmas greetings, you have to admit,' said Marion.

We expected him to be elderly and very correct, and pictured him living in ship-shape fashion.

He greeted us at the door of his old farmhouse. He was indeed the archetypal British ex-serviceman, very public-school, courteous, but brisk almost to the point of brusqueness. His wife, he explained, was out, she was bored to death by Sneyds! But once inside, it was another story. If we had thought Averil's kitchen untidy, his was beyond redemption. A bright red Aga stood in an inglenook, the floor was uneven brick and the walls invisible behind a jumble of herbs, old pots, empty birdcages, boxes and junk of every description; while bottles and lanterns hung from the massive beams. An ancient stone sink with one cold tap stood by the door, and, incongruously, a modern tin tray laid with glasses and bottles perched on the edge of the crowded table.

We picked our way across the uneven floors. The rest of the house was much like the kitchen; antique kitchen pots, 18th century porcelain, 19th century bric-a-brac, vases of garish modern silk flowers, silhouettes, oil paintings, books, papers and clutter on every conceivable surface.

'It must be freezing here in winter,' I thought, eyeing the threadbare rugs and the half inch gaps between the uneven floorboards.

Wild greenery from the garden fought for access through the windows and open french doors, filling the rooms with the warm wet smell of a Norfolk summer. The house, probably built in the time of Elizabeth I, barely acknowledged the 20th century.

Roger served us white wine and elderflower cordial and chatted about what he knew of the Sneyds - he was particularly interested in the relationship between the Reverend John Sneyd and his brother Tom. Roger was one of Tom's descendants. Family legend had it that the brothers were very much at odds. He showed us portraits - including the original of a splendid portrait of the Reverend John's ill-fated second son, Ralph Debank, on a black horse, with Sharpcliffe, the estate his father had bought him but which in fact he was never well enough to manage, in the background. We had seen black and white photographs of it at Keele, but the original was much more interesting. Roger had photographs and a few letters, but though we enjoyed his company, there was little that we did not already know. After a simple lunch we took our leave and headed for Debenham.

We looked round the town and visited the church. But it was the Vicarage we really wanted to see and we couldn't find it.

We headed for Norwich where we planned to spend the night, and in the morning went to the Record Office. Susanna's mother had been a Holley, and the Holleys were a Norfolk family - we hoped to find out more about them. It was a disappointing morning and after a couple of hours we decided to leave. This trip was proving unusually unproductive.

'I feel sure we should go back to Debenham,' Marion said, 'I don't know why, but I just feel we should.'

'Fine,' I replied, knowing, as we both did by then, that if either of us felt strongly that we should do something, that feeling should be followed without question.

'They are learning,' approved Susanna.

We were still looking for the old Vicarage and, on a whim, went and asked directions in an estate agent's. They told us where it had been and that the site was now being cleared for a housing estate. An old Vicarage was still there, all boarded up. But Ralphy had not been to school there, it was not nearly old enough.

'Oh well,' I said, 'let's go back to the main street and take some photographs. It hasn't changed very much, they'll do for the book, or for *My Dear Aunty* come to that.'

For some reason Marion felt she had to go back to the church. I let her. I don't like churches at best, I was forced to spend too much of my time in them as a child, and this was a particularly unattractive one - square and stolid, built of cold grey stone, with overpowering modern kneelers in unsubtle colours and banners with 'Jesus Saves' emblazoned in citrus yellow on a royal blue ground.

As Marion went into the church a lady in a blazer approached her. 'I felt this tingling sensation,' she told me later, 'not the awful drained feeling I get.'

I knew what she meant. Just before we met Colin and Joyce; at Keele when we found the cookery book; in fact, whenever we were about to make one of our more improbable discoveries, Marion would become lethargic and withdrawn, not quite with me. It was worrying sometimes. I didn't react in the same way but I had noticed that after our Staffordshire excursions, particularly the very eventful early ones, I was totally exhausted - not just ordinarily tired, as I would be after a strenuous holiday or a hard week at work - but completely, completely drained. Sometimes the feeling lasted for several days.

'Well,' whispered Susanna, 'no-one said this was going to be easy.'

Marion had arrived in the church a few minutes before the Mother's Union was due to meet. There would be a number of elderly members there, said the lady in the blazer, she could ask them about the old Vicarage. She did. One remembered it being burnt down in about 1920 when she was a child

'I remembers the flames in the night sky,' she said in her soft Norfolk accent.

That tallied. The house we had seen dated from the 1920s and had presumably replaced the one that burned down.

Then someone else mentioned a book. A book had been written about the history of Debenham, ages ago - but the local paper shop might still have a copy. They did. It was their last one.

Of course it contained a picture of the old Vicarage, pictures of Ralphy's teacher, Mr Cornish and his family and descriptions of his school!

But Susanna was **not** with us when we went to Preston.

'You're not going to like this,' I said one evening on the phone to Marion.

I had been at the National Record Archive in London that day, in connection with my PhD research, and, playing idly with their computer system, had keyed in the name 'Sneyd'. The deadline for *Thirty Pieces of Silver*, our book about the Reverend John, Susanna's father, was approaching and I had found another cache of records.

'The bad news is they are in Preston.'

'Not the dreaded Emily Jane diaries....?'

I laughed. 'No, it seems to be stuff from Tom's family, the ones in Devonshire. His daughter Emma, Susanna's cousin, married a Captain Gale. His home was Bardsea Hall in Lancashire, its that family. One of the sons, Richmond, was at Mr Cornish's with Ralphy, if you remember. There's probably nothing important. But I think we ought to see it just in case.'

Preston in January is not inviting. In fact Preston at any time of the year is probably not very inviting, but we made plans to go anyway. I had the name of the owner of the Sneyd material - it was only on loan to the Lancashire Record Office - and I rang Humphrey Scott-Moncrieff at Basford to see whether 'Mr H. Townley' meant anything to him.

'Yes,' he said 'that's my Uncle Humphrey, my mother's cousin. Lives in the Lake District.'

'Might he have anything else,' I asked, 'portraits, photos...?'

'Quite probably. I'll ring him if you like. I haven't spoken to him for ages. He's a nice old boy, bit of a Colonel Blimp, but I like him.'

A few days later I heard from Humphrey Scott-Moncrieff again. He had spoken to Mr Townley. They'd started off at cross purposes; a 'This is Humphrey,' 'No I'm Humphrey,' 'Humphrey who?' sort of conversation, but had eventually identified which Humphrey they each were and agreed that there were not many of them about. I sighed. If the old gentleman had problems identifying his own nephew it looked like we were in for a difficult visit!

'Not at all,' said our Humphrey breezily, 'it was all my fault. He'll be fine with you. I've told him you're not in the least like those other researchers; they bored the pants off him and Esther!'

It didn't sound promising. But as the Townleys had been led to believe that we were likeable and not in the least boring they had agreed to see us. Marion took over the arrangements; I was busy at work.

She rang Mr Townley. Yes, he had all sorts of things that were not in the Record Office; of course we could see them; we should come for lunch and did we like boiled eggs? Over the next few days boiled eggs featured large in Marion and Mr Townley's conversations - 'soft or hard?', 'three minutes or four?' 'bread soldiers or toast soldiers?' But somewhere along the line they managed to arrange a date and time. Marion had directions to find his house. Well it was a pretty part of the world in which to get lost, I thought....!

We spent a couple of days in Stoke en route during which we had a difficult session with Bruce's assistant Chris and her new computer, tea and sticky chocolate cake in Greystones and a bizarre birthday evening with Barbie in Stoke.

Barbie was fifty, though she certainly didn't look it. She was displeased with Ken - he had failed to mark her birthday with anything more original than a card. But that evening she was putting on a good face - streams of visitors passed through the tiny colourful house, bringing greetings, cards, presents and wine and tripping over Jack, her small grandson, who was with her for the evening. Thai retreated to my bedroom - several of the visitors had dogs. Many of them were bikers.

By now Barbie had acquired her own bike. A 'Virago' she told us happily - pleased with the name - and she was learning to ride it. She and Ken had joined a motorcycling club and their joint social life seemed to consist solely of rallies. Barbie would complain of stiff joints and an aching back afterwards but she did not let that deter her. We thought she was mad. She was determined that her fifty-first year would see her a motorcycling granny with a degree. Her test was booked and the degree in library studies that she had been working on throughout our project was almost complete.

We seldom saw her; a degree by distance learning combined with a more-than-full-time job and a healthy social life meant she was seldom home when we were. Ken worked long hours, trying to keep his ailing business on its feet. We were out much of the time, but most days we could have had the house to ourselves from morning to night. Poor Thai was clearly lonely, his Siamese ancestry had programmed him to need a great deal of attention from the people in his life and he wasn't getting it!

The next day we set out for Preston. It was not a difficult journey - at least not until we got there. We had a map showing the Record Office; it was in the town centre, near the station and the Town Hall. Unfortunately the layout and numbering of the roads on the map bore no relationship to the roads we were driving on. There were no signs at all to the town centre - the only signs to anything were to out-of-town leisure complexes. Indeed, there seemed to be no possibility of turning right off the ring road.

Round and round we drove, numbering our circuits by the number of times we passed Do-it-All, a hideous building with a squat pyramid entrance made of bilious green metal and dirty green glass. Time was running out; it was nearly mid-day and we still weren't there. Marion completed the laps ever faster. At last we spotted a well-concealed sign for the railway station - discreet to the point of invisibility. We drove into the car park.

'Let's walk from here,' said Marion, seeing that the road we probably needed was yet another one-way street.

Of all the Record Offices we had visited - and between us that was a great many - for sheer ugliness and user-unfriendliness Preston was unbeatable. It must have been built in the 1960s and was a prime example of the decade's architecture - drab, rectangular concrete blocks. Thirty years of industrial pollution had only enhanced its lack of charm. It was built on stilts so the reading rooms were reached by steep, narrow staircases and they were protected by uncomfortably small electronic turnstiles. The concrete was damp and stained. 'Practical too,' I observed, 'keeps the documents nice and moist!'

The space beneath the building was used for ......nothing at all. The car park, to which Marion moved the car when we had ordered our documents, was surrounded by a high barbed-wire fence. 'Colditz,' she said, as we sat eating yet another carbohydrate-rich picnic; naturally no documents could be produced for us over lunch time. We reverted to our 'Alternative Britain' game - this place was made for it.

The documents, when they arrived, were announced on an electronic board which flashed up seat numbers like a station departures board. It was probably efficient but it made the place seem very impersonal. The papers we had ordered were quite interesting, especially a précis John Sneyd had made of his father's pre-1792 diaries for one of his nephews. Those early diaries no longer survived. The nephew, Tom, had kept his own diaries, too, mostly accounts of big-game shooting. I found some useful bits to add to the family tree but there was nothing that greatly altered what we had already written. Our late arrival had not mattered but Marion was still rattled. She'd been unwell ever since we left home which did not sweeten her temper.

We set off to find the Travel Lodge where we had booked a room. We made several more circuits past Do-it-All before finding what we thought might be the right road. The A50 out of Preston was not a route that appealed to the local highway engineers and there were no signs to it! Marion was now incandescent with fury and lack of tea; there was no way we could have finished our work **and** broken for tea so I had put my foot down. Now I regretted it. At last we spotted the Lodge and drew into the car park. A bright young receptionist dressed like an exceptionally patriotic air hostess checked our reservation. It was the wrong Travel Lodge!

'Do you have a twin-bedded room for the night?' asked Marion. They had, we took it and got them to cancel our other reservation. Enough was enough - and besides, this one was cheaper.

Tea, several glasses of wine and some rather good cheese and salad later, we were both happier and more relaxed. We chatted, worked, and slept soundly.

Next morning we dressed carefully.

'Dotty eccentricity is the order of the day,' said Marion, lending me garments that she thought more suitable than the ones I had brought with me. 'Nothing boring, remember what the Townleys said about that other couple doing Sneyd genealogy. Flowing black with beads, I think.' I did wonder how appropriate this would be for a Cumbrian farmhouse on a wet day, but thought it wiser to say nothing. Sometimes Marion brooks no argument.

And it was wet. The beautiful views over the estuary at Grange-over-Sands that I had promised Marion - I knew the area fairly well - were invisible beneath a blanket of dripping fog. On the road up to Cartmel we could see only a few yards of hillside and the occasional soggy sheep. Fortunately we didn't get lost.

The Townleys greeted us warmly. Humphrey was definitely Averil's cousin; no sooner were we seated in his chintzy living room than he pressed glasses of gin on us. He was interested in what we were doing but vetting us carefully. I told him I had worked in a museum and he gave me pieces of porcelain and Staffordshire figures to identify. He had been an antique dealer - was I really what I claimed to be? Fortunately I was.

We gave him a copy of the short book we had written for the Oxford Record Office about the misdeeds of Susanna's ghastly brother Gustavus. The story was new to him and he chortled appreciatively. He had sorted out a box of pictures and documents for us and, now we had passed his scrutiny, was happy to leave us in his study with them.

After a while we were summoned to lunch. Not boiled eggs, but rich pork casserole, blackberry and apple pie, lots of cheeses. Esther Townley was another wonderful cook.

Susanna smiled happily at our appreciation of the meal.

'You know,' I said to Marion later, 'if people called on me out of the blue like this, I'd give them coffee and biscuits, probably, but not a meal like that.'

She nodded. 'And did you notice how time stretched again! Just think how much we got done, and there was still time to chat and have a civilised lunch.'

In Humphrey's box were many more photographs - Susanna, Ralphy aged eight, John Sneyd and Mary. How quickly Mary's good looks had faded, we thought, living with John Sneyd had taken its toll. And then, best of all, a photo of a portrait of Susanna's mother Penelope, a confident mature woman with dark ringlets and a fashionable green dress. And just as exciting, there was a photo of Freddy's portrait, painted when he was a schoolboy at Marlborough, a bovine young man in a top hat and tail coat.

There were more diaries of Tom's tiger shooting exploits, and, at the bottom of the box, a very familiar cloth covered diary. Marion recognised the handwriting instantly - it was John Sneyd's 1865 diary - and there was much information in it that we needed for the book; a whole new chapter, probably. We put the things that interested us to one side, wondering what to do about them.

Humphrey Townley wandered into the study and looked at the little pile of photos and papers.

'Those the ones that interest you?' he asked. 'Better take them and get them copied then, no hurry, I don't need them at the moment, send them back when you've finished.'

It was happening again. Why were people so willing to trust us? Thank you Susanna.

Chapter 14

# Ghastly Gustavus

'OK, back to Ralphy and Susanna at Basford - what happened next?'

'Well, at Easter 1881, when he was nineteen, Ralph left Mr Cornish's and came home to live.'

'Susanna must have been delighted.'

'Well, I'm not so sure. First of all they'd planned to have him home in the summer of 1880 but then he went off travelling with one of the Cornish boys in Belgium.'

'Paid for by Susanna?'

'I imagine so. He seems to have missed part of the autumn term by being abroad, came home for Christmas and went back to Debenham for a term. But he still had no job and no income; *'...when I live at home I shall go in hard for collecting things,'* he wrote in one of his last letters home. And that is just what he did.'

Basford Hall was a joyless place for a teenage boy. Susanna was overworked, struggling to maintain a large damp house with only two servants and to hold her quarrelsome family together. She was forty-seven. Her chief interests were Ralph, her church, her garden and her needlework. John William was fifty six, deaf, and troubled with a serious throat complaint that made talking difficult; he had no point of contact with his only son. Though his series of legal battles with Dryden had ended in June 1881 with a detailed legal agreement that sorted out the ownership of every last fence post and blade of grass, a true reconciliation between the brothers seemed unlikely. John William had become increasingly withdrawn and bitter.

Marion made a careful analysis of their social activities from 1863, that heady first year together in Armitage when Susanna and John William had ninety-seven social engagements together, to 1881, up at Basford Hall, when they only went out together five times. Age, illness and family discord had taken their toll. Though they lived in the same house, cared about each other and supported each other, Susanna and John William lived very different lives. Susanna visited the poor and spent the rest of her free time with her sister Emily or one of a small handful of old and trusted women friends. John William's only social outings were to shoot with Sir John Crewe, Captain Phillips or Captain Colvile. The couple were becoming more and more isolated.

Up at Basford Hall, as the 1870s became the 1880s, all the doings of the great world beyond Cheddleton - the first Boer War, the death of Gordon at Khartoum, the murders of Jack the Ripper in the East End - were far away and irrelevant, stories in newspapers which were as remote from reality as any novel. What mattered was the family.

One member of that family was causing Susanna enormous problems - and for once it wasn't Ralph. Her youngest brother, Gustavus, had been ordained in 1868. In January 1879 he became rector of Chastleton. Chastleton is a tiny, pretty village up on top of a hill in Oxfordshire, dominated by Chastleton House, which, by 1879 was home to Miss Mary Whitmore Jones and her nephew.

Chastleton was a good living - worth over £500 (£25,000) a year, but Gustavus was a foolish young man and he had not been brought up to live economically. For years he had been borrowing money from Susanna, mostly £10 or £20 at a time. In December 1876 he borrowed £70, in November 1877 he borrowed another £200. By the end of 1878 his total debt to her, including interest, was £459-13s-10d (£22,000). Susanna was beginning to get worried as his requests escalated. In February 1879 she wrote: *'I do not think it would be right of me to lend you £300 more without very good security so I must oblige you… to insure your life for £800 letting me have the policy and also letting me know yearly that you are paying the required sums to keep it up.'*

He agreed and on February 6th she lent him £150, on April 12th he had another £50 followed by £100 on April 15th and a further £100 on October 6th. Susanna did not record all the loans in her diary. It was not a private diary and perhaps she did not want others to know quite how much she had let him have.

Unbeknownst to Susanna, Gustavus's debts were much greater than the £860 he now owed her. Presents of birds' eggs and coins for Ralph and grovelling letters of thanks lulled her suspicions. And in 1878 in an attempt to pay off some of what he owed her, Gustavus gave Susanna one of his *'large dogs'*. He bred rough haired St Bernards and several of his dogs appear in the Kennel Club stud books. They were quite valuable. Susanna described their new pet in a letter to Ralphy:

*June 11th Your Uncle Gustavus brought the St Bernard last Thursday her name is Linda de Chamonie she is a very large and also very fat, she is brown and white, & has a darker brown head. The cottagers all turned out to look at her, the sheep stampede across the field when they see her & no dog dare to offer to fight her. She does not condescend to notice them, she cannot get through our small stiles, she likes to walk out with us, she is fond of water & perfectly good tempered. She ought not to be so fat as she is but she seems always hungry.'*

She was then four years old. A year later greedy Linda ate some poisoned bait and died.

'And Susanna had her made into a rug!'

'No!'

'Yes, look ....'

We hooted over the account books. 'It cost six shillings to tan the skin - what on earth do you suppose the tanner thought?'

'Oh look at this bit: Extra to do it well... 1s!'

'And to making up poor Linda's skin cost £1-13s (£76) - that sounds expensive.'

'And it took eight yards of carpet to line it. She was huge!'

'Just fancy having your pet made into a rug. It's macabre.'

'But typically Victorian. Think of all those tableaux taxidermists used to make; the kittens' tea party, squirrels boxing - we had umpteen of them at the museum. And I suppose its no worse than having the hair of your dear departed woven into a bracelet. Strange people the Victorians!'

'How do you suppose the new puppy reacted to its hearth rug ancestor?'

Gustavus had replaced Linda de Chamonix with an eight week old puppy, also named Linda.

'I doubt if it noticed; it probably wasn't allowed indoors anyway.'

In October 1879 Susanna visited Gustavus in Chastleton.

'It was a delightful village,' she reminisced, 'and such pretty country. Chastleton Rectory is a fine old house of honey-coloured Cotswold stone, situated at the bottom of the hill below the village. It has extensive grounds with a private lake and Gustavus had bought another piece of land next to the Rectory which he proposed to farm to increase his income. He assured me that the success he was having showing his dogs paid for the servant he employed to look after them. I was so pleased to see him happy. Now he had a proper income rather than the meagre curate's stipend on which he had lived for the previous eleven years he said he would be able to repay his debts to me with interest. It would just take a few more months for him to get on his feet. I quite understood.

We went for long walks, saw the Danish fortifications on Addlestrop Hill and visited Miss Whitmore Jones at Chastleton House. Chastleton House was built by Sir Robert Catesby who was one of Guy Fawkes's conspirators. It was dark and forbidding but very grand. Miss Whitmore was charmed by Gustavus; well, he was a gentleman; handsome, young, courteous and well-educated; and he always had a way with ladies. I could not but feel warmly toward someone who was so obviously fond of my brother.'

Susanna would have been less aware of the feelings of Gustavus's other parishioners. They, it seems, were much less enthusiastic about the dapper young clergyman with his long nose, his habit of quoting Greek tags, his peculiar big dogs and the pretentious way he always carried a furled umbrella even on the driest of days. Susanna went home happy, but Gustavus was in fact getting himself into serious trouble.

'It was another eighteen months before I became aware of the full extent of his debts. Early in 1881 he asked to borrow £1000. Well, I had to consult Mr Joseph Challinor. On March 3rd he sent me a detailed letter of explanation. It contained dreadful news:

*I ought not to conceal from you the fact that since the death of your father your brother has not only spent or lost one half of his legacy of £4000 (£200,000) but has also spent or lost the money he now owes you and the above sum of £1081. If you do not find him the £1000 he wants I think it not unlikely that the money lenders will take steps to sequestrate his living.....*

While a curate in Nottinghamshire, Gustavus had opened a stone quarry to provide work for poor men. In the fine tradition of Sneyd business ventures it failed, leaving him in debt. He had also stood surety for loans to two 'friends' who had defaulted. Foolishly he had tried to pay off all these debts with money borrowed at an exorbitant rate from Mr

Venables and Mr Rayler, money lenders. To make matters worse, on his arrival in Chastleton, Gustavus had taken out a £2000 (£100,000) mortgage on the parcel of land adjacent to the Rectory. He had used his advowson on Chastleton as security without telling the vendor, Mrs Nutting, his predecessor's widow, that it was already mortgaged up to the hilt.

'What's an advowson?' asked Marion.

'It's the right to appoint to a living; I suppose there must have been a formal document of some sort.' I only knew because I had looked it up.

'Who issued them?'

I didn't know.

'Well, what use was it?'

'Well, if you owned the advowson on a living you could appoint a relative, your son, say, or you could use it to make sure that your church always had a vicar who was high - or low - church, or voted Liberal or whatever. Old Mrs Debank had four, Draycott, Handsworth, Harworth and Norbury, total value in her will, £15,952-5s (£782,000). Actually, you know, Ralphy was left the advowson of Dalbury by his Grandfather Cotton. Of course, he didn't have a degree so he could never have been a clergyman; there was quite a bit of correspondence about it as his Aunt Fanny Stewart thought it was hers and left it to her stepson. That suggests there wasn't any sort of documentation, doesn't it? But he must have got it back. There was some correspondence in the 1930s to the effect that the patronage of the living of Dalbury - they'd stopped using the term advowson by then - was pretty well worthless. Nonetheless, Colin says Ralph De Tunstall left it to his youngest son, Billy. Anyway, Gustavus bought the advowson to Chastleton so he could have the living himself when old Mr Nutting died.'

'So how could he use it as security?'

'Well, they were expensive - it cost Gustavus £5,500 (£270,000)!'

'Wow!'

'So I suppose it was a bit like putting anything else up as security - it had a fixed value and the vendor could foreclose on it if you didn't pay what you owed. Mrs Nutting just made the mistake of trusting Gustavus because he was a clergyman, or her solicitor did, so no-one checked it out.'

Against her own inclination and against John William's advice, Susanna paid the £1000. Much of her money was invested in railway shares and she had to sell some of these to raise the money - it distressed her deeply to part with capital assets that she was saving to leave to Ralph. But there was worse to come. A matter of weeks after she had received this devastating account of her youngest brother's financial incompetence, Susanna had an even greater shock, though it took us some time to unravel what it was.

'What does she actually say?' asked Marion.

'Well, she's very discreet but there's all this correspondence with Miss Whitmore Jones.'

'Of Chastleton House?'

'Yes.'

'What's so odd about that? They knew each other didn't they?'

'Well, Susanna visited her several times when she was staying with Gustavus and wrote to her - a thank you letter I suppose - when she got home, but apart from that I don't think they had any contact. Then there were all these urgent letters:'

*1881 May 3rd Ralph  took Miss Whitmore Jones' letter to Emily, she came here to tea. Linda had a powder.*

'Linda?'

'The dog.'

*4th   Wrote to Miss Whitmore Jones.*

*5th   Emily dined here, she wrote to Miss Whitmore Jones....*

*6th  Ralph took a letter from Miss Whitmore Jones to Emily & Elizabeth* [the maid] *had to follow him with a telegram about poor Gustavus...*

*7th  Emily went to Chastleton.*

On the 10th, 13th and 17th more letters winged their way to Miss Whitmore Jones. On the 21st Mr Joseph Challinor travelled from Leek to Chastleton and on the 23rd he called at Basford Hall to report on his visit. Susanna wrote to him several times in June and he called four times *'on Gustavus' business'*. We were intrigued. Then, out of the blue, there was the diary entry *'I wrote to the Bishop of Oxford'*.

'I think I'll write to the present rector,' I told Marion.

'Why? What will you say?'

'Well, if there really was a scandal about one of his predecessors he may know about it,' I said, rather lamely, 'and I could also ask him if there's anyone in the area who has studied the history of the village. Come on, think of all the village historians we know. OK it's a long, long shot.....' I went on, seeing her face, '...but you never know!'

Within a week I had a reply from the local vicar - Chastleton no longer has its own rector - telling me that he had passed my letter on to a Mr Freer whose family had lived in the village for many years and who knew a great deal about local history.

By the next post I had a long letter from Mr Freer himself, page after page covered in large, sprawling handwriting. The son of the current owner of the Rectory - it had become a private dwelling many years previously - was a history student and had turned up some references to Gustavus Sneyd in Oxford Record Office. There had been a Consistory Court hearing, and Herbert Freer, our Mr Freer's grandfather, had appeared as a witness for Gustavus - he didn't know the details.

'See?' I said smugly. Susanna **wants** us to know what happened! Now, when can we go to Oxford?'

A few weeks later on a hot, sticky summer's day we braved Oxford's tourists and the one way system. Marion was still working on John Sneyd's diaries and had found a reference to an undergraduate diary that overlapped with his. It was in the Bodleian and she had made an appointment to see it. We had also arranged to meet the archivist at Brasenose College where John Sneyd had studied to see what information she could turn up for us about his time there. With our limited resources we felt we had to make the most of every excursion.

The Brasenose visit was interesting but not particularly productive. Marion went off to look at her diary and I went to the Record Office; we arranged to meet in a nearby pub for lunch. Sitting at uncomfortable wooden picnic tables on the pavement, blinded by the sun, jostled by passers-by and eating indifferent salads, we exchanged news of our morning's work.

'Mine was not much use,' said Marion, 'just a list of books and lectures - nothing to add to what the Rev J had to say. Waste of time really. And it was so hot and stuffy in there!' She sipped her drink. I watched her, realising that she had inveigled yet another bartender into providing her with orange juice and brown ale - a concoction of her own invention which she claims to enjoy. 'Not much different to lager and lime, really,' she assured me cheerfully.

I have tasted it and have to admit that it is not quite as revolting as it sounds.

'How about you?'

I grinned happily, sipping my lager, 'Just **wait** for this.....' I regaled her with my discoveries - which had been much simplified by finding a press cutting describing Gustavus's court hearing. But I hadn't finished; I needed her help that afternoon as there were two whole boxfuls of documents to work through - but I had the gist. The students at the next table stopped discussing their love lives and eavesdropped blatantly.

'Poor Gustavus' had indeed got himself into a scrape. Sometime in the autumn of 1879, shortly after Susanna's visit, he had seen, and fallen head over heels in 'lust', with Rose Elizabeth Marnes, then under-housemaid at Kitebrook, one of the local farms. Gustavus was thirty five, Rose Elizabeth was just fifteen. He had sent her letters which began *'My darling Rose'* and ended *'your ever loving Alfred'* - his full name was Gustavus Alfred - and which asked her to meet him in secluded places after dark. The inevitable had happened, and in March 1881, Rose Elizabeth had given birth to a daughter and named Gustavus as the father.

He had compounded his problems by first offering her money and then going back on his word, and her family had taken out an affiliation - a bastardy - order against him. He had staged a mugging of himself, and a burglary at the Rectory, both of which he tried to blame on the girl's family to discredit them. His attempts were so clumsy that even the local policemen did not believe his stories; one even accused him of *'painting his bruises'*!

In the afternoon we went back to the Record Office, a small, cramped space in the basement of County Hall. The staff provided us with white gloves to prevent our sweaty fingers contaminating the precious papers - a refinement we had not come across before. The boxes were crammed with papers relating to Gustavus, but they were in no particular order and each sortie to the counter produced the next three documents, regardless of what they were.

I had expected Marion to be irritated by the system; she is usually much more impatient than I am; but this particular afternoon she decided charm was the order of the day. She chatted to the young assistants and told them the story of Gustavus and the housemaid; soon they were as interested as we were, and they began to let us sort the documents at the counter so that we were reading the episodes in the sequence in which they happened.

Clearly our project was becoming the talk of the staffroom. As each new shift of assistants came back from their break or passed our desk they asked for a progress report, giggling delightedly at each new revelation of Gustavus's sharp practice or sheer idiocy.

'Well, it makes a nice change for them from people researching their family trees,' we decided, 'and everyone enjoys a juicy scandal.' And scandals did not come much juicier than Gustavus's.

We discovered that the Consistory Court did not meet until 1883 - two years after Rose Elizabeth's child was born. The Bishop of Oxford had at first turned a blind eye to the scandal surrounding the rector of Chastleton, but in April 1882 the parishioners had petitioned him to investigate *'the scandal under which this parish has for some time been lying'* and he could not ignore a direct request. The unedifying story was published in *The Times* on July 31st 1882 for all to read.

Gustavus was found not guilty - the evidence was old and inconclusive and his accusers were ordinary villagers while he was a gentleman - but he was reprimanded for his unseemly behaviour and the police officer giving evidence **for** him said that Gustavus had *'committed follies without end'* and condemned his love for Rose Elizabeth as *'unnatural and foolish'*. It was not an honourable victory.

'I was mortified,' Susanna blushed with remembered shame. 'How could he? Such a common girl!'

All the papers survive; sordid little letters from Gustavus to Rose Elizabeth; threatening letters from her father. The transcript of sixteen year old Rose Elizabeth's testimony, given before a jury of forebidding black-gowned clergymen and lawyers, was sickening to read:

Q: How and where did intercourse take place?

A: Standing with her back to the old oak tree in the meadow down by the brook.

Q: Did no-one notice mud and leaves clinging to her clothes?

A: There were no mud and leaves, she did not lie down.

Q: Did her mother not comment on her soiled underclothes?

A: No, Rose Elizabeth did her own washing.

Q: Did she not know she was pregnant when her periods ceased?
A: No she did not know about such things.

There were pages and pages of testimony and she did not falter. Either she was an exceptionally clever liar or she was telling the truth.

By contrast, Gustavus's account of the 'mugging', when Rose Elizabeth's letters to him were supposedly stolen, beggars belief. The men had a pistol and a dark lantern, unlikely accoutrements for countrymen who were not professional criminals. One of them looked very like Charlie Marnes, Rose Elizabeth's younger brother, another one reminded Gustavus of *'my brother Frederick, now dead'* - who, presumably, he could easily have described if pressed. Gustavus's watch and chain, which he claimed they also stole, were found in a hedge, only the letters disappeared; his horse made its own way back to its stable and miraculously unhitched itself from the trap; Gustavus was unconscious for some time but then just got up and walked home!

He did confess to meeting Rose Elizabeth, kissing her and being attracted to her, all very unsuitable for a man in his position, but would not admit that he had seduced her or promised to marry her. Only Miss Whitmore Jones believed him! The Marnes family withdrew the bastardy order because Joseph Challinor, acting for Susanna, paid them off. It cost Susanna £128 (£6,400), and interestingly enough, she never bothered to contact Gustavus to hear his side of the story. It was a sordid, depressing episode, made worse for Susanna by the fact that she was ill and bedridden at the time.

Susanna had saved Gustavus from public disgrace, at least temporarily. But he was not in the least grateful. His solicitor reported:

*The paying of the money led to a disagreement between Mr Sneyd and his family - the payment impugned his virtue and was part of the reason the Bishop became interested in the case.*

Certainly Susanna had brought the affair to the Bishop's notice.

'Yes, I wrote to him,' she thought. 'I told the Bishop he was innocent, of course, but really I was not so sure. Gustavus always had an eye for a pretty face. I remember how he flirted with Miss Macallister when the Macallisters were staying at Ashcombe in the summer of of 1864. Gustavus was home from university - he would have been twenty then. Papa was so cross with him, summoned him to account for himself.

But it was his debts that worried me most. I did not at all know what to do. He already owed me a great deal of money. Miss Whitmore Jones had written urging me to pay the girl's family not to serve the bastardy order; she believed Gustavus to be wronged. She was an admirable woman, of course, but perhaps a little, how shall I put it - innocent? She did not know Gustavus as I did. John William said I should save my money; Gustavus should lie on the bed he had made for himself. But Emily wished me to pay, to save the family honour - that always mattered to her - and to save Gustavus. And I wished to help him, I really did, but I feared the expense.'

The affair split Chastleton in two, the Whitmore Jones faction supporting the rector and most other people finding him guilty. Knowing he was unlikely to be offered as lucrative a living as Chastleton, or any living at all, given his record, Gustavus decided to sit it out and even fantasised about bringing an action against the Marnes family for defamation.

Then, as now, it was virtually impossible for the church to evict a clergyman who was prepared to defy his Bishop. To secure his position with Miss Whitmore Jones, Gustavus married her niece 'Mimi', Christabel Harris, a lady who seems to have been just as unpleasant as he was. It was against this background that the Parish Council approached their Bishop.

The result was unsatisfactory to them and within weeks the Bishop, too, must have regretted his leniency. The business of the much-mortgaged advowson was about to reach the courts and the Bishop and his staff were being bombarded with angry and distressed letters from old Mrs Nutting.

'What happened then?' I asked, 'Susanna doesn't explain.'

Marion had dealt with that part of the Oxford Record Office material. I had concentrated on the Consistory Court hearing.

'The living was sequestrated,' she answered - 'that's the ecclesiastical equivalent of the receivers taking over a business - and Chastleton endured a year of farce at the hands of incompetent sequestrators and cunning lawyers. None of the local farmers knew where they should send their tithes, for example, and the sequestrators took the Poor Rate so the Poor Law officials had no funds to distribute. That must have caused a lot of hardship in the village when you think about it. Then there were all the conflicting notices that kept appearing on the church door telling people who was responsible for what. And Gustavus disappeared to Devonshire for the duration. What a hero!'

I remembered the church door. We had visited Chastleton to see for ourselves the scene of Gustavus's disgrace. The door is protected by a porch and is still used for parish notices. It is pitted with hundreds of tiny holes made by generations of drawing pins.

Despite being incumbent of Chastleton for over forty years there is no trace of the Reverend Gustavus Alfred Sneyd in the little church that lies in the shadow of Chastleton House; no memorial, no gravestone. His Rectory still stands, now owned by a family from South Africa; a beautiful house, much restored and altered, secluded in acres of grounds at the foot of the hill on which the village stands.

'Susanna was helping us again, wasn't she?' said Marion dreamily, 'how many people do you know who would have done that amount of research into the history of their home?' Not only had the history student son of the family read up on Gustavus in the Record Office but his father had compiled a file - well an unpublished book, really - on the history of his home. He had talked to old people in the village, long dead by the time we arrived on the scene, who remembered Gustavus. He even had photographs of Gustavus, Mimi and Miss Whitmore Jones sitting on the lawn and photographs of the house as it was in the 19th century.

It was almost unbelievable. Sitting taking tea in the elegant drawing room looking out over the lake, now adorned with Chinese bridges and pagodas, it was easy to see why Gustavus had been so loth to give up his living.

Chastleton had one other sight we needed to see. Gustavus and Rose Elizabeth's affair had been conducted in the fields by the Kite brook. It was a glorious summer's day and the fields around the Rectory were golden with buttercups; through them meandered an insignificant stream, the Kite, and there, could it possibly be the same one - in the middle of a field stood a venerable old oak tree!

'Poor Susanna,' I said, 'the Gustavus affair dragged on and on.'

In December 1883 the Reverend Gustavus Alfred Sneyd was declared bankrupt and his creditors were awarded two shillings in the pound. The hapless Mrs Nutting received just £200 of the £2000 owed to her. Susanna received nothing, yet still she lent more money and she had been persuaded to 'buy' Gustavus's furniture to prevent the sequestrators getting their hands on it. Some of it must have been despatched to Basford, for a sickeningly bright little note survives from Christabel telling Susanna how they had *'re-arranged what was left'*.

Meanwhile Miss Whitmore Jones had handed Chastleton House over to her nephew. He had led the anti-Gustavus faction and she probably found it extremely uncomfortable to continue to share a house with him. She now moved in with Gustavus and Mimi and between them the two women exercised some control over the wayward Reverend Sneyd. They did not, however, ensure that he kept up the payments on his life insurance, Susanna's security for the first £800 of his debt to her, and it was some months before she discovered that the policy was now worthless. Her diary suggests that she then made the annual payments herself. As late as 1887 her diaries include references to visits to Mr Joseph Challinor about 'Gustavus' business'.

'He really was a little swine,' said Marion. 'Do you remember that picture of him we found in Averil's album?'

Usually young men sitting to have their portrait taken looked serious and responsible. But not Gustavus. He sat astride a chair, arms round its back, smirking boldly at the camera.

'Con-man in the making.'

'Wasn't he just? And there was more. Remember the falsified Sneyd pedigree. That was down to Gustavus. And Averil's stories of how he seduced a servant in the next room as Christabel lay dying?'

'And don't forget how he attempted to molest Averil. Remember how she dealt with it? 'I think I hear my mother calling' she said as Great Uncle Gustavus unbuttoned his trousers. She was eight! Talk about presence of mind!'

Gustavus, we agreed, had been a deeply unpleasant man.

Chapter 15

# 'When I am doing all that I can for Ralph's good'

In the winter of 1879-80, even before she knew about Gustavus's misdemeanours, Susanna became very unwell.

*1879 November 15th I was poorly all week.*
*30th Frosty. I stayed at home having side ache.*
*December 6th Fine. Dr Somerville came to see me for rheumatic gout. One of the pipes burst. I had a mustard plaster.*

All through January and February Susanna was ill. Dr Somerville called regularly. She had neuralgia, rheumatism, aches and pains and was generally weak and sick. Dr Somerville suspected heart trouble. He prescribed iron and quinine but there was no improvement. He brought in Dr Arlidge of the North Staffordshire Infirmary for a second opinion - to no avail. He suggested another a tonic; she was to drink port each day, an expense which troubled frugal Susanna.

*1880 March 1st I began my port wine 42s (£106) a dozen.*
*13th 2nd bottle of wine....*

Family and friends visited, but she did not get much better.

*23rd I came down to breakfast for the first time for 9 weeks*
*25th As I had rheumatism I stayed in bed for breakfast.*
*28th Easter Sunday. Mr Boucher sent his carriage to take John Wm and me to the 8.30 sacrament.*

A note survives from this period which gives us some idea of the warmth that existed between John William and Susanna. She was again ill in bed:

*My dearest kind treasure, Dr Somerville has forbidden me to be in your room on account of my bad throat. I am so very sorry. He says you must keep in bed. He will come again the first thing on Thursday morning. He says you must have rabbit, mutton and chicken broth, sago, tapioca and suchlike pudding, but not beef in any shape. You must be very careful. Bless you my dearest one, do take care & mind you have everything to make you comfortable & you think will do you good.....*

John William may have quarrelled with Dryden and been cantankerous with his son, but clearly he cared deeply for his sister. Indeed, to the modern reader, his note sounds more like that of a lover than a brother.

Throughout the summer of 1880 she continued to be delicate, seldom coming down to breakfast and spending much time sitting out of doors reading. No doubt the scandals surrounding Gustavus took their toll and the discomfort of living in a cold, damp house cannot have helped. And she worried about her other brothers and her nephew. John William had become increasingly paranoid and he had built a den, *'his lookout on Tatton's Bank'*, from which to spy on Dryden who he now referred to as *'that creature'*. Ralphy had at last left school and was himself becoming increasingly selfish and eccentric. Susanna was under constant stress.

'Perhaps being ill was her way of coping,' Marion observed, 'if she was sick no-one could expect her to deal with it all.'

'But she did have to deal with it,' I countered, 'she literally sorted out the Gustavus business from her sick bed; that's why she was writing to Joseph Challinor, not going in to Leek to see him. **Was** it just stress? Could there have been some underlying physical problem?'

'Whatever it was that I suffered from was real,' thought Susanna. 'I was often in great pain. Sometimes I could not even sew.' She glanced at her diary, 'I paid Minnie's daughter, dear Beatrice, to finish my 'Dignity and Impudence' - 3d an hour, we agreed. It was such a beautiful picture, after Landseer's painting, you know, it seemed a shame that I might die without finishing it. At that time even a walk down the hill to the Bath House was too much for me.'

Her 1880 and 1881 diaries record almost continual ill health. The 1882 and 1883 diaries are missing and by 1884 Susanna seemed to be rather better - although she was still coping with the aftermath of Gustavus's bankruptcy, John William and Dryden were still not speaking, Ralphy was becoming a huge worry, and her cousin Henry, son of her father's brother Henry who had been vicar of Wetley Rocks, had abandoned his wife, Marianne, and their daughter. Marianne was all but destitute and was pestering Susanna for money.

'Such a fiery young woman,' thought Susanna, 'Irish, she was a Swete Townsend, from County Cork. Henry did use her badly, of course, coming home from Switzerland and leaving her behind after one of their arguments. In the end he had to leave altogether, she was so bad tempered, he could stand it no longer. She had the eldest girl with her, of course, poor little thing. Marianne made such scenes, even applied to the Board of Guardians for poor relief! Such a dreadful thing for a Sneyd to do! I helped her a little, but I did not altogether believe her tales. She was hysterical, poor thing, but she had parents who could have helped her.'

The stress had not abated in any way but Susanna was better. Why?

We went to see Alun and Angela. If anyone could help us it would be Alun. We compiled a case study for Susanna's two years of illness, with details of what Dr Somerville had tried, and handed it to him.

He studied it carefully. 'Mmm,' he said at last, 'how about a connective tissue disorder?'

'What?'

'Well, it's to do with the immune system breaking down. Usually the body distinguishes between itself and invaders - germs - quite easily. But sometimes it seems to make a mistake and starts to attack itself in all sorts of different ways. So the patient can get a whole string of symptoms - migraine, arthritis, general lassitude' - Alun consulted his text book -'even skin lesions  - her chilblains could have been part of it. It could go on for years but the system sometimes recovered, there were remissions and relapses.'

Angela looked at him over the rims of her glasses. She too was a doctor - and clearly she was not convinced.

'Well, no-one can ever prove you wrong,' she said gently.

'What about lead poisoning?' Marion enquired. She had been reading up on it. 'After all, the pipes in the house were lead, they'd been installed fifty years earlier. And they were eating all that tinned meat and tins were soldered with lead.'

'Possibly,' Alun replied, 'but doctors in this area knew a lot about lead poisoning because it was so prevalent in the pottery industry. They would have recognised it.'

Marion looked unconvinced.

Even if her ill health had a physical basis, anxiety about Ralph must have contributed to Susanna's malaise. Once he left school he could devote as much time as he wished to his collections, arranging, sorting, sticking things in scrapbooks, listing, looking things up, pressing botanical specimens, arranging creatures in spirits - all to his heart's content. Boxes of curiosities arrived from friends and relatives around the globe. His first showcase had been joined by many others and on his return to Basford he was allocated his own sitting room and *'museum'*.

'I think they were in the archway room,' Humphrey told us on one of our visits to Basford, indicating an outside door that led to several rooms over the coach house and the arch that linked it to the main house. They must have been tack rooms and sleeping quarters for stable hands originally, but by the 1880s the Sneyds no longer kept a horse or ran a carriage.

'Of course, towards the end all the outbuildings were stuffed with Ralph's collections - box loads of items from his foreign travels that he never got round to unpacking,' Humphrey went on. 'And my mother remembers him coming round and looking over the house, pointing to things and saying "that belonged to me pore Aunt Susan" or "me pore Aunt Emily". My mother's Granny......'

'That would be Annie Brodie, daughter of Susanna's sister in Edinburgh - right?' I interrupted.

'Yes, she was always keen to get rid of him. Apparently he would talk and talk, never knew when to go.'

We nodded; someone else we had met had told us how his father used to hide whenever he saw Ralph De Tunstall approaching. Ralph could talk for hours, oblivious of the fact that others had work to do; after all he never worked himself.

Visitors coming to see Ralph's museum became a regular feature in the 1880s. They would take tea there and he would talk - probably at great length - about his myriads of specimens. No doubt the housemaids who had extra fires to light and rooms to clean were less than enthusiastic about Ralph's new territory. John William was even less supportive. Gone was the father who had encouraged his little son with gifts of fossils and letters about baby sharks and rare butterflies; the very mention of Ralph's museum could now make him incandescent with rage. On more than one occasion he took away the key to the museum door and refused to give it back.

'It took me days of pleading each time to get him to return it,' thought Susanna. 'Ralph never learnt to manage his father as I could. There was that time John William threatened to get rid of the collections - Ralph was so wilful, he went up to Ipstones and rented a room for a shilling a week. Whatever would people have thought?'

'When he came home from school he had a new, bigger bedroom on the top floor - after all he was almost grown up - but he made very little attempt to help us get it ready. It made me very cross.' She looked at what she had written:

*1880 September 10th Fine. Ralph took a book to Miss Colvile and another to Miss Phillips, he went to the fête at Churnet Grange. Mrs Bloor, Elizabeth and I carried Ralph's things to his new room the bedroom nursery.*

*12th I patched up the paper in Ralph's new room. Ralph helped a little. John Wm went to the look out.*

'I think 'a little' is the operative bit here,' I said to Marion. 'The womenfolk could lug things around for him while he swanned off to annoy the neighbours. Poor Susanna.'

By the 1880s Susanna's own social life was limited; she could see now that her diaries had become a chronicle of Ralph's doings. He was still entirely dependent on his father and her for every penny he spent. This did not in any way curb his activities. In September 1880 he had a holiday in the Isle of Man with Captain Colvile - for which she paid.

'He could be a so charming,' thought Susanna, 'and he was popular with our friends. He spent many nights in Leek with the Wardles, the Challinors or the Crusos when he went to dances or other functions in the town. I understood it but I missed him. And it made John William very cross.'

Basford was isolated and it was a long, dark walk home from Leek of a winter's evening to a cold house to be met by an angry, disapproving John William flanked by Susanna acting the patient martyr. It is not surprising that Ralph chose to spend many evenings away from home. Unfortunately these were often arranged on the spur of the moment, and, in the absence of telephones or a car with which to track down their errant child, John William and Susanna must have had many anxious evenings waiting for Ralph to come home, eventually going to bed hoping that he was safe somewhere.

One January evening in 1889 Susanna records that she sat up until three in the morning waiting for Ralph to come home after a dance in Leek. Sometimes Mrs Blore waited up. Inevitably he occasionally found himself locked out. John William was deaf and would not have heard his son knocking at the door and on at least one occasion *'poor'* Ralph slept in the outbuildings. It seems he was never deemed trustworthy enough to be given a house key.

As time went on Ralph became very friendly with Mr Faulkner, who had come to Ipstones as curate in the spring of 1880, and spent a lot of time with him discussing theology, especially High Church practices and Anglo-Catholicism.

'I worried about him', Susanna remembered. 'He was a very spiritual young man and would become extremely agitated and absent minded after these meetings. I tried to dissuade Mr Faulkner from entering into these long discussions. I remember writing - was it to Mrs Cruso?

*....Ralph has been so that he cannot remember anything, such as posting a letter or knowing what day it is - and on Sunday mornings not having the least idea of getting ready for church. I wrote to tell Mr Faulkner his memory was going & that he must keep him from so much High Church talk - we were told never to send him to a public school because of his weak brain & this church work is very bad for him.....*

But nothing I could say made any difference.'

It is 1884 by the time we catch up with Ralph again and his social life had become even more hectic and worrying for his aunt. Thomas Wardle entertained all sorts of people and in February Oscar Wilde came to Leek to lecture and stayed with the Wardles. Ralph was fascinated by him and for the next year or so went to hear him lecture whenever he could. Though he was actually nearly twenty-one Ralph was behaving in ways we would associate with a difficult teenager, making unsuitable friends, treating the house as a hotel, arguing with his father and aunt and generally being thoroughly selfish. Susanna wrote again to her old friend Mrs Cruso:

*I do value a little sympathy when I am doing all I can for Ralph's good - but now I have more anxiety about him than ever as he is so easily led wrong & my sister and Dryden do so very much harm to him and make John William's and my life so very unhappy, they encourage Ralph in not obeying his father's wishes. One of the things my sister says against us is*

*that we do not feed Ralph well - he has plenty of meat, etc, etc. - we are not
keeping him at home from any wishes of ours, my brother would have gladly
sent him to college or anywhere to learn something...*

'Sounds familiar to me,' I said sourly. My eldest son was at that time
resisting all our attempts to persuade him to train for any sort of proper
career. We disliked many of his friends and the case that had got him
arrested a year previously still had not come to court. We were getting
desperate too.

Susanna's relationship with Emily had obviously become strained.
Emily had spent many months staying with Gustavus. Instead of
applauding her sister's generosity to their problem brother she berated
Susanna for lending him money - thus causing him to incur the *'sin'* of
borrowing. The implication was that Susanna was grudging in her support
of Gustavus, and that she should have given him the money he asked for.
Emily, of course, had no money, so could afford to take this stance.

Feelings between the sisters ran high as this letter shows. It is from
Emily to Susanna, from Chastleton, dated July 11th 1881, though it is not
clear exactly what Susanna has said or done to make Emily so angry:

*Everything that I wrote in my letter to you was true & God knows it;
indeed if it had not been I should not have had these effusions from you - I
never wish to receive a geranium or anything else from anyone unless given
in a friendly spirit - I have known you from a day old & now say if I receive
another letter from you containing even the slightest abuse, I after it will
burn any letter sent by you...*

Now, it would seem, Emily was criticising the way Susanna and John
William were treating Ralph, and she had allied herself with Dryden. And
Ralph was being difficult. He was about to turn twenty-two and his
fascination with the Church of Rome was re-surfacing. Susanna makes
several references to his attending services *'at the R church'*. And in May
Ralph De Tunstall finally achieved the ambition that had caused so much
distress to everyone when he was seventeen. He was away from home,
staying with his aunt Bertha Palliser (née Cotton) and her husband,
Viscount Sherbrooke.

*1884 May 17th John Wm had a letter from Ralph to say he had fixed to
become a R Catholic.*

*21st  I heard from Ralph that he had become a Roman Catholic.*

'I was distraught,' whispered Susanna. 'I suppose I knew he would do it, he spent so much time with the priests at Cheadle - 'taking instruction' he called it. It started as soon as he was twenty one - we could do nothing to prevent it then.'

Having dropped his bombshell Ralph seems to have been understandably loth to come home and face the music. He spent almost three months away staying with various sets of relations including his Uncle Gustavus in Chastleton, Cousin Henry in Nottingham and old Uncle John Holley in Norfolk.

Knowing how much Ralph's conversion had distressed Susanna it seems strange that they all seemed to take his side. All three were Church of England clergymen and Gustavus and Cousin Henry Bamford had good reason to be grateful to Susanna. She had lent Gustavus enormous sums of money; and she had cared for Henry as his mother lay dying, entertained him at Basford and paid for him to go on at least one holiday with Ralph. She had written to them all for support when sixteen year-old Ralph had first expressed an interest in Roman Catholicism and it is unlikely that any of them actually approved of his decision.

Under the circumstances it is difficult to read their behaviour. Were they being disloyal to Susanna? Did they think secretly that she had treated Ralph unreasonably? Or were they simply unable to refuse him when he invited himself to stay?

Within three weeks of his return home, Ralph was off on another expedition, this time to Wales and Ireland.

'He knew Susanna would come round in the end,' said Marion. 'I expect he just wanted to avoid the constant nagging while she got used to the idea.'

'It's not as if she left him alone when he was away,' Marion continued, 'remember the letters.'

Susanna worried about Ralph's behaviour when he was away and bombarded his hosts with embarrassing letters and instructions. It was one thing when he was a young boy, out of school for the weekend at Uncle John's, to remind him to say please and thank you, not to talk too much, not to ask for gifts for his collection and to try not to leave his toothbrush behind; it was quite another when he was a young man in his twenties.

But Ralph **was** forgetful. Returning home from school for the last time he arrived *'without box or keys'*; several times a week at home he would have to retrace his steps to retrieve hats, coats, gloves or scarves that he had left at one or other house he had visited. In December 1885 he excelled himself by taking the St Bernard with him on a walk to Leek and losing her! She was found by the night watchman who charged an exasperated Susanna 7s to get her back.

Ralph's lack of money did not curb his spending and after his prolonged absences Susanna would find herself paying off moneys he had borrowed from his relations and conveniently 'forgotten'. Sometimes there were other complaints - in full spate Ralph was totally oblivious to other people's feelings - and while his relatives were usually tolerant his friends were less so.

Susanna's diary entries suggest how strained relations between them had become in 1884 immediately after his conversion. As ever, she is discreet and non-committal but there are a handful of uncharacteristically snide entries. Almost certainly these mask rows of volcanic proportions.

*1884 September 1st Fine. Ralph went to Leek and promised to pay 1s a week for a Roman Catholic chapel at Leek. He had supper with the young Wardles. Mrs Colvile called. Ralph made such a fuss about his things that I would not speak to him.*
*3rd Ralph would smoke at Mrs Cooper's so I left him....*
*16th Fine. I began to help Ralph with his room but as he was so wilful I left him.*

'It was worse when he involved others,' thought Susanna miserably. 'In 1885 Katie Fraser, Cousin Minnie's daughter, became a Catholic nun - Sister Monica, she called herself. Minnie and I used to have long talks - we could not understand them. Katie had been brought up in a good Church of England home, too - Dr Fraser, her father, was vicar of Alton. I know there's no evidence that Ralphy influenced Katie - but he did influence the servants. Not long after he joined the Roman church he took Mrs Blore to the ceremony for the laying of the foundation stone of the Roman Catholic chapel in Leek. And one summer day in 1888 I met him taking our servant, Annie Lomas, her mother, two of the tenant's wives and one of their daughters to church with him. And after all my efforts to turn my servants and the villagers into good Anglicans!'

We visited the Catholic church in Cheadle which had first aroused Ralphy's interest in Catholicism. St Giles's Roman Catholic church was built by Pugin, under the patronage of the Earl of Shrewsbury, and was completed in 1846.

'Its known as 'Pugin's gem',' said Marion, consulting the guide book as we arrived, 'and isn't it just glorious?'

Plainsong played softly in the background, piped but unobtrusive, as we wandered round the little church enjoying the richness of the painted decoration which covered every surface with geometric patterns in rich red and gold, subtle dark blue and green. Above the luminous alabaster high altar the tree of Jesse east window glowed in the afternoon sun. Even the inner doors were scarlet with huge, dramatic, gilded, lions rampant from the Shrewsbury coat of arms. It was a joyful place, a feast for the senses, colourful, mysterious, uplifting.

'Just look at this,' said Marion, 'and think of how it must have seemed to Ralphy. 'Think how drab his life was at Basford - with all Susanna's scolding and penny-pinching. Think about Ipstones church, or Cheddleton, so much more restrained, austere even - then imagine a service here - the vestments, the incense, the music.'

'He was a romantic,' I agreed, 'think of his fascination with the Knights of the Round Table. That must have begun back in the Trinity Aisle at Mavesyn Ridware when he was a little boy, looking at all those dead crusaders and imagining himself in armour, riding Jennetta into battle, his trusty wooden sword at his side. And Roman Catholicism was the old religion, the religion of the Middle Ages, the faith those knights rode off to defend.'

For the first time we began to understand Ralphy's fascination with Catholicism.

Even the Catholic church in Leek which we later visited was bright and colourful, Italianate rather than Mediaeval, with a pretty, sentimental statue of the Virgin, but still with the same sense that faith was joyful and life affirming rather than a solemn duty to be undertaken on pain of indescribable eternal suffering.

Over the next few years Ralph drove Susanna to distraction. He was socialising with all sorts of families the Sneyds did not know. His choice of friends seems refreshingly egalitarian to us but to his class-conscious father and aunt in the 1880s it was cause for immense concern.

In 1885 Ralph became interested in fortune telling and table tapping. A few years later it would be freemasonry, then spiritualism, then phrenology. Victorian society did not see these pursuits as in any way harmful; to Susanna they were probably infinitely preferable to Roman Catholicism. But when Ralph became a vegetarian it caused her a good deal of heart searching. Victorian society dismissed vegetarians as cranks - and it would make it difficult for people to entertain him. Nonetheless, she dutifully collected recipes for lentil cutlets, stuffed tomatoes, corn oysters and a whole host of other meat-free dishes!

'She should have been grateful that he still ate dairy products and eggs,' I said. My second son was then in his vegan phase.

'Being vegetarian was probably as difficult then as being vegan is now,' suggested Marion gently.

For a while Susanna feared for Ralph's health as he consulted his doctor about all sorts of real and imagined complaints and was prescribed quantities of pills and medicines. She contacted Dr Somerville herself to discuss what she considered to be Ralph's hypochondria - which, given the amount of time she had spent nagging him to take care of his health when he was a schoolboy seems somewhat inconsistent. Undeterred, Ralph consulted specialists elsewhere and became interested in what we would today call alternative medicine. For a time he swore by a mysterious potion called 'No 1'. He despatched bottles to all and sundry and in 1888 received a polite thank you letter from old Mrs Cotton, his grandmother. His grandfather was ill in bed and was most grateful for the medicine - but his doctor had advised him not to take it until he was better!

Ralph joined the Staffordshire Field Naturalists and went on outings with them. In October 1884 he decided to put some of his knowledge to practical use. He had been interested in toadstools since he was a little boy, bringing home puffballs and other edible species for the family table.

*October 2nd   Fine until evening. Ralph went to Belmont & Ashcombe woods for fungi..... in the afternoon Ralph gave his lecture on fungi & sang in the school at Cheddleton, about 12/- were received at the door, tickets were 6d & 2d, there were 13 dishes of cooked fungi & 3 kinds - wholesome, doubtful & poisonous,'* wrote Susanna.

'You mean he actually cooked the poisonous ones?' said Marion incredulously.

'Sounds like it.'

'And people went?'

'Forty or fifty of them. There wasn't a lot to do in Cheddleton of an evening. They got their money's worth - he sang songs to them in the interval.'

'Really?'

'He had quite a good voice by all accounts. He did quite a lot of this sort of thing; maybe he hoped to make a living at it, who knows? Susanna does record one 'rough meeting', meaning...'

'That his audience became bored and youths booed his songs?'

'Probably.'

Susanna's 1886 diary is missing, and by the spring of 1887 Ralph had found a new interest. He was reading Madame Blavatsky's *Isis Unveiled*. Later he visited her in London.

'Who was Madame Blavatsky?' I asked Marion.

We looked her up. Helena Petrovna Blavatsky was the guiding light of a movement known as theosophy or the 'wisdom-religion'. She was Russian born; her marriage had been conveniently brief, just long enough to give her an exotic name, and she had travelled widely, in Egypt certainly, in Tibet possibly, in Europe and America extensively. She was a gifted medium or an accomplished charlatan. Together with Colonel Olcott, an American journalist, she founded the Theosophical Society.

'We need to know more about this,' I told Marion, 'time for a trip to the British Library.'

*Isis Unveiled* proved to be two almost unreadable volumes of pseudo-scientific religious thought linking the tenets of most of the major religions and philosophies and twisting old 'truths' into new positions. The language was dense, there was an impression of scholarship that somehow felt spurious.

'It reminded me of von Danniken,' I told Marion that evening.

'Von who?'

'The chap who produced all sorts of evidence to suggest that spacemen have visited earth at various times in history.'

Madame Blavatsky's writings were impenetrable - and there were an awful lot of them. If nothing else you had to admire the woman's energy, but I had read other things and felt I was beginning to come to terms with what the movement was about.

'I found a pamphlet outlining the Society's rules,' I went on, 'published in 1879 by Colonel Olcott. A lot of them were about grades of membership, the right of individuals to belong to the society without anybody knowing, the duty of members to keep secret the various symbols the society used.'

'But it wasn't a secret society as such?'

'**Isn't;** it's still pretty active - look on the internet. Anyway, there were seven real objectives that emerged; hang on, let me get my notes. Right, these are my words, not his.'

'Why?'

'Because I use fewer of them.'

Marion laughed.

'A. To keep alive the belief that man has a soul.'

'OK so far.'

'Wait! B. To counteract bigotry - specifically including people being sceptical about miracles.'

'Oh.'

'C. To write and collect books for the Society's Library.'

'Which was where?'

'New York, I think. Or Madras. Stop interrupting, we'll never get through them all at this rate. 'D. '

'Sorry.'

'D. To learn about natural history, including the so-called occult sciences and folklore.'

'Mm-mm.'

'Quite! E. To promote feelings of brotherhood between nations. F. To promote the spread of non-sectarian western education. G. To assist individual members in their quest for intellectual, moral and spiritual self improvement.'

'Well, those seem all right.'

'Yes, but that's about as lucid as it gets. There are all sorts of publications that purport to explain theosophy in a few simple paragraphs but when you read them they stop making sense by the third sentence. I thought it was just me, but then I found this wonderful exposé called *Isis*

*Very Much Unveiled* written in the 1890s by Edmund Garrett. He writes a bit like, well *Private Eye* I suppose, with 19th century overtones. Listen to this. "Anything undraped in verbiage is considered nude, even to indecency." I like that. Or, "If there is one thing more than another which is deemed to be bad form in circles Theosophical it is to corner a Theosophist on definite matters of fact"!'

'You did have fun, didn't you?'

'Mmm! Then they were very much into eastern religion. HPB and Olcott spent some time in India. And there's lots of pseudo-eastern jargon - terms like karma, which we know, or akasha - do you want to know what that is?'

'Go on.'

'The subtle spiritual essence in space.'

'What's that?'

'I haven't a clue. Then there was dzynan - divine wisdom; manvantara - period of manifestation; pralaya - period of rest between manvantaras; mulaprakriti - the root of the matter. Dozens of them. When it comes to this sort of thing I'm a nastika!'

'Which is.....?'

'An atheist.'

'Me too.'

Susanna put her head in her hands. Was this what Ralphy was doing when he visited Madame Blavatsky? It was almost blasphemous. Colonel Olcott had come to Leek to lecture, she remembered, at the Nicholson Institute. Ralphy had introduced him, she'd written the introductory speech for him herself. When would it be now; 1889, November time. She'd heard the lecture; the bits about India had been interesting; dear Cousin Emma had been to India.

'But it gets better,' I went on. 'The Society for Psychical Research investigated Madame Blavatsky and found her to be a complete fraud, which caused quite a bit of fluttering in the theosophical dovecote. Various people looked into her history and found it didn't add up. She couldn't possibly have been in Tibet for the seven years she said she had and some of her other claims were pretty implausible too. She and Olcott had a bungalow outside Madras for some years - riddled with secret doors and concealed passages, apparently, to facilitate her séances. They ran foul of -

I think it was the English Missionaries, in Madras; letters appeared in the press and the Missionaries published a pamphlet denouncing her. It looks very much as if that was the nearest she actually got to Tibet.'

'So why was she so influential?'

'Hard to say. I suppose she had charisma, though it certainly doesn't come through in her photographs, she looks dumpy and sullen. Then, in the late 1880s it gets really smelly and there's a battle for presidency of the society between Colonel Olcott and William Q. Judge!'

'Splendid name!'

'Madame Blavatsky pulled the strings by claiming she was getting messages from her Tibetan guides, the mahatmas.'

'As in Gandhi?'

'Right. Well they went in for astral communication!'

'What?'

'Inserting cryptic messages, written on tissue paper, into ordinary letters that were addressed to the participants.'

'If you believe that....'

'People did. Apparently the originals are still in the British Museum.'

'Ralphy really did get involved with some weird people.'

'It's difficult to know how deeply involved he was. He certainly visited HPB and I imagine it was he who invited Colonel Olcott to Leek, and he was in touch with the Reverend Ouseley, who wrote *Mountain of Light* which was a sort of High-Church-meets-Theosophy text - and, incidentally has a chapter about how good it was for you to be a vegetarian.'

'Didn't Ralph stay with Ouseley in Brighton?'

'Yes. Ouseley later went out to Georgia and founded his own church - in Savannah, I think. Ralph certainly read quite a lot of theosophical literature; and tried to introduce some of it to Susanna. Remember *The Perfect Way*?'

'Susanna described it as *'a queer book'* - I remember that because she hardly ever commented on anything she read.'

'Well, I had a look at it - it was by Anna Kingsford and it tried to present Christianity in a theosophical light, by, I quote, "demonstrating Christianity to be a symbolic synthesis of the fundamental truths contained in all religions". The author said it "represented the result of intuitional memory, quickened and enhanced, we believe, by some measure of the divine influx". It's awash with quotations from the Talmud and the Koran, the illustrations include a section through the great pyramid at Gizeh and a diagram showing the Magical Molecular Poles in Health and Disease - little men with all-over spikes like hedgehogs!'

'I see what Susanna meant!'

'So did I.   Then there was *A Buddhist Catechism* - that was Buddhists-are-really-theosophists by Colonel Olcott, and *Psychometry*. Why do you suppose we never looked that up in a dictionary? That was by Colonel Olcott as well.'

'So what is it?'

'Psychometry is another name for thought transference - it was almost a parlour game. His scientific experiments consisted of wrapping objects in paper and placing them on people's heads and having them guess what they were while other people in the room tried to send them thought messages. And sometimes they guessed right!  Proof positive!'

Marion had gone uncharacteristically quiet.

'Susanna read *Psychometry*,' she said, at last.  'I would say it works **very** well!'

'Well **done**!' murmured Susanna.

Ralph remained interested in theosophy but he was not closely involved with the society for long.  Instead he decided to invent his own organisation.

*January 27th Fine. Ralph went to Leek to get candles & his cassock, he had a meeting at Mr Faulkner's at 7.30.*

*29th Fine. Ralph took his cassock to Leek to be altered.*

*February 8th Ralph brought 2 blue robes from Mr Godwin's.*

*12th Fine.   Ralph and Mr Jones went by the 2.8 to Mr Beardmore's at Bucknall.  Ralph made him Provincial Governor and another man joined the League.*

*26th Ralph took his vestments and candles to Tansley's & entered him in the League.*

'What on earth is he up to now?'  I wondered.

The cassock and candles cropped up at regular intervals throughout 1887 and, predictably, they caused Ralph to have at least one major row with his father. For a while we decided that the League must be some offshoot of the Theosophical Society, but then, in Colin and Joyce's trunks we found Ralph's pamphlet detailing the *Objects of the True Philosophic League or Order of the Round Table*.

*The Objects,'* Ralph wrote, *'are to promote in a practical manner the Happiness and Harmony of the Universe, and therefore to strive in every rational way for the good and welfare of the human race, and the furtherance of the principles of universal fraturnity.....*

'He still couldn't spell then,' I observed.

'Why?' said Marion. I'd forgotten that Marion couldn't spell either!

*.....and Amity. The Votaries of every Culture, consistent with these principles, and the members of every Race and Caste, of either sex, are eligible for admission to the Society.*

In particular the League sought to uphold true principles of philosophy and hygiene and oppose false ones; neither Marion nor I was quite sure what a principle of philosophy and hygiene was but it sounded harmless. It also set out to create an interest in art, poetry and literature, to perpetuate all *'beneficial Institutions and Usages...*

'Nothing like being specific,' I said unkindly.

*.....to benefit mankind by constructing and collecting beautiful and interesting objects and to prevent the destruction of animal and plant species and historic monuments and artefacts.*

'Tailor-made to Ralphy's own interests,' I said, 'especially the collecting bit. **And** he manages to invoke the knights of the round table in his pursuit of happiness and harmony.'

'The good citizens of Leek seem to have been remarkably tolerant of his foibles,' agreed Marion. 'Do you remember that account in one of the scrapbooks?'

Ralphy had saved a press-cutting from the *Leek Post* about one of the League meetings - it is undated so we cannot be sure whether or not it was the inaugural meeting.

Forty or fifty people assembled in the Coffee Tavern in Leek at about five o'clock, for tea and refreshments. The tables were decorated with scarlet geraniums, no doubt from the gardens at Basford. Silk banners with pictures of animals and birds (lent by Thomas Wardle) hung from the ceiling. A placard with the word 'Excelsior' above a crescent and a cross and the words 'Hail to the Lotus and the Jewel' was propped against the wall. One table was laid out like an altar complete with a white tablecloth, an incense burner, wax altar candles and peacock feathers.

After tea Ralphy read out the rules of the society - all forty-six of them - and explained them to the assembled company. He then talked about the need to preserve endangered species and ancient monuments - his chief target seems to have been the use of feathers and birds in ladies' hats - but it is apparent that by this stage the *Leek Post* reporter was becoming fairly confused. Ecological matters were not high on most people's agendas in the 1880s. Ralph's concerns were well ahead of their time.

The proceedings then turned into a typical Victorian social evening with songs, recitations 'sports' and some exercises in thought-transference. Ralph sang 'Dinah Doon', a negro spiritual and 'No, Sir!'; others contributed 'Nelly Gray' and 'My Mother Only Left Me The Old Armchair'! At nine everyone went home to their slippers and cocoa, leaving the reporter totally bemused 'after a most enjoyable and astonishing evening'! Ralph's commitment to his League was unswerving, but later meetings attracted fewer and fewer participants.

Nonetheless, compared to the rather unsavoury antics of the 19th century theosophists, the aims of the True Philosophical League seemed wholesome and laudable. Introducing one of Ralph's travel lectures at the Nicholson Institute in the 1880s, his old friend and mentor, Thomas Wardle, 'was sure that a young man who had nothing else to do could not do better than devote his time to such objects.'

On balance, we agreed with Mr Wardle.

Susanna was less convinced. What Ralph was doing was useful at best, harmless at worst, but it was definitely odd. People in Victorian Staffordshire did not like oddity. But despite her concerns, she did her level best to take an interest in Ralph's varying enthusiasms and he in his turn tried to educate her. At his suggestion she read Darwin's *Origin of Species* and *Sketches of the Rites and Customs of the Greco-Roman Church* by H.G. Romanoff, and Pastor Chinigny's *Fifty Years in the Church of Rome*.

'Such strange books,' thought Susanna, 'not really the sort of things I should have been reading as a good Anglican. But I tried to understand. John William just used to get so angry with poor Ralph.'

In August 1888 Ralph went travelling again, this time heading north via Edinburgh to the Orkneys. Susanna, who remained at home, patching and mending, of course paid for the trip, though she did send the occasional complaining letter (in true Susanna form):

*As I cannot imagine what you have done with all your large sums of money I will oblige you to write down how you have spent it as I cannot have my money wasted in this way & not know what becomes of it. I enclose a cheque for £4 (£250) which you must acknowledge by return of post & remember you are not to misuse people's money given to you on trust...*

On October 13th, when she had not heard from him for weeks and believed he was still in Scotland - '*A telegram came from Ralph, Christiania, Norway "Send £10 directly".*'

'I've got kids like that,' I said.

'No you haven't,' answered Marion. 'Ralph was asking for something over £600 in today's money - £626 to be precise.'

'Well, so would mine if they thought they'd get it!'

But in 1888, transferring money from country to country was no easy matter. There were no computers, credit cards or fax machines - and, not surprisingly, the local postmaster in Cheddleton had no idea how to operate those systems which did exist.

Two weeks later Ralph was home, pausing only to drop his luggage before rushing off to visit his Aunt Emily and dine with his Uncle Dryden.

'He had been from home for over two months,' thought Susanna, 'but he couldn't see how much his company meant to me. He could be so selfish. Then of course all the collections he had bought began to arrive - and I had to pay the carriage, his money was all gone; a spinning wheel from Orkney; boxes of wooden utensils from Norway......'

Again, Ralph decided to share his experiences with his neighbours and planned a lecture about his travels to be given at the Nicholson Institute. He also wrote and published a pamphlet illustrated with drawings of artefacts that he had collected. Desperate to find something positive to say about her errant nephew Susanna despatched copies of it to everyone she could think of.

1889, the last year for which we have a diary from Susanna, showed that her life had changed little. Ralph was still away more than he was at home and still spending her money thoughtlessly. Gustavus had the cheek to write to her and berate her for giving Ralph so much money - she replied promptly and one can only guess at the content. She was still paying, at that time, his life insurance for him! Emily Jane spent more and more time with Gustavus at Chastleton - so did Ralph - and one cannot help wondering if there was a degree of 'ganging up' on Susanna - the only one in the family with any money, to whom they were all, in varying degrees, beholden and of whom they were all, at heart, jealous.

Both she and John William were frequently ill. The house became damper as the winter closed in and on her rounds to take soup and gifts and church magazines to her 'cottagers' she recorded, uncharacteristically, that she had *'rested at another cottage where Mrs Pegg was making oatcakes.'*

Suffering though she was from neuralgia, rheumatism and chilblains and general debility Susanna did not give in. That winter she still attended Colonel Olcott's lecture at the Leek Institute, and, on Christmas Eve, still found the energy to walk all the way up to Ipstones church to take two baskets of flowers.

On December 31st she wrote in her diary, *'Mr Boucher had all the givers out of magazines at his house for early tea. I brought home 12 magazines and 15 almanacs.'* It was to be her last entry.

Humphrey and Judy Scott-Moncrieff.

Marion wearing the replica dress - but refusing
to wear the bonnet.

Lunch at Rock Cottage - Pam and Edward with Averil.

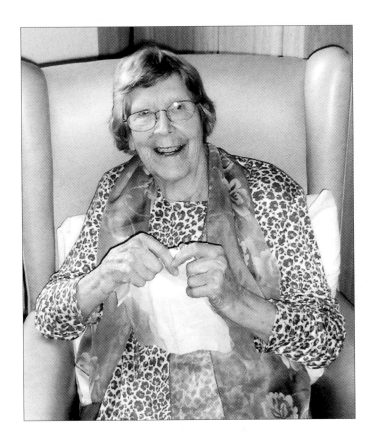

Averil Scott-Moncrieff.

Colin and Joyce Shenton with Ralph De Tunstall's hunting horn.

Dr John Sneyd surrounded by family memorabilia.

'Medicinal' adverts from *The Graphic*, illustrated magazine of 1887.

Chapter 16
# Shadows on the wall

Susanna pushed the stone hot water bottle away from her feet. While she was dozing it had gone cold and without its warmth the bed clothes felt damp. Downstairs a clock chimed - one, two, three, four, five. The fire in the grate flickered feebly, it needed more coal but Annie would be helping Mary get John William's supper, better not to disturb her. Besides, it was so much effort to reach the bell-pull..... Susanna lay still, trying to preserve the little heat her body generated.

The night-light under the food-warmer on her bedside table was still alight but the wax was now just a trace of liquid in its foil cup - soon it, too, would go out. Not that it mattered. The Nestlé's food in the covered cup on top of the warmer would have dried out by now - she'd only left a spoonful or two in there after lunch. Horrible stuff - could it really be good for you? Outside it was already dark but there were no stars, it had been cloudy all day. From her bed, all she could see was sky; she was becoming quite expert at forecasting the weather.

She felt so feverish, so lonely. If only Ralphy would come and see her more often - but he was out so much. He was young of course, so busy with his friends, his wretched League, the Roman church, services on saints' days, visits to the priests to discuss theology, appearing in plays in Leek, outings with the Field Naturalists, writing all those letters about theosophy - what must people think of his spelling now she no longer had the energy to check it.

And his collections were growing; people were so kind to him - he'd told her just the other day that he felt he was neglecting his museum, he had so much else to do. Perhaps one day people would come to Basford like they went to Lichfield Museum or the great museums in South Kensington. That would be something to be proud of. Susanna almost smiled. But she wished Ralphy would read to her - she loved the sound of his voice. It really wouldn't matter what he read, even one of those strange books he was so fond of, it was his company she craved.

Dear Beatrice had called, of course, and Emily. John William sat with her much of the time - he tried so hard, thought Susanna gratefully. But his voice was so strained now and he could hear so little. They couldn't talk and even before he developed that dreadful throat he'd never been much of a one for reading aloud.  And he was becoming strange, too, retreating into his silent world, becoming childish, forgetful, worrying about trifles, forgetting to wind the clocks, even to lock the front door so Annie had said. They were getting old, thought Susanna, he sixty nine, she sixty, and they'd had so much to bear.

Perhaps she would feel better soon. She'd caught a chill last week and it had settled on her chest; that was the problem. And she'd been flushed and feverish; Dr Somerville had come every day to take her pulse. But propped up on the pile of pillows she was finding it easier to breathe; lying flat made her gasp and cough - a dry, painful cough. The chilblains on her fingers were sore and itchy; Annie kept forgetting the alum water she asked for to bathe them in. The ones on her feet hurt less now that she'd not worn boots for a week, though her woollen bedsocks made them itch and lying in bed with nothing to do they were hard to ignore.

Her joints ached - rheumatism, Dr Somerville said, but her side pained her horribly, she couldn't understand why. It hurt to stay in one position - then it hurt to move. She'd had bad headaches all week, often she could not bear even the dull wintry light and had to call Annie to draw the curtains. But worst of all she felt weak, so weak - no energy to sit up, to read, to sew. She'd tried, but the words or stitches swam before her eyes; she couldn't focus and the effort made her cough and she brought up phlegm tinged with blood. But it wasn't consumption, Dr Somerville had been quite clear about that.

She'd had bad turns before, she comforted herself. She'd had them on and off for ten years nearly; they lasted weeks, or months, and then gradually, she would begin to feel better and then soon she'd be back to normal - and she'd only been in bed for a week so far this time. She sighed, knowing she'd probably feel like this for some while. Better think about something else. She shifted uncomfortably, shivering as her thin limbs moved away from the warm patch she had created.

She was getting so thin; no wonder she was cold. Dr Somerville had advised her to rest and eat nourishing food. But she was never hungry. Nothing could tempt her - soup, beef tea, milky drinks, scrambled eggs - of course they were all cold by the time Annie had slopped them upstairs from the kitchen. Eating was such an effort and to make matters worse she'd developed a cold sore on her lip. And she coughed so when she tried to sit up properly. Besides, the less she ate the less problems she had when she came to use the commode - those operations had not brought any long-term benefit.

But she was thirsty. A cup of hot tea would be nice, thought Susanna. There was a glass of water on the table; she decided it was not worth the effort of reaching out for.

She dozed fitfully. She had known this room all her life - Harriet and Emily had shared it when they were girls. Penelope and Helen had had the room next door. Poor dear Harriet, her children had grown up without her and she would never know her grandchildren. And Penelope dead too, all those babies and only four of them still alive. And all the others - Ralph Debank, Helen, Mary, Lionel, Freddy, Wettie - she could see the faces of her dead siblings as clearly as if they were in the room with her. Some had died in rooms along this very corridor. 'As I will', she thought, resignedly.

'There were so many of us,' she went on, remembering the squabbling and the giggling, the borrowing of ribbons and sashes, stockings and gloves, and the girls brushing each other's long hair, twisting it in rags to make ringlets. Somewhere there always seemed to be a baby or a toddler crying, and the little boys were so boisterous - except poor dear Wettie, of course.

'And now there are only four of us left,' she thought sadly. 'Of course we never see Dryden. Emily comes, but Gustavus - well, he and Mimi write but they only visit very occasionally and we're quite glad of that. Of course Ada is still alive too, but she was never really one of us - and she's so grand now, busy with Ponsonby and her little boys.' She remembered how Ada and Mary had looked down their noses the last time they'd come to Basford - it would be three years ago. They'd been staying with Dryden at Ashcombe, so it was all rather embarrassing, they hadn't brought the children and she'd been so looking forward to playing with little Bertie.

'Yes, Basford was always full of people when we were children.'

It seemed drier and warmer then, too. In the kitchen, fourteen servants ate their meals at the long table, seated according to their own strict hierarchy. Not that they ate well, Papa believed in a spartan diet, but the kitchens always smelled of food - frying bacon, roasting meat, simmering stews, baking cakes, burnt sugar in the soft fruit season when the cook and kitchen maids made gooseberry and blackcurrant jam, sharp citrus smells when they made lemon curd or marmalade, hot vinegar when they made pickles.

In the scullery there were always maids scrubbing vegetables, plucking birds - in the autumn there was an endless supply of grouse and pheasant to be prepared - or washing up in the big shallow stone sink, scouring the copper pans with wood-ash and sand, grating household soap to make suds in the rapidly-cooling water, washing the plates and glasses in separate wooden bowls.

Down at the Bath House, at the foot of the hill, another small army of servants serviced the big house, baking huge batches of bread in the bake-house and doing the laundry. Great wicker hampers full of soiled sheets and under-linen were manhandled down the steep track from the hall, others were lugged back up the hill full of fresh-smelling, neatly-folded, carefully-marked sheets and pillowcases, nightdresses and petticoats, camisoles and drawers.

There were fires in all the rooms in winter then, and one of the maids saw to it that they were always supplied with coal, always burning brightly. A piece of damp coal spluttered and spat out its flame in her own grate as a reminder of how times had changed. All the main rooms used to be kept clean and dusted - they used a goose's wing to do the books in the library, she remembered. Papa insisted; why, she couldn't remember. The room off the servant's passage that looked over the garden, that was the housekeeper's room. It was low-ceilinged, compared to the rest of the house, and easy to keep warm. These days she and John William used it as their own sitting room.

Everywhere was so silent now. And she was sure it would all be dirty. What would Mama and Papa think if they could see Basford now? Without close supervision, Annie did as little as possible. Their sitting room would be reasonably clean, but the girl was no good with fires and slapdash about black-leading the grates. John William grumbled - but she simply kept out of his way. Ralph noticed very little - if he was absorbed in a book or busy arranging his specimens he would never see that the fire had gone out, let alone think to ring for more coals. Mary Towill was a good enough cook - not like Mrs Bloor, of course, but their needs were simple. John William liked plain food, Ralph was often out for meals, her own appetite was poor and they never entertained. Visitors like Emily or Beatrice would be offered tea, a plate of bread-and-butter, home-made jam - seldom cake - toast, perhaps, if it was winter, a relish of home-grown salad in summer. It was all well within Mary's capabilities. And she was loyal, did not complain about Ralph using her kitchen to pickle his specimens, and seemed to keep the place fairly clean.

'Yes, we manage,' Susanna thought grimly.

'We're good at managing. We've had to be. There was Papa's trouble with the Welsh miners, my marriage and the terrible time I had in Oakamoor, poor dear Agnes's death, the dreadful feuds between Papa and John William, and John William and Dryden, Gustavus's scandals, our disappointments with Ralphy..... and so many, many deaths. You get used to it, sadness becomes a way of life. And once you've got used to the losses, the disappointments, the shame - well, you just have to carry on and do your best, remember you have a position, you're a Sneyd, people look up to you.'

In 1887 she had insisted that they light beacons for the Queen's jubilee. They were Sneyds, Conservatives, staunch monarchists, they should set an example. John William had agreed and they had started to build the fires together - Basford was on the top of a hill so the flames would be visible for miles - but he soon lost interest. Ralph was away in Stoke Gabriel, staying with that Mr Neville - so he could not help.

Harrison and the servants found less arduous but more urgent things to do whenever she asked for their assistance, but Susanna was determined that the beacons would burn. She remembered how heavy the wood had been as she dragged it up the slope, how she had struggled up the bank with load after load, only stopping for breath when she was sure no-one could see her, until she was satisfied that the fires would burn for long enough to show the world - this corner of North Staffordshire anyway - that the Sneyds were loyal subjects of the crown as they had been back in the days when Major Ralph Sneyd of Keele died for his king at the hands of a traitorous Roundhead.

Sometimes, though, she did wish they hadn't come back to Basford.

It was disloyal even to think it, of course, this was their home, Ralphy's inheritance, but they'd had so many friends in Armitage and Abbots Bromley - she thought wistfully of the good times they'd had with the Birches at Armitage Lodge, the dances at the Rectory, helping at the soup kitchen in Abbots Bromley. She'd felt needed, valued.

But she still tried to be useful. In the spring of 1889 she'd taken a course on 'First Aid to the Injured' at Cheddleton in the hope that it might make her a more competent nurse. Twenty-eight ladies took the course. 'But only nineteen of us were brave enough to take the test at the end,' remembered Susanna proudly, 'and I passed - well we all did.'

But however much she chose to pretend, Basford was not what it was. She was very aware of her father's shadow - still a dominant presence in the house. She suspected John William felt it though he'd never have admitted it. She could see it in the cottagers' eyes, too. She still visited the poor people, of course, as she always had, and they were polite, apparently grateful for the gifts of grapes or eggs that she brought, but somehow their deference seemed false, almost mocking.

They would talk about Dryden, though everyone in the neighbourhood knew of the feud between Ashcombe and Basford, or make veiled allusions to Ralphy's collections or his Roman Catholicism or his strange ideas. She ignored it, of course, impudent mischief-making, she would not give them the satisfaction of a response. And then there were all the references to the good old days 'when the old squire was at Ashcombe' or 'when your dear father was alive, Mrs Ingleby', memories of her family when it was powerful and influential, implying that they knew how much her circumstances had changed. None of that business with Mr Tatton would have happened in her father's day - Papa would have had him evicted, or imprisoned or both. People had feared Papa, but they all knew that John William had very little influence. It was quite safe to defy him. Susanna sighed.

In 1889 John William had quarrelled with his tenant in Sneyd Arms Farm about a right of way which the Tattons had used for years but which John William now decided constituted trespass on his land. Both old men were stubborn and Mr Tatton gave notice to quit. John William then realised it would be difficult to re-let the farm and asked him to stay on. Mr Tatton refused, and they both consulted their solicitors. Tatton's farm was just by the entrance to Basford Hall and was also a pub. Finally the case came to court and one hot August day John William and the gardener set out for the assizes at Stafford.

'Papa would have taken a gentleman friend or a brother magistrate,' thought Susanna.

She had been worried that her brother would make himself appear ridiculous in court - and Annie and Mary were already gossiping. She had taken Annie out of the kitchen and made her help polish all the furniture; it needed it and in her mistress's company Annie had to keep her speculations and opinions on the 'dotty old master' to herself. Besides, Susanna found the hard physical work distracting.

From the start the case went the Tatton's way. The jury arrived late so the case was postponed until the afternoon - John William and Harrison had got up early so as to be in Stafford by eleven, but that counted for nothing. The jurymen were all farmers.

'Papa would not have allowed that,' thought Susanna, 'he'd have complained to the judge.'

The jury was happy to support a brother farmer against an apparently unreasonable landlord - and Susanna had a sudden, sneaking, disloyal suspicion that John William had been just a little unreasonable. But the Tatton's reaction to their victory was unpardonable. They had ignored the sounds of revelry coming from the pub well into the early hours - well, she had, John William had been mercifully unaware of the boos and catcalls and noisy singing. But by the following morning a large red, white and blue flag fluttered from the pub roof, an unmistakable gesture of defiance. Within hours John William had hung a banner on the Hall gate.

'It was most impertinent of the Tattons to gloat in that way,' thought Susanna. 'But I did think John William should have ignored them - it would have been more dignified. People no longer respected us but we did not have to descend to their level.'

So few people of their own sort invited them out these days. Of course, John William was a difficult guest, unable to hear or to be heard, she herself was often unwell and had to refuse invitations. But it was Papa's legacy, she was sure, and respect for Dryden, that made them unwelcome visitors in so many local houses. Though they acknowledged her if they met in the street, people who had known her since childhood no longer called. Of course Basford was isolated - but in her parents' day that had made no difference.

Captain Colvile had been a good friend - they'd dined there on John William's last birthday. They missed him when he left Churnet Grange. No-one now invited John William to go shooting - since Sir John Crewe's death John William had had few invitations to practice his favourite sport. Dear Mrs Cruso in Leek was always pleased to see her. Mr Joseph Challinor was a friend as well as a lawyer, suave, urbane, supremely tactful, never giving a hint that he remembered the details of her terrible experience with poor Charles, or the horrible things Papa had said about John William, or the dreadful lies Gustavus had told. He was ageing, too - he'd been barely out of his teens when Grandpapa met him at Mr Catlow's in Cheadle. Later he had joined the family business in Leek. And he'd done well, very well indeed. Mrs Challinor was charming, too, her little boys were the same age as Ralphy, and she'd been so knowledgeable about schools, Susanna remembered gratefully.

Dear Phoebe Wardle had been a good friend too - but her brother, Mr Wardle - though he was kind to Ralphy, he and Mrs Wardle never requested her company or that of John William. Even Emily, old maid that she was, sour and embittered as she could be ('God forgive me' muttered Susanna guiltily) saw more people than she did. Emily spent a good deal of time at Ashcombe now. When she had fallen and cut her leg she had gone there to recover, to wait until the wound was sufficiently healed for the silver wire to be removed.

'If that had happened when we first moved in she would have come here, where I could nurse her,' she thought bitterly. 'Of course Emily said she didn't want to trouble me when I was poorly and John William was so difficult - but really she knew she would be much more comfortable at Ashcombe. She certainly stayed there long enough.'

Fanny Cowell wrote, but her children were grown and she no longer visited. Dear Mr Palmer - Susanna's eyes misted over - was married now, she seldom heard from him. She remembered how, for several years they had stored Mr Palmer's books and pictures and furniture at Basford - they'd been glad of it. They'd missed it when it was gone - the empty spaces always gave her a pang, reminded her of what might have been.

But she'd done her duty, stayed with John William and Ralphy. Duty was so important, she'd tried hard to impress that on Ralph. *'Leave as good a name behind you as one who did his best'* she'd written. Would he? Would she?

Church was her comfort. And she'd tried to support both Cheddleton and Ipstones churches, sending flowers and grapes for the harvest festivals, chrysanthemums, dahlias, great tubs of brugmansias, and decorating the altar rail in Cheddleton church - that was her special task. Holly and evergreens at Christmas - Ralphy was always so good at finding holly with berries, so cheerful in the cold midwinter; daffodils in moss at Easter - or primroses and violets, depending when Easter fell; lilies sometimes, too. Her garden was a great solace, soon, when the weather got warmer, she'd be able to walk there again, take tea in the greenhouse.

John William would be in soon, she promised herself. He would make sure that Annie got the fire going again and made her comfortable for the night and he'd sit with her till she slept. Often he'd nod off in the chair and be there all night. Dear boy! He always did his best but men were not much good in the sickroom - Susanna wished with all her heart that Aunt Mary could come back and look after her. But Aunt had been dead these five years and it had been many years longer than that since she had been able to look after anyone. Even Emily would have been a comfort - she'd have seen that the water on her bedside table was fresh, made her tea, helped her sit up to drink it, prayed with her, read the bible - soothing, familiar words.

God was good, thought Susanna, she should be more patient, more grateful for all His mercies, even this illness. He must have sent it for a purpose. But it was easier to talk to God in church, she'd always found. She remembered that letter Charles had sent her after she'd visited Cauldon Low with him and exclaimed about the bare room in which he held his services. He'd told her you could find God wherever you were, the place was not important if your mind was right - he was so Evangelical, almost a Wesleyan, she thought, so unlike Papa.

Cheddleton was the church she attended most often now. Dear Mr Boucher sent his carriage to take her if she was ill and it was one of the services he knew she would not want to miss. And he was always so grateful to her for helping with the parish magazine, she used to deliver it to farms all over the Ashcombe estate, it was good to have a reason to visit the old places again, places she'd known since she was a little girl. She'd done her rounds only last week. And if she was on church business John William could not object. She might even run into dear Dryden, one day, visiting his tenants, and if John William were not there, who knows? They might even be able to speak.

Susanna drifted off, she was walking through the fields, it was warm, summer, and Dryden was coming towards her, smiling......

She woke with a start.

'Aunty Susan? How are you my dearest?'

Ralphy was bending over her, looking concerned. He was such a handsome young man, thought Susanna proudly, so tall, that beautiful wavy hair.

'Did I wake you?'

'No,' she lied, 'I'd just closed my eyes.'

'Good, good,' said Ralph languidly, 'Dr Somerville said you should rest as much as possible. Annie will be up with some soup, shortly. And Papa will come and sit with you tonight.'

'Can't you stay a little while?' Susanna whispered. She felt strange, far away. 'Sit down, tell me what you have been doing all day.'

Ralph perched his long frame uncomfortably on the edge of the bedside chair. He wanted to get off, finish writing that poem. During the silent evening meal with his father he had thought of the rhyme he needed and he wanted to get it down on paper. And then he wanted to re-read that chapter about vegetarianism in Ouseley's book. His father had been making derogatory remarks about the lentil cutlets his son had had for supper - he himself had had a greasy mutton chop. Ralph grimaced inwardly. Ouseley had put it so well.

Now what could he tell Aunt Susan to keep her happy? He embarked on a recitation of his new poem. And a diatribe about his father. And a blow-by-blow account of the discussion he'd had with the priest at Cheadle about the precise date of Christmas.

Susanna relaxed back on to her pillow and closed her eyes. She wasn't really listening, it was just so nice to have Ralphy there, to hear his voice - she felt relaxed, peaceful.

'Good,' thought Ralph, 'she's asleep again.'

He dropped a perfunctory kiss on her forehead. It didn't feel so hot now and her face was paler. But her breathing was still rapid, her nostrils dilating oddly as she breathed, she had that nasty sore on her mouth and there was a bluish tinge round her lips - she really did look very old and ill. But she'd rally, of that he was sure, she always did.

'Good night, dear one,' he murmured.

Susanna opened her eyes with an effort. 'Ralph - the fire. My hot-water bottle.'

He hesitated. At that moment Annie Lomas bustled into the room with a tray, her cap awry, soup splashing on to the soiled tray-cloth, and a recently-filled stone hot-water bottle wrapped in grubby flannel tucked under her arm.

'Here you are Mrs Ingleby, sorry I'm late Mrs Ingleby, shall I see to the fire Mrs Ingleby?'

'There you are, Aunty,' said Ralph, a shade too cheerfully, 'Annie will make you comfortable, won't you Annie?' And he escaped out into the passage. Duty done for another night.

Annie set the tray on the bedside table. Clumsily she withdrew the cold hot-water bottle and pushed the new one against Susanna's feet. Then she tipped some coal from the scuttle on to the fire - there wasn't much left, she'd better make it last, she didn't want to have to fetch more before the morning. She poked the fire hopefully and a flame flickered, died and flickered again. Good - fires were the bane of Annie's life, they always seemed to go out.

Susanna did not want her soup. Annie was so rough when she helped her sit up - she couldn't face that tonight. It was easier not to eat, somehow, she just wanted to lie still.

'Thank you Annie, you may go now. Mr Sneyd will help me when he comes,' she whispered.

The girl scuttled away gratefully.

By the time John William hobbled into the room she was dozing again, breathing quickly and shallowly. He sat down stiffly, watching her face as the firelight flickered, worried, tired. Susanna stirred slightly in her sleep, her thin fingers gripping the edge of the quilt. John William leant over her and pushed wisps of her grey hair back under the cotton nightcap. The untouched cup of chicken soup still sat on the bedside table, cold and greasy.

'My baby sister,' he thought, 'my poor darling.'

It was late, dark, quiet. He had had a long day.

A few hours later John William stirred. The room was cold again, the fire almost out. Stiffly he rose to his feet and put another lump of coal on the embers. He could hear nothing - but he was used to that. Susanna seemed very still. Gently he laid his hand on her forehead. Cold. Cold.....

'Annie! Mary! Come quickly. Quickly!' he croaked from the doorway, banging his stick on the doorframe, desperate to be heard.

Bleary-eyed, Annie stumbled into the room.  Mary followed, wrapping a shawl round herself.

'I think she's....' John William sank to his knees beside the bed. 'Oh my love,' he sobbed, 'my own dear love. My dear, kind treasure....'

The girls watched, motionless. After a while Mary helped him to his feet and began to lead him away. Annie wiped the tears from her own eyes with the back of her hand.

'Mr Ralph, Mr Sneyd?' she asked tentatively. Ralph slept the sleep of the dead. The commotion had not roused him.

'Let him sleep,' replied John William bitterly, 'he'll know soon enough.'

'You've made that up!' said Marion accusingly. 'I always knew you were a Mills and Boon writer at heart! You told me that we couldn't invent things! For all we know Emily might have moved in to nurse her. Susanna might have died in a warm, clean bed, a roaring fire in the grate, happy, with Ralphy, John William and Emily by her side, reading the bible to her, comforting her, holding her hand. We don't know whether Annie Lomas and Mary Towill were still there, even.'

'Well, they were there when the census was taken at the beginning of 1891.' I'd done my homework! 'Susanna died on December 11th - and she'd been ill less than a week. John William was present - it says so on the death certificate. I like to think he popped in and sat with her awhile, then realised she wasn't breathing any more. Ralphy wasn't in there - remember the poem: *'Oh, sadly did I kiss her and bid good night; I knew that I should miss her ere morning light!'* Emily might have been there - but she didn't move in on any of the other occasions when Susanna was ill. And they always had huge problems with the servants - if it wasn't Annie and Mary neglecting her it would have been another equally dozy pair! Anyway, I've talked to Alun,' I said, clinching the argument.

'She died of 'cardiac disease' according to the death certificate - Alun thinks she probably caught a chill which turned to pneumonia and her heart just gave out - there were no antibiotics, of course.  Once it took hold you could be dead within hours - so she really could have talked to Ralph in the evening and been dead by morning.  It could be quite a peaceful death, especially if you were elderly -  sixty was a good age in 1891.  William Osler, the famous 19th century professor of medicine wrote 'Pneumonia may well be called the friend of the aged.  Taken off by it in an acute, short, not often painful illness, the old man escapes those painful "cold gradations of decay" so distressing to himself and to his friends.'  Alun suggests that Susanna might already have had heart trouble which speeded things up - remember Dr Somerville *'came to try my heart'* in 1879?  If he knew she had a heart problem that would explain why he recorded the death as cardiac disease not pneumonia.'

'So Alun thinks all this is plausible?  Hmmm.'

And the memories I gave her - they're all things she recorded in her diaries - about the beacons, the Tattons, the first aid course, Emily's leg, church, polishing the furniture.

'Fine.  I stand in awe of your research!  But the conversation with Ralphy, the grubby hot-water bottle cover, the soiled tray-cloth...?'

I looked sheepish. 'OK, well perhaps there was a bit of artistic licence!'

Marion smiled.

'So can we get back to the facts now?  Her obituary, for example!'

We looked again at the cutting from the Cheddleton Parish Magazine for February 1892 that Ralphy had pasted into his scrapbook:

Although she had not been at all well for many months, she used to surprise people by her energy and her quick walk up to the last.  In fact she was taking out her parish magazines to some distant farm near Ipstones the Saturday before she was taken from us - we must all feel deep sympathy with her brother and nephew who have so entirely depended on her and cannot but sorely miss her.

No doubt they did miss her a great deal.  Ralph carefully preserved all Susanna's papers, clothes and personal possessions, many of which remain in the family to this day, and he penned a number of sentimental poems in her memory.

Susanna left her entire estate to Ralph with the exception of a £50 a year annuity to Emily Jane. She forgave Gustavus the first £1,500 of his debt to her; the remainder was to be repaid to Ralph. Her household goods were to remain at Basford for John William's lifetime and were then to go to Ralph, who, she supposed, would inherit Basford Hall and the estate from his father.

But Susanna was not there to mediate three years later when Ralph met the woman who was to be his wife. This time, the rift between father and son would not be mended.

Miss Harriet Brookes worked for Messrs Sheldon and Fenton in Leek, giving out work and doing some book-keeping. Her father was a wood-turner and her mother and sisters worked in silk mills. Apparently Ralph had visited Harriet's family home in Belle Vue to see some curiosities which Sergeant Major Brookes, her brother, had brought home from India. Ralph took one look at Harriet and fell head-over-heels in love. Within a few weeks they were married, though even Ralph was able to see that their marriage was somewhat unorthodox.

It is hard to tell whether the Brookes were happy for their daughter. They despatched Harriet to Cheadle to stay with a married sister, telling the neighbours that she had gone there to further her education. Ralph put up at the Packhorse Inn in Stockport and visited his bride-to-be daily. Three weeks later the couple married at St Mary's church, Stockport, without their parents being present - though Harriet's young sister did come from Leek to be present at the service. Wisely, Ralph did not inform his own father until after the event.

It was a romantic love story which captured the public imagination - the *Leek Post* published an article entitled *The Leek Matrimonial Romance* with engravings of Basford Hall and the Brookes' cottage to illustrate the difference in Ralph and Harriet's social standing, and much speculation about Ralph's financial expectations.

Class-conscious John William was furious. He was seventy two when Ralph married, ill and reclusive, deaf and as-good-as dumb. He may also have been becoming senile. A letter to Emily a few years later from an old servant about the misdemeanours of a maid at Basford, '*a regular bad woman*', who was entertaining gentleman clients at the hall unbeknownst to her bedridden master, describes him as *'childish'*.

Ralph's marriage was one disappointment too far for John William. He settled £4000 of Agnes's marriage settlement on Ralph, then re-wrote his will, disinheriting his son of Basford, as, nearly fifty years earlier, his own father had disinherited him of Ashcombe Park.

Ralph and his bride spent their first years of marriage with seventy year-old Aunt Emily at Rose Cottage, Bradnop, while their own house, the small but grandly-named Fairview Hall at Onecote, was being renovated. Susanna had left the house and land to Ralph. It still stands, complete with the battlements that Ralph designed during the Second World War, the chapel in the front garden, the Druidical altar at the back and lengths of stone from the Giant's Causeway on the lawn.

Marriage did not change Ralph. Up at Fairview he could conduct rituals and ceremonies to his heart's content. A lengthy account survives of the blessing of his belt, sword and scabbard in the chapel at Fairview one New Year's Day, assisted by a Father Dominick. Ralph bathed, dressed himself in his robes and spent the night in prayer and meditation by his altar. *'I also made a solemn profession of knightly faith and devoted myself to the cause of God, and of the ladies; faithfully promising to protect the oppressed.'* he wrote.

'Meanwhile the real live lady in his life - Harriet - was alone,' I observed, 'she must have had the patience of a saint!'

He continued to keep scrapbooks - the newspaper announcement of the birth of his first child, Stella, Colin's mother, in 1896 is in the same book as notes about the alchemic sepharoth, an article on the Philosophical Egg, notes on the Tarot, a description of an Armenian mass in London, a picture of a Ju-Ju home near Benin, an article on snake worship, a note from the *Catholic Times* that aluminium was an acceptable material for sacred vessels..... and much, much more.

'Do you remember Colin's story?' I asked, 'about Ralph taking baby Stella to visit her grandfather. John William was bedridden by then and covered his face with a sheet so that he wouldn't have to look at his granddaughter.'

'Oh yes, and Ralph pulled the sheet back and shouted, 'You will look at this child!'

'But things did get better,' I went on. 'John William was reconciled to the marriage in the end. And Harriet seems to have been a wonderful wife to Ralph. She bore him four children, ran his home **and** acted as his secretary, dutifully copying out notes for him and getting involved in all his schemes. He travelled widely, to Africa, Australia and all over Europe, collecting curiosities. But he was always a bit of an oddball. In later life he became a Druid! The Leek paper carried all sorts of pictures of him in his white robes, up on the moors.'

John William died in 1904, partially reconciled with his brother Dryden, and with his son, but without having changed the will he had made ten years earlier at the height of his quarrel with Ralph. Consequently, on his death, Basford Hall passed to his brother Gustavus, who had caused Susanna such expense and embarrassment.

Ralph was as bitter about his disinheritance as his father had been over Ashcombe. In the hall at Fairview he kept a replica of the front door key to Basford Hall as a reminder of what should have been.

He died in 1947, and was buried, in full mediaeval armour, in Cheddleton churchyard in the grave in which Susanna and his wife already lay.

Ralph De Tunstall Sneyd officiating at one of his ceremonies in the 1880s.

An old Ralph De Tunstall Sneyd with some of his curiosities in the Fairview chapel.

Ralph De Tunstall Sneyd.

A Loving and devoted Sister, Aunt, and Friend.

"Blessed are the dead which die in the Lord, Yea Saith the Spirit, for they rest from their labours."

He giveth His beloved sleep.

---

In Loving Memory

OF

## Suanna Ingleby née Sneyd,

Born at Basford Hall, 9th July, 1831,
Died at Basford Hall, 11th December, 1891.

Interred at Cheddleton, December 15th.

## On the Death of Susanna Ingleby

List, for the wind moans sadly 'mid woodland shades;
Hark! for the storm howls madly in forest glades;
On, by the fields and fountains, where cattle low;
Far mid the craggy mountains where pine trees grow.

Over my dear one hovers the hand of death;
Soon to snatch from her body the vital breath;
Oh, sadly did I kiss her and bid good night;
I knew that I should miss her ere morning light!

Though hid from those around her, I knew full well
Death, by his power, had bound her with fatal spell;
Three loud raps on my casement, sharp and clear,
Filled me with dread amazement and lonely fear.

She died - the gentle lady, my soul did love;
But her spirit hovers round me, like Holy Dove;
My soul's true eye beheld her when days had fled;
I knew that she was happy, though seeming dead.

In a deep grave, reclining, her body rests!
And long did sad repining afflict our breasts;
But, surely, she is shining where angels stand,
Bright mystic flowers entwining in God's dear land.

I feel that I shall find her some day to come!
And, then, will I remind her of things of home;
That home she left behind her, now home no more;
I pray that I may find her on God's dear shore!

                                        Ralph De Tunstall Sneyd

## The Guardian of Childhood - Susanna

O thou who didst love me
In childhood's bright days
Still now do I love thee,
And sing to thy praise.

Oh, well didst thou soothe,
With thy beautiful smile;
And with tales of bright fairies,
The hours did beguile.

Thou didst mend my small garments,
And wisdom instil;
That wisdom that flows
Like a beautiful rill.

A rill, to refresh
The lone pilgrims that move,
Through the deserts of life
To the ocean of love.

Ralph De Tunstall Sneyd

## The Guide of Childhood - Susanna

Oft, by thy side, I've wandered'
Far in the woodland glade;
Love's dearest theme I pondered,
'Neath the dark pine tree's shade

Oft have I stood beside thee,
Where the bright river flows,
As, through the flower-lit meadows,
On to the sea it goes.

Sweet was thy face, my darling!
Sweet was thy voice to me,
Oh, when I hear thee calling,
Then will I go to thee.

No death the loved can sever!
Love fills our life with peace!
Oh, give me love for ever,
Love that shall never cease!

Ralph De Tunstall Sneyd

# EPILOGUE

For a long time we could not find Susanna's grave. No-one seemed to know where she was buried and though we combed the graveyards of both Ipstones and Cheddleton churches we could find no headstone bearing her name.

Eventually Colin remembered that his Uncle Billy had told him that she, Ralph De Tunstall and his wife were all in the same grave in Cheddleton churchyard. It was unmarked - Ralph had always planned to design a tombstone but never got around to it. Further enquiries produced a probable location in an unmarked plot. In a sentimental moment on one of our trips to Staffordshire we decided to put flowers on Susanna's grave.

We deduced from Susanna's account books that red was her favourite colour. It was too garish for a respectable woman to wear as a dress, but, given the chance, Susanna would trim her bonnet with scarlet feathers, brighten a drab dress with crimson ribbons or buy herself a red embroidered apron. We chose red flowers.

It was a gesture which appealed to both Joyce and Judy, and, as a result the family (Colin and Joyce, Judy and Humphrey, Dr John Sneyd and his family) decided to buy Susanna a headstone. By the time you read this book we hope it will have been erected, just inside the side gate to Cheddleton churchyard, on the right of the path. It is, we feel, a fitting coda to our project.

We hope it pleases you Susanna.

'Because we were so lucky,' said Marion, 'so very lucky.'

I agreed.

'And none of it would have been possible if we'd left it any later,' Marion went on. 'Think how much has changed in the last few years.'

It has indeed. Averil is no longer able to care for herself and is in a nursing home. Stephen, the Trubshaw expert, Humphrey Townley and Roger Wykes Sneyd are all dead. The Reverend Stanley Price has retired from Ipstones. New rules have come into force at Keele University library and items from the Special Collections can no longer be borrowed.

Barbie has moved away from Stoke, and I have a new lodger. Ken ran away with the girl next door who is half his age...

Of course, it is not all bad news. The condensate problem seems to have evaporated as quickly as it developed. Planning permission was withheld for the incinerator behind Colin and Joyce's bungalow. Humphrey's tenant moved to another farm and his replacement has a much more stringent lease. The sickly-sweet smell of condensate no longer permeates the Ashcombe valley.

I now have a PhD. Marion is vaguely contemplating doing one.

The Sneyd family still flourishes. Judy's twins are growing up fast - from the chubby toddlers we first knew Alexandra has turned into a sophisticated young woman, nine going on nineteen, and William is turning into a devastatingly handsome young man. Colin and Joyce's grand-daughter is now a beautiful teenager and looks set to become a talented athlete. Dr Sneyd and his wife have young grandchildren.

But the owners of many of the family homes are elderly. In the foreseeable future Ashcombe, Woodlands and Sharpcliffe may be renovated as Basford and Belmont have been, and new owners may be less interested in their history. Fewer and fewer people will remember Ralph De Tunstall Sneyd and his children. The links between our age and Susanna's are stretching; soon they will snap.

Yes, we were very, very lucky. Yes, thank you, Susanna.

'But what are we going to do next?' I asked Marion as we finished reading through the draft of this book for the last time. 'There's never going to be another Susanna, is there?'

'Probably not - she was a find in a million. But we still have *My Dear Aunty* to do. Then there are the five sisters I found in the 1851 census for Norfolk, all spinsters, living in Barton Turf Hall, a splendid house, miles from anywhere, and all moneylenders - there must be a story in there somewhere!

Or there's that diary of the young American school teacher in Albany in the 1840s that Maddy gave me. And that one you found in Leicester Record Office. Who knows what might turn up? In fact, I've brought this for you to see.'

She pushed a package towards me. 'Alan Bednall found it in a collection of documents he was using for his research and sent it to me.' Alan was a local historian we knew in Macclesfield.